a harem boy's saga - 1 - initiation

1967

young

A Harem Boy's Saga I: Initiation

The contents of this book constitute a work of NONFICTION. It documents the author's experiences, and is not intended as an expose'.

No portion of this book may be transmitted or reproduced in any form, or by any means, without permission in writing from the author or publisher, with the exception of brief excerpts used for the purposes of review.

This book contains substantial sexually explicit material and language which may be considered offensive by some readers.

Copyright © 2012 Bernard Tristan Foong

All rights reserved.

ISBN: 148266075X

ISBN 13: 9781482660753

This memoir is dedicated to sissy boys the world over.

"It takes courage to grow up and become who you really are."

e. e. Cummings

Table of Contents

PART ONE: Kuala Lumpur, Malaya

Chapter 1	The Foong Family	3
Chapter 2	On the Queen Mary	7
Chapter 3	The Chinese Year of the Water Snake 1953	13
Chapter 4	My Birthday Bash	19
Chapter 5	Fashion Recruited Me	23
Chapter 6	The Little Ballerina	29
Chapter 7	This Boy Just Loves to have Fun!	35
Chapter 8	On the Good Ship Victoria	43
Chapter 9	Club Chop Suey at Griffin Inn	53
Chapter 10	Macho Mary goes to Town!	61
Chapter 11	Catch a Falling Star	69
Chapter 12	Wear a Mini Skirt	79
Chapter 13	A Land Far Away	85

PART TWO: The United Kingdom, London

Chapter 14	"I've Never Done Before"	93
Chapter 15	Daltonbury Hall, School for Boys	97
Chapter 16	Hold Your Head Erect	105
Chapter 17	The Kipling Society	113
Chapter 18	No Distance between Us	121

Chapter 19	Christmas in London	131
Chapter 20	Creeping Up Softly On Me	139
Chapter 21	The Young Ones Shouldn't Be Afraid	147
Chapter 22	Outgrown My Shoes	153
Chapter 23	Love to Love You Baby	161

PART THREE: The United Arab Emirates, Red Sea Riviera

Author's Note		169
Chapter 24	E.R.O.S.	173
Chapter 25	Initiation and Incantations	179
Chapter 26	Up, Up and Away	187
Chapter 27	Bahriji (Oasis) School	193
Chapter 28	The Art of Seduction and Flirtation	199
Chapter 29	The Art of Body Language	205
Chapter 30	Drop Dead Gorgeous	211
Chapter 31	To the Souq	217
Chapter 32	Art of Sensuality and Foreplay	223
Chapter 33	Love Knows No Boundaries	229
Chapter 34	On the Red Sea	233
Chapter 35	On The Kahyya'm	239
Chapter 36	Cruising The Red Sea Riviera	245

PART FOUR: The KOSK Household, Tunisia, Florence, Venice, Tuscany

Chapter 37	Seeing Clearly Now	253
Chapter 38	Is It An Empty Experience?	259
Chapter 39	This Thing Called Love	265
Chapter 40	Orgasmic Interlude	271

Chapter 41	The Sahara	279
Chapter 42	The Parades	285
Chapter 43	The Races	291
Chapter 44	The Caravan	297
Chapter 45	On Board the Simorgh	305
Chapter 46	The Peacock Chamber	309
Chapter 47	The Kosk Household	313
Chapter 48	Confessions Within The Mansion	319
Chapter 49	Talkie, Talk, Talk	325
Chapter 50	Fashion! What Fun!	329
Chapter 51	In The Mosque	335
Chapter 52	Redesigning Women	341
Chapter 53	"Pussycat, Pussycat I love you"	349
Chapter 54	Night Clubbing After Sunset	355
Chapter 55	Educating a Naughty Boy	363
Chapter 56	An Encounter with the Libertine	369
Chapter 57	At the Palazzo Della Gherardesca	375
Chapter 58	At Gallerie Dell Accademia & Ponte Vecchio	383
Chapter 59	At the Ristorante Santa Elisabetta	391
Chapter 60	In Anticipation Of Things to Come	399
Chapter 61	Notte Sadomasochistico	407
Chapter 62	The Rape of Shanghai	413
Chapter 63	Romeos and Juliets	421
Chapter 64	At Albergo Danieli Venezia	427
Chapter 65	At Terrazza Danieli & Ponte Di Rialto	433
Chapter 66	At Regata Storica	437
Chapter 67	Ristorante Da Raffaelle & Beyond	443

Chapter 68	Lido Excelsior Di Venezia & Plazzo Contessa Rosa	449
Chapter 69	Teatro La Fence & The Gondola Experience	455
Chapter 70	At Mercatino dell'Antiquariato & La Cupola	461
Chapter 71	That's What Friends Are For	467
Chapter 72	The Two Brothers	473
Chapter 73	The Rite of Passage	479
Chapter 74	Sex Before Circumcision	485
Chapter 75	Fitrah and Khitan	489
Chapter 76	Eid al Fitr & The Nubian	493
Chapter 77	Merci Beau Coups and The Visitors	499
Chapter 78	Ludwig, Oberon and Nirob	505
Chapter 79	Kismet and Friends	511

PART FIVE: Oasis, Daltonbury Hall, Paris

Chapter 80	Back At The Bahriji	519
Chapter 81	Oscar! What Am I To Do With You?	525
Chapter 82	My Mystery Lover	529
Chapter 83	Ou La La Mon Paree	535
Chapter 84	A Haute Couture, Chanel, Dior Emanuel Ungaro	541
Chapter 85	J'Aime Mon Paree	547
Chapter 86	Un Spectacle Historique de Beaute a Paris	553
Chapter 87	Café De Flore et Le Folies Bergers	561
Chapter 88	Les Maisons de Givenchy, YSL et Jean Patou	567
Chapter 89	Au Revoir Mon Aimee	573
Author's Biography		573
Acknowledgements		573

Introduction

The story I will tell you is a story of a boy whose unique upbringing and extraordinary educational experiences are so uncommon and surreal that you might think it impossible. My story is one that has been experienced by very few. Only a privileged few have been offered an opportunity as uncommon as mine: to be educated in life's varied forms of love, sensuality and sexuality in a sheltered, secret society that, to this day, is unknown to the Western world.

Basically, my story is this: I had a privileged upbringing that played out in England and the Middle East, including a unique - and perhaps startling to many - private school education that included being inducted into a clandestine organization. My story has been kept under wraps for close to forty-five years. It is ready to be told.

My family sent me to an exclusive private school in England. I was one of the students selected to enter a secret society within the school, from which I was sent to an even more exclusive, privately run Middle Eastern school in The United Arab Emirates. For four years, unbeknownst to my family, I willingly and happily was part of a Harem.

I pledged an oath of confidentiality and allegiance to the society and to my mentors, vowing never to reveal this establishment to the public. This unique school taught me more than the regular school subjects; we were schooled in many aspects of carnal knowledge. Once I agreed to partake, I was groomed and prepared for three months, before being sent to Arab Households.

I served wealthy aristocratic families in various parts of the Emirates. In short, I was in different Middle Eastern Households' male harems for a period of four years. Some might jump to the conclusion that I was sold into slavery; to me, it was nothing like that, as my story will reveal.

During my time in The United Arab Emirates, I was very well treated and received an abundance of financial gifts and gratuities which, after I left the boarding school, served me well by paying for my graduate and postgraduate education in England. Without this Harem experience, I would never have been able to afford a Master degree in fashion design at The Royal College of Art in London.

I have decided to tell this story because I feel the correct moment has arrived to make known this unique and clandestine education and to reveal how it made me the person I am today.

I am truly grateful to have had these experiences; to be one of few to have attended such an unorthodox school and to have had phenomenally valuable lessons studying a variety of human behaviors. I am grateful, and have remained humble during the entire learning process. The school I attended still influences me in my daily growth. It continues to provide me with strength, resilience, humility and compassion as a human being, searching for meaning in a human world.

The story I will tell, my story, taught me an understanding of vastly different expressions in the art of love. It taught me how our upbringing and our place in the world shapes our world view. This knowledge has kept me open, in mind and spirit. It taught me to be patient in learning every situation and experience by looking inwardly before assembling any immediate conclusion or relying on the preconceived judgments of another. As Jesus of Nazareth so rightly spoke to this effect - Let those who are unblemished cast the first stone at the sinner.

In many ways this is a Love Story, a love that is woven upon layers of intrigue - both in carnal knowledge and educational knowledge of life's many unrevealed mysteries - which not many adolescents have the privilege to experience. It is also a story of coming of age in a world that was, until then, foreign to me. I had the luxury of coming to know myself in a loving, structured environment, while learning how other parts of the world lived, worked and played.

I ask that you not be quick to leap into culture-driven reproach or plunge into judgment. Listen to my story. Hear my heart. Learn from my soul. Learn from the inner space where pure positivity and love reside. This world would be a very different place if we were non-judgmental of other cultures, of other drummers and of other dreams. As Sir Paul McCartney sings, 'Let it be.'

PART ONE

Kuala Lumpur, Malaya

CHAPTER ONE

The Foong Family

Beginnings

I was born into a wealthy Chinese household in Kuala Lumpur, Malaya. My father, S. S. Foong, was a successful business entrepreneur. He had his hands full running a talk-of-the-town nightclub by the name of Griffin Inn. He had also bought a large recreational complex with a huge public swimming pool, a basketball stadium and several in-house restaurants that came with this expansive property on top of a hill.

Members paid big bucks to join this recreational facility in hopes of meeting and networking with high flyers of the Malayan social circle, the Who's Who that frequented this expensive establishment. My father's business acumen extended beyond the hospitality and entertainment industry. He was also a developer and a builder.

Mr. S. S. Foong was a handsome, smart, intelligent young entrepreneur, and a great opportunist. While studying at a local Chinese public school, he met my mother, Miss K.L. Ho, on the basketball courts when both were representing their respective Malayan States in inter-state basketball tournaments. They fell in love and married on March first, 1941.

1941 was not an easy time to be married. The Second World War was in progress and Japanese troops had occupied Malaya. Because Foong had a good business head on his broad athletic physique, he benefited much by associating with the expatriate community residing in Kuala Lumpur.

After learning sufficient English skills, he became friends with several well-heeled British expats in the city. He garnered a reputation within the local expat community very quickly, as an enterprising entrepreneur. His nightclub business flourished and he became a wealthy businessman as the years passed.

Mother, on the other hand, was a typical Chinese lady of her era. For those who have read the well-known book The Joy Luck Club, you would have recognized Mrs. K.L. Foong, my mum: a genteel, well mannered, stay at home, adoring mother.

In the early years of my parent's marriage, they had a loving relationship. But, sadly, by the time I was born, their relationship had deteriorated. Mother already had two beautiful young boys in her care, my elder brothers, Hal and James. Although my family was wealthy enough to hire full-time nannies, a live-in maid, and domestic help to assist with the household chores, Mother was always there for her children. She was a marvelous mother; we remember her fondly.

Accounts & Reports

From what my aunties and older cousins told to me, our extended family was a daytime Soap Opera. With Dad out socializing, spending an incredible amount of time on his numerous business ventures, it was just a matter of time before the news of his infidelity became common knowledge.

On Mother's side of our family, we had many aunties and female cousins, often visiting and staying at our large five-bedroom house.

Annie quickly became a well-known household name among my female relatives. According to Aunt Tai Yee, Annie was our home wrecker; she was my father's gold-digging lover. She was The Griffin Inn nightclub singer who held a tight rein over Daddy, S. S. Foong. She was the femme fatale, the coquette, the whore to the women of the Foong household; there are endless other names I cannot remember.

You must realize I wasn't born during the period when Father started womanizing. Eldest brother Hal had left to study at an English boarding school at age thirteen. British friends of Father's were official guardians to Hal during his student days in England. Mother would travel regularly to the British Isles to visit her eldest child. During summer vacations or long school breaks, Hal would return home to spend them with his family in Kuala Lumpur.

James, my second brother, was studying at the Methodist Boy's School in Kuala Lumpur. Since we had numerous aunties and cousins staying with us regularly, Mother was able to travel extensively with her wealthy female friends.

A year before she became pregnant with me, Mum decided to be away from my father. She ran away from all her marital stress and unhappiness. Her marriage seemed to be falling apart at the seams.

Her relationship with my father had deteriorated into a love-hate relationship. There were times when major fights and quarrels would break out, but, soon after, kisses and 'I love you dearly' moments would occur. It was a pattern that happened over and over again.

She seriously wanted to be away from her husband during that period in her life. She was considering a divorce. In her heart, she continued loving my dad even though his infidelities had taken a toll on her, physically and mentally. She already had two handsome healthy boys, but she desperately longed for a daughter of her own to love and cherish.

She packed her luggage and off she went on a world cruise on the famous RMS Queen Mary.

CHAPTER TWO

On the Queen Mary

Departure

Towards the end of August, Mother left for Singapore with a couple of her peers (her elite, well-to-do women friends) on the RMS Queen Mary. Travelling on the Queen Mary was a luxurious experience, especially first class. Mother, like many wealthy women of her time, had trunks and boxes of luggage to load aboard the vessel.

Mother kept a Chinese language journal during those early days. A page in her journal read:

This ship is larger than I imagined, spanning three stories in height - an indoor swimming pool, salon, library, children's nursery, an outdoor paddle tennis court and the ship's kennel. Ang Gi, Si See and I boarded with several porters who transported our luggage to our individual staterooms.

Our rooms are spacious and beautifully Art Deco. Our individual maids, who attend to us whenever we ring the bell for assistance, greet us. Fresh flowers in our sitting room and on our dressing tables are beautiful - roses, gardenias and camellias. So enchanting! A fragrant rose scented bath was prepared by my maid so I could bathe and be dressed in time for dinner at the Captain's Table in the Grand Salon.

Tai Yee and Ying Yee came on board to see me settled before the whistle blew, informing our guests of imminent departure. We stood on deck before setting sail, throwing confetti and streamers to my sisters below. It was emotional, festive and full of good cheer. I am sad leaving my family and friends - tears started down my cheeks. Si See was by my side calming, comforting and cheering me. She said it's time to put my troubles aside and we'll have a great time on the trip. Unfortunately, deep within my heart aches, I already miss James and Hal and my relatives.

We had a marvelous evening during and after dinner. The food was fabulous and the dancing was fun. I met a handsome English gentleman, James R. Pinkerton, who is very polite, charming and he spoke fluent Mandarin. He is divorced, travelling with a couple of his business acquaintances and a senior executive with the Hong Kong & Shanghai Banking Corporation.

We sat overlooking the ocean, and talked for hours. He is a wonderful man; I like him. Lying on a comfortable bed and already missing home! I must catch some sleep.

On Tour

My mother loved to shop and she went to towns and cities just for shopping. Mother bought dolls and baby clothes from every corner of the world. Away for six months, she soon built a substantial inventory of dolls and baby clothes. There were antique dolls, baby dolls, dolls dressed in national costumes, dancing dolls, wind-up talking dolls, beautiful dolls, pretty dolls, smiling dolls, even ugly dolls! Mother even concocted and documented names for a beautiful baby girl in her journal: Li Lee, Yin Hua, Swee Ling, Mei Li, and more. All sweet names she had dreamed up on vacation.

Baby Clothes

Mother's excuses to friends for shopping for dolls and baby clothes were, "These are gifts for aunties and cousin's children" or "These are presents for my friend's kids". But the too thinly veiled reason for the extensive buying spree was the hope of a daughter. She wished to ensure that this girl child would have a beautiful wardrobe as soon as she arrived in the world, with lots of pretty dolls to see when her little eyes first opened.

She bought beautiful clothes to dazzle the little beauty as she was welcomed into Mum's world. A pretty baby she'd have a chance to love and dress up: that is what she often visualized.

When she returned home, she would design a pretty pink chamber in her five-bedroom house for this baby girl (as recorded in her journal). Magazine pictures and interior design photographs of girl's rooms all had been accumulated, collected, and photographed on her trip. She kept her prizes in a neat, tidy folder under lock and key in her private dressing room drawer. These pictures were the precursor to my bedroom, when I finally arrived.

Mrs. K. L. Foong was a beautiful woman. Full of vitality, and with a great love for living, she was elegant, sophisticated and very pleasing to the eyes of her beholders. No wonder she had many admirers. Men were drawn to her for her beauty, wit and charm. Women loved her charisma, sincerity and no-nonsense honesty. A good listener and clever conversationalist, she made friends easily. As a result, she had a wonderful cruise; as her trip came to an end she decided to give her marriage another try.

Chapter Two

Home Not So Sweet Home

Mr. S. S. Foong, on the other hand, had plunged deeper into his affair with the already infamous (among our household anyway) Annie, after mother left on tour. But the week after mother's return, Father played the role of an attentive husband, skillfully and splendidly.

He was home nightly, every evening of that first week, the week I was conceived. Mother, being the kind woman she was, had bought presents for every member in our family. Aunt Tai Yee, eldest of Mother's sisters, received a pair of pearl earrings. Aunt Ping Yee, Mother's younger sister, a gold bracelet. Mother's best childhood friend, Ying Yee, a tiny, crusted moonstone brooch. The list went on for all the cousins, relatives, and close friends, including the servants, the chauffeur and the gardener. There was great excitement in the household upon her return.

Sadly, the household bliss was temporary. The following week Father fell back into his habitual routine of spending the majority of his time with Annie.

Mother, discouraged and disheartened, wanted a divorce, but her husband would not agree to sign the divorce papers. A couple of months later, my mother discovered she was with child. She was incredibly elated, hoping to give birth to the darling daughter she could finally claim as her own.

On the other hand, she was sad, melancholic and extremely disappointed that Father continued his womanizing and did not agree to a divorce settlement. But now she had a new life in her and with that, new hope.

In those days, Malayan divorce laws were different than they are today. Both divorcing parties had to consent to the separation before divorce papers could be served. If one party did not agree, the other party would have little choice but to continue in the confines of their marital agreement. If one party decided to separate illegally - which was not a solution my mother would consider - he or she would not be able to remarry if not granted a legal divorce in the eyes of the Malayan law.

My aunties consulted with Mother and urged her to remain in her marriage. After all, they reasoned, Mr. S. S. Foong was a responsible financial provider for her and her children. Mother would not have to worry about money as long as she remained married to Foong. Her children's futures would be secure (so they thought at the time.) Turning a blind eye to this betrayal was a respectable way of dealing with the unpleasant situation, advised my aunties.

In early April, Mrs. K. L.'s private physician officially confirmed she was with child. One thing her gynecologist could not predict was the sex of this baby. Mother prayed diligently for a healthy baby girl.

CHAPTER THREE

The Chinese Year of the Water Snake

1953

1953 was a very good year. The English Princess, Elizabeth, became Queen Elizabeth, II, of the United Kingdom and the Commonwealth Nations. At the opposite end of the world, in a vastly different country, another "Princess", or so my dear mum hoped, was born. Mother was in labor for a long time. It was a most difficult birth.

Finally at 12:40 p.m., on December eighth, her baby emerged into the hands of her mid-wife. A slap on the baby's butt, and the room immediately filled with the loud wailing cry of the infant. Mum, too exhausted to ask the sex of her child, fell into deep slumber. The baby was washed, cleaned and wrapped warmly in pink blankets, and brought to the mother to behold. This beautiful child was a healthy ten pound . . . boy!

A boy, not the beautiful baby girl Mrs. Foong had prayed would be delivered into her bosom. Although my mother was disappointed her baby wasn't a girl, she did not show any sadness. Instead, she celebrated her love for this child. She was happy and delighted her chubby baby was healthy, and very cute!

Dolls, Dolls, Dolls

The moment I opened my little eyes, a room full of dolls greeted me! Dearest Mummy had placed all the dolls she bought on top of dressers, sofas, chairs, settees, and dressing tables. They were on the floor, on shelves, and on every possible surface. They were everywhere!

Wherever I looked, there were dolls, dolls and more dolls. All toys under the category of dolls were represented in mother's feminine bedchamber, which was later transformed into my playroom. Looking back, I guess that was my first introduction to a career in fashion. As I grew up, designing clothes for these beautiful dolls, especially the ugly ones (which most required my creative design) became my passion.

Nanny, the mid-wife who delivered me, was a wonderful lady who loved and cared for me until I was six. Nanny and I enjoyed a marvelous relationship for many years, until she died in the early 1970s. I called her Amah because that was a name most nannies used in those Malayan days.

Mother, being Mother, had endless charitable functions and social events to attend. She didn't care about these events, particularly, but, because of her social standing, she was obliged to attend. Her favorite pastime was playing Mahjong with relatives, friends and aunties.

Most of my early days - from birth to approximately three years of age - were spent mainly with Amah. Being the baby of the family, I was spoiled by Amah, my female aunties, and cousins and, of course, the darling Mrs. Foong.

Since Mother had bought girls' outfits when on tour, I was dressed in pretty frocks, beautiful dresses and color-coordinated outfits, all the time. According to Mother and Amah, a baby is a baby and no one will notice or care if I was wearing girls or boys clothes.

Or would they? Of course not! I, for one, didn't mind at all. In fact, I loved when my dear Amah pushed me around the neighborhood in my frilly candy pink pram, dressed in sparkling clean pastel-colored baby outfits with matching colored bonnets tied to my head. I adored and savored the moments when strangers stopped to play and oohed and aahed because I was so adorably cute. They often cooed, fawning over the cute baby. Many thought I was a girl.

Amah at times would correct their misunderstanding. I didn't mind in the least what people thought. I was enjoying the adoration.

The only person who did not care for my pretty baby garb was Mr. S. S. Foong. In my baby mind, he was an unlikeable party pooper! I didn't care for him at all. Whenever he came close, I wailed and cried until he left me alone.

Mr. S. S. Foong wasn't home most of the time. He was at his mistress' most evenings, and returned home only a couple of nights a week. Those who had come to know my father will tell of a temperamental man, an alpha male who liked his sons to behave like macho men. Both my brothers were well-behaved, gentlemanly boys. If they stepped out of line, they knew punishment would be close, if and when Senior Foong found out.

The Wrath of God

This is an incident aunty Tai Yee related: God, in the form of Father Foong, descended upon my brother Hal one afternoon at a fun family picnic. My parents and their two boys were enjoying a warm afternoon outing in our garden. Boys being boys, James and Hal were playing, running around and making a lot of noise. Father told them to be quiet, but Hal continued with his fun and games and would not listen to Foong Senior's warnings.

After several scoldings, Hal continued to be bratty; he did not listen to our father's admonitions. Suddenly, Senior Foong raised his hand and slapped Hal hard across the face. The sweet potato Hal was chewing flew from his gaping mouth and landed on one of our dogs, sending the innocent creature squealing and scrambling fearfully across the lawn. Poor Brownie must have thought a gigantic meteorite had landed on him!

Hal was so stunned from the slap! The side of his face was completely red with Dad's handprint. Hal's jaws dropped and he sat motionless for several moments before tears started rolling down his handsome face. He certainly learned his lesson that day; not to mess with Father.

Of course, sweet Mummy consoled her firstborn with stern reprimands, telling him he should have behaved when told. After this Wrath of God incident, both brothers hung attentively to every word Daddy said. Never again did they venture into defiance and brattiness when Senior Foong was around.

Water Snakes

According to ancient Chinese wisdom, having a Snake in the household is always a good omen, since the sign of the Snake means the family will never starve. Whether due to their shrewdness in business, intuition in their dealings, or tenacity over their assets, one way or another Snake-born folk managed to attract money. It is therefore not surprising that Snake folks are known as the guardians of the treasure. True to this ancient advice, when this Water Snake - Moi, arrived into the Foong family, Foong Senior prospered even more greatly in business and in his extramarital affair with Annie.

Following Chinese astrology and tradition, at the first month of a baby's birth, a celebratory feast and elaborate party for friends, business acquaintances and family is held in honor of the birth. My first birthday was a major event, catered in the expansive garden at the Foong Family residence. It was a coming out Party for this sassy Snake child!

CHAPTER FOUR

My Birthday Bash

Party Time

January 8 was a good day! It was the day I was officially presented to my parents' family and friends. I was there to witness all, yet I cannot remember a single thing that happened at this eventful function. But my aunts and older cousins told me all that occurred, in later years.

Er? Indeed!

The morning of January eighth began with the hustle and bustle of activities around our house. Maids polished the silverware. Fresh linens required ironing. The household was made ready for more than a hundred fifty guests who would descend upon our house later that evening. Uncles assisted in setting up the tables on the lawn, while aunties and female cousins busily prepared themselves for the evening's festivities. I was the most relaxed of them all, deep in peaceful slumber in my rocker, dreaming of my debut, my "coming out party," I'm sure!

Guests started arriving through the iron gates of our property around 5:00 p.m. By 7:00 p.m., the band from the Griffin Inn was playing Nat King Cole and Cole Porter tunes while guests mingled, chatted, drank and, true to any Foong celebration, gambled! Various types of card games like poker, gin rummy, and 21 were played. Mahjong was also a favorite at Foong parties.

Male guests in the front of the house were having a "good ole boys' club" get-together. Behind the kitchen a very different scenario played out. Aunties and female cousins from Mother's family busied themselves filling jars and containers with water, loading them into cardboard crates and boxes to be carted out by servants and the gardener to the iron-gate driveway.

They were preparing an ambush, readying themselves to begin the War of the Roses. A reliable source had informed Mrs. K. L. Foong that Ms. Annie would be arriving at our house to sweep S. S. Foong away from his son's birthday party. A few weeks earlier, my father had bought a brand new sports car for his beloved Annie to zoom around in.

At 7:30 p.m. sharp, when our guests were being seated for dinner in the gardens, a fancy, open-top sports car came down the road. In the driver's seat was Ms. Annie. She was dressed in a striped red and white open neck blouse with a matching floral red head scarf. She began honking madly for Senior Foong. She yelled for her lover to drive away with her. She wanted my father to herself!

Mother had her ammunition hidden in the shrubberies by the gate. Aunties, cousins and allies rushed to the gate picking up the bottles, ready to commence battle. As soon as the signal came from Mother, their commander-in-chief, the gardener threw open the wrought iron entrance and Mother's troopers rushed out in battle formation.

They hurtled water grenades, bottles, jars and whatever they could get their hands on, at the beautifully polished sports car, aiming chiefly at Annie. She was drenched! Her 'welcome' from Mrs. Foong left her a wet mess. Annie stepped on the gas and sped off without turning to look behind, in case more bottles came flying her way!

Father and the guest were totally stunned - speechless - and taken by surprise! They could not fathom what had just happened. Silence fell over the entire party. One could hear a pin drop, if not for my loud screaming cry. I did not enjoy the brash commotion that fell on my baby ears. All I wanted was admiration and adoration from those in attendance.

Quick to the rescue, breaking the icy cold silence, the Griffin Inn Band started up with happy Big Band dance music, mitigating the awkward situation. Soon the festive mood returned, or at least appeared to, on the surface. It was as if nothing unusual had happened.

Everyone sat politely through dinner. Liquor flowed. Toasts were made to congratulate my birth, and guests were back to oohing and aahing at the beautiful baby. I was the only one at my party who was completely and utterly oblivious to the evening's drama.

Life Went On

Life went on as normal, albeit superficially, after my birthday party. Father spent less and less time at home. I did not know my father during those early childhood years. It seemed that every time he was around, the household staff would do a disappearing act, so as not to be near Father Foong. If they could avoid him, so much the better, they reasoned. That was their unspoken creed.

Mr. S. S. Foong was a temperamental, intimidating man who often scolded those around him. He was reprimanding and demanding when he wasn't in a good mood, which was often the case. I was scared of Father and did not care to be close to him, or near him. If I was able to avoid his presence, I was a happy camper! If not, I was a cry-baby.

I was the complete opposite around Mum. I sought out her attention and affection. She was lovingly protective of her newborn, adoring me like I was her precious little Princess. She loved to dress me up like her Princess Doll in pretty clothes and show me off. Since James was in school most of the day and Hal was away studying in England, I was the cute baby Mother doted over, constantly.

Cute

I mentioned earlier that Mother had amassed quite a collection of magazine cutouts, pictures from periodicals and interior design photographs of baby girls' bedrooms during her extensive travels. My room was newly refurbished and decorated when I arrived into the Foong family. While visiting the classical French chateaus and cruising up the Rhine, mother fell in love with the French, German and Bavarian castles that lined the hilly cliffs of European rivers. Mrs. Foong could have designed the now-famous Cinderella Castle seen in every Disney theme park, movie and film. Mother had a stylized wall mural of The Swan King's Bavarian Neuschwanstein Castle painted by a local artist on one of my bedroom walls. It was well before the Disneyesque image of Neuschwanstein became a cliché.

I loved my bedroom. I spent many hours playing with my fabulous dolls in the play-wing of my fairytale bedroom. I was completely enveloped in a fantasy world within the walls of my pretty suite. For security reasons, I did not have many play pals.

My chief playmate was my dearest cousin, Pinky. She was a year older than me, and we got along splendidly. Mother loved her like a surrogate daughter and she unofficially became 'my beloved sister in crime' while growing up. She was my confidant for years, until I left for further education in England.

CHAPTER FIVE

Fashion Recruited Me

Aunt Tai Yee

Aunt Tai Yee moved into our house after my third birthday, to keep her sister company. Father wasn't home most of the time. My fourth birthday was a relatively quiet celebration compared to my first birthday celebration. Father, Mother, James, Pinky, Tai Yee and several close relatives came to our house for a ten-course meal. If I had a say as to whom I would have liked to invite to my birthday party, I would have ruled Father OUT! Unfortunately I was too young to have a voice. I had no choice but to put up with his presence whether I liked him or not.

Tai Yee brought a Singer sewing machine with a foot peddle. One of her favorite hobbies was making patchwork quilts as gifts for family members, for charity organizations to donate to the poor, and for the homeless who needed warm coverings for chilly nights. Her civic conscience was a great example to me then, and it still influences me today. Her creativity, however, was limited to cutting scrapes of woven fabrics into small triangles, rectangles and squares, before assembling the pieces and sewing them into colorful intricately patterned bedspreads, pillow cases and quilts.

Our chauffeur drove us to the home of tailors and seamstresses where Tai Yee gathered bundles of scape fabric which they discarded as rubbish. After we had enough finished items, Tai Yee, our chauffeur, and I would make the rounds to the various charity organizations and homeless shelters to drop off our donations. This act of generosity fascinated me.

A week after Tai Yee became a permanent fixture at our house; I started my apprenticeship with this amazing woman, assisting with scrape fabric cutting so the pieces would be ready for her sewing projects. My creative eyes and hands soon began mix-matching florals with stripes, plains with paisleys, and polka dots with gingham. The list was as limitless as the twinkling stars above the night sky.

After three months of watching and assisting her work, I progressed from fabric mix-matching to learning the art of simple sewing. It was fun peddling on the foot machine and more fun when decorative projects took form and shape in my little hands. Eight months from the day I commenced my apprenticeship, I was officially promoted to be Aunt Tai Yee's assistant.

At age four, I was an avid sewer, although I was limited to simple hand stitching techniques and sewing on the ever-fascinating foot peddling machine. My short legs had difficulty reaching the pedals.

Tai Yee liked what she saw and trusted my fabric mix-matching judgments. On my fourth birthday, I was presented with a congratulatory gift. It was a pretty dress, for her favorite sewing assistant. I was elated! I loved the dress.

Holy Smoke!

Another favorite pastime for Tai Yee was smoking cigarettes. When sewing, she would puff away like a flame blower to get her energy going. She must have gone through a minimum of two packs per day – every day! As much as I disliked inhaling the secondhand smoke, I continued to trail her every move. She was my teacher and mentor.

Being a child of four, I did not feel I had the right to advise an elderly lady to quit her lifelong smoking habit. So, I diligently sat through class inhaling cigarette smoke and putting up with the smell. I often mentioned to her I didn't care for the cigarette smell, but her response was always the same: "You're too young to know what I'm going through."

I've come to understand the emotional stress she endured throughout her difficult life. Her rogue husband disappeared when she was a young bride. Left with three girls to care for, she managed with assistance from my mother throughout the years. Her daughters grew up to be responsible ladies and married reasonably well before she came to live with us, permanently.

On the exterior, she showed a happy face. But I could often detect her sadness. At four, I did not understand the inner demons that were slowly destroying her. Aunt Tai Yee died of cancer six years later. It was a sad experience when Mother took me to visit her in hospital. The grand lady I adored was an emaciated, fragile skeleton of a woman. I did not recognize her.

After the visit, I wept, alone, in my fairytale bedroom. I had deep sadness in my young heart. She passed several days later, in her sleep.

Pinky

Pinky was my mother's favorite niece; she came to visit often. We were only a few months apart and we became great play partners. Usually, we played with the dolls that filled my playroom, dressing and changing their outfits. We played all the girlie games little girls play. Sometimes when Mummy was out playing Mahjong or with friends, we would secretly venture into her boudoir to raid her extensive closet, trying on Mother's clothes and shoes. We competed to see who was the fairest of them all.

My favorite thing to do was to put on Mum's beautiful cheongsams made from colorful silks, brocades, satins and jacquard prints. We also tried applying her make-up, and dabbed ourselves with fancy perfumes which were sitting on her beautiful mirrored dressing table. My favorite scent was definitely Chanel No. 5. It was also Mother's favorite. Nothing but the best for this pretty sissy boy!

Leong Lin

Pinky's mother, Aunt Lok Kam, owned Leong Lin, near Kuala Lumpur's Chinatown. Mother went there often for her hair treatment, sometimes twice or more a week, depending on the number of social events she had to attend.

Upstairs on the mezzanine floor, Auntie organized a small Mahjong den for her customers. After having her hair done downstairs, Mother would play a few games of Mahjong before leaving. More often than not, I would follow her to Leong Lin.

The glorious bouffant hairdos that came out of that salon were a sight to behold. 1950's rouge, lipstick and eye shadow were applied, and clients' nails were painted. It was amazing to watch. I looked, I observed, I learned and at times, I was taught by Lok Kam's staff. I learned techniques and tricks in the hair and beauty trade.

Since I was an eager learner of all things beautiful, the staff was delighted to teach me to do hair. Leong Lin had many used hairpieces and wigs which the professionals were happy to loan me for practice. In addition to my sewing training with Tai Yee, I also became an unofficial underage hair and make-up apprentice at Leong Lin.

Crocheting Prodigy

The moment I picked up my first crocheting needles, I knew I had found a new path of creative expression. From the mid 1950s, to the early '60s, the girls at Leong Lin would organize crocheting parties, and I was allowed to attend.

Women exchanged techniques and methodology at these events, and I paid attention. They taught me the art of crocheting raffia handbags, purses, mini-skirts and halter tops that were popular then. A quick learner, I would have crocheting competitions with the Leong Lin girls to see who would be the quickest to crochet an item from start to finish, without mistakes. The majority of the time, I won.

My work was never shoddy; it was retail quality. Before long, Lok Kam made a business deal with me. She wanted to sell the bags and items I crocheted. The salon would take 50% commission from the net, and I could keep the other 50%. The cost of materials, such as raffia, yarns and accessories, was covered by Aunt Lok Kam.

It sounded like a good business arrangement to my five-year-old mind. So, I crocheted my heart out, enjoying every moment. When Leong Lin marketed my crocheted items, customers were told a five-year-old child prodigy made the pieces. The items flew out the salon door, like hot cakes sold fresh off the griddle! I couldn't keep up with the demand.

The ladies who bought my creations loved my color combos and the creative way I mixed and matched different patterns into unique items. I was crocheting day and night.

It was only a matter of time before Mother put a stop to this madness. I had to go at a slower pace, she said. It was soon time to commence primary school. Of course, darling Mother had other extra-curricular activities planned for me after school hours, which were very exciting!

It is strange how life's circumstances present themselves. Fashion recruited me before I had a chance to say "No!"

CHAPTER SIX

The Little Ballerina

Sissification

To be sissified is not as easy as one might imagine. A "sissy" or "sissy boy" is a boy who does not comply with traditional male gender roles. He is, generally, more interested in traditional female hobbies or activities.

One might think, having read these past chapters about my upbringing that my aunties, Mum or Amah, feminized me, but that was not the case. A newborn male is initiated into this exclusive boy's club by birth and through birth only. It is nature rather than nurture that creates our uniqueness.

Sissy boys were described by the Ancients as "God's gift to humankind." For "us," the sissification process is natural, coming from a boy's inner soul and manifesting itself in his mannerisms, personality and character.

It is definitely not a lifestyle choice, as some believe, which can be avoided or reversed. Many sissy boys are known for their intuitive, sensitive and creative spirits. More often than not, they are open and liberal in their outlook on life, and accepting of others who also do not conform to society's norm.

Sissy boys are certainly not weak; rather, we are strong, resilient individuals who are unafraid to stand out in a crowd. We have demure, soft-spoken and genteel voices. Yet, our souls are giants, waiting to burst forth with valuable contributions to the world.

It is a sissy boy's birthright to dance, rejoice and sing his own song, set to his own music. The Ancients consider these unique souls as special beings, capable of guiding the populace's return to divinity. There is no special rhyme or reason to this sissification phenomenon. It just is. I'm privileged and proud to be a sissified boy!

Ballet

While Daddy Foong was busy making babies with the vilified, vicious, vanquished Annie, Young Foong was busy with my gay (no pun intended) hands and happy feet. Dearest K. L. had enrolled her son in ballet class. This was my after school activity.

During her trips to London visiting Hal, Mummy would often catch The Royal Ballet and The Royal School of Ballet performances at Covent Garden, Royal Opera House or at The Royal Albert Hall where they danced Swan Lake, Giselle, Sleeping Beauty and The Nutcracker.

Mother adored watching the dancers' grace, beauty and ease of movement during performances. Therefore, it came as no surprise that she wished her final child to acquire similar grace in everything he did. Since Hal was studying in England and James was a great swimming competitor in the State of Selangor, winning many gold and silver medals for school and State, I was the only suitable candidate in our household to be initiated into the fine art of ballet. K. L.'s motherly intuition served her well; her little boy adored ballet.

Mother had also enrolled Pinky. Not a born dancer, she dropped out after two lessons, much to my mother's chagrin. I thoroughly enjoyed dance classes, and continued until grade four in ballet. When I was the only boy pirouetting in an ocean of twenty girls, I hung up my ballet shoes for good, and I regret it to this day.

Dancing Queen

God bless Mummy Dearest Heart! K. L. loved to watch me dance. She was a proud mother when her young son danced, danced and danced some more. And dance I did! At home, I would practice plies, pas de chat, pas de deux, changement, battlement and much more.

After my regular school and homework, I'd switch on the gramophone, put in the black vinyl ballet record and away I would go! Sweet Mummy and Aunt Tai Yee would clap and cheer me on. The maids and servants stood on the sidelines smiling and swaying to the rhythm of the music.

It was a fun time until someone would hear Father's car drive up the driveway. Suddenly everything would stop. Maids and servants scrambled away as fast as their legs could carry them. Mummy and Tai Yee would switch off the gramophone and stash away the records while I made my great escape upstairs, untying my ballet shoes while disappearing into the study. I would sit at my desk pretending to do homework, in case Foong Senior walked in to inspect.

Daddy Poopy Doo-Doo!

There were a couple times when my team of staunch and enthralled supporters and I got caught red-handed. All hell broke loose! First, the maids and servants received a scolding for wasting time and not working at their never-ending domestic chores. Next, "Daddy Poopy Doo-Doo" would yell in a loud and condescending voice for Tai Yee to leave the living-turned-rehearsal room so he and Mother could have a "talk" about their "sissified" son.

There was a time when their 'talk' turned into fists of fury! The arguments turned into fights. Inquisitively, I would peer between the staircase railings, straining to hear and see what was happening below. Once, what I saw startled me. I never wanted to witness it again.

Mother was beating on Father's chest! She screamed obscenities at him while Tai Yee and our Filipino maid did their best to separate them. Our gardener, Ah Choi and Bakar, our Malay chauffeur, were both pulling Father away from K. L. The scene was wild, and too much for me as a 7-year-old to witness! I bolted into my bedroom, locked the door and cried in shock until the commotion below died down.

Yet, after my parent's disagreements, Mother continued to send me to ballet classes. Besides being the odd man out, the male "Lone Ranger" in ballet class, I was often teased by boys in my regular primary school. Other children called me "Sissy" or "Girly" or worse. They flung horrible names at me which were not nice to call anyone.

James, my older brother, would be a horse's ass and call me those names when he wanted me to perform some task for him, after I refused. I did not have to deal with his insults for too long. Once James was out of the country, Mummy pampered me more than ever.

Swan Lake

In my third year at ballet school, the Australian Ballet Company performed in Kuala Lumpur. My sweet yet stern ballet teacher, Mrs. Mary Lee, wanted her students to experience a large-scale professional ballet performance. Since Mother was a patron of several Performing Arts organizations in Kuala Lumpur, she secured tickets.

The excitement on the day of the show was simply too much for my little heart to bear. It pounded and thumped in great expectation and anticipation! Although we were attending a matinee performance, to me it was like an opening night premiere. I had never experienced a live performance of Swan Lake and certainly had not experienced ballet on this scale. For this little aspiring 'ballerina' boy, it was an incredible experience!

As Bakar drove our car to the main entrance of Stadium Negara, we saw crowds of people trying to gain entrance. Mrs. K. L. Foong and her sissy boy son breezed through security into the open arms of other board members who were present to meet and greet guests in the stadium's foyer. Uniformed ushers guided us to our front row seats, just two rows from center stage. Mummy made a special request for these seats so I could have a perfect view of the dancers' movements, expressions and their body language.

As soon as the Swan Lake overture started, I sat mesmerized in my seat throughout the entire performance, even though I was dying to go to the boy's room to pee. I held it in because I didn't want to miss any part of this enchanting show. The gorgeous sets, the fabulous costumes, the beautiful orchestral music, the superb lighting and the perfect sound system took me into a fantasy world I didn't want to leave.

The male dancers' performances were the best. They completely captured my imagination! I was engrossed in the world of ballet! When the curtains finally came down amidst a rain of red roses, bows were taken by the dancers. I sat in awe, clapping my tender palms till they were red and sore. I knew then and there, I wanted a career in ballet. Little did I realize then that life had a much different agenda for this little sissy boy.

Pretty In Pink

Before I leave this part of my story, I'm going to tell you a little secret of mine that I've kept hidden for years. Those in ballet know that male dancers wear black flat ballet slippers. Maybe we'll wear cream or off-white, but hardly ever pink, unless it's for a unique dance segment which calls for this pretty color.

Although I had several pairs of black ballet slippers which I wore in dancing class, I pestered Mother to purchase a couple of soft pink and peach slippers, because they were so beautiful, so wonderfully pretty to look at. These I kept for my rehearsals and practices at home. I also insisted Mother buy a pair of "point-toe slippers" because I wanted to dance on my toes like the beautiful female ballerinas.

After I hung up my black ballet slippers, I kept the pink pair I loved the most and used for practice. Now they sit in a box at the top of my shoe closet. When I want to re-live my ballet memories, I bring out these beloved pink friends to cherish and hold. Beautiful memories of my ballet years flit back to action reminding this "older, but wiser" ballerina that he is still dancing his dance for the world, and will be doing so for a long time to come before his final, fabulous Swan Song.

CHAPTER SEVEN

This Boy Just Loves to have Fun!

A Wedding

Summers came. Autumns went. Winters departed and Spring was in the air! What better time of year to have a wedding celebration than the merry month of May! Cousin Yun Wah's marriage to her long time beau, Foo Kor, was scheduled. Wedding planning had begun immediately after their announcement was made in November. When Yun Wah asked if I would be her Page Boy at the wedding, I was absolutely delighted and honored to participate! I quickly agreed. I began the process of finding the right outfit to match the two Flower Girls, Pinky and Ah Fong.

Chapter Seven

For six months I fussed over what I should wear as a Page Boy. Tai Yee said she would make me an outfit. Mother said, "No! We should go shopping to find something nice."

The one and only department store in Kuala Lumpur was Robinson, named after the British owner who created the establishment. We searched high and low but could not find anything suitable. Mummy wanted me to wear a white shirt with black dress pants. I wanted to be in all white. I must have been thinking it was my virgin wedding debut! Since we could not reach a compromise and the clothing selection was terribly limited, Mother had Bakar drove us to Singapore to continue our clothing search.

Singapore has always been considered by Malayans to be a more vibrant city than Kuala Lumpur. The chances of finding something suitable on this cosmopolitan island seemed more viable to Mrs. K. L. Foong. Off we went to pack for our journey across the Straits of Johore Bahru, to Singapore.

I had never been to Singapore. It was an exciting proposition for a boy of seven. I must have packed clothes for a week instead of for two days, because mother left two-thirds of what I loaded into my suitcase out! We departed at the crack of dawn so we could arrive at our hotel at the latest by 6:00 p.m., that evening.

On our way out of the city, we passed tin mines and numerous rubber and palm oil plantations. It was definitely an educational trip, as I had never seen real rubber or palm trees before. Bakar, born and raised on a rubber plantation kampong before venturing to work in the city, was a perfect tour guide.

As he drove, he taught me everything there was to know about rubber and palm oil production. Explaining in Malay or Bahasa Malayu, he gave me an explanation of the production of rubber. From tree planting, collecting the sap right through to the processing of the sap into all kinds of rubberized products (such as car tires and rubber bands) Bakar seemed to know it all.

Malaya, now Malaysia, is one of the largest producers and exporters of rubber and palm oil in the world. I didn't know before Bakar's wonderful tour. Although I was taught a little in school on this subject, it could not be compared to this field trip where I could witness it with my own thirsty eyes. Throughout the journey, I had my head out the window like a dog enjoying the wind blowing on its face. I was absorbing the Malayan country scenery as we drove past plantation after plantation. We also saw a number of tin mines, while mother napped.

In Malacca City we stopped for lunch. We ate authentic Nonya food, which was spicily delicious and suited my taste buds splendidly. As we proceeded towards Johore Bahru, we passed padi (rice) fields, which I'd never seen, either. Driving across the Johore Bahru causeway, we finally arrived on the island of Singapore.

You'll never guess where mother booked us: the famous Singapore Raffles Hotel! Wow! What a fabulous Christmas treat!

Raffles Hotel

Bakar drove to the front entrance of The Raffles Hotel. Before our car came to a complete stop, two bellboys in pristine starched white uniforms with tiny matching pillbox hats on their heads saluted our arrival. The Indian turbaned Bell Captain in a black, white, and red uniform came to Mother's side of the passenger door to open it for her. He extended his white-gloved hand to assist Madam out of the car. He greeted Mrs. Foong by her married name and led us through the grand glass doors into the foyer.

I didn't understand how the Bell Captain could possibly know Mother's name. Then, it dawned on me that Mother had stayed at Raffles when she was in Singapore eight years ago while waiting to board the Queen Mary.

Management made a point to remember those who had stayed at their luxury establishment throughout the years. That's how the "Ah Char" Indian Bell Captain knew Mother's name. By now, the two young bell boys were standing at attention, waiting for Bakar to open the trunk for them to collect our luggage. I held onto Mother's hand the entire time.

The lobby was opulent and superbly decorated. An enormous floral bouquet sat atop the lobby's large teak wood table. Glass skylight panels lit the hotel's interior with a golden glow giving one the feeling of entering a holy sanctuary or a grand Cathedral. I had to strain my neck to look skywards at the many floors lining the sides of the lobby foyer.

White marble flooring stretched for miles. It was covered, in places, by large Persian rugs in hues of deep orange, red, serpentine blue, aquamarine, and saffron yellow gathered together in paisley motifs. Dark brown wooden pillars and beams shimmered when light from antique chandeliers reflected on their polished surfaces.

I wasn't aware that Mr. "Ah Char" Bell Captain was standing next to me, smiling his welcoming toothy grin. He led Mother, me and my Teddy Bear towards the double wrought iron gated elevator doors. I was speechless, starring at Mr. "Ah Char" with eyes wide open.

The uniformed elevator boy closed the gates, and we ascended to our room. Our spacious room, a suite with high ceilings, a bedroom, and sitting room, reminded me of our house.

The two bellboys soon brought in our luggage and Mum tipped them four ringgit each, which was a lot of money in those days. I shared the huge, teak four-poster bed with Mummy. The bed sheets were the most luxurious I'd slept on in my young years. Totally comfortable and snug, I didn't want to get out of bed the next morning. I wanted to lie in luxury for hours.

Mother, on the other hand, had plans for us. After an exquisite breakfast at the open air Inner Courtyard Restaurant, we headed to town - SHOPPING! Yes, one of my favorite things to do is shop till I drop. And that's what we did on December 23rd.

Shopping

Shopping in Singapore was one of my favorite experiences. There were plenty of venues and choice selections. Our first stop was Orchard Road. Orchard Road then was quite different from what it is today. At that time, the majority of shops were housed in traditional Chinese style buildings owned largely by local shopkeepers. Even the department stores on the same street were locally owned and operated.

We walked, we shopped, we lunched, and then we walked and shopped again, until we finally agreed on a pair of long, off-white colored pants for me to wear at Yun Wah's wedding. Convincing Mother to make the purchase wasn't difficult. After all, she knew her son had an unusual taste in clothing choices. And this pair of trousers could certainly be considered unusual.

After much bargaining with the shopkeeper, she bought the off-white pants with appliqued cartoon characters on the knees. I liked the appliques because they were characters from Mother Goose, and they were so cute to look at. Our special task accomplished, it was time to have real fun eating local delicacies and visiting places of interest. That day was the best day in Singapore so far!

High Tea at Tiffin

I have to confess the most memorable moment of my Singapore trip was having High Tea at Tiffin in Raffles. The following day, after our wonderful shopping bonanza, Christmas Eve was upon us. Raffles was decorated like a fanciful fairyland. Christmas trees lit every floor. Decorated with hundreds of tiny twinkling lights, the trees were hung with pretty toy ornaments sparkling on pine branches in twinkling kingdoms.

K. L. told me early in the day that there was a surprise in store. At 4:00 p.m., we headed down to Tiffin. Through the large wooden doors, I entered Tiffin's Magic Kingdom! At the front of this huge dining room sat an enormous Christmas tree, every inch covered with delicate pinks, reds and white faerie ornaments. It was the most enchanting Christmas tree I could have ever imagined!

Beneath the tree were boxes of colorful presents wrapped and tied in an array of patterned ribbons and iridescent strings.

Toys of various shapes and sizes sat next to these enchanted gifts. Jolliest of all was Good ole' Santa, siting high on his golden brocade chair having photos taken with children of all ages.

A string quartet played Christmas tunes and carols by the tree. Every table was covered with pink, red and white tablecloths sprinkled with glittering fairy dust around the table's floral centerpiece. Sweet scented candles flicked in little glass containers, illuminating the room like dancing faerie circles in the depth of a winter wonderland. The antique chandeliers were draped with swirls of white, pink and silver heart shaped tinsel. Oh my God! A true-to-life Magical Wonderland for Mummy and me to enjoy and have fun! How fabulous!

Enjoying every moment wrapped in the confines of Tiffin's Magic Kingdom, I had completely forgotten about High Tea until finger sandwiches arrived on tiered silver trays. Strawberries and cream came in tiny glass bowls with shaved chocolate sprinkled on top of cream caramel. Jam and scones were delivered on silver platters. Cupcakes, chocolate cakes, lemon meringue pies, and custard tarts arrived at the tables. Towards the end of the festivities, raffle tickets were drawn. When the announcer called my name to receive a golden fluffy teddy bear, I was in Heaven and utterly thrilled with High Tea at Tiffin!

All fabulous things must come to an end, but memories are etched in our minds forever. This was certainly the most memorable Christmas's party of my childhood era. Little did I realize that this special annual Christmas event was organized by the hotel as a thank-you gesture to their guests for their patronage to this historical Grand Dame - The Raffles Hotel of Singapore!

Fancy Pants

When wedding bells rang in the merry month of May, I was dressed and ready for my walk down the aisle with the two pretty Flower Girls. All the members of my family were present including Mr. S. S. Foong, Mrs. K. L. Foong, Hal and James, who had both returned from England to attend Yun Wah's wedding. The marriage ceremony was held at the Petaling Jaya Marriage Registrar. Immediately after the ceremony, family and guests proceeded to Chin Woo's to attend a reception at the grand hall of this private sports club.

When the bridal limousine arrived at Chin Woo's entrance with the bride, the groom, the two bridesmaids and I, family and guests had already been seated and were waiting for the wedding march to begin. The bridal party was to proceed from the grand entrance towards the stage. In the limo I had the urge to pee but was so excited with the wedding ceremony, the picture taking, smiling, posing, and all the trappings of being a fancy Page Boy that I decided to postpone going to the boy's room even though I needed to, urgently. Mistake!

Since we were running late, as soon as we arrived at Chin Woo's main entrance the bridal party wasted no time and was ready for the procession down the red carpet. At this juncture, I had difficulty holding my pee and had to release and let go. Down the aisle, to the accompaniment of Clarke's The Prince of Denmark March musical fanfare we walked, while pee slowly trickled out of my white underwear, down the side of my leg, soaking my crisp white pants. By the time we reached the stage, my pristine white pants were completely drenched.

I was about to burst into tears from embarrassment when Mother came to her young son's rescue. She was sitting at the table closest to the stage. Up she jumped, taking me gently by my hand and led us towards the side exit. Once outside, she whisked me to the nearest restroom to release myself. Unfortunately, my fancy pants were already soaked and could not be worn until washed and bleached. Thank God good old Bakar, my 'Super Hero', came to my rescue. He drove home as fast as his ancient body could, got a change of trousers for me from the maid, and came speeding back.

But, oh no! I was not happy because the trousers Bakar delivered were not the ones I wanted to wear. The color did not match my shirt. "No! No! No! Not at all color coordinated! These simply will not do!"

I created a huge fuss in the restroom, flatly refusing to put on the pants Bakar delivered. I would not come out of the restroom until poor Bakar drove home again to fetch another pair. "This time, the trousers better match my shirt," I screamed.

Mother did her best to plead and reason with me, saying it was OK. No one will notice the difference between the white and the colored pants, she suggested. "This will never do," I said. "I cannot appear in front of so many people and not be color coordinated! No! No!" I cried kicking and screaming, refusing to come out of the stall I'd locked myself in. Mother threatened to call Father to put a stop to this madness.

"Father or no Father, if my outfit doesn't match, I am not making an appearance," I yelled. By the time Bakar returned with the correct trousers the wedding reception was almost over. So sad! I missed all the fun in the grand hall while screaming my bratty lungs out. I was, and still am at times, a spoiled brat and probably always will be.

CHAPTER EIGHT

On the Good Ship Victoria

VICTORIA

Choo, choo, choo, sounded the ship's horn. Mrs. Foong was yelling below deck for her son's attention, telling him to hurry and board the cruise liner, The Victoria. Hal and James were busy flirting with a pretty girl whom they had just met, by the Singapore dock. She was walking up the gangplank as my brothers followed like puppy dogs, listening attentively to her every word. I was busy running around deck to check out the facilities on our journey to Hong Kong.

For our annual vacation, Mother booked her family on a twelve-day cruise up the South China Sea. Senior Foong drove his family to Singapore to board the Victoria. He left the family's Bentley in the care of the Singapore Raffles Hotel until our return two weeks later. Father had promised me a stuffed toy two weeks prior to my ninth birthday, but my present never arrived. Every day I would pester Mother, asking if my present had come, but the daily answer was always negative.

Mummy had given me ample warning not to expect much from the promises Senior Foong made. Yet, in my boy's heart, I continued to believe Father would bring the gift. I waited and waited, but no present showed.

By the time we boarded The Victoria, I had given up on seeing a birthday present from my father. Although he had always given me birthday presents, there were times when his gifts were late. Never had they been completely forgotten. It was now two days after my birthday and no present. Though disappointed, I did not mention my disappointment to him. "Maybe he is too busy with his work to remember," I thought. Mother, being a sensitive woman, always knew when I was unhappy. She hinted that my gift would be arriving soon. Since there were many exciting adventures to experience on board this large vessel, I promptly forgot about the birthday gift.

After a wonderful luncheon buffet at one of the ship's many restaurants, Mother and I went for a stroll below deck to look at the galleries and shops. In one of the store, were two stuffed faux fur toy poodles. They were displayed in the window. There was a black one and a white one with red leather leashes fixed around their cuddly necks. It was love at first sight! I fell for both doggies in the window.

They had coats of curly fleece except for their knees, which were trimmed short, similar to the fashionable way real poodles were groomed in the 1960s. Mother saw me admiring them, and asked the sales lady, "How much are the doggies in the window?" As much as I loved the puppies, I didn't pester mother to buy them since I was told there was a playroom on board The Victoria. There would surely be sufficient toys to play with for the duration of the trip.

Wrong! The room was more a library than a toy room. In those early days of cruising, passenger ships catered to adults rather than children, unlike today, when ships are for the enjoyment of the entire family. Liners in 1961 had few facilities for children. In the toy department there were hardly any notable items for a child of nine.

I had started school and was reading children's books such as The Chronicles of Narnia by C. S. Lewis and the Enid Blyton Famous Five series. These were all marvelous books I loved. Complete sets were stocked on the library shelves, so I spent hours reading on deck, sitting on the sunning chairs by the First Class pool or inside the spacious library room, which the ship's librarian kept silent.

My brothers were busy cruising - and cruise the pretty girls they did! They often used me as bait to lure the ladies they fancied. Hal and James knew older girls had a soft spot for cute little boys. I was excellent at discussing girly topics. Subjects such as fashion trends, styles, crocheting, knitting, ballet, art, design, hair and make-up were my forte.

I had kept my eyes and ears tuned to learning all things fashionable and trendy. These were topics ladies loved to discuss and I was comfortable discussing them. They adored and loved me. Not many nine-year-old boys knew about fashion. When James and Hal came across a girl they were interested in getting to know, I would be pushed like bait to lure a fish.

My job was to strike up a conversation with the chosen girl, often with an opening line such as: "You are so pretty! Your skirt (dress or blouse) looks beautiful on you. You have such a great sense of style. I love your look! I'm hoping to be a fashion designer when I grow up and I would appreciate it if I could get some fashion advice from you. Do you have time to sit and talk?"

More often than not, they would agree and we would sit on the deck chairs and talk shop. We would become fast friends, laughing and giggling like I was their little long lost brother. That's when Hal or James would make their appearance and I would introduce them. Voila! Once that was done, I was to excuse myself on the pretext of having to visit the boy's room. I would leave my brothers to their flirtation with the "catch."

Being of use to my brothers had its perks. They were much nicer to me when I helped them, and they, in turn, would collaborate on goals I wanted to achieve.

Besides being engrossed in my books, I went swimming and played indoor and outdoor games in the liner's numerous facilities. Because there were not many children travelling first class, I was often bored. There were a few kids in Tourist Class but my parents didn't like me wandering too far away.

I ventured, secretly, below deck to check out the beautiful doggies in the window, admiring them and wishing I could own one. I asked Mother to buy one, but she said I had enough toys at home and didn't need another fleecy toy dog in my possession. But my love for these dogs was too strong. I devised a plan to have either Mum or Father buy one.

My brothers and I shared a sleeping cabin. There were two single beds which Hal and James took, while I slept on a smaller pull-out bunk bed which folded into the wall during the day. Sometimes, I would return to the cabin during the day, but the door would be locked. When I banged on it, one or both my brothers would yell to shush me off. I knew they were smooching gals inside and didn't want me around to disturb them.

Although my parents knew of their flirting, the rule was not to bring girls to the cabin. If caught, they would have to sit through an awful lecture by S. S., our tyrant dad. Now, I had a reason to blackmail my brothers. I could threaten to expose them if they don't conform to my wishes. I bribed them into finagling my parents to purchase one or both the doggies for me. To keep me from exposing their secret, they agreed to put in a good word on my behalf.

Sure enough, the next day I had my belated birthday present sitting by my 'drawer' bed, compliments of Father. It was the sassy black poodle that had been sitting in the shop's window, below deck. At last, Father remembered my birthday! My beloved brothers found a way to fulfill my doggie dream. Darlings!

But this is not the end of the story. I had told my brothers I wanted two poodles, not one. Since I have two brothers keeping two secrets, I deserved two doggies. A fair bargain, no?

I gave my father a hug to thank him for the present when we met for breakfast that morning. Later the same day, Mum, my brothers and I were below deck. The white poodle was still sitting in the window looking extremely forlorn, now that its companion had been sold. The stuffed puppy looked at me with such sadness. I wanted it badly now! James saw me staring at the puppy and said to Mother, "You should buy this for Yoong (my Chinese name.) It seems a shame to separate the two dogs; they should be together."

Hal agreed, and added, "The two looked great together and shouldn't be separated. Mum, you should buy the white poodle so they can be together as a couple." They did their best to appeal to the lady's soft spot. Mother wasn't sure if it was a good idea since I had already received the black puppy.

Hal continued his gentle persuasion, "If you are not going to buy it, maybe James and I will buy it for Yoong. After all, they look good together as a pair," he said, thinking K. L. would not let them purchase it since they were "poor" students. But she did not fall for their trap.

A day passed and I was losing hope. After tea, I ventured downstairs to visit the white puppy to check if it was still available. Tears flooded my eyes when I saw the shop lady giftwrapping the white dog. I thought to myself, "Oh no! I'm too late. Somebody bought the dog. It's gone, gone! I'll never see it again!"

The sales lady saw I was by the entrance. She knew me by now, since I came to visit the doggies daily. She took my hand and led me to the counter, smiling the entire time. She requested I wait by her side until she finished wrapping.

I waited till she finished. Bending down with a charming smile on her face, she handed me the gift. "I know you love these two dogs very much. Your dad bought you the black one and now your lovely mother bought you the white one. Here is the present your mum asked me to wrap. She knew you would be coming and I'm to give this to you. Go say thank you to your mother," she said.

I was totally elated, overjoyed and in shock! Taken by surprise! I couldn't believe I was getting two doggies! The sales lady gave me a loving hug and sent me running to thank K. L. for her gorgeous present. When I found Mother she was with her other sons. I gave her a big hug. My brothers gave me knowing winks -- their way of telling me to keep their secrets under wraps. Deep in my heart, I knew my brothers loved me, though they never admitted they did.

Sampan Vendor

Cruising into Victoria Harbor was a lot of fun! Sampans and Chinese junks surrounded the sides of Victoria, welcoming the passengers and flaunting their wares. The sampan vendors were always present when international cruise liners arrived and departed from the port. Sometimes vendors would be allowed to come aboard and install temporary counters to sell their products.

It was fun rummaging through the clothing and crafts on display. There was a particular vendor who sold fur products: fur-lined coats, jackets, hats, caps and everything and anything else made with fur. With my deciphering eyes, I spotted a fur-lined child's jacket hanging on a bamboo rack.

For those who know Malaysia, you know it is a tropical country. No winters, no snow, no sleet, certainly no ice or anything remotely connected with cold damp winter weather, except freezing air conditioning inside hotels and cinemas. A fur jacket would be the silliest thing a Malayan child could ask for. However, this child was no ordinary child! He was a sissy fashionista and when he fell in love with a fur jacket, he wanted it and he got it! Unfortunately for this child, he had no cash in his pocket to make any purchases.

Off to pester Mrs. Foong I went. Mother did not sway to my way of thinking, though she did agree that the jacket was nice and well made. "Where would you wear this"? She inquired. My lame excuse was to air-conditioned places such as the cinema and restaurants. I could not think of any other venues. Of course, Mother didn't give in to my nonsense to buy the jacket. As much as I loved the garment, there were no justifiable reasons to make the purchase. For once, I gave up and was a sensible child - but not for long.

Hong Kong

The five days we were in Hong Kong, we went everywhere, from Aberdeen Jumbo Kingdom for delicious seafood to shopping on Nathan Road, Kowloon. We went all the way across to Central, down to Causeway Bay around Hong Kong Island.

One of Father's great loves was eating and dining. So eat and dine we did, from the hole in the wall Char Siu, or Roast Pork rice plate eateries, to fine dining restaurants in The Peninsula Hotel. The only word in my vocabulary to describe those five glorious days of gastronomical indulgence is SUPERCALIFRAGILISTICEXPEALI-DELICIOUS! We ate, shopped, went sight-seeing, and ate and shopped some more!

The Peak

One of my most memorable outings was to The Peak. Catching the Peak tram up the steep slope was exhilarating, scary and tremendously exciting! In those days it cost approximately thirty HK cents for a one way ticket for adults. Children's tickets were fifteen cents. It was a beautiful ride before Hong Kong became over built.

On the way up and down the mountain I had a view of the entire island. The tall Kowloon clock tower was visible from high above the clouds. The view from The Peak was spectacular. There was a Peak restaurant where visitors could dine and walk around the area to enjoy the spectacular mountain-view and landscaped gardens. It was located in an expensive residential area. The majority of colonial style residences were owned by wealthy expatriates and rich local business owners.

I could also see The Victoria docked at the harbor below. We did not stay at a hotel, since board and lodging were provided on the ocean liner. A motorized ferry carried passengers daily between Victoria, Kowloon and Hong Kong. At an allocated time, the ferry would collect the passengers returning to ship.

Repulse Bay Hotel

The Repulse Bay Hotel was another charming destination we visited on the island. It was built by the side of a cliff; one could walk to the beach below down a long flight of stairs. The hotel itself has a storied history and is now classified as an historic preservation.

We had lunch sitting on the terrace overlooking the ocean. Cruising below were yachts owned by the rich and famous. The beautiful and expensive cars parked outside the hotel were as fancy as their clientele, who came to stay and dine. Hong Kong movie stars and starlets of the day loved to see and be seen at the Repulse Bay Hotel.

Mother was a great fan of the Chinese Silver Screen, and especially loved movies directed and produced in Hong Kong. She and I were in awe admiring the star-studded cast who passed by our table every few minutes. "There goes Ms. Lin Dai with her new beau." She'd whisper. "Sitting under the umbrella is Ms. Yam Kim Fai and her lesbian lover," she'd say. "Over there lounging on the balcony is Ms. Betty Loh Ti and Ms. Margaret To Chuan!"

It was quite a sighting for us Malayan visitors, who practically worshiped these popular Hong Kong actors and actresses on the Big Screen. Mother and I were certainly the privileged few who saw them for real -- not just in the movies, but also as breathing human beings. Unfortunately, most of the actresses we saw that day met untimely deaths, some committing suicide, which many celebrities seem to have a habit of doing even in the twenty-first century.

Furgalomanic

Before I knew it, it was the last day in Hong Kong. Remember the fur jacket I wanted? The vendor was back on board displaying her products before The Victoria was to sail. Although we had done a lot of shopping, to me there was always room for one more item in my suitcase no matter how much I already bought.

I had to devise a plan to have Mother buy it without realizing the jacket was for me. Again, I solicited Hal's assistance. I pestered Mother to go with me to check the stalls again, to see if the vendors had brought anything new and exciting. Hal made an excuse to join us, saying he had to find a gift for his English guardians, the Andersons, who had been so hospitable to him. It would be a nice gesture to buy the couple and their two children gifts from Hong Kong.

The three of us trotted off, looking at products on display. When we arrived at the fur vendor, I gave Hal a sign, so he would know which jacket I wanted. Hal casually mentioned to Mother that the fur jacket sitting on the bamboo rack would be a perfect gift for the youngest Anderson boy, Paul, who was similar in age to me.

Hal took the garment, and handed it to me to try on for fit and look. Hal got K. L. to buy the fur jacket for Paul, as one of his gifts for the Anderson children. He convinced her that Paul would find good use for the fur jacket when winter hit, and the boy would have a great Christmas present from the Foongs. It would be a token of appreciation for the family looking after my brothers in London.

Hal would temporarily hold on to the jacket after our return to Kuala Lumpur. When he returned to London, he would conveniently forget to pack the jacket and I would keep the garment. Everything went according to plan. Hal flew to London without Paul's gift. I kept the jacket and wore it once to an air-conditioned cinema to see a cartoon movie with my cousins.

The following year, when Hal returned to Kuala Lumpur on vacation, I surrendered the fur jacket, which he then gifted to Paul a year later. I was a happy boy because I got to wear fur for the first time in my life. Since then, I have owned many fur garments.

CHAPTER NINE

Club Chop Suey at Griffin Inn

Flower Drum Song

"Bien Venue, Ladies & Gentlemen! Welcome to the fabulous Club Chop Suey at Griffin Inn where all the women are beautiful, the men are handsome and the nights are forever young!" announced the MC through the old fashioned microphone on stage at the Griffin Inn nightclub. It was the first of many themed events that Mr. S. S. Foong organized at Griffin Inn. Father had always had great panache and showmanship. During Griffin Inn's heyday, there would often be elaborately themed parties, costumed soirees, and an abundance of black tie events at this Kuala Lumpur talk-of-the-town nightclub.

Griffin Inn is no longer open; the Selangor Turf Club now occupies its address on Jalan Ampang. It was a beautiful nightspot with its Coral Bar and good sized dance hall decorated with three-dimensional coral, sea shells and mother of pearl underwater murals. It boasted a staff of thirty five cooks, dozens of waiters, busboys and other employees for the large main dining and dance hall -- the garden restaurant and the pool bar.

This was also an era of great movie adaptations of stage musicals by Rodgers & Hammerstein. One of the first, the movie version of South Pacific, premiered in 1958. It was followed by Flower Drum Song, which premiered in 1961. These were international blockbusters. Foong Senior seized the perfect moment to create a themed event at Griffin Inn, aptly named A Night at Club Chop Suey. Father's creative mind went as far as to gather my many female cousins to perform a song and dance number at the Club Chop Suey. Who was nominated to be the choreographer and costume designer for this performance? Me!

Father knew I was extremely good at dancing and he also knew I had been watching all the Rogers & Hammerstein musicals that Mother had taken me to see on the Big Screen. I was glued to these early musicals and watched them many times at the local cinemas. As much as Father wanted me to butch-it-up and behave like a macho boy, he knew I was gifted in the creative department. My assignment from S. S. was to train a group of ten female cousins to perform a professional dance routine to the song "I Enjoy Being a Girl" from the hit musical Flower Drum Song. It was a perfect little girly boy's dream to choreograph a dance routine to this campy musical number.

The first item on my agenda: Round up all ten of my female cousins to watch the movie musical Flower Drum Song. I made them watch the movie until they were sick and tired of watching the same show over and over again. I familiarized them with every detail, nuance and gesture of the sexy female lead in the movie.

My cousins complained about having to watch the movie over and over, but I put my foot down and insisted they follow my instruction or else I'd give a bad report to the Big Boss, Mr. S. S. Foong. None of my cousins wanted a bad report card. As much as they moaned and groaned about having to sit through the show repeatedly, they wanted to give a good performance, so they ended up watching the movie until they memorized the show in its entirety.

Second item on my agenda: Put the cousins who were great dancers in front and the not-so-good ones at the back of the chorus line. Four cousins with dance training were the leaders of the pack. The remaining six were followers, who learned from watching the four girls in front.

I was glad several of my older cousins had studied ballet and that the rest had some form of ballroom dancing background. We were able to devise a routine in which each dancer could work within her range of dance skills with reasonable ease.

The third item requiring my attention: Teach my cousins who were not good actors to strike 'Vogue Poses.' I devised a method of getting the cousins who were good at posing to work with those who did not possess this natural flair. I showed them many poses since I knew what I wanted.

I had been browsing movie magazines (especially the Asian movie gossip magazines, which had plenty of photos of Hong Kong movie stars striking poses for the paparazzi) and looking at fashion magazines since I was six. Showing the dancers how to strike 'Vogue Poses' came as easy as A, B, C for me. The task was teaching them timing, and when in each song segment a specific pose was required.

Number four on my work list: To show my cousins how to be more overtly feminine than they already were. This job was much harder than I imagined but proved to be a lot of fun nevertheless. The majority of my cousins were stiff and inflexible when it came to body movements. Because of my dance training, it was easy and natural for me to move in graceful exaggerated gestures. They thought it was hilarious that a boy of nine could outdo the gals in the art of being a girl.

The rehearsal sessions were two hours every other day for a period of two months. We often ended rehearsals with roaring laughter, having a fun time, constantly running beyond our scheduled time. We spent numerous hours and days of grueling, hard work even for professionals, let alone amateurs whom I had to train from scratch.

Fifth item on my agenda: Hair and make-up. Aunt Luk Kum's salon, Leong Lin, sponsored hairdressers and make-up artists and provided us with wigs and hairpieces. Thanks to her we were ready to roll. My job was to advise the hairdressers on how best to style the dancers' hair. I wanted a unified look for all of the performers, so they wouldn't look uncoordinated on stage.

We had several make-up and hair runs prior to dress rehearsal. A few of my cousins wanted to do their own hair and make-up but I put a stop to that! I knew even at that age that I could not let the girls do their own hair and make-up if I wanted a consistent, 'total-look.' Every dancer had to do as I commanded!

I'm glad my cousins had faith in that nine-year-old who took charge. I suspect they all believed I would grow up to be in the design business since I was always so fussy and detail-oriented!

The sixth item on my work sheet: Collaborate with the Griffin Inn stage manager on the backdrop I required: basic black drapes. The audience should concentrate on the dance and dancers and not be distracted by gimmicky stage tricks.

For me, the two most important stage requirements were excellent lighting and sound. The professional lighting & sound technicians at Griffin Inn performed well without any of my input. If anything, I should have been learning from them rather than giving them directions. The sound and lighting turned out excellently as I imagined on performance night.

And last but not least, the costumes! Besides Aunt Tai Yee being our seamstress-in-residence, Cousin Lai Ngor, an accomplished professional dressmaker and also a Club Chop Suey dancer, was also involved in making the costumes. She was an excellent seamstress. She set up shop at our house as a private tailor and dressmaker and sewed outfits for airline stewardesses and secretaries, privately.

I was seven when my cousin arrived to take up residence at our house. She proved to be a perfect teacher who furthered my sewing education. I assisted in picking up pins and doing menial tasks for her while she did her pattern construction, fabric cutting, sewing, fittings, and garment finishing. As in the rest of my creative apprenticeships, I learned by watching, progressed to apprenticeship and finally to assistantship. I absorbed many sewing and pattern cutting techniques from Cousin Lai Ngor over the years until I left for school in the United Kingdom.

It went without question that Tai Yee, Lai Ngor and another cousin Yee Mei were the designated seamstresses, responsible for all costumes for the Chop Suey girls. Although I knew how the outfits should look, I wasn't skilled enough to advice on costume alterations and fit. I learned on the job by watching the three dressmakers fit the outfits onto each dancer. I stood, watched and gave comments on basics, such as pant or dress lengths, styling, color co-ordination and accessories.

Besides being the choreographer, I was also the costume designer. Designing costumes was the easy part, as I had lots of ideas to put into use. During the late '50s and early '60s, A-line mini dresses were the fashion rage, along with knee length capris, and hot pants were gaining popularity.

Cousins who didn't have a 'perfect' figure wore A-line mini Go-Go dresses. The ones with great legs and slim waist wore hot pants. The dancers with decent legs were in caprices with ribbon fringes dangling from their trouser hems. They wore matching bolero jackets over their one-piece skin colored swim suits with curvy-suave circular frills sewn on them.

The girls that had great boobs wore low scooped one-piece swimsuits, to show off their assets. The cousins with flat boobs wore padded, low-cut bras sewn into their fitted body suits. Voila! We had a group of Folies Begere pretenders, ready to take center stage at the Griffin Inn Club Chop Suey Revue!

Festivities

We rehearsed, rehearsed and rehearsed for hours and days on end. With sheer determination and the spirit of teamwork, we finally made it to show day. The nights before my big debut, I couldn't sleep due to the excitement. After all, it was the beginning of my career as a theatrical costume designer and choreographer.

The local press, The Straits Times, and The Star newspaper sent reporters to review the opening night premier. It was the first time a nightclub in Kuala Lumpur had been the venue for such an extravaganza, according to their entertainment news reports.

Foong Senior had organized street stalls and vendors to be set up around the Griffin Inn lawn. There were stalls selling Chinese fans, crafts and trinkets, paintings, auspicious calligraphy, parasols, and even a stall which sold miniature stuffed toy pandas. The evening started with the lighting of firecrackers which was followed by lion dances. The finale was a dragon dance, which I missed due to exhaustion.

The same twenty piece ensemble that played at my one-month birthday party also performed for this event. Guests, with drinks & cigarettes in hand, mingled while checking out the stalls (and each other).

Ms. Annie Low, Father's not-so-secret lover and the resident singer at the nightclub, sang songs from the movie Flower Drum Song. Guests danced the evening away; the fox-trot, quick step, cha-cha, mambo, and salsa were popular dances of the day.

My parents, apparently, had reached an agreeable understanding that there would be no fighting or bickering over Mr. Foong's affair with Ms. Annie Low. She had been in his life for close to ten years. By now, mother had mellowed and had pretty much accepted the fact that Father wasn't going to leave Annie or her. On social occasions such as the Club Chop Suey soiree, all involved parties behaved in a cordial and civil manner towards each other.

It was my "Big Night". Mother came to give us her moral support; she was not there to pick a fight with Ms. Low. The evening festivities proceeded without any drama outside of that found in my choreographed routine, performed on stage.

The Show

The show went splendidly well. The girls struck 'Vogue Poses' and looked entirely professional; their hair and make-up were perfect. The costumes looked fabulous on stage. I was the only nervous wreck among the sea of people who came for the event!

I hadn't eaten all day because I was too excited. I ran around like a mad "queen" checking on everything, to be sure we were on schedule. The hair/make-up team arrived fifteen minutes late. I was up in arms, legs and all other body parts, cursing them while fussing over costumes and accessories before the dancers went on stage.

I was standing by the backstage exit, next to a full-length mirror so I could perform last minute adjustments before the dancers went on stage. I was like the girls' mama san checking to make sure they didn't forget their fans, feather boas or whatever else that required last minute attention.

Before the dancers could change out of their costumes, the newspaper and magazine reporters were already lined outside the changing rooms waiting to photograph and interview the Chop Suey girls and the choreographer. My adrenaline was pumping, over time. The crash was going to happen sooner or later and thank God it was later, after the press photos and interviews. I threw up, and then I blacked out from hunger, insufficient sleep, and stress. An ambulance arrived and took me to the hospital.

When I came round, Mother, Tai Yee, Lai Ngor and Pinky were by the hospital bed. The doctor told Mother it was over exhaustion and that I would be fine after a few days' rest.

The next day, both local newspapers had very positive write-ups on the "marvelous" performances at Griffin Inn. It was great publicity for the nightclub.

The following year we collaborated on 'I'm Gonna Wash that Man Outa My Hair', from South Pacific. I am grateful to my father for giving me these opportunities to shine. I did shine, with panache and style!

CHAPTER TEN

Macho Mary goes to Town!

Ooh, la, la! Isn't he cute?

Father decided enough was enough regarding my feminine pursuits. He increased his efforts to butch me up! "No more dance classes for my son," he said. "Time for some serious man action!" S. S. enrolled me in Karate class at Chin Woo, the gymnasium and stadium Father owned.

When he told me I was enrolled for Karate, I tried to figure ways to escape this drudgery. At first I pretended to be sick, but that only lasted a day. When I couldn't put it off any longer, I had to attend.

Karate Boys

When I walked into the gymnasium's grand hall, there were approximately ten boys between the ages of eight and twelve. Father walked to the podium and started talking with one of the men, who later introduced himself as the karate instructor, Master Chen. There were several boys I immediately took a liking to; my testosterone was working overtime!

I kept it to myself that I found boys attractive. I was afraid someone would find out what was in my mind. I certainly wasn't educated in the facts of life or about homosexual thoughts and finding other boys attractive and sexy.

Philip

Instructor Chen had all the boys seated cross-legged in a circle. He asked each person to introduce himself by name and age. I was a shy boy and spoke very softly, and I was hardly audible in this huge hall. I was asked again to speak louder, so the class could hear. Instead of doing as I was told, I became tongue tied and felt scared of all the eyes staring at me. It must have been this frightened puppy gesture which drew Philip, an older Caucasian boy, to my side. He was one of the older boys who worked as a teaching assistant to Master Chen.

Philip sat by me and held my hand in his. With an assuring, gentle, masculine voice he told me I didn't need to be frightened. With this handsome guy by my side, I regained confidence and proudly announced my name to the class.

Since most of the boys were young lads and first-timers at public speaking, Philip knew it was a daunting task for us to face a large group of unfamiliar faces. He took the role of the understanding older brother to whom the boys could go if they had difficulties, questions or problems.

My problem was that I was mesmerized by Philip's good looks, masculinity and gentleness. You might say it was lust at first sight! I kept staring at him all through class.

Although there were several older boys who were handsome, it was Philip's charm and charisma that attracted me. He was the kindest person, I thought. Every time I had difficulty performing a warm-up exercise, he would be at my side, teaching me.

The first classes were simple warm-up exercises. Then we rehearsed hand-chopping techniques. Philip always came to my assistance when I had problems with any of the tasks. By the third session, I was already 'in love' with this handsome guy. I couldn't take my eyes off him when he did karate demonstrations. I was glued to his every move, wondering what it would feel like if he ran his hands over my body. Of course, I didn't tell any of my naughty desires to anyone, especially not to Father, although I think he must have felt something unusual about my infatuation with Philip.

Most of the time, Father sat on a bench in the hall, watching my progress. Because it was his idea for me to learn karate, Mother insisted he be responsible for me during each session.

In the fourth class we were taught 'knife-hands.' Every time I tried the chop, I would yell "Ouch!" Like a sissy boy, and the rest of the class would laugh and giggle. Philip would appear by my side, patiently teaching me the technique. He would hold my hands in his, encouraging me to work on the motions, slowly.

His closeness overwhelmed me! I could smell his masculinity and felt intoxicated in his presence. I fantasied that he wouldn't let go, that we would perform the knife-chop with his hands on mine. I would often create excuses about not understanding certain moves in order to have him demonstrate it again and again. My mind ran wild; I imagined being caressed and held by him lying next to me.

Before long, Foong Senior figured I was hooked on Philip, not on karate. By the fifth class, old Foong decided my karate days were over. His excuse - my karate chops were disastrous and extremely painful for him to watch! Listening to me yell "OOOUCCHH" during practices was unbearable for his macho ears!

I think he figured out that I was infatuated with Philip and not karate. That ended my karate career once and for all. I missed Philip miserably, until the next cute boy came along!

Judo

Yes, Judo! Another desperate attempt by S. S. to butch-me-up. One day I was happily minding my own business when Father came into my fairytale room and announced he had enrolled me in Judo classes. I would be driven to class in an hour, he informed me. Oh God, I thought! Dreading another ordeal, I desperately tried to find an excuse not to go. Unfortunately, no good excuse came to me so off we went to Judo class at Jalan Pudu.

This Judo training facility was a wooden shack. The floors were covered with padded Japanese straw mats. A small office with a waist-high glass wall provided a lookout for staff to keep their eyes on the classroom.

There were fifteen lads between ten and thirteen years of age, and six boys between fourteen and seventeen. Mr. Thomas Chen was the instructor. There were two assistants - Eric, a nineteen-year-old hapa-haole boy, and Lee, a twenty-three-year-old Chinese man.

In class, I was the quietest boy. I sat behind the students, mainly to avoid being called upon as demonstration material! I hated Judo. Without Philip for me to salivate over, life was a misery in Judo class. For some unknown reason, I seemed to attract handsome boys when I needed help.

Eric knew I was shy. Whenever students were pairing to rehearse throws or strikes, Eric always partnered with me. I would create excuses to be next to him, waiting for all the other boys to find partners. Seeing me alone, Eric would have no choice but to choose me.

I loved being thrown around by Eric! He tried, over and over again, to teach me how to resist, and defend. I would purposely let him get the upper hand so he would land on top, straddling me with a firm judo lock. I could smell his handsome masculine scent. His cute face would almost touch mine, if only for a brief moment.

I would fantasize that his mouth was on mine. I could envision him French kissing me with his tongue. At ten, I couldn't make sense of why I was sexually aroused by Eric. I didn't understand the strange stirrings happening in my groin. He would immediately release his grip on me, and pull away, like he was afraid of letting his guard down. He seemed to put his emotions in check, not wishing to proceed further. There were times I had to run to the restroom, so my erection would not be noticeable.

After the sixth lesson, Father struck me off the Judo list. He didn't expect that his attempts to "butch me up" would back fire. I think by now, he suspected this girlie boy was as Gay as a Goose! Once again, I missed my young man mentor. I felt miserable because I wouldn't see Eric any more.

Before Father removed me from the judo class, Eric gave me a photograph of himself giving a demonstration. I had given Eric some lame excuse about needing a picture to better remember a Judo move. I believe he secretly knew the reason I asked for the photo. I placed it by my bedside so I could adore his handsome face and body. I could at least fantasize for a while, until some other cute guy caught my fanny. Oops, sorry, I meant, "Fancy!"

Martial Arts

Father just wouldn't give up! After Judo he enrolled me in Kung Fu classes. For goodness' sake, would this man never learn? This son wasn't going to be the macho dude he envisioned! I played along, without letting the old man know my thoughts. I'll give you three guesses why I went to class. Correct: To meet handsome guys. Off to Chin Woo, not for Karate this time, but for Kung Fu.

In order to increase Chin Woo club membership, a variety of sporting classes were organized for members. The stadium's manager, Mr. Fang hired overseas instructors to conduct special classes. The class I was signed up for was conducted by two well-known martial arts practitioners from Hong Kong. They had collaborated with the famous martial arts actor Bruce Lee, choreographing several of his Kung Fu movies.

I loved looking at the Martial Arts teachers. I had seen advertisements of them in local magazines and these two were as handsome as they came. I rated these cute Asian guys high on my list of good-looking people. They both had great bodies to salivate and fantasize over; I definitely wanted to be in their class!

As it turns out, the class was over booked and filled to capacity. A good try, Father, but your scheme failed miserably, again! There is a gay son in the family, so deal with it, Mr. Foong!

One Enchanted Evening

It seemed ironic and contradictory that, on the one hand, Foong Senior tried to convert his son to be a macho boy, and, on the other commissioned him to work on a dance routine based on a song from the South Pacific. It was aptly named, "I'm Gonna Wash That Man Right Outa My Hair!"

After the success of Club Chop Suey at Griffin Inn, Father realized he had a gem in his hands and he might as well put his boy to good use generating business and publicity for the night club. I'm glad Father hired a team of professional dancers from a local dance school to work with me on this second big event. The new dance number called for a group of boys to sing and dance with Annie, the lead singer. I had a marvelous and relatively easy time choreographing this dance sequel. The ten male dancers were experienced, compared to my female cousins who had performed in the previous presentation. Naturally, it was more pleasurable for me to work with the boys than with my female cousins.

The boys showed up on time for all rehearsals and seldom moaned or groaned. We discussed choreography ideas openly and easily. I'm fairly certain that a couple of the dancers were gay even though they wouldn't admit it. My young boy 'gaydar' could detect a homosexual man miles away! Don't ask me how. It's an inborn mechanism that most gay men possess.

Although the dancers were considerably older and more experienced than I was, we enjoyed working together and had mutual respect for each other. I learned many techniques from these guys even though I had already hung up my ballet slippers. Several of them befriended me after the show. We lost touch years later when I left to study in Great Britain.

Father Foong recruited my female cousins as servers for the numerous huts and stalls on the Griffin Inn lawn. There were booths with crafts from coconut leaves, stalls that sold hula skirts and paraphernalia, and vendors selling trinkets. The male dancers lei-ed me, though I would prefer if they 'laid me' instead, after the show.

All my cousins wore colored raffia hula skirts sewn together at the waist. Underneath the skirts were one-piece nude swimsuit bottoms bought from the local department stores. Numerous full flower leis adorned their necks.

I outfitted the male dancers in tank tops I bought at a local Chinese Emporium on Batu Road. They wore their trouser legs rolled three quarters of the way up their sexy legs.

This time, I did not black out from exhaustion, hunger or stress. Griffin Inn was certainly a memorable part of my childhood. Last word: I "washed all the men outa my hair" when I left for England, only to replace them with new ones who were even more beautiful and sexy.

CHAPTER ELEVEN

Catch a Falling Star

Methodist Boys' School

I shot up like Jack and The Bean Stalk while I was at the Mehodist Boy's School; I was mostly stalk. Both my parents were tall by Malayan standards. I was already five foot ten and still growing.

My voice was changing and so was everything else. I was becoming a young man. I hated the Methodist Boys' School I attended because I was constantly teased and harassed for behaving like a sissy boy. Being bullied relentlessly by the older boys was a misery, my own "Nightmare on Elms Street." I prayed for the day when I would be ready to leave for England.

I loved my mother, aunties and cousins, but I longed to see the wider world. Each day, I looked skyward like a frog waiting to jump out of the small pond (Kuala Lumpur) to catch a panoramic view of the large ocean (London, England.) I knew it would happen soon. Foong Senior was a great believer in sending his sons abroad for further education and I was next in line.

To me, my days at Methodist Boys' School were a phase that I had to endure for a short period. Thank God classes were only half-day affairs. Every morning before classes began, a half hour student assembly was held in front of the school's main building out in the football field. All students stood at attention while Malaya's national anthem played over loud speakers. The Head Master would stand at the podium providing the usual boring school agendas and current affairs. The boys would be fidgeting, or up to their mischievous behaviors.

The Gang of Four

There was a gang of four boys in the same class as I who constantly bullied me, making silly remarks and calling me girlie names whenever they got the chance. I was a timid and shy boy, certainly not one to retaliate or tell them to go f**K themselves! I was, in every sense of the word, a nice, polite well-behaved boy.

One day, KiWi, the most handsome one in the group, threw a tiny pebble on my back during assembly. When I turned around to check on the culprit, he started making silly girly faces at me. Ignoring him and his stupid innuendos, I tried to think of a quick escape route to the classroom right after assembly. I was too scared to think of the consequences if he cornered me.

Too bad - I wasn't fast enough. He caught up and started insulting me. He was extremely obnoxious, threatening me that he and his gang of rascals would get me during our fifteen minutes mid-morning break. I hated him and his gang of four!

KiWi

True to his word, when the recess bell rang and all the students filed out of the classrooms, he and his gang cornered me. I ran as fast as my legs could carry, trying to make my great escape.

I thought I would lock myself in one of the toilet stalls until the bell rang for class to resume. Unfortunately, I didn't run fast enough, and fell while they were chasing after me.

I was caught outside the school hall. One of the bullies who had pushed me down locked the door and threatened to pull my pants off to check if I was a girl or a boy. They teased relentlessly, saying that if I were a boy I would get an erection if they played with my butt.

I hated these guys and desperately tried to escape their hurtful hands. Managing to pull free after a lengthy struggle, I ran towards the door but I couldn't unlock it quickly enough. One of them threw me on the floor again, tackling me over behind, while the other three tore at my pants.

I was like a frightened rabbit trapped in the paws of the 'Hounds of Baskervilles,' doing my best to save my life. As much as I secretly fancied KiWi, I definitely didn't care for his friends. Those malicious bullies were zooming in for the kill. Desperately trying to get free of their grip, I kicked and screamed and shouted for help. No one came to my rescue.

KiWi had me in a Judo lock, almost choking me, when the school bell rang to resume classes. Saved by the bell, the bullies reluctantly released me, warning that they would get me soon enough. They ran off to their respective classes, giving me malicious snares.

I was doing my best to recover from this dreadful attack. From the corner of my eye, I noticed KiWi was still there. Was he making sure I was OK, I wondered, or was he there to be perform another abusive prank? I felt like he was afraid I might have choked to death or that something else too terrifying to comprehend had happened. I was desperately adjusting my clothes, doing my best to brush the dirt from my soiled white uniform. I was sure Mother would give me a good scolding when I got home.

KiWi stood by the door and didn't leave. My heart was thumping wildly, wondering if KiWi was going to abuse me further, or possibly rape me. There was only one entrance and exit out of the hall, so there was no escape route. I had no choice but to face up to this guy, which was extremely terrifying for a gentle boy like me.

When I reached the door, thinking I would have to push my way through, KiWi leaned over, pulled me to him and kissed me full on the mouth! I was completely taken by surprise! I didn't know how to react. I was stunned when he did it again! He did not wait for my reaction. He fled down the hall, disappearing from sight.

I stood there speechless, wondering if a meteorite had hit me. Honestly, I wouldn't have known what to do if he had stayed. This was the last thing I imagined would happen between me and this handsome swimmer who was every adolescent schoolgirl's heartthrob.

I slid to the bottom of the door in complete and total shock until I heard the bell ring, announcing the next class would start in a few minutes. I got up and ran to class as fast as I could, not knowing which lesson I was supposed to attend.

As much as I enjoyed KiWi's kisses, I was at a loss! A few moments before, he had been a hateful bullying tyrant trying to molest and possibly rape me. The next moment, he was kissing me on my mouth! What was happening to my world? It was going topsy-turvy.

For the remainder of the day, I couldn't get his kisses off my mind. I could not figure out what to make of this guy. It seemed completely contradictory, like a surreal dream.

Bakar drove up the school entrance to collect me. As I was getting into the car, a hand suddenly reached for me. Turning round, to see who it was, I froze. KiWi was standing by the car door. He whispered, "Meet me outside the main gate of your house at 5:00 p.m. this evening." He quickly released his grip, and fled. I became more puzzled by the minute.

When I arrived home, mother saw my soiled clothes and asked what had happened. I made an excuse, "I tripped and fell on the ground and dirtied my clothes," I said. I didn't dare mention the truth to anyone, lest one of the bullies was hiding in a corner listening to my conversation, about the assault by the Gang of Four. I certainly wasn't going to mention KiWi's mouth-to-mouth kisses!

The rest of the afternoon I paced restlessly and felt helpless, in my room. I couldn't concentrate on my homework. I watched the clock tick away. I didn't know what to expect when 5:00 p.m. arrived. Was the Gang of four waiting at the main gate to assault me? It was too unfathomable for my young mind to comprehend!

Earlier in the year, Father had bought a bicycle for me to ride around the neighborhood. Being older, my parents were less paranoid about kidnapping possibilities than some. On the pretext of riding my bike to the neighborhood shop to purchase ice cream, I rode to the iron gate. Sure enough, waiting on his bike was the boy who earlier in the day had tried to molest and maybe rape me. KiWi did not utter a word as we rode our bikes in silence.

Behind my house was a vast tropical rainforest, covered with thick carpets of under growth, surrounded by tall monkey-pod trees and huge shady banyan trees. Kiwi led me into the forest. We arrived at a small clearing.

We left our bicycles hidden behind some tall leafy bushes and walked into the forest, undetected. Without saying a word, KiWi leaned me against a huge tree trunk, and began French kissing me. My heart was thumping hard and fast. I could hear its boom boom sounds echoing in the silence. I shut my eyes, surrendering myself to KiWi. He was a good kisser. I was sexually aroused; my mind was racing a mile a minute. It was a fantasy, come true!

As much as I had fantasized about Philip, Eric and other cute boys, I had never believed my fantasies would play out. Although many times I had uncontrollable erections thinking of those boys, sexually, I had no idea what to do in real life.

In the past I waited for my manhood to subside, and continued with my life. Now for the first time in my young life, I was confronted with an opportunity to actualize my dreams.

KiWi did most of the work, as he was older. He was my sexual teacher but he was not very experienced in the art of lovemaking. Our stay in the woods didn't last long. The entire process was over in less time than I imagined.

We dressed without speaking. He biked home and I went on my confused way. My head was reeling from the experience. More confused than before, I realized that I liked what happened in the woods, yet I didn't know what the hell I was supposed to do.

All my sexual urges were present and highly activated. So were his. He ejaculated. I didn't. I enjoyed being intimate with a boy but I did not have an orgasm. I didn't know what an orgasm felt like.

The following day in school was a complete turn around. KiWi's gang no longer harassed me. I never knew what he told them or what he didn't tell them. I only knew that the harassment suddenly and mysteriously ceased. When we met in the school corridors, canteen or classroom, KiWi and the gang were cordial, and they left me alone.

Those days, our class teachers would pair up the boys to work together on various school projects. KiWi voluntarily came over to partner with me, which in our 'pre-sex' days would never have happened. We put on a facade of being regular friends, in school. But out of school, it was a different story; we became f**k buddies.

He, of course, never let on to his gang that we met after school, and were intimate. We did continue to meet daily at the exact same time in the exact spot in the woods, and did similar things each time. There were times I was invited to his home, since he lived half a mile from my house. During our rendezvous we seldom exchanged more than a few words. We did what we set out to do. When done, we dressed and went our separate ways, much like the Last Tango in Paris.

KiWi came from a wealthy family. His elder brother was in a British medical school studying to be a physician. His father was an accomplished local entrepreneur and attorney. The times I visited KiWi's home, on the pretext of working in partnership on our prescribed school projects, we would lock ourselves in his air-conditioned library and be at it again, again and again, until we were spent, while his mother napped in her bedchamber. She was unaware of what was going on behind the library doors.

There was usually no one else in KiWi's house in the late afternoons. His father was at work, and his chauffeur was busy in the garage working on their Mercedes and Bentleys.

Within a month after our initial forest rendezvous, I became a fixture in his house and at the Royal Selangor Club; KiWi's father was an honorary member. KiWi had the privilege of using the club's Olympic size pool for his swimming practice. I would go with him, like his 'boyfriend,' encouraging him on.

Mother knew I had a friend with whom I collaborated on projects. She was curious to meet him. When I told her KiWi's parents' names, she knew who they were. They moved in the same social circles. Kuala Lumpur was not a metropolis, back then. Mum wasn't worried that I was spending time with KiWi because she knew his family's background and she assumed I would be safe in their son's company.

One day when K.L. was out playing mahjong and Father was not home, (Tai Yee and Lai Ngor were busy with their sewing projects in their sewing rooms and the maids and servants were fussing in the kitchen,) I invited KiWi to our ohana.

Father had converted part of our large garage into an air-conditioned guest room. Most of the time, the ohana was vacant. It had air-conditioning; noises from within were undetectable when the air was switched on.

I locked the ohana's door and Kiwi and I proceeded into our sexual zone. One day, half naked, with our pants on the floor, our lovemaking was interrupted. There was an urgent banging on the bedroom door, and it shocked us back to our senses. We didn't have sufficient time to dress and so I wrapped a sarong round my waist and went to check out the commotion. Who should be standing on the other side of the door but a furious S. S., shouting and barking like a dog with his head cut off!

He took a look inside the room, and commanded us to get dressed immediately. He screamed at KiWi to leave the house right that minute. We were caught red-handed in the heat of our boy love session! To this day, I have no idea how father got wind of my secret rendezvous at the ohana.

All hell broke loose! I would never hear the end of it! Father carried on for weeks about how disgusted he was with the way I behaved! I was sick and tired of old man Foong so I prayed diligently that I would be banished to a British school ASAP!

Of course, I was forbidden to see KiWi after the ohana drama. Father threatened to inform KiWi's parents of our sexual misconduct but I doubt he ever did. After all, he couldn't admit his third son was gay. It would have been difficult to tell his peers this scandalous secret. It would jeopardize his standing in the local community. The Chinese are fond of not losing face!

With all the fuss and drama going on, KiWi and I still met secretly in the forest. By then, Tai Yee, Lai Ngor, and, of course, Mother knew about my sexual escapades with KiWi.

I have a feeling Mother knew of my sexual liaison before father so rudely interrupted us. Mummy never said anything negative about my relationship with KiWi, because she loved and accepted me just the way I was, unlike Father. He was narrow-minded and could not come to terms with what he feared most -- his own sexuality being threatened. Since Father's outburst, I hated him more than ever. When he was home, I would lock myself in my fairytale bedroom, refusing to come out for dinner until he left the house for the evening. Mother, being the kind, gentle woman she was, brought food to my room and urged me to be more understanding of my father. I would not. I wanted nothing to do with this man!

England

Shortly after this dramatic episode, KiWi told me one day he was leaving to attend boarding school in Belfast, Ireland. It was a sad day for me because I knew, in my heart, that our affair was coming to an end. After school that day, I locked myself in my room and cried. I was infatuated and 'in love' with the beautiful swimmer boy! I saw KiWi a couple more times. We made passionate love; by then, I sort of knew what I was doing.

KiWi had taught me a few tricks along the way, before he departed. After he left, I was devastated and fell into a miserable state. I didn't feel like eating and I wept constantly, thinking of our times together.

Mother, Tai Yee and Lai Ngor comforted me, reminding me it was puppy love, and that all first time lovers go through this. Soon, they counseled, I would learn to live without him. But I did not get over this sexy handsome young man for a long time. We continued our relationship for another year before it faded, becoming just a memory.

The following summer, KiWi came home for his summer break, for a month and a half. My parents had no idea KiWi was in town. I had been corresponding with him throughout the year.

We picked up where we left off. I was happy as a lark to see my boyfriend again but the winds of time had slowly changed the course of our lives. I was no longer passionately 'in love' with KiWi. I had moved forward with my life while he was away. I didn't tell anyone that I was seeing KiWi that summer. It was none of their business and I preferred to keep it that way.

I was the happiest boy, when Foong Senior told me I had been enrolled in school in the UK. I was overjoyed by the news. Within six months, I would be a free man doing all the fabulous things I want to do! No Father Foong to tell me what I could or could not pursue.

The few months before leaving Kuala Lumpur, I promised myself I would not return to that 'small pond' if I could help it. I would, rather, soar high like a condor, with winds beneath my gigantic wings, pushing me forward to achieve great and marvelous goals, only to glance below when I happened to fly pass Kuala Lumpur! I would circle long enough to send kisses to those I loved, below.

In my own way, I'm glad I caught a falling star when I did, and that I put it in my pocket. Memories of KiWi never waned nor faded, and I will cherish him in my heart, forever. Past experiences are what make us who we are, today. What I learned with Kiwi contributed to the oceans of love I have to shower upon those who are willing to open their arms to The Gift of Love!

CHAPTER TWELVE

Wear a Mini Skirt

Busy People

After KiWi left for Ireland, I needed to keep myself busy so I wouldn't wallow in misery. I couldn't ask for a more understanding Mother than Mrs. K. L. Foong. She knew I was missing KiWi. Being an astute Mother, she also knew I loved everything connected to art and design. To ease my mind from thinking of my beloved, Mummy made sure she kept me busy. She enrolled me in several classes she thought I would enjoy.

Mother was a well-traveled, artistic woman who loved classical music, show tunes and the popular music of her genre. When visiting my brothers in England, she often attended concert performances in and around London. An admirer of art, she visited the world's great museums and galleries to view famous paintings, learning the history of art and literature of the Western and the Eastern world.

Piano

We had a grand Steinway piano in our house for as long as I could remember, but it was seldom put to use. On rare occasions, when a piano-inclined cousin visited, the beautiful sounds from the Steinway would float through our house. So it came as no surprise that the first order of Mrs. Foong's agenda was to enroll me in piano lessons.

As much as I loved listening to music, I wasn't gifted in the music playing department. After a couple of piano lessons, I quickly became a piano music appreciator rather than a pianist.

Art

Like Mother, I loved art. Mother had converted to the Methodist faith and had begun attending the Chinese Methodist Church opposite my school grounds. At Sunday Service, she met a well-known artist, Mrs. Koo.

Mrs. Koo was an accomplished Chinese painter and calligrapher who gave private art tutorials at her home to students she believed had talent. She taught Eastern and Western paintings, Art History and Art Appreciation. I was enrolled as one of three of her students, and quickly became her prodigy.

Although I had drawn at school, it was very basic compared to what I learned from Mrs. Koo. The classes were two afternoons per week. We met for a couple hours each session. The year I studied under her tutelage we studied various styles of painting, from contemporary to classical, as well as art appreciation. Mrs. Koo taught us the names and styles of Western Art movements, throughout history.

I was completely immersed in my studies and looked forward to her classes. When I first commenced drawing, my techniques were primitive. By the end of the year, I came in third in a local art competition sponsored by the National Art Gallery of Malaya.

I particularly loved Orientalism and Orientalist Art of the early Victorian and French eras. The Pre-Raphaelites, Art Nouveau and Art Deco movements all stimulated my creativity. After regular school hours, I would head straight to the library to look at art and design books. I adored drinking in the opulence depicted by the artists; their wide range of color usage and the beautiful compositions of masterpieces inspired me to create works of my own.

Fashion

One day, inside the air-conditioned library as I was researching various art books and pictorials, I came across a book written by a famous model, Jean Patchet. She had modeled in New York, Paris and London for many of the top fashion houses, from Christian Dior and Chanel to Givenchy. I absorbed myself in the contents of this book, especially the glamorous photographs taken by well-known fashion photographers, such as Louise Dahl-Wolfe, John Rawlings and Irving Penn. I borrowed the book from the library numerous times so I could learn and memorize all the names of the fashion designers and photographers, their signature styles and looks, and the art of fashion photography.

From this point forward, fashion design became my number one career goal. I was hooked on fashion for life, promising myself I would craft a fashion design career no matter what might come my way.

Fashion Show

The Methodist Boys' School had a Music, Fashion and Variety Show organized by the student body. A couple of my friends and I volunteered to do a "Slipping and Sliding" dance routine. This was a time of great creativity and self-expression. When Brother James came home for vacations from England, he demonstrated the newest dance crazes that were 'groovy' at the time. He showed us the Twist and many of the Motown dances, such as the Mashed Potato, and the Soul. There were many new dance styles to learn, and so little time to master them all!

It was often difficult to keep apace of what was new and what was passé. I decided to put all the dancing styles that James had taught my cousins and me into a three minute choreographed routine, which I termed "Slipping & Sliding." We were to perform on the day of the Music, Fashion & Variety event. Girls from our sister school, The Bukit Bingtang Girls' School, were also invited to showcase some of their talent along with us boys. The local press gave us rave reviews.

With so many extra-curricular activities happening in my life, there was hardly time to think of KiWi. Every day, my diary was jammed full of activities. If it wasn't art classes where I had to hand in paintings for Mrs. Koo for critique, schoolwork was due. After school was "Slipping & Sliding" dance rehearsals, and Fashion Show modeling practice in the school hall. I had also signed up to be a male model.

I was confident I could do remarkably well as a male model, and I was right, judging from the adulation showered on me by the audience at the event. I became a workaholic without knowing I had become one. My lingering feelings for KiWi were soon upstaged by all of my various projects and activities. Mother seemed to know what was best for her children and certainly knew how best to chase my blues away. True to Mother's prediction, my dark cloud of depression left a week or two after KiWi boarded the jet plane for Ireland.

Flower People

Flower People were in full bloom as were the Beatles and Hare Krishna chanters; swinging London was pulling me towards the city like a magnet. A boy of only twelve, I was also 'California Dreamin', wishing I could go to San Francisco to experience the Flower Power phenomenon that was taking root.

Everything happening in the larger world seemed so exciting in my young mind. I dreamt of strolling down Carnaby Street with my bell-bottoms and fitted floral shirts, a headband tied round my head and love beads around my neck. I wanted to experience it all!

I had a local tailor sew my clothes every week. You might be wondering how I got the money to have clothes made weekly. Well, the best way to save money is to not spend it on trivial things. Clothing and fashion accessories to me do not fall into the category of trivial things. To me they were a necessity!

Mummy gave me money for school lunches, which I saved. Every weekend I was happily trotting off to my tailor with designs in hand for outfits. Voila! The following week, I'd have a new outfit based on whatever struck my design fancy.

Shoes filled my bedroom closet. I had them in all the colors of the rainbow, lining the shelves. My dolls were moved to make way for clothes and shoes. Where children's fairytale books once stood, one would now find British, French, and Italian Vogue, Harper's Bazaars and an entire host of Japanese fashion magazines. I followed the latest music of the Beatles, Bee Gees, and Mamas & Papas. If you named any popular group, I had their twelve-inch vinyl records. In short, I was a fashion and music junkie. And it was fun. Fun! Fun! No wonder I couldn't wait to travel to London. I wanted to experience and be a part of it all. And, finally, I did after several years of waiting.

CHAPTER THIRTEEN

A Land Far Away

"All my bags are packed, I'm ready to go. I'm standing here outside your door. I hate to wake you up Daddy to say goodbye. The taxi's waiting and blowing its horn..."

To London

It wasn't the taxi waiting and blowing its horn; it was Bakar, loading our luggage into our family Bentley, ready to take us to the airport. Mother came along for two weeks in London, and a day on the Isle of Wight, to settle me into boarding school.

I had already said my goodbyes to my immediate relatives at a dinner party organized by my parents, for my departure. It was pointless to wake the entire household to say "Sayonara," again. We had to catch an early British Overseas Airways Corporation (BOAC) flight. Off we went to the Kuala Lumpur airport!

Chapter Thirteen

Air Travel

Travelling on a jet plane was a luxury in those days, especially since we were travelling first class. The hospitality services were splendid. The air stewardesses were beautiful and remarkably well groomed; they were attentive, young and very pleasing to my young eyes. Unlike travelling these days, which is a chore, a first class long distance flight was in and of itself an experience to savor.

We were served roost beef and Yorkshire pudding, with cooked vegetables. The food wasn't bad, although I wasn't a big fan of English cooking. The desert tray was scrumptious, with different selections of cakes, tarts and fresh fruits served with tea or coffee. En route, the plane made a couple of refueling stops in Bahrain and Frankfurt.

Landing at Heathrow Airport a little after 8:00 p.m. the following day, I was exhausted. Mr. James Pinkerton, whom Mother met on the RMS Queen Mary, picked us up in his brand new Silver Shadow Rolls Royce. They had kept in touch over the years, and whenever Mother was in London visiting my brothers they would renew their friendship. We were his guests for the duration of our one week London stay. He or his chauffeur drove us around the city, sightseeing. He was most hospitable. James was my English guardian.

James traveled frequently on business between England and the Far East. He was divorced, and his son was also in boarding school, so the town home was largely left vacant.

Mr. Pinkerton was a wonderful 'fella' and I liked him the moment Mother introduced us. He was humorous, easygoing and full of laughter. I could tell right away that he liked me as much as I liked him. James, in every mannerism, was the opposite of Foong, Sr., whom I feared. Over the years, I had wondered, "If my parents had divorced, wouldn't it be nice if mother married Mr. Pinkerton?" Then I would have had a wonderful relationship with a stepfather I could truly admire and look up to as my role model.

But that was just wishful thinking. I presume K. L.'s relationship with Pinkerton was platonic. I was too young to ask questions regarding such matters, and it was none of my business, anyway. I was overjoyed to be in London, the city of my dreams.

Travelogue

After a good night's rest at James' three story townhouse in Mayfair, we drove to the Savoy in the Strand for brunch. Since it was Sunday, James had time to show Mother and me (more me, since it was my first visit) the city. Along the way, we drove through Hyde Park, past Speakers Corner where a large crowd had gathered. A couple had placards hung around their necks announcing that Armageddon had arrived. The world was coming to an end! Others stood on boxes, trying to outdo each other while voicing their opinions on the state of the British government. There were hippies and flower people dancing in the park. It was wonderful to watch -- it was my first time to witness such happenings in Hyde Park or anywhere, for that matter. It was a beautiful, hot summer day and the tourists were out in full force. Londoners were sunbathing on the grass, shirtless or in their bikinis. Some were kissing and rolling around the grass in intimate positions. People were strolling around and frolicking on rowboats in the Serpentine. I was totally in love with London; I already knew it was my city.

We drove by Kensington Palace and Buckingham Palace while the Changing of the Guards was in progress. I was hoping James would stop, allowing us to see the pageantry, but mother said there would be another time for that. James had reserved a table, and we were already five minutes late. Everything was extremely exciting to me! London offered more than I could ever have imagined. I knew I would live there one day.

Fabulous

A doorman greeted us at The River restaurant. The wait staff wore spotless uniforms of black and white, with touches of

Parisian Pink. We were escorted to the outdoor terraced seating area which was as beautifully decorated as the elegant and charmingly chic interior.

White porcelain plates with circular lines of black framed a fine gold interior with the River Restaurant's monogram embossed on the edge. Everything on the table was pristine, from the neatly folded white linen napkins to the layered tablecloths. Highly polished silver cutlery gleamed next to crystal salt and pepper shakers. The appetizers and entrees were amazingly prepared and delicious. The desserts were heavenly!

Groovy

After our delightful brunch, we were ready to rock and roll. James drove us to Westminster Abbey. We had the opportunity to attend an early evening service inside the ornate Cathedral. I marveled at the grandeur of the interior and the gothic architecture.

The last week of our stay was a whirlwind. We went everywhere! I was enthralled by the animals at the London Zoo as well as by the people shopping on Oxford and Bond Street. We had high tea at Fortnum & Mason, and later experienced groovy King's Road and swinging Carnaby Street.

Carnaby Street

"Bed, bed, I couldn't go to bed. My head is too light to try and to set it down. Sleep, sleep, I couldn't sleep tonight, not for all the jewels in the crown. I could have danced all night; I could have danced all night and still have begged for more. I could have spread my wings and done a thousand things, I've never done before. I never know I made it so exciting; while all at once, my heart took flight". (My Fair Lady)

I only know that when Uncle James told me he would take me to Carnaby St., King's Road and Kensington High St. for a visit I was beyond the moon. No wonder I couldn't sleep that night. I was too excited for the next day to begin.

Oh my God! Carnaby Street was right in front of me. The boutiques were playing the current songs I had been listening to on LP's in Kuala Lumpur. Every shop had a different psychedelic theme. English and Irish pubs lined the perimeters. Longhaired, mustached males were outdoors drinking their pints wearing hipster bell-bottom pants and fitted floral and colorful shirts. The gals had the shortest mini skirts and dresses I had ever seen. Carnaby Street boutiques weren't Mother's idea of a shopping paradise. She preferred sophisticated, elegant, and classy stores. I wanted to shop at psychedelic, trendy, groovy boutiques. I didn't care if the clothes were cheap throwaway, worn one minute and discarded the next. I wanted the look of the moment. I wanted things that were fashionable on Carnaby Street.

Mother was afraid I would go Ga-Ga over everything "Flower Power" or "Hippie Dippy." She feared exposure to the pot smoking and free-loving youth culture might cause me to begin "dancing in the streets!" Uncle James had a different take on the matter; he thought I should experience everything. Besides, I'd only be in town for a few days before departing to the Isle of Wight. He thought it hilarious that Mrs. Foong should worry about her boy getting high on Ryde (Rye!)

Laura Ashley's boutique windows were filled with feminine cotton dresses in pretty tiny floral prints resembling the English countryside. I was in 7th heaven checking out all the shops; Lord John, I was Lord Kitchener's Valet, Tuffin & Foale and Mary Quant, the swinging sixties iconic queen of fashion, were on this short but fabulous street.

James was a good sport, venturing into every shop and boutique that caught my eye. It was no wonder I wanted him to be my stepdad. He accepted me as I was. We had a lot of fun, joking and laughing, and he even stopped to buy us pink and turquoise lollipops. He was, and always would be, a wonderful figure in my life.

Later, Jeffrey transported us to Fortnum & Mason to meet Mother for High Tea at the Fountain Restaurant. Afterwards, we visited all the major stores from Harrods to Harvey Nichols. Since winter fashion choices were miserable and limited in Kuala Lumpur, Mother suggested we shop at Selfridges. There was such an extensive selection in this cosmopolitan metropolis! I wanted to buy this, I'd love to purchase that, and it would be wonderful to own these! I'd buy the entire store if I had the money! Our list of exciting things to do seemed endless.

PART TWO

The United Kingdom, London

CHAPTER FOURTEEN

"I've Never Done Before"

London

After a hearty bacon-and-eggs breakfast prepared by Uncle James' maid, we went to Kew Gardens for a morning of sightseeing and picnic. It was another beautiful summer's day and the flowers at Kew were in full bloom. Roses of numerous varieties grew in the garden's spacious landscaped grounds, creeping along walls and climbing trellises. The centerpiece of this impressive garden was a massive glass greenhouse, resembling the Crystal Palace built during the Great Exhibition of 1851, at the height of Queen Victoria and Prince Albert's reign. The Palm House was an impressive glass structure housing an array of lush flora.

We brought a picnic basket. James, Mother and I spread a gingham cloth under the lovely sunshine. We ate finger sandwiches and drank tea which James' maid had packed. It was a glorious time of the year to be in England. I loved and adored Uncle James. Once again, I fancied the thought of Mother marrying this educated, cultured and kind gentleman.

The Tube

When James's Silver Shadow pulled up to Sloane Square there were pedestrians walking everywhere. The Rolls Royce could hardly move; it was so crowded. James' chauffeur, Jeffrey, dropped us outside of Peter Jones so we could walk down King's Road. We inched our way slowly down this busy street. We did not stay long, as it was too crowded, but we did go into the famous Mary Quant boutique.

James informed Jeffrey that we would be taking the tube to Kensington High Street. I had never been inside the London Underground, and Uncle James said it would be a good opportunity for him to show me how to use the tube.

My initiation was a scary but exciting experience. I had never seen, much less ridden, an underground train. Especially unforgettable was the descent down the flights of stairs, because the elevators were temporarily out of service that afternoon.

Electric information boards informed passengers of each train's destination. All the people were walking too hurriedly for a Kuala Lumpur boy. James urged me to board the train quickly, before the door closed. A voice announced, "mind the gap", an admonition for travelers, so they would not be trapped between the platform and the train. It was completely foreign yet amazing to me that passengers could remember where to alight and disembark in this massive underground labyrinth. Uncle James held my hand so I wouldn't be lost in the shuffle.

After 20 minutes, we saw daylight again. Before long we were at Kensington Church Street where even more trendy shops and boutiques were located. I fell in love with the fabulous Biba boutique, down Abington Street.

(Biba moved to the now defunct Derry and Tom's department store in 1971, where Biba filled all five floors with fashions, and furnishings. Biba had an amazing 1930s Art Deco ballroom - 'The Rainbow Room' which was renovated to a Tea Dance restaurant. I later worked at this venue as a bus boy during one of my school vacations staying at Uncle James' house in London.)

Unfortunately, my school wasn't situated in London. It was at the very tip of Southern England. I was sad having to leave London, Uncle James and mother. I was feeling homesick before we even said our farewells.

CHAPTER FIFTEEN

Daltonbury Hall, School for Boys

Isle of Wight

Mother and I arrived at Gatwick Airport to board Daltonbury Hall's private plane, which would fly us to the Isle of Wight. (On future trips, I would travel by train from London Waterloo station to Lymington, Portsmouth or Southampton, before catching a ferry across the English Channel and arriving at one of several coastal towns around the island.)

The private jet was a small 30-seater plane with ten new boys and their parents or guardians. The school laid out the royal treatment to welcome the new boys from different parts of the world. A few 1930s vintage Rolls Royces were dispatched to collect us. Four passengers were settled into the back seat and the seat next to the chauffeur was filled with our luggage.

Most boys' escorts left after spending a day at the school, ensuring that their child was settled before departing in the evening.

Dormitories

As soon as we arrived at Daltonbury Hall, several footmen and valets were waiting at the entrance to assist with the luggage. We signed in with the school matron at the reception office. She advised us on school rules and regulations before the footmen and valets directed us to our respective dorm rooms. I shared a room with two boys: a freshman a year older than me and an eighteen-year-old senior.

All the dormitory rooms were similarly arranged with two "junior" boys accompanied by a "senior." We were not officially advised that the senior was our role model, but that became evident after a short period of living in such close quarters. If we had any difficulties or problems, we were encouraged to seek our 'big brother's' advice. All the seniors appointed as prefects were handsome in their own unique ways. There were other common threads. They were personable and easy to confide in, as well as being good looking.

The dormitory rooms were fairly spacious, accommodating three people, easily. Juniors had bunk beds while our 'big brother' slept on the single bed opposite us, in order to observe us with ease. Each of us had our own desk with locking drawers for our personal processions. Every morning when we were in class, the manservants would clean our rooms. We were responsible for making our own beds but the tasks of dusting, emptying wastebaskets, and cleaning the floors were left to the help. No personal televisions were allowed, although we could each have a small radio and an alarm clock. We spent most of our free time studying, or in the common recreational facilities.

Every floor of the three dormitories had a communal shower, with separate urinals and toilets in and adjacent area. Boys showered together without any dividing partitions. Approximately 18 juniors together with five or six 'big brothers' would be bathing or showering, naked, at the same time.

Each dormitory had an individual name which we referred to as our House. There was the Yates Fraternity, Kipling Society, and Tolkien Brotherhood. All three Houses competed with each other in sports, games and other extra-curricular activities. Although students could mingle and participate in different activities, the majority of the boys preferred to stick to their own assigned House's activities.

The Yates Fraternity consisted of boys who were passionate in writing, science and mathematical pursues. Debates, discussions of the latest political/scientific research and mathematical developments were the specialty of this House. Students and staff belonging to this dormitory organized political debates, science fairs and mathematical contests.

The Kipling Society recruited boys who were great at outdoor activities. All categories of sportsmen belonged to this House: swimmers, cricket players, football and polo players and more. This group was responsible for the organization of hunts in the nearby forest. Kipling graduates were excellent sportsmen, and often become international sports figures. This dormitory and their physical education teachers were also amateur archaeologists, participating in professional digs around the world.

The Tolkien Brotherhood boys were the artsy crowd. Their interests were artistic pursuits such as musical recitals, concerts, music appreciation lectures and seminars. Subjects related to art and design were the focus of this House. Residents of this dormitory sponsored field trips to museums, historical sites and galleries. Renowned painters, artists, sculptors and designers were invited as speakers by the Tolkien Brotherhood and their professors.

Recreational Areas

There were three common rooms in each of the boarding Houses where boys could play Ping-Pong, billiards and a variety of board games. Social meetings, discussions, debates, and other general affairs were conducted in these communal facilities. Many friendships were established and a sense of camaraderie was fostered among students in this setting. At certain times of the year, school dances were held and our sister school's students were invited to participate.

Daltonbury Hall had an Olympic size indoor swimming pool, several outdoor tennis courts, squash courts, badminton courts, cricket fields and a couple of football/soccer fields. There were acres of outdoor gardens, parks and lawns where students could hike, bike, jog or stroll. The school was on approximately 550 acres of land in the rolling English countryside. One side of the property faced the English Channel, and the other side overlooked hills, flatlands and farms.

There was an ample sized stable for horseback riding. A good number of stable-boys and groomsmen were available to assist students who rode as well as those who were learning to ride. They also organized hunts, on occasion.

Classrooms, the Hall, Facility and Staff

A large Assembly Hall, the classrooms and the library were adjacent to the dormitories. The school's helipad was above the Assembly Hall. Classrooms were on the lower levels of the building. The windows were soundproof. When classes were in session there were no exterior noise disturbances. Two canteens serviced the student body with another catering to the staff. Canterbury was a self-service cafeteria, and The Hobbit was a sit-down dining facility. If students were running between classes and hungry, they could catch a quick snack at the Canterbury. Students desiring a proper sit-down meal would dine at The Hobbit. They proffered an excellent selection if a student chose to eat lavishly.

The staff's restaurant, the Winchester, was located in their residential building, a structure located some distance away from the students' dormitories. A small in-house Clinic with several full-time nurses and a live-in doctor was located on the far side of the dormitories. Any pupil experiencing discomfort or sickness could report to the Clinic for a check-up with Doctor Hunton, aided by nurses Mary and Felicia. All boys and staff referred to the Clinic as 'The Rabbit Hole.' The term was derived from the children's book Alice in Wonderland - where Alice fell into the rabbit hole and drank from medicine bottles, which caused her to become tiny, and later, extraordinary large.

There were approximately seventy-five faculty members teaching one hundred and fifty boys a traditional English secondary school curriculum. Besides the teaching staff, there were teaching assistants to tutor boys who had difficulty grasping a topic. These teaching assistants were, generally, between the ages of 23 and 26 years old. Like our 'big brothers' (Valets), they were handsome, educated and patient with all of the students. Whenever any junior had a problem with his studies, an assistant would be assigned for one-on-one tutelage. These assistants could be stern at times if students stepped out of line, yet they were never angry or abrupt. Most were alumni of Daltonbury Hall. A minority joined the school from other countries, as teaching apprentices, to learn from Daltonbury Hall professors and teaching assistants.

Ninety percent of the cosmopolitan enrollees were foreign students. Australians, Asians, Canadians and Europeans from outside of the UK comprised the majority of the student body.

Although students were not officially informed about the source of the school's educational funding, it was speculated that a substantial amount of monies were donated by countries in the United Arab Emirates. Wealthy Arabians with an abundance of oil reserves invested in many areas within the United Kingdom, including educational institutions, during the Oil Boom. Although this information was not officially documented, many speculated that the benefactors of Daltonbury Hall had strong ties with other educational institutions in the Middle East.

Chapter Fifteen

Towns & Villages

Isle of Wight is a truly scenic island. If one enjoys peace, tranquility and a quiet living, this is a great locale. The villages were called Shires; they resembled cottages in Tolkien's trilogy, The Lord of the Rings. The homes or cottages were charming from the exterior, but inside they were small, dark and cold. The windows were tiny, allowing limited sunlight to penetrate the structure.

In Spring, Summer and early Autumn the island's scenic beauty was spectacular. Bicycle riding, walking and horseback riding were great ways to absorb the splendor of the Isle. Sheep, lambs and goats flourished. They could often be seen travelling alongside vehicles. Farm land was plentiful in this part of the world. Both villagers and town folks were friendly and if one were a regular, one could easily obtain an invitation to the villagers' humble dwellings for a meal and small talk.

Pubs are located on practically every street corner, whether large or small. These are social venues where locals and foreigners meet to share stories, gossip, and chit chat with friends, neighbors and strangers.

The island had a handful of adequate hospitals and clinics to service run-of-the-mill illnesses, but for advanced medical treatments it was best to travel to the nearest city, preferably London.

Ferry across the Channel

Mother left shortly after I settled into my dorm room under the care of Nicholas, my 'big brother,' (Valet) who assured Mrs. Foong I would be well looked after. I soon came to love and cherish Nikee, as I would learn to address him. Nikee was a superior young man who took great care of me.

As much as I loved my new environment, I was homesick for the first few months. But soon, I grew accustomed to life in my new home, Daltonbury Hall. A new chapter in my young life was unfolding as I plunged forward, full steam, to face what was in store for me. When school broke for Christmas, that year, I took the ferry across the English Channel and caught a train to London's Waterloo Station, to visit dear Uncle James.

"Life goes on day after day. Hearts tone in every way. So Ferry cross the Channel because this land is the place I love and here I'll stay. People, they rush everywhere. Each with their own secret care. So Ferry cross the Channel and always take me there, the place I love. People around every corner, they seem to smile and say. We don't care what your name is boy; we'll never turn you away. So, I'll continue to say. Here I always will stay. So Ferry cross the Channel, because this land is the place I love and here I'll stay. And here I'll stay and here I'll stay. Here I'll stay." Ferry Cross the Mersey

CHAPTER SIXTEEN

Hold Your Head Erect

"Whenever I feel afraid, I hold my head erect and whistle a happy tune so no one will suspect, I'm afraid. While shivering in my shoes, I strike a careless pose and whistle a happy tune and no one ever knows I'm afraid. The result of this deception is very strange to tell. For when I fool the people I fear, I fool myself as well. I whistle a happy tune and every single time, the happiness in the tune convinces me that I'm not afraid. Make believe you're brave and the trick will take you far. You may be as brave as you make believe you are. You may be as brave as you make believe you are." The King and I

I was indeed shivering, not just from the chilly English morning air, but also from the daunting prospect of having to undress in front of a group of boys for our scheduled morning communal shower. No one had seen me naked since I was five years old besides Mother, my nanny and Kiwi, my ex-lover. "What am I to do, I thought? Whistle a happy tune?"

Personal hygiene was stressed at Daltonbury Hall. Every night, boys had to brush their teeth and wash their hands and faces before jumping into bed. We could either sleep with pajamas, or naked. Most juniors wore pajamas. Seniors were a different breed. They seemed to like sleeping naked. They said it kept their bodies warm when naked between the comfortable cotton sheets and duvet or blankets. Self-generated body heat keeps one more warm and cozy than sleeping with clothes. Most juniors, being brought up in conservative homes, were not used to the idea of sleeping naked, although many learned quickly and were soon sleeping in the buff, or in their underwear.

At 6:30 a.m. each morning, the school chapel bells would ring a total of six times, informing all dormitories to ready themselves for morning showers, cleaning, and dressing in our school uniforms. At 7:00 a.m., the bells would sound again, reminding students to proceed to breakfast at either the Canterbury or the Hobbit. Breakfast was self-service, and students queued in an orderly manner, food trays in hand, for their allocations. By 7:45 a.m., the chapel bells chimed again, informing us that it was nearly time for our classes, which commenced at 8:00 a.m. sharp. Mid-morning tea break was between 10:30 a.m. and 11:00 a.m. Five rings from the bells signaled that classes were to resume. Lunches were later served at each restaurant. The remainder of the day was reserved for extracurricular activities. Participation was mandatory; and all boys were given opportunities to choose up to three of their favorite activities.

Five rings at 5.30 p.m. called us to dinner. We had an hour and a half for dinner before the kitchen staff cleared the dishes. The restaurants reopened at 7:30 p.m. until 10:00 p.m. for students who desired a later supper or snack.

Regular classes did not resume until a week after I arrived. Big Brothers were at the school early to receive all of the new boys. For one week, I had Nikee, my 'big brother', all to myself. John, the second year student who would share the room with us, arrived the following week.

Sleeping Beauty

The evening after Mother left, I was very lonely, missing home more than ever. Nikee showed me the Shire, Tolkien Brotherhood's communal recreational room, so I could get acquainted with the newly arrived Tolkien juniors and their 'big brothers'. The six new students and three 'big brothers' were introduced to each other. The BBs (Valets) prepared tea and biscuits for us. We were reminded that if we had any questions or problems, we could go to any of them for advice, as they were available for us anytime.

That evening I slept poorly, twisting and tossing in bed, doing my best not to disturb Nikee. He was a light sleeper. He knew I was homesick, and understood the sadness I was going through while leaving home for the first time. He had gone through a similar experience when he first arrived at Daltonbury Hall.

When my tossing and turning continued, he came over and whispered in my ear, that I could sleep with him in his bed. He held me to help me fall asleep. No one had ever done that for me, and it was certainly a proposal full of promise. I wanted to be next to a warm body, especially one as handsome as Nikee. He was half naked, wearing only a pair of white briefs; I was in my silk pajamas. In bed together, he proceeded to wrap his muscular arms around me. We were both on our sides, facing each other. The stirring I had when I was in close proximity to Eric and Philip (from Judo & Karate classes) returned. My 'man-hood' steered to attention and my heart began beating hard and fast. I could smell his cool, clean masculinity close to me. I tried squeezing my eyes as tightly as possible, but his intoxicating aroma was too overwhelming. The more I tried to force my hardness to subside, the more it stood to attention. I feared he would find out what was going through my mind and throw me out of bed. The more I tried to control my thoughts, the harder I got. No matter how desperately I whispered a happy tune in my head, my erection would not subside.

Nikee did not stir; he kept his arms wrapped round me as if I were his little teddy bear. My face was on his chest and I could hear his heart thumping like mine, loud and clear. I could feel his hardness pressed against me. His eyes were closed peacefully and he appeared content, gently patting my full head of silky black hair like I was his little puppy. I was awestruck.

When I sneaked a peek at his peaceful handsome face, under the dim night-light, I detected a smile on his beautiful, upturned lips. Nikee's other hand gently, softly, stroked the small of my back. We remained like this for hours. He gently patted and stroked me into a sweet, safe peaceful slumber. When I woke the next morning, I found myself back in my own bed.

Bathing Beauties

Chapel bells were chiming in the distance, awakening us to a new day. It was time for all of the boys to take a morning shower. Nikee had on a pair of boxer shorts, with a towel draped across his broad shoulders. He came to my bed, smiled, and took my hand to help me out of bed. With a towel wrapped around my waist, wearing an undershirt, we proceeded to the communal shower room. Now, my heart was really thumping fast, faster than last night when I was next to Nikee. I was frightened about revealing my nakedness in front of a group of boys! I had never done anything like this before. A voice in my head reminded me to whistle a happy tune, which I had often heard Anna (Deborah Kerr) sing in the King & I. Nikee sensed my fear, which increased with each step I took, drawing me closer to the shower room. With an amused grin he said, "Don't be afraid, Young." (For some reason, it was difficult for foreigners to pronounce Yoong - my Chinese name; it always turned out sounding like 'Young.') He continued, "They are all friendly fellas, and, most likely, the juniors are just as frightened of getting naked as you are. We are not here to judge any of you; stop being afraid. We don't bite! We are here for you." His words were certainly reassuring for a while, yet fear persisted. In my naive head, I kept thinking:

"What if I don't match up in the 'size' department, down below? I would be embarrassed if the other boys were better endowed! What if I get excited in the company of these naked boys? Would they laugh and make fun of me, like KiWi and his gang? What if I can't take my eyes off the cute boys? Would I be banned from the school? What would my parents say, then?"

There were so many "what ifs" running through my head! Before I knew it, we were at the entrance of the shower room. I felt like turning to run, but my wonderful BB, Nikee, sat me by the bench outside the entrance and told me to close my eyes. He said, "Inhale deeply several times and imagine going into a communal swimming pool, plunging into the pool naked, enjoying your own company, swimming and frolicking on your own and never minding the others."

Several deep breaths later, I had relaxed considerably. We entered the shower room. It was steamy and hot, like a Turkish steam bath. I could not make anything out when I first entered. By the time we undressed and stood under the shower my eyes had adjusted. I noticed the other juniors I met the previous evening. They appeared to be as nervous as me. Most cupped their hands in a futile attempt to cover their privates, while the seniors joked and talked, without a care in the world. All of us were naked as jaybirds! The seniors were having fun, mucking around, hitting each other with their wet washcloths. There were six juniors including me, and five seniors. Our BBs assisted in scrubbing our backs and helping us feel comfortable with our bodies. I soon learned that there was nothing to fear except fear itself. Everything terrible I imagined before entering evaporated. I, too, was having fun swiping the juniors and seniors with my wet washcloth.

By the time we finished in the washroom, I realized my endowment was adequate for a young man my age. I did not get sexually excited during the shower, though my eyes did stray, checking out the naked boys. The BBs didn't mind whether the juniors stared or not. They were comfortable in their skin and with their sexuality.

All our 'big brothers' (Valets) had beautiful physiques. They were very friendly with juniors, showing no prejudices regarding different color, race or nationality. To them, we were simply their younger brothers who were under their care and tutelage.

Nikee taught me to shave for the first time in my life. I had little facial hair then, but I stood and watched Nikee's demonstration. The more I looked at him, the more I liked him. This was not solely due to his incredible good looks. I liked him as a person. Memories of Nikee holding me came flooding back. I found myself getting erect. The refection in the mirror told no lies. Nikee noticed the bulge pulsating beneath the towel tied around my waist. He smiled and without saying a word continued shaving. Then, we dressed in our casual clothes. School uniforms were not required until classes commenced the following Monday.

At breakfast we sat on benches at a long dining table with juniors from other Houses. After eating, Nikee took me on a tour of the campus, showing me the interiors of each dormitory, classrooms, library, etc. He explained each building's historical significance and how the various Houses came to be, educating me in the history and geography of the school and its setting.

It was during our half hour mid-morning tea break, while sitting at Canterbury, that he mentioned, with amusement, my erection in the shower room. He explained that it was normal for boys to get excited, especially at my age as we were growing into young adults. There was nothing to worry about or be embarrassed about because I would soon learn to be comfortable in my own body. "It is all right for a boy to like another boy, because sexuality comes in many varied forms," he explained. He continued to expound on my maturation process and sexuality in general, promising me that I would figure out what form was best for me as an individual as I progressed down life's highways and byways. "All varieties of sexual preferences are created equally," he emphasized.

During the human sexuality class, conducted by Professor Nuein, I had the chance to learn, in depth, about different kinds of love and sexuality. His only caution was that feelings of infatuation could be misinterpreted as "love." I received admonitions about 'falling in love' with males or females, because some juniors are groomed for greater and more exciting things to unfold in our lives.

I didn't understand what he meant by 'being groomed for greater and more exciting things to unfold in our lives.' But there were other things he spoke of which seemed a riddle to me at the time. He promised he would look after me while I was in his care, and that he would teach me many things during our time together, but I was not to fall "in love" with him. I could love him, but I could not be "in love" with him. Unfortunately, I was already 'in love' before we even began!

I meekly promised I would do my best, all the time wondering how I could not be in love in the company of such a beautiful, gentle, caring soul. It was an extremely difficult task!

School Buildings

After our friendly chat over tea and scones, we walked the school grounds and I became acquainted with the buildings and venues. The Assembly Hall, where students had their Monday morning briefing before classes began each week, was located in the main building where the chauffeur had dropped Mother and me off when we arrived. Inside the entrance on the left were the office and reception rooms. The headmaster's office was located next to the reception room down the long corridor. Next to the headmaster's suite, there were 3 large staff rooms. On each staff room door hung name placards from each of the 3 Houses. Teachers of each House were given office space in one large staff room dedicated to their particular House. Within each staff room were smaller rooms partitioned off to the sides for the tenured professors, who had private offices.

Further down the corridor on the ground floor were storage rooms and the two restaurants, Canterbury and The Hobbit. An in-house Barber Shop (known as The Shaver) was just past the restaurants. Mr. Stanley Stanton, the barber, and an assistant barber provided students with either a short crop or a crew cut. No long hair or facial hair was allowed. All students had to maintain a neat, tidy and clean appearance at all times.

Chapter Sixteen

This floor also housed mathematical laboratories and science research classrooms. The second floor was comprised of art studios where painting, drawing (live drawing classes were conducted), and pottery-making took place. Outside the pottery workroom, there was an open-air courtyard with a firing kiln for the ceramic studio.

The third floor was the school library, stocked with books on all subjects. It was one of the best private school libraries in the United Kingdom. The top floor was the Assembly Hall with a large stage. This space was also used for performances; musical concerts, theatre, and dance recitals were conducted here. To the side of this great hall were smaller lecture theatres, reserved for debates, or presentations by visiting scholars and dignitaries.

During spring, summer and early autumn when the weather was warm and hot, the double-glazed glass roof, slid open, revealing sports facilities, a swimming pool, and a gym. The rooms in the basement were used as storage for the school's historical relics or used furniture from previous eras.

The day's tour, guided by my handsome and charming 'big brother' (Valet), flew by quickly. Before long came washing up and bedtime. That night I was tired, and I fell asleep in my own bed. My dreams did not lie about my conscious thoughts; I did not sleep peacefully that night.

In my dream, Nikee was holding me close, kissing me on my mouth; a passionate lingering kiss on my ears, eyelids, and nose. He performed a slow dance over my naked body with his lips. I felt sensual kisses over my smooth body. His masculine scent intoxicated me to hardness. His erect pressure against my hardness took me to the point of no return. Without lifting a finger to touch my hardness, I surrendered my dream Self to him fully. Holding me close, breathing on my tender neck, his silky smooth muscular contours jerked me awake.

I found my naked torso sticky and wet. I quietly sneaked to the washroom to clean myself, and returned to my bed. But the still small voice whispered, saying, "Nikee was awake," though the room was quiet. I just knew Nikee was always observing my every move whether I was awake or asleep.

CHAPTER SEVENTEEN

The Kipling Society

Although classes had not commenced, without me being aware my lessons had already begun, with Nikee, the evening I arrived. The following days, Nikee and I continued my tours, increasing my familiarity with the school's facilities. The school grounds were quite expansive, and there were many departments with which I needed to be acquainted.

The rest of the week was as busy as regular term days would be. There were numerous classroom locations I needed to learn in order to know where to go for each course subject when classes began. Some tutorials were held in the lecture theatres in the assembly hall, and others were in classrooms housed within the three dormitories. Nikee provided historical accounts of each House and the faculty. There was a lot to learn in a short amount of time, for a newbie from Kuala Lumpur.

I jokingly asked if I would be quizzed on what Nikee had been telling me. In his good-natured manner, he said I would have to hand him a detailed report by the week's end. I thought he was serious for a minute. Then he smiled and said he was just giving me a hard time. As we progressed towards Kipling Society, he turned and said, "In a few years, you'll be in a position to be a 'big brother'. You will know how from my tutorials. There are few suitable candidates that possess the qualifications required to be a BB (Valet) and I believe, Young, you have the potential."

I giggled and thought he was joking, but he wasn't smiling; he was looking directly into my eyes in complete seriousness. I replied, "I know nothing about being a junior, let alone be a 'big brother.' Maybe it's someone else you have in mind; it is definitely not me!" Nikee turned away and said nothing. That was the end of our conversation on the subject.

Kipling Rowing Club

The Kipling Society, the house with athletic sportsmen, was originally used as a shed for row boats during the Victorian period. Students and townspeople could paddle in either of the two lakes (Swan and Goose.) One evening, Nikee related, after dinner, a couple students were strolling by Swan. Hearing screams, they ran to the water's edge and discovered a lady crying for help. She had fallen into the lake by accident and couldn't swim. The boys disrobed, and jumped into the lake to save the drowning woman. A couple of boys raced to fetch a rowboat to bring them all in, safely. Unfortunately, the small boat capsized when the boys were trying to lift the woman into the wooden vessel. Her cumbersome crinoline caught the base of the boat as they were hoisting her up, and they were pulled into the water with her.

A quick-thinking student with a penknife sliced the entangled material from the lady's dress away from the boat. In the process her under garments were revealed. In Victorian society, this was considered an indecent display of nakedness. She climbed into the vessel, rowing herself away as fast as she could, while her rescuers swam in the buff to shore. They were gallant, giving the lady sufficient time to reach dry land and be covered by women on the shore who had towels and blankets, to protect her modesty. Only after she was hastened away did the boys come ashore.

Word of the incident spread hastily. Running out to Swan, other boys cheered and hailed the rescuers as heroes. The boys, in their birthday suits, were carried on the shoulders of the cheering student body. The students continued to row naked, in honor of the quick-acting nude rescuers, who saved the drowning lady. Nude rowing at the Kipling Rowing Club became a tradition. The rowing teams won numerous competitions over the years for Daltonbury Hall.

When Nikee and I arrived at Kipling Society, the rowing club students were just getting their boats out to practice for an upcoming competition. The competitors returned to school a week prior to commencement, for practice. I caught an eyeful of naked rowers when we went into the boathouse. Nikee knew several of the seniors from Kipling; he gave them friendly hugs, in their birthday suits. I felt embarrassed, but only slightly. Often, during the course of the school term, gazing out of the classroom windows, I would see naked rowers on Swan.

Nicholas

Nikee's grandparents were descendants of a powerful and wealthy Austrian aristocratic family. His grandfather was an Archduke, who fled Austria during World War I. They took what wealth they could and left for England, seeking political asylum from the British monarchy. Starting over from scratch, Nikee's grandfather, a shrewd entrepreneur, quickly built a business and forged a comfortable living for his family in Wales. Nicholas Senior, Nikee's father, continued in the family business, becoming a wealthy landowner, operating a successful Welsh supermarket chain.

Nikee, one of two siblings, was enrolled in Daltonbury Hall. He studied at Daltonbury before beginning a three-year duration of travels to and from the Middle East. It was a student exchange program, which required him to commute between Bahrain and Daltonbury Hall. He had just arrived from Bahrain a couple of days prior to our meeting.

Nikee kept to a regimented daily workout schedule. When he had first arrived at Daltonbury Hall, Nikee's 'big brother' (Valet) had encouraged him to participate in a bodybuilding workout class as one of his extracurricular activities. He encouraged me to enroll in the workout program as well, which I happily did. Under his guidance and support as my workout partner, my physique morphed from a skinny beanstalk to that of a muscular and defined man. Working out had never interested me, nor had any sport, for that matter. But, these workouts seemed quite pleasant compared to Foong Senior's unsuccessful attempts to butch me up with Judo, Karate and Kung Fu.

Whatever Nikee suggested, I willing participated in, including horseback riding. He was my constant companion, cheering me forward with moral support. I was falling 'in love' with my 'big brother' more and more each passing day, despite the admonitions I had received. I had no idea that I was secretly being groomed for a special mission.

When I was in class, Nikee was engaged in private tutorials with Daltonbury Hall professors. He was also diligently preparing applications to prestigious United Kingdom universities for the following year.

John

"Time flies when you're having fun," they say, and for me, at Daltonbury, that was so true. The next few days of becoming acclimated, with Nikee as my guide, went quickly. Before I knew it, Monday, the first day of class, arrived. John, our roommate, returned Sunday afternoon. I took an immediate liking to John as soon as we met. Like Nikee, he had a sweet, charming personality with an open and accepting demeanor.

A year my senior in age and grade, he seemed mature for a teenager. Other boys I had known in Kuala Lumpur who were his age were gawky, geeky, or full of themselves. Most of them had faces full of acne and pimples. John was one of the most beautiful boys at Daltonbury Hall. He had a certain je ne sais quoi, which was extremely attractive.

I knew we would get on well sharing the room together and becoming friends.

John, like our BB, had just returned from a 3 month student exchange program in the Middle East. He had been based in Abu Dhabi, instead of Bahrain. He was a Spanish/Filipino mix; his smooth, boyish skin had a beautiful light brown glow. I felt certain his beautiful smiling face could charm birds down from trees.

His father was a wealthy merchant who made his fortune in planting and processing tobacco products in Venezuela, for distribution worldwide. Being the only child, he was spoiled, bratty and pampered from birth. He was travelling down the path to being a 'bad' boy, while living in Manila. He had fallen in with some sordid schoolmates who had become a nuisance to the local community. His parents removed him from his unsavory companions, and enrolled him in Daltonbury Hall. This proved to be an excellent move; John's transformed rapidly after his arrival. In the care of his 'big brother' and the teaching staff at Daltonbury Hall, he quickly became a better-behaved young man. The boarding school provided him with a regimented routine as well as with loving attention, which he desperately lacked in Manila.

John's first year BB, Jonathan, had departed Daltonbury for his higher education in France. John was now assigned to Nikee's care. It wasn't long, however, before he was back in the Middle East. Whenever he returned to Daltonbury Hall, we would easily renew our friendship. Later, our lives took different routes and we lost touch forever.

Jealousy and the Look of Love

The few days before classes commenced I had Nikee completely to myself. Although we didn't cuddle every night, the nights that we did were heavenly! From him I learned patience. Every time we slept together, I fell into safe, peaceful slumber as Nikee held me close. I wanted the sensuality to proceed further, but he maintained a stable equilibrium. Our sexual arousal continued each night we spent together.

Sometimes Nikee bent over to kiss me goodnight, on my lips, leaving me desiring more. But that was as far as it went. I felt that he wanted to carry our brotherly love to a new level, but he was training me to develop patience, to wait. At times, he would whisper softly into my ear, telling me, "Be patient young man. Be patient. Patience reaps many rewards if you practice control. Patience is a virtue. Wait and all wonderful things happen when the correct time arrives."

With that he would stop and let our passions subside but he would continue to stroke my hair and lower back while I snuggled into his muscular body, inhaling his clean manly scent. Eventually, I would fall asleep, in his arms. In the morning, I would be back in my own bed, never remembering how I got there.

Our dynamics changed when John arrived. Everyone was busy with classes, schoolwork and projects which required all of our concentration and energy. By the end of each day, I was exhausted, retiring early to bed.

One night I awakened to go to the restroom. In the dim night-light by Nikee's bedside table, I could barely make out a figure cuddling next to him. It was John. The green-eyed monster of jealousy rushed to the forefront. I felt an angry sense of betrayal and was filled with envy. I wanted Nikee for myself and myself only! I didn't want to share him with another. I returned to bed quietly, but the growling, nagging, pestering jealousy wouldn't leave me alone. It was eating me alive, tearing at me.

The pain within me was extremely difficult to comprehend because I was so young and inexperienced. I wanted to get up and push John out of 'my' place in Nikee's bed. Yet I remained still and silent. I tried shutting my eyes tightly to eliminate the jealous, ugly thoughts from my head. Still, they lingered, like blades of steel piercing into my heart. The tighter I shut my eyes, the more hatred rushed forward, relentlessly.

I lay still, trying with all of my might to be nonchalant about what I was witnessing. I opened my eyes a little; I couldn't resist looking to see what was happening on Nikee's bed. I was confronted with Nikee's piercing blue-green eyes staring at me. I quickly shut my eyes again, feigning sleep. Curiosity took hold, and I opened my eyes just a slit, to see what was transpiring. Once again, Nikee's eyes pierced me, unmoving, as if he were telling me that everything was all right, and that I need not be upset or jealous.

This time, I opened my eyes and saw BB's (mentor's) handsome face, filled with love and serenity confronting the ugliness of my jealousy. His beautiful eyes were arrows of fire boring through my soul, flooding my interior with sweet molten love. His eyes spoke a thousand words that night. Without blinking, he made love to me with his eyes, penetrating my very heart. I was filled with an indescribable depth of love, tapping into a serene, inner peace I never knew I possessed. My jealousies shattered into broken fragments, and my envious hatred subsided in Nikee's beautiful, wholesome love. That night, BB (guardian/Valet) initiated me into the 'art of making-love' through the seductive enchantment of his eyes.

By the time I fell back asleep I was assured that Nikee loved me as much as he loved John, even though John was in his arms. From that moment forward, when I saw them together in bed I understood that the ugly green-eyed monster could be kept at bay. With sufficient love, will power and mind control, I could conquer any dark jealous hollows, harnessing their satanic powers, transforming them into beauty and truth. Nikee educated me well with each passing week. I was a fast learner.

There were nights when the three of us slept together in Nikee's bed, BB holding each of us by his side. I soon came to love John as I did Nikee. Through all that transpired, BB (Valet) was grooming me for a role I wasn't aware of at the time -- a role for which I was observed, daily. A role whose success depended on my behavior, reactions and conduct. A role that required patience, self-control and, most importantly a clear understanding of the Art of Unselfish Love.

CHAPTER EIGHTEEN

No Distance between Us

Tolkien Brotherhood

I was accepted into the Tolkien Brotherhood because my resume stressed my interest in art and design. Mother and Father provided an impressive background on my ballet dance and dance choreography work at the Griffin Inn shows. Father's discreet failure to mention that he was the owner of the nightclub probably helped. I was accepted on the merit of my creative talents.

My parents also provided Daltonbury Hall with impressive letters of recommendations from Mrs. Koo, my former art teacher, who informed Daltonbury that I had won Junior Art competitions while under her tutelage and that I excelled in painting. I also had a glowing letter from Uncle James, an alumnus of Yates Fraternity. He wrote a personal letter to the school's

Headmaster, with whom he was friends, giving him an excellent account of my behavior and character.

My grades from The Methodist Boys' School were more than satisfactory. My whole-hearted involvement in the organization and participation of the boys' fashion shows and the variety show dance performances were sufficient for me to be considered for acceptance into the school. The school had vacancies to be filled in the performing art dormitory when I applied. I was lucky to be given the opportunity to enroll in this prestigious institution.

During the Victorian era many artists came to the Isle of Wight to capture the scenic beauty of the island. Daltonbury Hall acted as host to many well-known artists of that period, particularly artists from the Pre-Raphaelite Brotherhood. Painters such as John William Waterhouse, Arthur Hughes, Sir Lawrence Alma-Tadema, Dante Gabriel Rossetti, together with a host of other famous Victorian painters, had been artists stationed at Daltonbury Hall. By the turn of the 20th century, the Tolkien Brotherhood had already established an artistic educational institute for boys who were aspiring artists, painters, sculptors, and designers. Many well-known artists, photographers and designers of the 20th and 21st century were alumni of the Tolkien Brotherhood at Daltonbury Hall.

Tolkien Culinary Society

The Culinary Society at the Tolkien Brotherhood would organize special events to educate students in the Art of Fine Dining. Since the majority of students came from wealthy, established families, this extracurricular course of study was considered part of the finishing school education for society boys. We were educated in gentlemanly etiquette in preparation for our emerging roles as society's leaders, movers and shakers. Naturally, etiquette and proper manners would be required in our social and business duties.

Formal Dress

A week before school closed for the Christmas holidays, Nikee suggested we attend the school's end-of-term culinary evening organized by the Culinary Society to celebrate the advent of Christmas. It was held at the Assembly Hall on a Saturday evening. Young ladies from our sister school were invited, together with staff, faculty members and their spouses. Ever since the day Uncle James and mother took me to the River Restaurant at the Savoy, I was hooked on the "Art of Fine Dining." A sucker for British and European pomp and circumstance as well as society's dining etiquette and manners, I was glad to have the opportunity to dress up for an evening of gourmet cuisine and great dancing.

I liked the fact that Nikee and I were attending a Ball together! I had seen photos of formal functions and the attending guests' attire, but I'd never attended a Ball and knew absolutely nothing about dressing for such an occasion.

Uncle James knew there would be formal occasions at Daltonbury Hall during annual festive seasons, and the task of suiting me up fell into his hands. When I was in London, he took me to Saville Row to have me fitted for a dinner suit. Mother knew next to nothing about bespoke tailoring, and it was pointless for her to come with us. We went to Geives & Hawkes, where James had his suits made.

As soon as we entered the shop, I was struck by the degree of English snobbery. A mature gentleman greeted Uncle James and me with an Edwardian air. He gave me a cursory glance, and then ignored my presence until Uncle James formally introduced us. James was a regular customer at Geives & Hawkes. The man soon understood that I was a potential client and it would be advisable for him to be polite. If I had ventured into the shop by myself, "Old Smith" would not have given me the time of day. Race and class prejudices were very much alive in England, in the sixties. I had stepped further back in time, in that shop, entering the era of the Gilded Age.

With assistance and advice from Uncle James, I selected an appropriate black wool gabardine fabric for the suit. I wanted something a little trendy, yet classical in cut. We also ordered a custom-made white dress shirt, especially crafted to fit my teenage frame. Since my favorite color is pink, Uncle James picked out a black and pink striped satin bowtie to match my ensemble. We also selected a pair of formal black patent lace-up shoes. Before I left for the Isle of Wight, I had a fitting at the shop. The clothes and shoes were hand delivered to Daltonbury Hall by Geives & Hawkes. It arrived in an elegant black box, with my full name embossed in scripted gold letters on the box cover. Inside, were soft white tissues, with Geives & Hawkes' logo, printed in gold. The Ball was the perfect opportunity for me to shine in my gorgeous attire.

The Ball

Nickee looked stunningly suave! If John had been present he would have looked spiffy, too, in formal black-tie attire. Unfortunately, he left for the Middle East shortly after a month at Daltonbury Hall.

The Assembly Hall was transformed into an elegant dining room for this festive occasion. The table settings were artistic and tasteful. A beautiful Christmas tree filled with Victorian antique ornaments and fairy lights was placed on the side of the entrance. It reminded me of the Singapore Raffles Hotel Christmas Party to which Mother took me when I was six years old. This venue really was an actual 19th century Victorian ballroom built in that era. The spacious domed dining hall, with its ornately painted ceilings, glowed in the soft candle light, carrying me back to an era of English aristocracy, when society's gentlewomen and gentlemen danced the Viennese Waltz.

Music students from the Tolkien Brotherhood's Music Society formed an eight piece stringed orchestra, playing melodic classical music while guests, students and staff sat enjoying their dinner.

Before Nikee and I entered the Hall, our names were announced to the guests who were already in the room. Although alcohol, wine and beer were served to staff and seniors over eighteen, juniors like me knew better than to try to sneak a sip of alcohol under the watchful eyes of our Big Brothers, professors, teaching staff, and their spouses. It would be a punishable offense if we were caught. The prefects send offenders to scrub toilets and shower areas after school, or on Sundays.

Long tables with place cards for each guest were beside the dessert silverware. Males and females were seated opposite each other and side by side. I was seated opposite a young lady by the name of Amelia and my immediate left and right were occupied by two other charming ladies, Georgina and Carol. They were students at Hattonfield Abbey School for Girls, our sister school on the Isle of Wight. On the left of Amelia was Nikee and to her right was a male senior student by the name of Aris, from the Yates Fraternity. This formal arrangement provided the boys with an opportunity for social conversation with the ladies, and vice-verse.

In the middle of the large rectangular dining hall was a dance floor where waltz music played after dessert was served. Male students had a chance to invite the females sitting next to or opposite them to dance without leaving any ladies to be wallflowers. It was un-gentlemanly to leave a lady sitting on her own; proper etiquette dictated inviting her to the floor, even if for only one dance. The Tolkien Brotherhood Dance Society had offered extracurricular ballroom dance classes for students who wanted to learn the "Art of Ballroom Dancing," which Nikee and I had participated in prior to this evening's festivities. It was relatively easy for me to master ballroom dancing, since I already had studied ballet. I had learned the basic dance steps and took to the floor with ease and grace. Nikee also had previous experience in social dances. It was not a surprise that many female students wanted to be waltzing in Nikee's arms. With his handsome looks and charismatic personality, he had no problem finding dance partners throughout the course of the evening.

Traditional Christmas formal black-tie affair or not, the Teddy Bares, an all guys band of five students from the Yates Fraternity, took center stage when the stringed orchestra retired for the evening. Popular dance music of that era was bound to make an appearance in one form or another! It was truly a delightful Christmas Ball at Daltonbury Hall.

Celebration of Love

It was close to midnight when I walked to my room. Nikee was still at the celebration, dancing the night away and chatting up the female students from Hattonfield Abbey. I wanted some solitude and a chance to catch a breath of fresh, night air. It was hot and stuffy inside the Hall; I wanted to chill on my own for a while. It was the dead of winter and the night sky was beautifully lit by a full moon. Although the air was slightly chilly, it wasn't damp or cold like England usually is during the winter and early spring months. Maybe I had danced too vigorously, but coming out of the heated Hall into the refreshing night air was such a wonderful relief. It was one of those rare evenings on which peace, calmness and serenity reigned supreme. The gods had created the midnight sky with such brilliance and beauty that it seemed a shame to retire to the four walls of my dorm room. I decided to continue walking towards the boathouse by Swan Lake where I sat quietly, drinking in the enchantment of the evening.

I sat on the wooden pier absorbing the beauty that surrounded me. My mind couldn't resist wondering what my future had in store. Deep in concentration, I felt a hand touch me on my shoulder. Turning around, I found Nikee standing behind me. Surprised to see him, I asked why he had left the party and how he knew I was by the boathouse. He did not reply to any of my questions. Instead, he lifted his index finger to my lips, indicating that he wished for me to be quiet. I kept still; he did not utter a word. Kneeling beside me, he turned my head towards him and kissed me, full on my lips.

Taken by surprise, I did not move a muscle. His tongue pried opens my lips, exploring my emotions of longing. I had dreamed of this for months. He was doing exactly what I had yearned for, but I wasn't expecting it. I didn't think my longing would ever be fulfilled.

Not releasing his grip, he held me closer than he had before. His tongue continued probing my mouth until I received him willingly. I had ached for his passionate kisses and now it was happening. Yet, I was afraid. I held onto him, breathing in his intoxicating masculine essence. My mouth opened in response to his passionate determination. Lifting me to a standing position, Nikee held my head with his strong hands, drawing me closer to him, wanting me to return his loving desire. His kisses sent electricity coursing through every cell of my body, drawing me to him like the gravitational force of the Sun. I had no choice but to give myself willingly to this bewildering experience. His beautiful bluish-green gaze never left my eyes. This reminded me of his tender love during my fit of jealousy early in the school year, over John. Under the silvery moon, I felt his fiery arrows bursting through my soul again, filling me with liquid honey between my longing thighs. Nikee, my 'big brother', frightened me in many ways; his loving actions and stare bewitched me completely, melting my boyish body into his masculine embrace.

Finally, he released his grip, telling me to sit and wait while he went into the boathouse to gather some warm blankets and towels for us. As we stood by the lake, he began to slowly unbutton my dress shirt, placing his hands on my naked body, caressing my soft skin. Slowly he reached his hands below, caressing my hardness beneath the fabric of my pants, unzipping my trousers and letting them drop to the ground. I could feel the chilly air brush against my naked skin, but with Nikee's warm body next to mine, the chill dissipated into the night sky. I slowly undressed him, just as he had undressed me, until we were both nearly naked with only our white briefs between us. He reached into my briefs and began stroking my erection, sending sparks of electric currents coursing up and down my naked body. I reached into his briefs to touch his manhood, ready to be unleashed from its confines.

Suddenly he took my hand and plunged us into Swan's icy water! As I came up for air, Nikee lifted me out of the water and wrapped us both in warm towels. Taking off my wet underwear, he dried our bodies before wrapping us in the warm woolen blankets he had laid on the grass. My spinning uncertainty was starting to slow down after being submerged in the cold water. Everything looked clearer than ever. We sat by the water's edge, admiring the tranquility of the night in a warm embrace. He turned my face to his and continued where he had left off, planting his longing kisses on my accepting mouth. This time, his tongue moved downwards towards my tiny nipples. Playing, circling and teasing the tips to erection, this stimulation aroused me, arching my body towards his strong arms which supported the small of my back. Feeling his warm body next to mine, I gave in to his every wish. His kisses were soft and gentle, biting, teasing and caressing. Our hardness stirred between the nakedness of our thighs. The more intense his adoration, the more aroused we became. My hands touched his strong muscular V-shaped back, stimulating my hardness to release stickiness onto my belly. Big Brother reached his fingers to my groin, feeling my excitement pressed against his masculinity. His fingers scooped my wetness for us to taste, driving me insane with sexual ecstasy as he lunged his tongue back into my mouth, I could taste my sweet salty liquid mixed with his saliva; it was delicious! His hard, muscled buttocks moved in rhythm to my continual pleasure, rocking us into Oneness.

He leaned above me so I could inhale the essence of his groin. His muskiness drove me wild. I opened my mouth to draw him in. His hardness plunged deeply into my mouth, unrelentingly. I wanted him pushing and pulsating in me. Lifting himself to a push-up position, he fed me his hardness, withdrawing occasionally for me to taste the muskiness below his erect length. He lifted my legs to his shoulders, spit into my virginity, and prepared my opening with his sweet saliva before easing himself inside the very depths of my being. I surrendered to bliss.

Tonight, I was finally his and I knew he wanted this to last. I was in heaven! My head was whirling as if the beauty of the Aurora Borealis had descended upon Swan Lake. The indescribable ecstasy sent shivers and goose bumps over my young body. We rocked back and forth steadily to a rhythmic slow love dance. I didn't want this wonderful sensation to end. Seemingly knowing my thoughts, he continued our dance in slow motion. We became one with the universe. Nothing mattered except the fusion of our souls into a single loving entity. Finally, our bodies could no longer stave off the inevitable. I involuntarily released, covering my belly with a wetness that slid off my slim waist and trickled onto his muscular thigh. The excitement was too much for him to hold out any longer. With a loud moan he gave himself to me, releasing deep within my core being.

Our moans and groans merged into a solidified oneness throughout the course of our union. His body jerked with intensity as he pushed his masculinity deeper into me, a gift I was only too happy to receive. I wanted his love to fill every part of me. We kissed for a long time after making love, not wanting the night to end.

That night, we sealed our union many times over before the wee hours of dawn greeted us. After jumping into the cold water to wash, we dressed and snuck back to our room.

CHAPTER NINETEEN

Christmas in London

Parting is Hard

The week after Nikee and I had our passionate rendezvous, he gave me further lessons on the Art of Making Love, both in and out of bed. Little did I realize I was in training for a mission that would soon change the course of my life. I was happily in love with my BB (Valet). I wasn't looking forward to our two week separation over the Christmas holidays. Nikee was returning home to Wales to spend the festive season with his family, and I would be crossing the English Channel by ferry, going to London to be with Uncle James.

I felt horribly sad leaving Nikee, even though we would soon be reunited. There was a strange emotional turmoil happening inside of me. He was my first true love and I was in love with him, but Nikee had repeatedly stressed that I should never allow that to happen.

Chapter Nineteen

On the day of our departure, Nikee accompanied me to Portsmouth Ferry Terminal to say farewell, reassuring me that we would see each other soon and encouraging me to enjoy my time in London with Uncle James. He promised to contact me when he was in Wales. Tears rolled down my cheeks when the ferry began pulling away from the harbour as I watched Nikee wave good-bye from the pier.

This time round, going to London didn't seem as exciting as my first visit had. What had happened? Within a short span of three months, I had grown up, considerably. I was no longer an immature boy; I was a young man, in love with a charming, handsome twenty-year-old man.

On the ferry, as the beautiful harbour lights slowly morphed into distant twinkling stars, I could not help but compare Nikee to KiWi. As much as I liked KiWi, I was never in love with him. We were too immature to understand love. There was no "lovemaking," really, with KiWi; there was nothing comparable to the experiences I shared with Nikee.

KiWi's idea of lovemaking was oral sex or mutual masturbation. There were no romantic gestures or any deep intimacy. There were hardly any words exchanged between KiWi and myself, since we were not trained in social communication skills.

I was beginning to understand the difference between the two experiences. It was little wonder when Nikee came into my life that I fell head over heels for this "Love God." He had good looks, charisma and was a connoisseur of the art of making love.

That afternoon Uncle James came to Waterloo Station to collect me. The moment I stepped off the train onto the station's platform, Uncle James said that I had grown taller and had matured from a, wide-eyed boy to a cute fella. During the journey to Mayfair, he said we could do many things together which I had never done before. He promised we would explore London together during this Holiday Season.

I enjoyed my time with Uncle James more than I thought I would. We did go to many exciting places, but as much as I tried to put on a happy face, Uncle James detected something was amiss; I wasn't my normal, cheerful self. I was missing Nikee horrendously. At first, James pretended he didn't notice my melancholy, when we visited places of interest.

Sight Seeing

We queued for 30 minutes at The Tower of London to get a chance to admire the Crown Jewels, which were indeed spectacular. I was glad we waited in line to view the sparkling diamonds, rubies and sapphires.

Our outing to see the Changing of the Guards at Buckingham Palace was spectacular. It was something I had hoped to experience when we first drove by The Palace, on our way to the Savoy for brunch with Mother. I was a sucker for the guards in their black furry bear hats and red, black and gold braided uniforms displaying traditional English pomp and circumstance, with such panache. Unfortunately, all I could think about was my BB Nikee, instead of enjoying the moment of the fancy procession parading before my eyes. I kept thinking, "If only Nikee were here watching and enjoying this with me." Nikee remained my constant companion, in my head every minute of every day and night! I tried to shake him away, but the memories of him wouldn't leave me alone. I kept reminding myself to enjoy what was before me, yet, the moment I turned my head, his face would loom large in the foreground. I couldn't shake him out of my head or my body. I hated this bothersome feeling!

Being a worldly man, Uncle James knew something was amiss. But he did not utter a word regarding my uneasiness, and wouldn't, unless I brought it up and wanted to talk to him about it. He was every yard an English gentleman who would not pry, even when he knew something was up. Night was the worst. I couldn't get to sleep, and when I did, Nikee was in my dreams. I often had sleepless nights, tossing and turning.

Chapter Nineteen

Conversation with Uncle James

It was futile trying to get Nikee out of my head. Finally, a week into my London stay, I plucked up the courage to talk with Uncle James, who would understand. After all, he was my guardian and mentor. I trusted him, and I was positive he would understand. That evening, when he treated me to a belated birthday dinner at L' Oranger, I finally told Uncle James everything. I shared all that had transpired within the past three months at Daltonbury Hall. I told him about my sexual relationship with Nikee.

James listened attentively, making no comments until I finished. Smiling, he said he had already suspected that something or someone was eating at my tender heart. He was glad I had confided in him. He said, "There are greater things in store for you besides your regular studies at Daltonbury Hall. You must take every situation in stride. Decide wisely for yourself what you should or should not undertake. The Ball of Life is always in your court."

Uncle James certainly did not object to my relationship with Nikee, because he understood it was part of a boy's coming-of-age process. "At your age, it's natural for a boy to explore his sexuality. I am glad Daltonbury Hall is providing a safe and secure sanctuary, giving young boys the opportunity to pursue their life's journey to adulthood, with grace and non-judgment. Very few educational intuitions provide this," he said as I listened, intently.

Uncle James continued, "You are one of the lucky few given this special gift. You are guarded from harm's way during this crucial exploration period in your life. It sounds as if you are taking full advantage of your time at Daltonbury Hall. Learn, absorb and experience all you can, because time will fly by quickly. Before you know it, this period of your life will be a distant memory."

Of course, Uncle James was correct; my time spent at Daltonbury Hall is, indeed, a distant memory now. But it shaped my worldview. I saw things in an entirely new light because of my boarding school experiences.

When I told James that I liked boys, not girls, he said he already guessed as much when we first met. It did not bother him if I preferred men, women or both. "Homosexuality is as old as history itself. The ancient Greeks and early Romans loved their male counterparts as much as they loved themselves," said James, before citing a brief history of homosexuality throughout the ages.

He was glad I was honest and that I had told him how I felt. He advised me to accept the person I was and to be true to myself at all times. Uncle James certainly accepted and loved me as I was. Before we left L' Oranger, he gave me his solemn oath to keep our conversation private, as it was his gentlemanly honor to do so. That is why I loved Uncle James, because he was a man of his word and a dear fatherly figure to me. He would never tell my parents what we discussed that evening.

I felt such relief after speaking to Uncle James. This was a conversation I could never have had with Foong Senior. Father would never have understood what I was going through and would, more likely than not, have sent me to a quack institution in hopes of converting me to 'normal,' whatever that means. I have witnessed the devastating results on others from such efforts. Far too many men who entered these 'reform intuitions' later committed suicide, or were unable to accept themselves after returning to regular society. The overlay of shame and judgment often compelled them to live a life of deceit and lies. A terribly sad situation indeed!

That night, in my room, I felt much better than I had the entire week. I was relieved that I had talked with Uncle James. I needed advice from an experienced man. Yet, as good as I felt that evening, the nagging infatuation with my BB continued to haunt me throughout the duration of my stay.

"Why hasn't Nikee called"? I wondered. It had been five days since we said "au revoir." He had promised that he would contact me when he was in Wales. My never-ending, unsettling feelings returned with a vengeance. "I beg you, get out of my head PLEASE!"

James R. Pinkerton

Uncle James was a widower whose estranged Chinese wife died in a tragic car accident while she was living in Australia. Their divorce was about to be finalized when the shocking news of Angela's death reached Mr. Pinkerton in Hong Kong, where he was CFO at the Hong Kong & Shanghai Banking Corporation.

Their only child, Paul, a young man approximately two years my senior, was studying at a boarding school in Scotland when his mother died. After boarding school, he was accepted into an Australian University. We were acquainted briefly, during the times I spent at Uncle James' Mayfair home.

James R. Pinkerton was an alumnus of Daltonbury Hall. Later, he graduated with Honors from Cambridge University. He joined The Royal Air Force Regiment and became an Air Marshal during World War II, before assuming his prestigious position at Hong Kong and Shanghai Banking Corporation.

James was truly a gentleman of honor and integrity, and I respected him. Without Uncle James' presence in my life, it would have been a difficult transition from my teenage years to adulthood.

BB did telephone me twice from Wales, and we shared a couple lengthy conversations. Once he rang to tell me Merry Christmas, and on the other occasion he called to wish me a delightful and Happy New Year! He was enjoying the Holidays and hoped I was, too. I was happy to know his family was well. I did not tell him I was going out of my head over him. I was just glad to hear his sexy, loving voice over the phone.

It was nice to spend Christmas with Uncle James, and to bring in the New Year with him, but I was elated to board the train bound for Portsmouth. I bid 'sayonara' to my dear guardian and caught the ferry to cross the channel to be with Nikee, again.

Nikee promised to be at the Portsmouth Pier to meet me when I arrived. It was a delightful and heartwarming reunion. I was overjoyed to see his handsome smiling face, waving to me as the ferry pulled in to dock. I could not resist running to his embrace. Bending down, he kissed me full on my lips in front of everyone. Dear BB Nikee never failed to surprise me.

CHAPTER TWENTY

Creeping Up Softly On Me

Equestrian

Spring had sprung in the Isle of Wight. The air was cool and the sun was out. So were the yellow daffodils, the white crocuses, and blazes of colorful tulips growing wild in the woods, surrounding Daltonbury Hall. Nikee continued to educate me in various techniques of lovemaking. I trusted and listened attentively to BB's advice not only because I was in love with this charismatic man, but also because he was older and more experienced than me. Therefore, he took charge in situations.

He was also showing me how to be a 'big brother' (Valet) when the time came for me to step into his shoes. Although he did not say he was grooming me to be a BB, he was monitoring my actions, reactions and responses to situations and circumstances, observing me to see how I handled myself.

I wasn't aware I was under surveillance by Nikee, nor did I know I was also under the watchful eyes of other 'big brothers' (Valets) and staff during the course of my first six months at Daltonbury Hall.

I was one of eight candidates who had the potential to advance towards a special mission in the Fall. The school would select five students out of the eight candidates. Unaware of this selection process, I was simply absorbing and learning everything a regular boy would, during life in a private school.

The day Nikee suggested we go horseback riding was a perfectly beautiful Spring Sunday. We had the stable boys saddle a couple of the school's horses for us for a cross-country ride. Under Nikee's advice, I had enrolled in riding classes as one of my extracurricular activities. I was able to trot and canter pretty well, but when it came to galloping, I fell short. I was afraid I might fall off the horse if the animal went too fast.

BB showed me some tricks about galloping, so my fear of falling would dissipate. "If you know how to handle the reins to control the horse, you should do just fine," Nikee advised.

Riding

We changed into our equestrian habits and headed beyond campus grounds on our horses. We trotted in the beautiful open fields for approximately half a mile before Nikee suggested we go faster down a country lane. It was wonderful to feel the cool air blowing on my face. I turned to look at BB (guardian), who was beside me. He laughed and said, "Let's race!" With a light tap on his stirrup to the side of the horse, the animal started galloping ahead. Though I was afraid of speeds faster than a canter, I wanted to catch up to Nikee to show him I was up to the challenge. I tapped my horse's side lightly with my crop and away I went, racing next to Nikee. It was such an exhilarating experience to be flying on horseback, next to the person I loved. We laughed as we chased each other for a few miles before slowing to a trot. We were nearing a forest, and our horses were taking us onto a woodland trail. Panting from our spirited race, we slowed our horses to a walk. As the trail got narrower and the undergrowth got thicker, we dismounted, leading the animals to a pond Nikee said he had been to before. Thick carpets of wild flowers were imprinted by our riding boots as we ventured further towards the fresh water pool. We needed to give our horses a drink; we had been working them hard. There, we could have a rest.

I was hot from the race. Taking off my show coat, gloves, and hat, I unbuttoned my shirt to my waist, to get cool. I had never been to this part of the school grounds and was curious to explore the shady forest. English woodlands and forests have always held a divine mystical, magical and enchanting power over me, especially during Spring, when new life is being birthed, all around. One of the reasons I fell in love with Pre Raphaelite Art was that many artists of this genre depict English forests in their paintings. The abundance of draping, twirling ivies around huge ancient trees gave the forest an air of romance.

Creeping Up Softly

Finally, we arrived at the pond. A beautiful waterfall cascaded from a slope above. It was picturesque. Suddenly, I felt the urge to go skinny-dipping in this enchanted pool. I tied our horses to a tree, stripped naked and plunged into the refreshing water.

Nikee sat on the grass, enjoying the lazy sunshine slipping in between the leaves of the forest trees creating a chiaroscuro on the forest floor. I was a happy boy, enjoying a delightful afternoon. A stable groom had packed us a warm blanket, in case we stopped for a rest along the way. We spread the blanket and I lay on the woolen tweed next to Nikee, enjoying the beauty of the forest. Looking up at the half-hidden afternoon sky, I closed my eyes, enjoying the moment, lost in time. When I turned to look at Nikee, his brilliant greenish blue eyes met my gaze. As he reached over to kiss me on my lips, I closed my eyes to enjoy

Nikee's warm embrace. One kiss led to another, and suddenly, Nikee was kissing me passionately. I gave myself to his caresses; his loving hands always seemed to play tricks on my body. His masculinity never failed to send shivers and goose bumps up my spine.

I felt what seemed to be another pair of hands stroking my groin. It was a pleasurable sensation, and I did not want it to end. Though my eyes were closed, the curiosity of wanting to see who the person was prompted me to take a peek. I could only see Nikee's handsome face smiling down at me, as he was leaning on his side, partially on top of me. The pair of massaging hands felt amazing on my naked body. Waves of sensual ecstasy flowed through me. I arched my back towards the delightful caressing hands, which slid underneath my buttocks. I felt a warm mouth encircling my hardness, engulfing it. It didn't feel like Nikee's sweet lips because BB's tongue was in my mouth, kissing me. Wave after wave of electrical currents charged through my tense body. I enjoyed these wonderful feelings, wanting everything to continue. I could feel my sweet boyish scent being inhaled. The pair of masculine hands held me, lifted me. His hardness inquired, probing me.

When I finally opened my eyes I saw a handsome naked male figure kneeling between my splayed legs. Andy. The good-looking senior rower from Kipling Society, whom I met when Nikee took me on my campus tour. Andy had smiled and winked at me a couple of times that day, before BB and I left the rowing team to their practices. Being a naive junior, it didn't register that his wink was a flirtatious signal. I thought he was just being nice and friendly.

Nikee's mesmerizing eyes stared into mine, assuring me that everything was all right, under control, and that I need not be alarmed by Andy's presence.

With both mouths caressing me, the sensual stimulation was delightful. I didn't want them to stop. Nikee undressed while Andy moved to kiss me, licking and planting sweet kisses on my closed eyes and earlobes. His sinewy rower's body was on top of mine, pressing his hardness against mine. I felt Nikee's sensual breath between my thighs, licking and kissing my pressing roundness below.

These sensations were too electrifying. I wanted to taste Andy's masculinity and stoke his erectness as I often did with Nikee. Reading my thoughts, Andy lifted himself to a straddling position, over my chest, feeding me his engorged manhood, while BB did the same to my boyhood. My hands reached to caress Andy's muscular physique. I felt his taut definition. My groans of pleasure encouraged his hardness; he thrust deep into my throat. The alpha muskiness of his groin was intoxicating, sending me over the edge. BB leaned forward, sharing my creamy wetness which was trickling down the sides of his lips.

Andy flipped me onto my stomach, spit in my opening, and eased into the core of my being. I tilted my pelvis upward, to receive him; I wanted his hardness inside me. BB's (Valet's) kisses in my mouth were soon replaced with his stiffness. Their synchronized movements brought them to the inevitable. Their ecstatic cries came simultaneously as they released their manly liquids inside me. Their love penetrated deep into my being, flowing unceasingly into the very center of my soul. It was pure ecstasy! Eventually their heaving slowed, subsiding to gentle moans before they lay next to me, one BB on each side. They gave me gentle loving kisses as we dozed into a lazy embracing slumber.

Andy

Andy was approximately the same age as Nikee, maybe a few months older. Although a student at the Yates Fraternity, he joined the rowing team when he was a junior. He was a German Jew; his family escaped Brandenburg, Germany, before the Nazis came to power. They fled to Sweden where they had relatives.

Andy's father was a wealthy merchant who made his fortune in the 1920s by investing heavily in the automobile industry. He deposited his financial fortune in a Swiss account. When they left Germany for Sweden, Andy's family was able to live comfortably off his investments. By the time Andy entered Daltonbury Hall, his father had accumulated more wealth than his family could spend during their entire lifetime.

Andy was the third child. His life was secured with a Trust Fund in his name which he could access when he reached the age of twenty one.

Andy's passion was engineering, especially designing and building bridges. Yates Fraternity offered great opportunities for pre-University engineering students. Andy's other passion was rowing, as a recreational hobby as well as an exercise regime. It kept his six foot and three inch muscular, sinewy frame in excellent condition. He was a 'big brother' (Valet) to a couple of juniors at Yates, as well. He and Nikee became friends when they spent a year in Bahrain in the student exchange program.

Questions & Answers

By the time Nikee and I arrived back at Daltonbury, it was dinnertime. We cleaned and changed before proceeding to The Hobbit for our evening meal. I was curious to know how Andy found us at the pond. Nikee smiled and asked if I enjoyed myself and asked if I would consider doing something similar again. Would I consider having liaisons with other boys? "Yes." I told him the experience was very pleasant and that I would be open to other experiences, depending on the situations and circumstances.

He continued to divert my questions regarding Andy's appearance by the pond. He had many questions for me, that evening. I found it a little unusual that he was so terribly persistent in his many inquiries. I didn't understand at the time where our conversation was heading. It was as if he were conducting a survey of my sexual habits, preferences and inclinations for a written report. I felt like he was collecting data for a paper. I answered him with honesty, and with an open heart. Yet, he avoided answering my questions regarding Andy's presence by the pond. I let the matter drop.

I'm sure Nikee recorded my interview actions for his report to our superiors. I believe that this deed I had participated in, with Nikee and Andy by the pond, contributed to my being one of the eight juniors short-listed for a special student exchange mission in the Fall.

It was a year before I found out the reason for Andy's presence by the forest pool, along with many other answers. Everything was made clear to me, when I went on a unique exchange program abroad.

CHAPTER TWENTY-ONE

The Young Ones Shouldn't Be Afraid

Artistic Photographer's Muse

On a late spring day, a notice was posted at Tolkien Brotherhood which read: American artistic photographer seeking male models, for an upcoming nude photo shoot on Daltonbury Hall campus grounds. Auditions will be held at the school's Assembly Hall, Lecture Theatre 2, at 2:00 p.m. on Saturday May 25th. Interested applicants, please contact Ernest Haas at...

I was keen to apply, as I had done modeling before and I thought it would be a fun project. After eight months at Daltonbury Hall, I had outgrown my shyness and was beginning to come into my own. I had learned to love my body as much as I loved Nikee's. Therefore, posing nude was not a

Chapter Twenty-one

problem for me. With Nikee's encouragement, I signed up for the juniors' workout class at Kipling gym with Nikee as my workout buddy. As I mentioned before, my body was morphing from a skinny beanstalk to one that had definition.

On the scheduled modeling audition date, I went to the Lecture Theatre 2, where the audition was being conducted. There were approximately twenty-five boys queuing up to be interviewed. Mr. Haas was looking for a maximum of five juniors for the shoot. I was nervous, since I considered most of the other applicants better-looking than myself, with nicer physiques as well. I wasn't sure if I would stand a chance competing with these boys.

My urge to be an artistic photographer's muse was very strong, prompting me to devise a plan to garner Mr. Haas and the selection team's attention. Haas' photography work was well known at the time; I came across some of his images in an American journal. He had enclosed a couple of artistic male nude photographs in the audition advertisement, so applicants would have an idea of what would be expected of them. The poster mentioned that the shoot would be in the style and genre of a famous late-nineteenth-century American painter by the name of Thomas Eakins. I loved his work; I went to the library and found his paintings of adolescent boys to be intriguingly beautiful. There was a naive quality which he captured in his pictures.

Each model was given five minutes to present himself in front of the five-person selection team. Mr. Haas sat in the middle. To his left sat his male assistant, Andy Hanson and his female companion at the time, Ms. Grace. Daltonbury Hall's art teacher Ms. Coupper, and our school's photography teacher, Mr. Owens, sat on Mr. Haas' right. All of them were situated behind a long table, where they had an unencumbered view of each applicant who entered the room.

The candidate could either stand or sit on the single chair positioned in the middle of the room. It was a solemn and daunting affair; the applicants appeared to be judged from head to toe. This seemed odd to me; I assumed it would be a casual, artsy meet-and-greet audition.

Although Nikee accompanied me to the audition, I did not tell him my plan, since I wasn't sure whether I would have the courage to carry it out. When my turn arrived to enter the lecture theatre for my interview, I was as ready as I ever would be.

The lecture theatre was partitioned with glass soundproof walls. The candidates who were waiting outside in the Assembly Hall could see into the interview room, but they couldn't hear a thing. It was a weekend, so students did not have to wear school uniforms. I had decided to wear a casual sweatshirt, and sweatpants with a drawstring tie.

When I entered the room, a couple of the panel members were busy jotting down notes from the previous interview. The others burrowed their eyes into me. It was as if they were trying to see into my soul, to determine if I were the correct candidate for the position. Before they started with their questions, I plucked up my courage, lifted off my sweatshirt, and untied the drawstring on my pants. I let my trousers drop to the floor. I was completely naked.

I purposely had not worn underpants. I was nervous in the beginning, but not being selected was not an option. I wanted the job desperately and would have done just about anything to get it.

Stark naked, I stepped out of my sweat pants and did a few poses that were similar to Thomas Eakins' adolescent boy paintings. I could hear both of my teachers gasp in shock that an applicant would do such an outrageous thing! Their initial shock soon turned to grins.

Life drawing classes were conducted weekly for students to study human anatomy in art and photography classes. Ms. Coupper and Mr. Owens were used to seeing naked boys like the one now standing before them. However, they were not expecting an applicant to drop his pants in front of the selection panel! The reactions from Mr. Haas and his entourage indicated that they were impressed, and amused. I knew from their smiling faces that I had won them over and that I would be selected for the role. No words were exchanged throughout my entire performance.

After my poses (which seemed like hours to me) I dressed and left the room. Nikee and the boys waiting outside clapped and cheered. A few boys wolf whistled. They had seen what I did through the glass panels. Nikee asked how everything went, and I replied, "I believe I got the modeling position." The suspense was unbearable since results would not confirm my belief until the following afternoon. Of course, news of my stripping naked in front of the selection panel leaked to other students in the school. A couple of sour-puss bad losers called me a bitch when they passed me along the school corridor. I wasn't bothered by the silly name calling; I was delighted to be selected. I was soon to be a naked muse for a famous photographer!

Summer Frolick

In early summer when the English weather turned warm, especially in southern England, students at Daltonbury Hall participated in quite a bit of outdoor activities. Most of my peers in my junior class had grown stronger, mentally and physically, since entering Daltonbury the previous fall. The majority of us was unafraid of our bodies and no longer bothered by being naked in front of other boys. We saw each other naked in the communal shower rooms as well as while swimming and playing outdoor games under the lovely warm summer sun.

After class, we would sometimes swim in Swan or Goose Lake. The seniors and 'big brothers' (Valets) also organized outdoor naked wrestling matches and tug-of-war games, where we could have fun and play together. Those were wonderful halcyon days at Daltonbury Hall.

Summer Holidays

I was sad to leave Nikee and Daltonbury Hall when the school's long summer holidays finally arrived. I was scheduled to return to Kuala Lumpur for a month and a half to spend time with my family. Kuala Lumpur did not hold the excitement for me that it did when I was a small frog living in a small pond. I was now a small frog living in a big pond! The idea of jumping back into the small pond, if only for a short while, was unattractive to me. I did, however, want to spend time with my family. I especially looked forward to visiting Mother and Aunt Tai Yee, whom I loved and adored.

Nikee returned to Wales to spend the summer with his family. I had grown accustomed to his face, and to his always being there for me. I was terribly sad to leave Nikee, even though it was only temporary. In those days, of no emails, text, or Skype, we relied on the art of letter writing and telephone calls. These were few and far between. I couldn't wait for my Kuala Lumpur visit to end so I could return to England, back into Nikee's loving arms.

I had no idea that when I returned after the Summer Holidays I would have far more exciting adventures than before, at Daltonbury Hall, and abroad.

CHAPTER TWENTY-TWO

Outgrown My Shoes

Tear Drops on My Lips

I reluctantly boarded the BOAC economy-class flight from Heathrow to Kuala Lumpur, arriving late at night, the same day I departed. Mr. S. S. Foong and Mother, driven by Bakar, came to fetch me, at the Kuala Lumpur airport. It was a strange phenomenon; whenever I was in the company of S. S. Foong I retreated into my shell, becoming a scared, shy boy. I never knew what to say to Father, and I had a fear of him, which I cannot explain to this day. Maybe his temperamental character frightened me, or perhaps his domineering mannerisms made me afraid closeness to him. I never could understand it.

I was tongue tied during our drive home. Sitting next to Mother, I tried to make myself invisible to him, leaning behind her. I definitely could not confide my inner secrets to this man.

I couldn't tell him the things I discussed so openly and easily with Uncle James. Father would not never ever understand, nor would Mother or any of my many relatives, cousins or aunties. I only kept in touch with a few of the relatives, who were close to me. I got on with my nieces, my half-brother and half-sister better than with any other members of my family.

Again, my heart yearned for Nikee. This time, I had to bear my heartache on my own, and my grief manifested itself in bouts of tears, alone. At night I would think of the beautiful times Nikee and I (and sometimes John) spent over the nine months we were together.

I dreamed of our equestrian rides by the long stretches of sandy beaches on the Isle of Wight, and of horseback riding through the beautiful tranquil countryside. I wistfully recalled jogging and roller-skating around the campus grounds. These memories now seemed like a distant dream.

Under the hot and humid Malayan sun I was thrown into depression, if only for a few days. Thanks to Father Foong's agenda for me, I was enrolled in a six week long Dale Carnegie How to Win Friends and Influence People course at a local educational institution. Father, being Father, felt that the scared and shy boy once again in his household still had much butching-up to do. He wanted me to live up to being a man's man, and to follow in his footsteps. He had not noticed my depression. All I really needed was someone to understand me, someone in whom I could confide. Father never could understand me the way Uncle James did.

In the end, I was glad S. S. enrolled me in the self-improvement course. At least I was able to engage myself mentally instead of constantly reminiscing about Nikee every moment of every day and night.

Dale Carnegie Course

The full-time (except Saturdays and Sundays) course was interesting and I learned much that assisted me throughout the course of my life in ways I was not consciously aware of at the time. There were thirty students in the class, including several middle-aged local businessmen and a handful of male executives who had been sponsored by their companies. The rest of the eighteen students were females in their twenties and early thirties. The majority of the ladies were secretaries or receptionists, working in law firms, the health industry or other local businesses. Approximately five of the young ladies were university students. I was the only young man and the youngest of all of the students. I easily became friends with all of the ladies.

They soon learned of my fashion interest, and, before long, they were turning to me for fashion advice, which I dished out willingly. I became the Dale Carnegie Summer Class Fashion Consultant. I don't know whether it was my cute, wide-eyed, doe-like appearance and gentle voice, or my fashion advice really worked, but they kept coming back for more. They also came to me to be an ear, to listen to their 'men problems.'

By the fourth week, all the women were my friends and confidants. They told me about their dates or their relationships with husbands or boyfriends, asking for opinions on what they should or shouldn't do. The casual conversations we had after class soon became relationship consultancy classes, with me as their adviser.

These activities kept me busy, leaving me little time to miss Nikee, until the quiet evenings set in. I couldn't possibly tell the women about Nikee, or Andy, or John. They wouldn't have understood. Most nights I cried myself to sleep when the house was quiet. I would shine a small torchlight on Nikee's handsome naked photographs and reminisce about our times together.

Fashion Show Debut

Since I started acting as a fashion and relationship consultant to the women in my class, it was only a short time before a couple of the ladies suggested we have a fashion show at the Dale

Carnegie graduation ceremony. The rest of the women loved the idea and asked if I would design one or two outfits for each of them to model at the show. As much as I loved these ladies, they were definitely not model sized 2's or 4's. They were 'normal' females, ranging from size 6 to 16. I was a busy young fashion designer working away on my assigned fashion project.

I knew a number of local tailors who made my personal clothes and my cousin, Lai Ngor, was a professional dressmaker. I encouraged the women to use my sewing team to make the outfits that I designed.

All the ladies were generous, paying for their outfits and fabric costs. I contributed free design consultancy services in exchange for name recognition on the advertising pamphlets, and announcements, publicizing the Dale Carnegie graduation event which was only three weeks' away. These brochures were distributed to the general populace as one of the publicity methods Dale Carnegie used to recruit new students into their fold. Family, friends and supporters of the current student body were invited guests. The event would be held at one of the city's revolving restaurants.

On the day of the ceremony, I was a nervous wreck. I had not eaten for most of the day due to the excitement of my fashion show debut. I had also selected the fashion show music and choreographed the movements. The most trendy fashion shows in London no longer employed announcers. Multi-media sound and visual effects were the latest trend for these presentations. Dancing was de-rigueur. I spent two weeks on rehearsals.

After each Dale Carnegie class, the girls would train under my tutelage on the premises. When the models began to run out of steam I would still be going, going and going. It was only a matter of time before exhaustion set in and the crash occurred.

The show went as planned. The ladies did well and the audience loved their friendly interactions, as they danced and modeled by the tables. Good old Foong Senior was clapping and cheering the women along! It was one of the rare occasions when I saw that my Father was proud of me. When I peeked out from behind the changing room curtain, I saw a delighted, proud father acknowledging his youngest son's amazing achievement. A sense of accomplishment and satisfaction filled my being at that moment. He finally had come to the realization that his sissy son was, indeed, excellent at something.

That fleeting moment of seeing my father, proud, was one of my few positive memories of Foong Senior. Mother, being Mother, was always supportive, no matter what befell me. She, too, beamed with joy when she saw Father clapping enthusiastically at the end of the show, calling for me to appear for my Designer Bow.

The excitement, together with my sleepless nights thinking of Nikee, was too much for me. I collapsed on stage when I came out for my bow. I felt a bright light appear before my eyes, and then nausea took over every fragment of my body. I fell to the floor. The next thing I knew, I was on a hospital bed. A saline solution was hydrating me, and when I awakened, food was bought for me to eat. Of course, Mother was by my side, making sure I was alright. Bakar drove us home from hospital.

I rested for a couple of days, before an invitation came from some classmates from my old Methodist Boys School. They requested that I join them on a day trip to one of the outlying Malayan Islands for a visit to a fishing kampong (village). I had never been to a Malayan fishing village. I accepted the invitation immediately.

A Different Place and Time

Nine months away from Kuala Lumpur seemed more like nine years had passed. I could no longer communicate on the level of my ex-classmates with whom I grew up in the Methodist Boys School. I had nothing in common to discuss with them. I had become a loner. The culture in which I grew up seemed foreign to me. I did, however, enjoy the outing to the fishing village.

It was good for me to experience and see how the less fortunate lived. We toured the kampong; wooden huts and sheds were built on stilts on top of the brown dirty water. The sanitary systems were basically holes, paneled with four planks of plywood as coverings. It was a raw and startling experience.

I realized I was one of the few blessed and privileged people. The lifestyle to which I had grown accustomed was a world away from the children living in this floating village. Despite their poverty, the villagers welcomed us with open arms. This experience touched me. I broke down behind my pink sunglasses, and wept. I had to walk away, quietly, to a corner, and cry out all of my pent up emotions before being able to return to the entourage.

The rest of the group seemed to be having a jolly fun time throughout the trip, while I was extremely sad, within. Malaya wasn't my home anymore. I knew it in my heart. I kept all of this to myself, and by the time I found myself back in our family Bentley, sitting behind in the passenger seat while Bakar drove, my heart sank deep into depression. I was living in a land of two completely vastly different, polarized worlds: abject poverty on the one hand, which I had witnessed that day, and extreme wealth on the other. I was emotionally torn by the disparity. That night I cried until I was exhausted before falling asleep.

Port Dickson

The final week before my return to England a few of my cousins organized a weekend retreat for our Mother's close-knit side of the family. Mother's family loved to organize recreational activities. The cousins took charge of renting several vacation bungalows in Port Dickson to, accommodate our large party. Port Dickson is a coastal resort town that is popular with local Malaysians. It is known for gourmet seafood, especially the delicious home-made chili crabs, fried with lots of garlic and hot sauce. I missed the spicy hot Malayan food that came in many different varieties since it was a multi-racial country with huge Malay, Chinese and Indian populations. One simply expects that the local gourmet delicacies would be hot and spicy.

With so many relatives together, some aunties and cousins were bound to ask how I had fared during the past months at Daltonbury Hall. I had to lie. I couldn't tell the truth regarding my relationship with Nikee, or the truth about my other sexual encounters, nude modeling, or about much of anything that had transpired over the past nine months in England.

I lied and made up palatable stories that were considered polite conversation. It was one of the most difficult things I had to do that summer back in Malaya. I believed, then, that no member of my family would understand the experiences or heartaches which were coursing through my mind.

The majority of the time I smiled, laughed or joked, revealing little. The longer I stayed in Malaya the more I resolved to return less and less often. I had grown apart from Malayan culture and from my early upbringing. I no longer belonged. As much as I loved my family, I could not live a life of deceit and lies. I yearned for my return to the United Kingdom, which occurred in the middle of August. I was delighted to be back in Uncle James's London townhouse for a few days, before journeying by train, then by ferry across the channel to Daltonbury Hall.

CHAPTER TWENTY-THREE

Love to Love You Baby

Conversation with Uncle James

It was wonderful to see Uncle James again. He had been in London for the previous week on business, and was on his way back to Hong Kong. I stayed at his townhouse for a couple of days, before travelling back to the Isle of Wight.

During my holiday in Malaya, Nikee had written to me requesting my presence at Daltonbury Hall a week prior to class commencement. He said that I had been shortlisted for a student scholarship exchange program, and that he had recommended me. There were eight juniors under consideration, and I was one of them. If I was interested I must return to Daltonbury Hall before class began. The school would select five students to enter this special program.

I was terribly excited to learn about the scholarship, but Nikee's letter was brief, saying I would be provided further information upon my return.

I told Mother I was being considered for a scholarship student exchange program. Since my parents had designated Uncle James as my guardian, they handed the reins of my school activities to him. Besides, Mother knew I liked Uncle James, and that as my guardian, he was a reliable gentleman, whom my parents (especially Mother) trusted. Mother said the decision to enter the program was entirely mine. If I wanted to pursue the scholarship I should consult Uncle James to obtain his opinion. It was pointless to consult Father; I found it difficult to communicate with him. It was best for me to discuss it with Uncle James.

Uncle James and I had dinner at the B.B.C. Restaurant in The Langham, London the evening of my arrival. It was an elegant, charming restaurant. We found a quiet spot, so we could have a conversation. After ordering our food, Uncle James asked me how my progress at Daltonbury Hall was and if I had a fun time in Kuala Lumpur. With a sigh, I told him the truth about how I felt upon returning to Kuala Lumpur, mentioning that I did not belong in that country anymore.

He nodded and replied, "Yoong, I knew that would happen sooner or later. It is very difficult for any young man to have experienced Daltonbury Hall and then return to his previous life without being deeply affected. I felt the same way when I was entering boarding school. Eventually, we are bound to outgrow our roots, and become our own person. The one thing you must remember is that no matter how difficult you find your Father, he is providing you the opportunity to experience and grow into the handsome, suave young man seated in front of me, now. For this, you must be grateful to him. He is a good person."

He continued, "I know you are having a difficult time understanding him. There is a generation gap, like I have with Paul, my son. It is often easier to discuss intimate matters with someone outside of your immediate family. You must understand, your Dad is a busy man. But I know he wants only the very best for you."

I listened intently as he continued, "Yoong, although we have only meet a few times, you are dear and close to me. I consider you as my prodigy. Besides, your lovely Mother has bestowed her trust upon me to look after you, to be your guardian, while you are away from home. Therefore, I have a personal responsibility to her and also to your Dad to make sure you are not in harm's way and to know you are well cared for." I nodded, grateful for his support and belief in me.

Uncle James went on, "I'm glad you trust me as your confidant. You can open up to me about any subject. I give you my solemn oath: I will not betray your trust. If there are things you don't want me to tell your parents, I will keep them to myself. But, you must always be honest with me and discuss issues that bother you be they school problems, health issues or anything else. Only then can I do my best to assist you."

That evening, over dinner, I told Uncle James more about my relationship with Nikee and how I truly felt about my BB (Valet). I omitted my three-way sexual encounter, which included Andy. I did mention to James about my potential student exchange scholarship abroad. He smiled and said, "If you get selected, this is a once-in-a-lifetime opportunity. It is a decision that you alone can make. If you decide to enter into this program, you will be initiated into an exclusive club that, during your course of studies at Daltonbury Hall, will open many doors for you. You will learn a lot more than you would at your current school. But you must tread with care, because some paths include uncharted territories."

"What do you mean by 'uncharted territories'?" I asked.

James replied that there was nothing to worry about. He explained that if I were selected, my headmaster, Dean Dawson Higgins, would give me a briefing, and provide me and the other candidates with all the necessary information. "For now, continue to enjoy your few days in London. Your 'big brother' will always be by your side. If, at any given time, you feel uncomfortable, you can always say the word and your 'big brother' will come to your aid."

I was so relieved to be able to confide my deepest secrets, emotional turmoil and pent-up feelings to my mentor. Although my time spent with Uncle James was short, our private conversations instilled an incredible amount of confidence in me. Because of his friendship and support, I would continue to grow stronger and more resilient as a person. This was something I never had the opportunity to experience with Foong Senior. I'm so glad Mother entrusted me to Uncle James' care.

The Workout

I was delighted and relieved to be with Nikee again after being away from each other for seven weeks. Nikee said the school would have the results of the scholarship by the end of the week. He insisted we both get back to the gym for our workout sessions since we hadn't done any exercises over our summer holidays. Regular classes had not commenced, therefore the gym room would be relatively quiet. Only a handful of juniors and their BBs were on campus.

On the second day of my return, Nikee and I went over to Kipling Society's gym for a workout. When we were in the locker room changing into our shorts and tank tops, a couple of the BBs suggested we work out naked. The gym wasn't air-conditioned. Ceiling fans were the only means of a cooling device. There would be nobody to disturb us, and it would be cooler. Working out in the buff was a welcome suggestion. Besides, we could better admire our muscles, flexing in front of full-length mirrors. Several inhibited juniors wanted to wear their shorts, which they did.

In The Gym

During our workouts, the BBs alternated in spotting the juniors when we did bench presses or other free weight exercises. When I laid down on the bench to work on my bench press, BB Colin was spotting me. While I was doing my presses, Colin stood naked above me. Colin's cock began growing. He smiled, making no excuses and continued spotting me as I was heaved and pushed on the heavy bar.

By the end of my set, Colin's organ has grown fully erect, and was throbbing against his washboard stomach. He grinned, looking at me again. My heart was pounding from the excitement of watching Colin's erection. When I glanced sideways to see the students' reactions I saw a couple of our BBs already kissing the naked juniors whom they were assisting.

The three juniors who were clothed retreated to a corner. Although their excitement showed beneath their shorts, they did not seem comfortable with what they were witnessing. Before long, one of the BBs who brought them asked if they wanted to leave. They left the gym with their senior. The five naked juniors and four nude 'big brothers' continued to workout. The sexual tension intensified with each passing moment.

Andy and another BB, Aaron, were assisting Tom and Eric, both juniors, with their push-ups. Both the BB's were rock hard from watching the juniors. Aaron had moved behind Tom, in a kneeling position. Before I knew it, we were an entanglement of limbs and torsos, on the floor mattresses and leaning over weight racks. Everyone in the room was engaged, in the throes of passion, exchanging partners when the need and urge arose. Our savoir faire orgy lasted a couple of hours before we were spent, from too much fun.

The juniors and seniors who stayed in the gym that day were obviously uninhibited. I found out later not all present were 'gay.' Two out of the four BB's were bisexuals; Nikee and Colin had girlfriends outside of school. The other two, Andy and Aaron, were gay. As for the juniors, Tom, Sach, and Blake liked boys and girls, while Eric and I were one hundred percent into men.

Love Grows

Something unusual happened which I hadn't anticipated during our fun and games at the exercise room. I saw Andy casually when we passed each other on campus after our three way rendezvous. We were always friendly and polite, giving each other hugs and exchanging regular student conversations. We never had any inappropriate conduct in front of other people. I always considered our forest liaison to be a casual encounter, nothing serious.

He never failed to wink and smile at me during our passing encounters, but I brushed it off as Andy being Andy, the nice and friendly 'big brother' (Valet). Since Nikee was constantly at my side, I never had a thought that Andy might like me any more than any other junior at the school.

During our entanglement of limbs and body parts in the heated workout session I sensed Andy's closeness to me. I could feel him watching my every move, even when he was actively engaged with other boys. He would glance over to see who I was playing with, as if he wanted me solely for his own enjoyment.

It seemed odd to me that I only noticed this aspect of Andy six months after our forest rendezvous. Maybe I was too in love with Nikee to acknowledge Andy's secret desire, or perhaps I was completely oblivious to the ways of love. Had Andy kept his secret so well hidden? Since I was under Nikee's care, maybe it was one of those unspoken 'big brothers' rules that BB's had to keep their hands off of others' juniors. The answer was unclear to me. But one thing I was beginning to realize was that Andy wanted more from me. He made that clear the afternoon of our entangled gym session.

Personally, I was sure that as much as Nikee cared for me and loved me, it was his 'big brothers' (Valet) "job" to do so. That was the reason he kept reminding me not to fall in love with him. He could never return the kind of love I had for him.

Secondly, Nikee was assigned to me as my "Art of Love Making" trainer, whereas Andy, I eventually came to understand, desired me, not just as a sex buddy, but as something deeper. Andy wanted a love relationship with me.

Nikee and Andy differed in many aspects. Nikee knew he was a very handsome, charismatic, and spontaneous man. With a snap of his fingers, he could make any boy or girl fall in love with him. He was an extrovert who loved to show off his prowess, and to preen. He was a peacock who enjoyed being admired and desired.

He was very versatile, sexually. He could go from being active to being passive, as a sex partner. Nikee was considerate, honest, kind, loving and passionate. Those who only knew him superficially might sometimes incorrectly assume he was an entitled, well-educated spoiled brat.

Andy kept many things to himself. His timing was impeccable; he always waited for the right moment before revealing his thoughts or taking action. He was a deep thinker who considered his options carefully, like a chess player before making a move. Although Andy came from a wealthy and powerful family, he didn't flaunt his status like many nouveau riche boys did.

Unlike Nikee, who could at times be flighty, Andy was completely reliable, and a man of honor. If he gave one his word, he kept it. In many ways, his character was similar to Uncle James'. Andy was one hundred percent 'top,' the active partner, when it came to sex. He was also one hundred percent gay. He loved deeply, truly and totally when the right person came into his life. He was sublime, subtle -- a gentle and kind gentleman, always.

In more ways than one, the gym day was a turning point in my young love life. I was curious to know Andy better, rather than just being casually acquainted. I did not reveal any of my thoughts about Andy to Nikee.

The student exchange scholarship results were announced on the last Friday in August.

PART THREE

The United Arab Emirates, Red Sea Riviera

AUTHOR'S NOTE

During the second part of my boarding school studies, my student life took an unusual detour. Under the auspices of a student exchange scholarship, I was enrolled in an exclusive private school in the Arabian Peninsula. I was transported to a secret location in The United Arab Emirates, joining a select few who were also scholarship recipients. There were many opportunities and pitfalls on this journey; it was not a road for the faint of heart.

There were rules and regulations which were not to be violated. It was an intriguing game, when played well. The rewards were rich and rewarding. This game, played behind closed doors by the rich and the powerful, is as old as time. Many believe it has become extinct, but it will always be there, morphing to accommodate or avoid the standards of the day, sometimes going underground. I am grateful to Daltonbury Hall for providing me the opportunity to play in this area. And play, I did.

CHAPTER TWENTY-FOUR

E.R.O.S.

"The secret of the greatest fruitfulness and the greatest enjoyment of existence is: to live dangerously!"
Friedrich Nietzsche

Scholarship Announcement

On a Friday, two days before classes commenced for fall semester at Daltonbury Hall, the student exchange scholarship results were released. The boys who had been short-listed were summoned to the office of the Headmaster, Dean Dawson Higgins, for a briefing. It was a lengthy, two-hour interview, with many questions for the eight candidates, their accompanying 'big brothers', and three staff members. Each potential scholarship student was called into the Dean's office separately; the candidates had no idea who the other shortlisted students were.

Chapter Twenty-four

I was dressed in my prim and proper school uniform. When the time came for my interview, I went into Dean Higgins's office with Nikee. The seating arrangements were formal. Three staff members, one from each of the school's 3 Houses, sat behind a long desk next to the Head Master's high desk. A chair for the interviewee was placed in the center, facing the panel of interviewers. My 'big brother' stood next to me.

The Dean welcomed me and began, "Mr. Foong, you come highly recommended by your 'big brother', Nikee, and by three staff members who have been observing your progress these past nine months."

He continued, "We are very pleased with your academics, your extracurricular and 'other' performances. We have selected you as one of the candidates for this special program at the Oasis School. If you choose to accept this scholarship, you will have the opportunity to have a much broader education than what is offered at Daltonbury Hall." I listened nervously, keeping my eyes fixed on his.

"Besides your regular studies", Dean Higgins explained, "Which will be tutored by our capable staff at the Bahriji, you will also be trained in many forms of carnal knowledge which you will have the opportunity to put into practical use. Your 'big brother' or Valet will always be present and close at hand to aid and assist you if you ever feel uncomfortable during the practical training sessions. You and your 'big brother', your Valet, Nikee, will be living with different elite Arab Households during the time you are in service. If, for any reason, you choose not to provide any of the requests your Household Master and his entourage make, you can always inform your Valet, and he will come to your aid, or take you out of the situation.

"If your services please the Household Master, or members of his selected inner circle, you will be rewarded handsomely. Rewards will either be financial, or gifts of jewelry. You are not to accept monetary presents directly from them. The school will open a savings account on your behalf in a Swiss bank, into which your Master can deposit the gifted amounts. It is for your future use, after you leave Daltonbury Hall. The financial rewards cannot exceed a certain sum, per deposit. Your 'big brother' will see that your rewards are safely transferred into your account. Jewelry will be ensconced in your safety deposit box, at the same bank. These gifts are yours to keep. The school does not withhold any rewards of your reciprocity."

I was listening intently, but I am not sure how much I heard or understood at the time. I just know I felt special. Recalling Uncle James' words of encouragement, I was extremely honored, and hopeful.

After a brief pause, Dean Higgins continued. He said that if I decided to accept this scholarship, I would have to take an oath of confidentiality and a pledge of allegiance binding me to a promise. I was never to reveal my new life to anyone. Ever.

"The society you are about to join is an exclusive private club. Members are carefully selected to be a part of this special scholarship program. Your membership initiation begins, as soon you sign the oath of confidentiality and the allegiance pledge."

He repeated and emphasized that if I signed I could never reveal the study locations or any information about the program. Not to members of my family. Not to friends or confidants. Not to anyone. He mentioned that I could discuss the program with the club's past and present members, who were available to assist me with any questions.

"If the school finds that you have broken your vows of silence regarding this program, the school and the society will deny all allegations and charges. Be mindful always, the club holds no responsibility for your actions. If you choose to make any of the club's activities public Daltonbury Hall will file legal action, claiming false accusations against the school.

"Mr. Foong, consider very carefully before you take the oath of confidentiality and pledge allegiance to become a lifetime member of this elite club. You will be given one day to consider our proposal. If you decide to accept, we will provide you with detailed information regarding membership rules and regulations. Daltonbury Hall will handle the logistics. The final decision will rest entirely in your hands. Nikee will advise you with details if you require further information to make your decision."

During the course of the interview, one of the staff members, Dr. Nuein, the school's sex education professor, mentioned that a 'big brother' (Valet), Andy, had given me high scores and also had recommended me for the program. Andy, evidently, thought I would do well in the exchange program.

The school I would be attending in The Middle East would consist of fifty freshmen students from different locales. It was a smaller campus than Daltonbury Hall, located many miles away from the city of Dubai. In the Bahriji School, the Big Brother who had been with a student throughout their first year at Daltonbury Hall would accompany the student, for their first three months.

I also learned that after three months, when I was assigned to a Household, a different Valet would accompany me to live at the Master's compound. We would reside there for another three months, before transferring to another Household, or back to Daltonbury Hall. During lengthy school holidays, I would be free to return to my home or wherever I chose to go, during my school breaks.

Decisions, Decisions, Decisions

Until this point, I had never had to make a major decision like the one with which I was now faced. In the past, my parents made all my decisions. At Daltonbury Hall, Nikee made most of my major decisions. The inevitable moment had arrived and I had to decide for myself. What was I to do?

I consulted my voice of silence within for the answer. It was difficult in the beginning, with all the chitter chatter that went on in my head. It took a long time before I finally managed to quiet my mind down from all the excitement and scenarios playing wildly through my head. There were so many questions I wanted answered. Nikee did his best to answer them, but more questions would pop into my mind. Finally, I told my mind to 'shut up,' and that was when the answer arrived, in the form of a dream.

When I finally fell asleep a masculine angel appeared before me. He had the most beautiful, kind and loving eyes; he was looking directly at me. He had glowing, white, gigantic outstretched wings. He kissed my forehead and in a gentle voice, whispered, "Go, be on your way. I will be at your side, always. I will not abandon you; I will come to you when you call out my name. I am here to protect you from harm and to see you through difficult times. All you have to do is speak my name and I will be present for you. I am always by your side. Do not be afraid. Go."

The next morning, my decision was made. I told Nikee I was accepting the scholarship. Nikee was delighted to hear the news and immediately made an appointment for me to see Dean Dawson Higgins, that Saturday morning.

It was a relatively short meeting, with Dean Higgins and Nikee filling me in on the scholarship program requirements. The initiation ceremony would be held Sunday afternoon at 3:00 p.m., at the school's Chapel. The four other freshmen who had accepted the scholarship would also attend, with their 'big brothers' (Valet). Chaplin Samuel Hollinger would conduct a half-hour initiation ceremony, consisting of an incantation and a welcoming speech into E.R.O.S: The Enlightened Royal Oracle Society. I was to show up in school uniform with Nikee at my side, fifteen minutes before the ceremony.

The Enlightened Royal Oracle Society

E.R.O.S. was founded in the early 1800s by the well-known poet, Lord Byron, a leading figure of the Romantic Poets. During his travels, while fighting against the Ottoman Empire, he fell in love with the Turkish way of life. He was especially fascinated with the Harem, a tradition in Middle Eastern cultures. After the Greek War of Independence, Byron returned to England secretly, spending time in the Isle of Wight to recuperate from injuries he suffered during the war. While on the Isle as a guest, at Daltonbury Hall, he created E.R.O.S., an exclusive secret poets' society.

From the mid-1800s forward, English and French Orientalist painters were initiated into E.R.O.S. Well known painters of Middle Eastern Harem life, such as Jean-Auguste-Dominique Ingres, Fernand Cormon, Jean-Leon Gerome, John Frederick Lewis and Frederick Goodall were members of this furtive group. Due to taboos associated with the painting of nude women and men during puritanical Victorian England, artists and painters of nudes joined this elite society in order to have the freedom to practice their art.

By the time the Pre-Raphaelite Brotherhood was initiated into this private society, Daltonbury Hall had already established an artistic student exchange program with wealthy elite Arab and Turkish Nations. Selected student members travelled to the Middle East to experience their culture. Some students became part of a Harem.

There was an extensive history of student exchange programs between England and the UAE, offering a rare view into the private world of Arab elites. Student sponsorship funding came largely from The Emirates' wealthy and aristocratic families. As a handpicked member of E.R.O.S., I was given the rare opportunity to become part of the Harem and to experience and learn the Middle Eastern cultures and hidden way of life in a traditional Arabian Household. I was granted the privilege of becoming a part of their inner sanctum.

I had chosen wisely and had made the right decision. I was rewarded generously by the Masters and their aristocratic inner circles. The financial rewards gifted to me during my services at the various Households provided the necessary funding to later pursue my Master degree at The Royal College of Art, London.

CHAPTER TWENTY-FIVE

Initiation and Incantations

LORD BYRON, Manfred

*And the power which thou
dost feel shall be what thou must conceal.*

Medical

The five boys who were being initiated were required to see Dr. Hunton, Daltonbury Hall's physician, for a medical examination. Nikee accompanied me to the school's clinic, the Rabbit Hole, to be tested. Felicia, one of the nurses, performed all of the basic procedures, recording height, weight and heart rate, before ushering me into the examination room to see Dr. Hunton. Nikee waited at the reception foyer until I finished. Dr. Hunton, a handsome man of about thirty-five, was kind and gentle, with a friendly demeanor, making it easy for patients to confide in him. He asked, "Mr. Foong, who have you had intercourse with since you arrived at Daltonbury Hall?" he inquired.

I replied, honestly, "Nikee, Andy, and two 'big brothers' and some Juniors who participated in the gym room orgy." He checked me for signs and symptoms of venereal disease. I was given a clean bill of health. Then, he proceeded to vaccinate and inoculate me, employing the usual preventatives required for students travelling to Middle Eastern countries. I passed my medical examination with flying colors.

Chapel Service

And on thy head I pour the vial which doth devote thee to this trial;

The morning of my initiation into E.R.O.S., I awakened early and decided to attend the hour-long chapel service at the same venue where the initiation ceremony would later take place. I had never been a religious person, but that morning I felt the urge to attend chapel. Maybe it was an unconscious effort to sanctify and purify myself. The service was nondenominational, but being on English soil, the spiritual service tended to lean towards the Christian faith. The sermon that Chaplin Samuel Hollinger gave serendipitously addressed many of the feelings that were going through me that day. He spoke about the many forms and aspects of Love. Quoting a verse from Alfred Tennyson: "Tis better to have loved and lost than never to have loved at all."

By the end of the service, I had come to the realization that the Divine dwelt within me. "I am God" meant "I am Love." I came to the conclusion that everything I undertook needed to be performed, wholeheartedly, with love. By loving, I release Divine energy into the Universe. Chaplin Hollinger's sermon gave me a sense of confident divinity. Since I was God, I was fearless, as long as everything I did was done with Love. I was ready for the initiation into the Enlightened Royal Oracle Society. I knew then that I was a Divine being summoned to perform a Divine duty.

Initiation Ceremony

At 2:45 p.m. that Sunday afternoon, I arrived at the chapel for my E.R.O.S initiation ceremony. The inner sanctuary of the Chapel was lit with many white candles encased in red and gold glass containers. The afternoon sunlight illuminating the enclosed room became a prism of rainbow colors, pouring through three ornate, stained glass windows. The highest center panel had artistic depictions of Love. The two shorter panels were an artist's interpretations of Faith and Hope. The round baptismal fount at the far end of the room was slightly raised, and could accommodate a full grown person submerged in its water. Pews were designated for current and past members of E.R.O.S.

Current members included a handful of eight Senior 'big brothers', including Colin, Aaron, Andy, Nikee and Troy. The five freshmen being initiated were Tom, Eric, Sach, Blake, and me, (the same five boys who opted to stay for the orgy.) It suddenly became clear to me that the orgy was specially set up as the final freshmen scholarship selection test. The three inhibited boys who left the gym were the students who did not make the final cut into E.R.O.S.

The exchange program recruited boys who were uninhibited, unafraid of their sexuality and comfortable with their bodies. These young men could enjoy the task at hand and were unafraid to explore uncharted territories.

Uncle James had been down this road and was a senior member of E.R.O.S., hence his sound advice to me over dinner at the B.B.C. Restaurant regarding uncharted territories. James could not divulge further information when I asked what he meant, because I was not yet in the secret society. I was eager to ask him questions regarding E.R.O.S., now that we were members of the same secret society.

There were also four second and third year students at Daltonbury Hall. One of them was my roommate, John, who had returned that Sunday morning from his summer vacation. He would travel with us to the Bahriji School where he was stationed, when not assigned to a Household.

In addition to the four juniors, the four BBs, several E.R.O.S. teachers from the three Houses and Dean Dawson Higgins, there were five freshmen, and their accompanying Big Brothers who witnessed the ceremony. Chaplin Samuel Hollinger conducted the initiation proceedings.

Incantation

The Chaplin began the initiation with a welcoming address to all the E.R.O.S. members, followed by a blessing of hope. All the freshmen were seated in a circle with our respective BBs standing behind us, to our right. After a minute of silence to honor members who had passed, I heard a faint sound from the pipe organ being played in the main chapel; it was a haunting piece of music.

Chaplin Hollinger gathered the freshmen, prompting us to stand around the baptismal font, telling each of the initiates to recite a verse from Lord Byron's, Manfred Incantation. Since there were six verses, he would commence with the first verse, and then proceeding clockwise, each boy would read a verse. When my turn came, I read:

> *Though thou seest me not pass by,*
> *Thou shalt feel me with thine eye*
> *As a thing that, though unseen,*
> *Must be near thee, and hath been;*
> *And when in that secret dread*
> *Thou hast turn'd around thy head,*
> *Thou shalt marvel I am not*
> *As thy shadow on the spot,*
> *And the power which thou dost feel*
> *Shall be what thou must conceal.*

As I read the verse, I looked up, momentarily, at Andy who was standing behind Tom, the junior in his charge. Andy's adoring eyes stared back at me. With unspoken dialogue, he conversed with me, using only his eyes. He conveyed clearly that the verse I was reading expressed the exact feeling he had for me. I quickly returned to the verse and continued reading.

My heart was pounding from this emotional surge. I recited the incantation. I knew, then and there, that I was developing a strong, illicit, emotional bond with Andy. It was beyond anything I had ever felt with Nikee. It was a bond in which no words needed to be exchanged.

This bond was illicit, because I was Nikee's Junior and Andy was Tom's 'big brother'. Tom and I were both in training under our respective BBs. It was an unspoken rule between 'big brothers' that when a Junior was under his charge, he would remain loyal to the Junior in his care until the training was completed. Only then were both parties free to pursue other love interests. For now, I was under Nikee's care. It was inadvisable for me to develop feelings for Andy. The same applied for him.

It was true that we had a threesome in the forest, but it was a test; Andy was invited by Nikee to participate. That encounter was simply a learning process and not meant to be taken seriously by me. I was being trained by Nikee to play the field, to see how I would react to a three-way sexual situation. And I passed the test.

That encounter was not designed for Andy and me to develop a 'love' relationship. Juniors are not allowed to fall in love with 'big brothers' while in training. That was the reason Nikee kept reminding me not to fall in love with him.

Andy and I could only carry out our secret adoration in the depths of our hearts. Yet, I was falling into an abyss which was excruciatingly painful.

Unfortunately, our time was not ripe.

Spiritual Baptism

When all the freshmen had finished reciting the incantation, Chaplin Hollinger called each of us, individually, by our given names. When our name was called, we had to strip naked in front of all present before being led by Chaplin Hollinger down the steps into the font.

He plunged each freshman, one by one, backward, into the water, before lifting us back up. Then, he placed the palm of his hand upon our wet head, reciting the Oath of Confidentiality and Pledge of Allegiances. The Initiates repeated the Chaplin's words and the process was complete. It was like a séance. We were then wrapped and dried with a warm towel by our respective BB, and led back to our place. On each seat was a fresh thawb for us to wear.

As I stood naked before the witnesses I glanced at Andy. Again, he stared into my eyes with a grin on his face, licking his lips subtly with the tip of his tongue. He was secretly caressing my nakedness without laying a finger on me. His subtle nuances excited me, sending shivers down my naked spine. I looked away, quickly. The heavy, intoxicating perfumed incense, together with the haunting organ music, the smoke filled room and the enchanting evening light transported me into a surreal world of sensuality.

I was afraid of BB Andy; I didn't know how to handle him. I was enchanted by this handsome man who wanted to love me. I wanted him to love me. But our love was forbidden and I didn't know what to do. His gaze continued burning into every part of me. I was getting hard. Quickly dispensing with the towel I threw on the thobe to hide my involuntary excitement.

I could not resist glancing at this handsome man. His mesmerizing eyes never left me for a second. He would respond to my every look with his seductive stare. Unfamiliar electricity coursed through my body, sending me into waves of unexplainable shivers. Andy was making love to me, just as on the night of jealousy, when Nikee seduced me with his eyes. I had to adjust my erection between my crossed legs, in lotus position, so no one would notice. I dared not look at Andy, yet I wanted to steal a glance.

I was afraid. The courage I had when I entered the inner sanctum was dissipating, quickly. I had fallen under Andy's bewitching spell. I was desperately trying to resist, but could not. His flirtatious stimulation was too strong for a freshman of thirteen to conquer! I closed my eyes, allowing the surreal surroundings to envelop me, only to vividly visualize Andy's lovemaking in the forest, as if it were happening now. I struggled to resist the unseen forces that were drawing me deep into a dark abyss.

When I opened my eyes, I was met with Andy's lovemaking stare. I was already under his sexual control, as if by magic. Everything around me seemed to be rotating in slow motion. With a few spasms, I shot my uncontrollable excitement into the inner folds of my kandura.

I was scared; I dared not open my eyes, in case the small congregation discovered my secret. I stayed immobile for a few minutes before I plucked up the courage to open my eyes.

No one seemed to have noticed. I thanked God. The final freshman was just coming out of the font. When I glanced, helplessly at Andy, he blew me an air kiss and winked at me! He knew what he had done to me. He knew he had me in his control. He knew I was already his. I had let him into my being, and he knew it.

When the spiritual baptismal ritual finally drew to a close, the circle of freshmen and their 'big brothers' joined hands, in a circle. The Chaplin said a final prayer of gratitude, adjourning the ceremony. The members hugged each other or gave each other kisses on both cheeks, a sign of welcome into the E.R.O.S. Secret Circle.

When Andy came over to hug and kiss me on my cheeks, I wanted to run and hide. Yet my legs disobeyed my commands. I was glued to the floor. I had goose bumps under my kandura. The stirring between my loins began to grow once more. I hated what this man was doing to me, yet I wanted him close. Andy hugged me longer than the rest of the other members. I could feel he did not want to let go of me. I was feeling the same way. He bent his six-foot, three-inch frame down, kissing me on both cheeks. His kisses were slow and lingering. I could smell his intoxicating masculine scent, and it sent me into uncontrollable trembles. He hugged me closer, holding me for a while longer before finally releasing his grip.

I plucked up the courage to look at his handsome face. He smiled at me and whispered an almost inaudible 'welcome into the club' in my ears. With that, he released his embrace. It is strange how physical contact speaks a thousand words. I wanted Andy and Andy wanted me.

Yet, we could not consummate our forbidden love.

CHAPTER TWENTY-SIX

Up, Up and Away

Departure

The day of our departure for the Middle East fell on a Wednesday, three days after my E.R.O.S. initiation ceremony. We departed Daltonbury Hall in the school's vehicles. We arrived at the Isle of Wight Airport to board the school's private jet to Dubai. During the seven hour flight, I had a chance to talk with John, my roommate. I had wanted to corner him after the E.R.O.S. Initiation Ceremony, but by the time I finished my welcome rounds he had already left the chapel. I wanted to get John's perspective on the Bahriji School and I wished for him to provide me some insights on the Households which he had been assigned to serve. I sat next to him; Nikee was busy chatting with another BB.

Chapter Twenty-six

Conversation with John

"Hey John, I haven't had a chance to talk with you, since you got back from your holidays. How did it go?" I inquired. John said he had a wonderful vacation in Manila and inquired, politely, about my summer. I told him I had a difficult time readjusting to my former Malayan life and asked if he had the same problem adjusting to life in the Philippines, after being at Daltonbury Hall.

"Young, I had similar problems the first time I returned to Manila. Everything seemed so different after being at Daltonbury Hall. Then, after a year at the Bahriji and a couple Households I decided there are too many things in this world I want to try my hand at. I won't return to Manila anytime soon."

I asked him why, and he continued, "After being initiated into E.R.O.S., I had learned so much. In the past, while living in Manila, I was lost. I didn't get much love and attention from my parents. They were always too busy with their lives. I felt so lonely. That was when my rebellious side took hold and I fell in with some unsavory classmates. I started trying different types of drugs, hard liquor and was slowly drawn into the seedy side of Manila life."

He took a deep breath and looked directly at me. "When my Dad enrolled me into Daltonbury Hall, I resisted. I didn't want to attend a school in England. But the old man told me I should at least go and check out the school, to see if I liked it. When I arrived, Jonathan was assigned to me as my 'big brother'. He was so caring: he helped me find my way back to myself. I've never been loved with the kind of love Jonathan showed me, as my BB. I was very sad when he left Daltonbury Hall. He was my trainer and my dear friend. I miss him terribly."

We were quiet for a minute. I wanted him to continue. "Although sexually I swing both ways, I prefer males to females. I can relate to a male companion more easily. I have a girlfriend in Manila, but she is naive and very needy. I like the Oasis School because I get to have practical carnal training with some of the females from the girl's school. They are in the same situation as we are; they have been taught how to please men sexually.

It is such a big difference to make love with one of them, compared to my girlfriend back home. All she wants is for me to do everything for her. In return, she doesn't know how to please me. My parents like her, because she's from a wealthy and distinguished family. They would like me to marry her after I finished college. But in the bedroom, she still has a lot to learn. My experiences, both here and at Daltonbury Hall, have given me the chance to sow my wild oats, and play the field before settling down into marriage. When I'm ready to start a family, I will have no regrets for not having had many sexual experiences with many different, fascinating, interesting people."

I shook my head vigorously, indicating my interest, and my desire for him to tell me more.

"You see Young, Daltonbury and E.R.O.S are providing us with a safe environment to experiment, which is unusual, especially at our age, when our sexual urges are so strong. We need some form of release. I don't know any other school or place where students are so well guided and guarded while being taught the Art of Love Making. We're trained by the crème de la crème. We have top notch educators and 'big brothers'. If I am going to learn something, I want to learn from the best. My current Valet, Andrew, is an excellent teacher. You'll get to meet him at the Oasis. I'll introduce you."

"What are the Households like?" I asked. John laughed and said, "Some of the Masters are quite kinky!" I had never heard the word kinky, so I asked John what the word meant. John continued laughing, seemingly finding it funny that I didn't understand the term.

He said, "Get your 'big brother' or Valet to explain it to you." Before I could speak further with John, Nikee was at my side, so our conversation ended abruptly.

Conversation with Andy

Since Andy and I were on the same plane, I made a conscientious effort to avoid eye contact with him. I was scared that my emotions would rage if I looked at him or went near him. I feared that I would not know how to react, or what to do. I tried to avoid Andy every moment. Yet, his stares continued to follow me and haunt me every step of the way. I could not escape his pursuit. There was nowhere to run, no place to hide, and nowhere to magically disappear.

I was a nervous wreck whenever I caught glimpses of him watching me. Why wouldn't he leave me alone? Why do I feel like this when he is present? Why does he have this kind of hold over me? Oh, why, why, why?

Before I could utter another why, Andy was sitting next to me in Nikee's seat. Nikee had gotten up to chat with the pilot and air steward. Andy snuck up stealthily, without my noticing.

My heart nearly jumped out of my chest. It was thumping so loudly I could hear it. I was sure Andy heard it, too. With a grin on his seductive face he asked, "How are you doing?"

"Well. I am looking forward to my new experiences at the Bahriji," I replied.

He smiled and said he was also looking forward to being back at the Oasis, and that it would be a lot more fun this time, because I was going to be there. I didn't know how to response to that remark. I turned and looked out the window. All the while, I was trembling inside.

Andy seemed to delight in teasing me, knowing I was afraid of being so close to him. He leaned against me with the side of his head almost touching mine, pointing his finger out the window on the pretext of explaining the scenery. His manly smell was making my heart thump faster. The more I was afraid of him, the more he took pleasure in teasing me further. If I had turned my head to face him, our lips would have met. My mind was reeling, trying to find a way to escape this embarrassing situation he purposely created. I could smell him breathing on my hair. I took a few deep breaths. It worked a little. I was slightly less nervous.

Basic Rules and Regulations

Finally, I thought of something with which to divert my fear. I asked, "What are some of the rules and regulations for freshmen and Valets at the Bahriji and at the Households?"

That sudden question seemed to throw Andy off guard. "Well, should I list them out, point by point for you?"

I quickly said "Please do," just to throw him off my nervous scent.

"Ok, let me start with these:

A. No photography or filming once we land at the Bahriji School. It is private property and no one is allowed to take any photos or pictures of the property, unless authorized. If you want photos, you can take aerial shots from the helicopter. Otherwise, photos and filming are strictly prohibited. Since we will be flying over desert for an hour or more you will not recognize the exact location. Everywhere you look are seas of sand.

B. When we are travelling by vehicle to and from the Oasis or Households, we will be blindfolded by our accompanying teachers or local Household guides. We are not allowed to know the location of the school or the Household. This is a precautionary procedure to protect the privacy of the Bahriji and the Households. So, every time when travelling on wheels, we are always blindfolded. All I know is it's a bumpy ride over rough, sandy terrain. All I can tell you is the school is approximately 3 hours away from Dubai city. You don't have to worry about being blindfolded, because your accompanying BB's will be right next to you, making sure no harm will befall you.

C. Your current BB will be stationed with you at the Bahriji School for three months after your arrival. Then another BB or Valet will take over.

D. The accommodations at the Oasis for the 1st three months will be similar to Daltonbury Hall: One BB with one freshman and one junior. When the freshman is allocated to a Household, then his Valet or BB will share his room.

"Anything else you'll like to know?" Andy asked.

Chapter Twenty-six

"What if my parents come to visit me at Daltonbury Hall or the Bahriji and discover I'm not there? How would the school answer to that?" I asked.

"My dearest boy, you don't have to worry. Daltonbury rules state that parents visiting their child must give twenty-four hours' notice before turning up at Daltonbury Hall. That boarding school rule is quite clear." Andy smiled at me.

"Secondly," he continued to explain, "When Daltonbury Hall is informed of a parent visitation, the E.R.O.S. student serving abroad is flown back on the school's private helicopter and plane immediately, so they can be there to meet their parents or guardian. Even if there is an emergency within the student's family, parents still have to provide a minimum twelve hours' notice before they can collect their child.

"Therefore, my darling boy, you don't have to worry about your parents knowing where you are. As long as you keep to your oath of confidentiality and pledge of allegiance to safeguard E.R.O.S. you will do just fine. Leave the rest to our Senior Executive members at Daltonbury Hall to manage your parents and guardian."

Before long, the plane was making its descent into Dubai International Airport. However, we did not land at the main commercial passenger terminal. We touched down at a private airstrip, set up especially for the United Arab Emirate V.I.P.s. Chauffeurs, two local Oasis guides and long, black, highly polished limousines met us.

They drove us to a private heliport location at the Dubai International Airport, where we boarded three separate helicopters. We did not have to go through immigration customs. Our passports or travel documents were collected by the local guides when we entered the limos. By the time we arrived at the heliport to board the helicopters, our passports and travel documents had already been stamped and returned to us. We were treated like Royalty, because we belonged to the Enlightened Royal Oracle Society.

CHAPTER TWENTY-SEVEN

Bahriji (Oasis) School

Welcoming Party

As the helicopters landed at the Bahriji School, or Oasis as it was also called, three Valets and three Abds (servants) welcomed us. As the Abds carried our luggage to our respective dorm rooms, we checked in with our 'big brothers' and the Valets at the reception office. Since our 'big brothers' and the four returning juniors already knew the school's Valets, they greeted one another like pals who hadn't seen each other for a while. After our registration, we retired to our lodgings. Joseph, the junior who was to share our room, was currently at a Household, so Nickee and I were the only ones in the room for the first month.

I noticed that when the Abd, a local Arab boy, fourteen or fifteen years old, brought our luggage to our room he kept his head bowed the entire time. He never looked directly at Nikee or me. When he left our bags he made a low bow, stepping a couple of steps backwards, before turning round to leave the room.

I was curious about this act of submission, like he was our slave. Nickee smiled and said, "Young, the Abds are at our service and they are available to serve us any time we require them. They are usually from poor families from the countryside hired to work at the Bahriji. If you need anything, just ring the little bell by your bedside table and an Abd will appear to serve you. They will fetch your balgha, your djellaba, thawb or anything you require. When you are ready for service in the Households you will have a couple of your own Abds at your beck and call."

I continued, "Why do they bow when they leave, and why don't they look directly at us?"

Nikee smiled and jokingly replied, "Because he is our servant slave-boy! And slave-boys are not allowed to look directly at their Masters unless commanded."

I was surprised to hear that remark. I told Nikee, "We don't have slaves where I came from." He laughed and said he was only joking. But I gathered there was an element of truth in his remark. It must be an ancient Middle Eastern tradition passed down from the old culture. After all, it was the 20th century; I didn't expect to find slaves. But then, I didn't know E.R.O.S. existed before I became initiated into the society. I guessed there were many things in the Universe I didn't know. I had a lot to learn.

Moorish Architecture

The Oasis compound was a fortress and an encampment for high Turkish army officials, long ago. Built around the late 1600s, it became a command post for the Ottoman Empire, hence, the beautifully ornate Moorish mosaic inlays around the Bahriji buildings. Since photography of the school was not allowed, I can only describe the school's marvelous historical architecture by reference to other structures that vaguely resembled the school's architectural splendor.

When I entered the walled school through the fortress gate, I was greeted with a large fountain in the courtyard. Going through a set of beautifully carved passageways, I arrived at the school's main entrance, where the office and administration rooms were located. The spacious Professors' offices and staff rooms were in the same building.

There were only fifty students in the school at any given time. The juniors were currently providing services at different Households; the total number of Bahriji students was approximately one hundred boys per year.

Although Bahriji was a Co-ed school, a high wall separated the girls' section from the boys. It was really two separate schools located on the same expansive oasis compound. This dividing of the sexes is a standard practice throughout the Middle Eastern world.

Professors

The student-teacher ratio at the Bahriji School was one to one. Most of the teachers were former Valets who returned after their University studies, to serve at the Bahriji School. Their strong affiliation with the Oasis inspired them to dedicate their careers to guiding E.R.O.S. juniors, assisting them in achieving the greatest success possible during their adolescent journeys to adulthood.

Most of the school's teachers and professors were very accomplished, and of a high caliber. Their pedagogy was based on methods utilized in their own education. Personal grooming, health, diet and nutritional care were part of the curriculum.

Just as the Valets were especially selected, our professors and teachers were carefully chosen. They were well groomed, and most had great personal flair, panache and style. Each was incredibly distinguished in his or her own way, possessing confidence and individualism. They were charming ladies and gentlemen.

Almost all of the Oasis professors, spouses and life partners were alumni of the Oasis girls' or boys' schools. Or they were graduates from a different E.R.O.S. school, located in other parts of the United Arab Emirate. Most of them met during their Household service years and developed strong emotional ties during the course of their service. It was therefore not uncommon for a male professor to be teaching at the boys' school and for his wife to teach at the girls' school.

There were separate staff apartments and living quarters on campus. These accommodations were located between the dividing walls that separated schools. The staff apartments were strategically designed to prevent members of the opposite sex from entering each other's dormitories. In an unofficial way, our teachers and professors acted as security guards, (even though there were round-the-clock security personnel guarding the campus.)

Teaching Assistants

Some of the Valets who were at the Oasis were also Teaching Assistants. They intended to return to the Bahriji as qualified teachers and professors after graduating from their respective universities and colleges, once they had completed their Master or Doctorate Degree. They were currently at the Oasis to learn from the tenured professors. There was, approximately, one teaching assistant for every two professors.

School Facilities and Routine

The classrooms where our regular studies were conducted were office-sized rooms. Every morning, we had personal tutorials from 8:00 a.m. to 12:30 p.m. A twenty minute tea or coffee recess was held between 10:00 a.m. and 10:30 a.m. Most of the professors taught a variety of subjects unless they were specialized in a specific field of study, such as physical education, nutrition, diet, grooming, or sex education. Group training sessions were held for physical education and sex education, which sometimes required several students or seniors to train together.

We would meet at specific locations within the campus. For example, a group of swimming students would meet at the school's landscaped swimming pool. A section of the Olympic size pool had an adjoining grotto with cave-like structures built for our sex-education sensual training sessions. A Harem etiquette training class would meet at the school's Harem Spa, which was adjacent to the swimming pool.

CHAPTER TWENTY-EIGHT

The Art of Seduction and Flirtation

Love is a moral drunkenness; and, whilst it lasts, the shrew seems gentle, the tigress a dove, the flirt constant, and the fiend an angel.

CHARLES WILLIAM DAY

The thrill of seduction is in the chase, rather than in the conquest. Those graced with an abundance of self-confidence seem particularly fond of being pursuers. Their strong self-belief increases the likelihood of their success.

Eyes

It is said that the eyes are the doorways to the soul. In order to titillate the soul, I had to learn the art of using my eyes. The first lesson in the Art of Seduction was to train my eyes to charm, drawing on divine charisma. The Look must be mesmerizing, drawing the beholder into fantasies about the sensual delights which are to come. Training my eyes to bewitch was an art.

Dr. Andrew Henderson was a handsome man, approximately thirty-five years old, with a slight tint of grey in his otherwise fair head of hair. He was an extremely personable teacher; I generally felt secure, while in his presence. Professor Henderson initiated my 1st lesson in the Art of Seduction, by telling me to look into his eyes. I was embarrassed, nervous and shy. I felt vulnerable in the beginning, and dared not look directly into Dr. Henderson's eyes. He continued to entreat me, and I was finally able to stare into his lively, greyish blue eyes. I didn't know what reaction I would receive from the eyes that looked back at me. I tried turning away. My professor kept turning my head towards him. He said, in a kind voice, "Young, don't be afraid to look at me. I'm not going to devour you. I'm teaching you to make love with your eyes. So, young man, look at me adoringly. Speak to me with your eyes!"

After several unsuccessful attempts, I was able to look directly at my teacher. My vulnerability dissipated as I followed his lead, learning to look into his mature eyes with confidence, staring at him unblinkingly.

He said, "Put love into your heart, Young, and you will exude love." Slowly, I injected love into my heart and sure enough, my blank stare transformed into looks of love.

"Next, allow sensuality into your heart and you will transmit sensuality. The same is true of all thoughts and feelings you inject into your heart. Your inner feelings reflect outwardly, through your eyes," continued Dr. Henderson.

As courage began to build within me, I stared at my teacher with a sensual, seductive desire. I tried to duplicate 'the look' that Nikee gave me the night of my jealous fit back at Daltonbury Hall. I was beginning to understand the deeper meaning of 'the eyes as windows into the soul.'

Practice makes perfect, and I became better and better at using my eyes to tempt, seduce and lure my beholder into my lair of forbidden sensuality. I could titillate with a glance. I could look demure and passive or fierce and lustful. By the end of my three months' eye training with Dr. Andrew, I was great at the art of eye seduction.

Revenge

One day during my training period with Dr. Henderson, he suggested I practice my Seductive Look, to learn if my diligent practice would pay off. I decided to give Andy a try, without his knowledge. Andy's stare had always intimidated me; now it was time to turn the tables.

I noticed Andy walking alone, down a passageway. Plucking up my courage, I followed him. He did not notice I was trailing behind. As he turned a corner into the courtyard, he noticed me, several paces back. Turning around, he smiled, and waited for me to catch up. As I walked towards him he eyed me with his usual lustful, intimating stare, as if he saw me naked through my djellaba (our Bahriji school uniform.) Normally, I would have avoided looking into his eyes, afraid of being sexually aroused. Today was different.

I returned his stare with unblinking eyes, and a smile on my face. Deep within, I was nervous as hell! My awareness of my new seductive power gave me the confidence to continue. Giving him my look of sensual desire, I began speaking to him without any dialogue. I used my eyes to titillate his libido.

His eyes never left mine. Time seemed to dissolve. I was in complete concentration. I wanted to arouse him, as he aroused me at my E.R.O.S. Initiation Ceremony. Licking my lips lightly and fixing my gaze on his handsome face, I informed him of my sexual desire. I wanted all of him!

When we finally embraced, he wrapped his muscular arms around my waist tightly. I thought I was being crushed. He didn't release his hold; we continued looking into each other's eyes. I didn't pull away as I had in the past. When he leaned down to kiss me, I turned my head and leaned against his muscular chest. It was extremely tempting to return his kiss, but the point of my exercise was to seduce him and to leave him desirous. I left him pining for me.

I thought of Dr. Andrew's words, "Tease him! Make him wait! Have him imagine what delights are to come!" I could feel his already erect manhood beneath his thawb. He tried kissing me again. I gave him a peck on both cheeks and pulled away. It was difficult; we found each other incredibly irresistible. I kept reminding myself that I must win this round, conquer him and make him submit to me!

I had practiced my new found art; I made him long for me and I made him wait. We exchanged some pleasantries and I told him I had to run to meet Professor Henderson, as I was already late for class. Blowing him an air kiss, I ran, not daring to look back to see Andy's reaction. I was afraid that if I did, I might turn around and head right back into his warm embrace.

I reached Dr. Henderson's office breathless; he asked me why the hurry. I told him I had just practiced my eye seduction on a 'big brother' and it had worked. He laughed and patted my back saying, "Well done, Young! You are a fast learner. We'll have you located in a Household sooner than expected."

The Art of Flirtation

When used for seduction, flirtation is a means of keeping the other person interested and aroused. It also informs the other party that they are unlikely to be rejected. Men, who are generally the pursuers, are highly dependent on signals to reassure them that they are "onto something good." Playing hard-to-get isn't particularly attractive. Men require signals to assure them that the chase will be worth it, in the end.

Dr. Henderson taught me that the best clues come from reading body language. "Body signals are far better indicators of how he feels about you than anything he may actually say. The eyes are the biggest give-away when it comes to seduction. If he returns your gaze, and especially if he holds eye contact with you longer than usual, then chances are he's interested. Trust your instincts and you'll 'feel' whether he's interested or not. Look for small gestures and pay attention to the tone of voice. These will guide your understanding, about what another feels towards you."

"Remember this, Young; two people who may have been attracted to each other visually may not have the right chemistry to move along the road of seduction. Once you've talked a little, does he still seem interested? Look for signs of acceptance or rejection. If you pick up on any signs of rejection, don't waste your time on something that is unlikely to happen, no matter how much you fancy him. The right man is out there just waiting to be seduced by you!" advised Professor Andrew.

I asked, "What if I know he is already interested but I desire him to play along with me for a while? What should I do then?"

Dr. Andrew replied, "I suggest planning and setting up the time and the right place knowing you will be alone. A "wrong" time and place may well add to the thrill. If you're getting the right feedback from him (flirting), the fact that he is interested but you can't do anything about it can increase the feelings of arousal and excitement. Let them linger," replied my professor.

"How long should I let the interested party linger?" I asked, insistently.

"Once you've made it known that you are attracted to him, you'll need to let him know where the encounter is likely to be heading. People have very different ideas of what sex should be, so it's important that you both know that you're looking for the same things and headed in the same direction.

"The subtle approach is more likely to get you what you want. Remember, though, an alpha man generally takes the lead in this area, asking questions and trying to determine whether you'll make a satisfactory sex partner. Follow his lead. The questions are often framed in self-disclosure. He tells you something, you have the opportunity to tell him something; this creates trust. Try discussing sex in a light-hearted, abstract manner.

"How shall I proceed if the seduction is successful?" I inquired.

"If the signals are good, it's time to make your move. One of you must surrender. In all probability it will be you, because even if you initiated the seduction, he will probably have taken over the role of pursuer somewhere along the line. The roles of 'hunter' and 'prey' have been decided through thousands of years of evolution, and fall naturally into place," Dr. Henderson said.

"Seduce, surrender and enjoy!" were the final words from my sensual education professor at the Bahriji School.

CHAPTER TWENTY-NINE

The Art of Body Language

"Love is the flower of life, and blossoms unexpectedly and without law, and must be plucked where it is found, and enjoyed for the brief hour of its duration."
D.H. LAWRENCE

Like an actor preparing for a movie role, I was groomed for my role as a Male Courtesan, or Cicisbeo, to be of service to the Arabian elite and aristocratic Households. Cicisbei or Courtesans were, historically, highly learned and educated companions of the Royal Courts. More often than not, Cicisbei achieved a high quality of life, gaining worldly influences and respect. This is something an average person seldom would have had the privilege to experience. Besides their regular education, Cicisbei were taught the Art of Human Intimacies, Seduction, Flirtation, Health, Fitness, Grooming, Dress, Beauty, Sensuality and, of course, Sexuality.

Cicisbei were groomed in the Art of Giving and Receiving pleasure in all aspects of life. In my opinion, a Courtesan or Cicisbeo is as noble a profession as any profession in the world, despite many modern day negative connotations. There was far more to being a Courtesan than simply acting as a plaything of the Courts.

Fitness

"It is exercise alone that supports the spirits, and keeps the mind in vigor," wrote Marcus Tullius Cicero.

Participating in different sports and exercise regiments was an essential part of a student's training at the Bahriji. I had been working out with weights regularly with Nikee at the school's gymnasium, and I swam daily. I decided to enroll in a Fencing class with Professor Richard Lichman, a world champion fencer in his heyday; he competed in the Olympics.

There were six Juniors, including myself, enrolled in Professor Lichman's class. I had always loved the Art of Fencing. Having a chance to learn from a professional, world-class trainer was indeed a treat.

I enjoyed the class tremendously.

Art of Fencing

"The sport of Fencing is divided into three weapons," Professor Lichman taught us during my first lesson in beginner's Fencing class.

"A foil is a light thrusting weapon which targets the torso, including the back and shoulders, but not the arms. Touches are scored only with the tip; hits with the side of the blade do not count, nor do they halt the action.

Touches that land outside of the target area (off-target) stop the action, and are not scored. Only one hit can be scored by a fencer at one time. If both fencers hit at the same time, the referee uses the rule of right-of-way to determine which fencer gets the point," said the professor, as we watched and listened, attentively.

"The sabre is a light cutting and thrusting weapon that targets the entire body above the waist, except for the hands. Hits with the edges of the blade as well as the tip are valid. As in foil, touches that land outside of the target area are not scored. However, unlike foil, these off-target touches do not stop the action," continued our instructor.

"An Épée is a heavier thrusting weapon that targets the entire body. All hits must be with the tip, and not the sides of the blade. Touches by the side of the blade do not halt the action. Unlike foil and sabre, Épée does not use right of way, and allows simultaneous hits by both fencers. However, if the score is tied at the last point and a double touch is scored, nobody is awarded the point." Professor Lichman said, finishing his fencing instructions.

My fencing lessons went well while I was stationed at the Madrasah (school.) The Professor often demonstrated when I was unsure of certain postures. He was very thorough, taking me step by step through the techniques of attack and defense. As the days progressed, I began to take a liking to Professor Lichman, who possessed a strong personality. He was a gay gentleman, living alone, in one of the male teachers' apartments. When students were selected to enter the Bahriji School, our confidential files listed each E.R.O.S recruit's information including our sexual preferences, and all of our personal details. All of the professors at the Oasis School had knowledge of each student's sexual orientation. Out of the six boys in my fencing class, three were heterosexual, and two were bisexual.

I was the only gay boy, and I was the most determined fencing student. I enjoyed the Professor's teaching methods and techniques. I liked his personality, and I felt motivated by him. He was a handsome man, and there were times when I fantasized about him being my lover.

I wanted to try out my newfound seduction skills and practice the Art of Body Language on Professor Lichman. If he fell prey to my seduction, then my theoretical lessons with Professor Henderson would have a proven track record of effective, practical application. If the practical exercise "glamoured" him, I could forget it and continue to move forward with another candidate as my sex education tutor had advised. There would be no harm giving Mr. Lichman a try, if the correct circumstances arose.

Dr. Henderson provided me with pointers regarding body language:

- Observe people and look for the clues
- Notice how others communicate with movement and positioning.
- Don't just hear what others say, but "see" how they say it.
- What is stated may be contradicted by body language and gestures.
- Remember that we all try to fool other people from time to time.
- Communicate with your whole being.

As a final reminder, my professor advised, "Young, don't forget what you are projecting; you are constantly giving clues that others can see."

Body Language

One day after fencing class I was showering, in the communal shower room, when Professor Lichman came into the locker room to use the urinal. The last of the students from our class was on his way out. I was the only boy left, and I was just finishing my shower. Mr. Lichman was surprised to see me, because he thought all of his students had already departed. Now would be my chance to try out my body language seduction experiment, and see if my fencing professor would swoon under my bewitching spell.

While he was standing at one of the urinals he turned his head towards me and said, "I'm surprised to find you here. Don't you have another class to attend?"

"No. I'm free for the rest of the afternoon, until dinner time. Do you have another class to conduct?" I asked.

"I'm done for the day. I'm about to clear out the fencing room and store away the equipment before leaving," he replied.

"Do you need some assistance? I can help you clean up."

I looked at him during our conversation, and I purposely stood facing him, with an erection, while under the shower. Pretending it was completely natural for me to be speaking to him in this condition, he tried not to look below my waistline, but his eyes occasionally wandered to my crotch I caught a glimpse of his growing erection. I continued to present my throbbing cock to him, under the running water. I had a feeling he was likely prey, from his body language.

My instructor continued, "Sure, I could do with some assistance to tidying the room. Thanks for offering to help."

I replied, "No problem Sir! I'm at your service!"

That remark got him more excited. By now he was having difficulty urinating since his erection was pointing skyward. If he started peeing, it would have shot above the urinal stall.

His body language was definitely telling me he wanted more than "help tidying up the fencing room." I sensed my professor would like a helping hand in other areas, as well.

I stepped out of the shower, and began to walk towards him while toweling myself dry. I stood close to him. My towel was not wrapped around my waist. I stood next to him, naked. I subtly started stroking my erection to see what Professor Richard's reaction would be. By now, he was terribly excited from all of my sexual signals.

He didn't turn to leave. Instead, he stared in my eyes, probably wondering if it would be advisable for him to proceed further. Smiling, I reached down to stroke his manhood. We continued looking at each other without uttering a word. We knew we wanted to take our liaison to the next level beyond just tidying the fencing room.

I broke the silence and said, "Let me put my wet towel away, and I'll give you a helping hand storing your equipment."

He laughed. "OK! I'll wait in the fencing studio for you."

CHAPTER THIRTY

Drop Dead Gorgeous

"It's not what you wear - it's how you take it off."
Bernard Tristan Foong

A month into my studies, the Bahriji Madrasah invited a well-known male model, Rick Samuel, as a guest lecturer for a one-day seminar in men's grooming. Since grooming was one of my favorite topics, I signed up immediately for the course. I was excited to learn from someone well-known in the fashion industry. Rick Samuel was a name I knew; he was a famous model, appearing in numerous mens' fashion magazines.

Nine students showed up for this event, which was held in the Lecture Theatre. I heard the faint whirring of a helicopter landing on the helipad outside, as we waited for Mr. Samuel to appear. He entered the theatre accompanied by our regular Bahriji health and grooming professor, Dr. Sherlock Grjotheim.

I was completely mesmerized by the six-foot two inch tall, strikingly handsome Rick Samuel. As he passed through the Lecture Theatre doors he looked like he had just stepped off of the pages of L' Uomo Vogue; he was the most attractive and polished man I had ever set eyes on. I had seen many good-looking men at Daltonbury Hall, and at the Oasis, but Rick Samuel's panache and impeccable grooming made it impossible not to take notice of him.

All eyes gravitated towards him, regardless of sexual orientation. There was great strength and seductiveness in his deep, blue, piercing eyes. His glowing golden tan reminded me of the angel I dreamed of the night I decided to accept the E.R.O.S. scholarship offer.

He wore a loose-fitting white pinpoint Oxford shirt, unbuttoned down to his waist. I caught glimpses of his muscular chest when he moved. His shirtsleeves were rolled above the elbow, showing off his hairy arms. He could easily seduce his admirers, making them long to have his arms wrapped around their bodies.

I fell in love with the image this man projected. He was the personification of everything I wanted in myself. I longed to be like this man, in every way. I saw my own best attributes through the person of Rick Samuel (which was both narcissistic and inspiring). His chiseled face and neatly trimmed beard made me think of Apollo, the Greek God of Beauty and Perfection, until he opened his mouth.

Art of Grooming

"I flew in from Milan, after a hectic photo shoot for an Italian fashion house," Mr. Samuel began. As soon as he uttered his first sentence, the soprano ring to his voice destroyed the macho image I had of him when he first entered the room. His voice sounded as if he were about to break into an aria. This distracted me greatly and I had difficulty following his teachings. The model's voice did not match up with this hunky man. It was like watching a macho Drag Queen lip synch. Despite this oddity, Rick was excellent at delivering good grooming advice to the students.

"Before providing you with the grooming suggestions, I will begin by showing you some of my modeling photos which demonstrate the importance of good grooming. Some of you might have already come across these, in men's fashion magazines," continued Rick, as he began advancing the slide carousel.

Images of him in numerous poses were projected onto the screen as he clicked away, explaining his regular regiment. Then, he gave us ten grooming tips:

Point 1 - Trim the nose hairs. This is something very basic that makes a world of difference. Believe me when I tell you, this is something people notice.

Point 2 - Trim the eyebrows. I would recommend getting them professionally done in order to open up the eyes. Remember to brush them up before you leave for the day. This opens up the eyes, giving the face a more alert, aware appearance.

Point 3 - Remove the hair from your ears and neck. This is something your barber can do for you monthly. The sight of hairy ears or neck hair around the collar of your shirt is never appealing.

Point 4 - Keep your nails short and clean. Dirty, long fingernails require no explanation of why they don't work. If your schedule permits, try a monthly manicure/pedicure to have someone take care of this for you. I also recommend buffing your nails to keep the healthy shine without it looking artificial.

Point 5 - Brush and floss your teeth daily. I've always believed that it doesn't matter if your teeth are not perfectly straight and white, but please, keep them clean. It is quite unappealing to speak to someone and see built up plaque or food stuck between their teeth.

Point 6 - Have your clothes tailored to fit your body. Regardless of one's individual shape, the right fit makes everything look so much better.

Point 7 - Stand up straight. Your Mom always told you "posture counts," and she's right. You create a sense of confidence and pride when standing tall. You display to everyone that you are secure in the man you are," he continued.

Point 8 - Cleanse your face on a regular basis with a facial soap. I have many male friends who use the same soap on their bodies that they use on their faces. Most body soaps are too harsh for the face. Invest in a cleanser that is just for the face, as the facial skin is much more sensitive than the skin on the body.

Point 9 - Remember, less is more when it comes to fragrance. Remember not to bathe in it. Fragrance is such a personal preference; you really must find what works best for you.

Point 10 - Match your belt with your shoes. This one is really simple and it makes a world of difference. If you are wearing black shoes, you don't wear a brown belt. This basic tip makes everything you wear look that much better," finished our lecturer.

Rick Samuel, the Person

As Rick flashed image after image of himself onto the screen I noted that most of the pictures were of him posing nude, or nearly nude. He kept asking us if we liked what we saw, wanting us to confirm how gorgeous he looked in the photographs. It dawned on me that this drop-dead-gorgeous hunk was an insecure man. He seemed to need accolades and praises, from teen-aged boys, to remind him that he was a handsome stud.

I sensed that he was afraid of losing the outward beauty which accompanied youth. He needed affirmation from his audience that he was still desirable and sexy. I came to the conclusion that this good-looking guy had no depth, and that his beauty was only skin deep. He was in love with the images, his superficial self.

Accepting one's beauty within and without makes a person truly beautiful! True beauty, from within, shines the brightest. Be well groomed on the exterior, certainly, but be better groomed on the interior. That was my takeaway from the lecture. I'm sure that was not Rick Samuel's intention!

Questions and Answers

When class was over I managed to corner Mr. Samuel to ask him questions. "Sir, why, in the majority of the images, were you scantily dressed, half naked or fully nude?"

He smiled and replied, "Good question! When one has a great body, like mine, photographers, advertising agencies and fashion houses love viewing one in the raw! You see, Young, (he had asked my name) I have become a sex symbol to my audience. As you may or may not know, sex sells. When I pose sexily in front of the cameras, my audience loves me. They imagine all kinds of sexual fantasies, which, in turn, help sell the products I'm paid to promote. I've learned to make love to the camera. That's why I am a successful model."

"Of course, I only pose nude for photographers who project my image in tasteful and artistic ways. I maintain creative control of the content and personally approve all nude images. I don't want to be misinterpreted as a pornographic model," he exclaimed.

At thirteen, I didn't know what 'pornographic' meant, so I asked him for an explanation.

"You see, Young, there are many publications and businesses which cater to the adult entertainment industry. Most of these are unrefined and distasteful. They are not what you would call 'above board.' These are not companies to whom I release my nude images," he replied.

I continued, inquiring, "How do you determine whether or not an image is tasteful and artful rather than . . . vulgar?"

"I thoroughly check out the companies and photographers. If my research leads me to believe that they are reputable and their projects legitimate, then I take the job. My instincts have served me well."

I did not see Rick Samuel again until I bumped into him several years later at a London dance club in Charing Cross.

CHAPTER THIRTY-ONE

To the Souq

"Our image is the mental picture we hold dear; with effort, thought, awareness, it can be clear that we hold ourselves in a good, honest light; with healthy self-acceptance, our life is most bright."

Bernard Tristan Foong

Professor Sherlock Grjotheim and Professor Mark Jobeck, (the school's performance arts teacher), organized a field trip for a few of the freshmen and their 'big brothers' to the local marketplace, or Souq.

The purpose of the trip was twofold. Professor Sherlock wanted to enlighten us about healthy eating, so he decided a good place to start would be with delicious Middle Eastern cuisine, at the Souq. Professor Jobeck wanted us to practice speaking what little Arabic we had learned. This was a chance to apply our knowledge and practice communicating in simple Arabic with the stall keepers and street vendors, at the Souq.

On a Saturday morning, three of the Freshmen, their big brothers and our two professors climbed into the school's air-conditioned minibus. We were blindfolded, with padded eye masks which completely blocked light from entering our eyes. These masks were fastened behind our heads with leather buckles, secured with a tiny lock. Each blindfold had its own individual key. They could not be removed, easily.

For me, it was an exciting experience; I had never been blindfolded. Our BB's were sitting next to us and we knew and trusted our professors; there was no reason to be afraid. The overland journey, as Andy had mentioned on the plane, was rough and bumpy. Against the window ledge, I could feel the stifling dryness of the desert heat seeping through the windowpane. Three hours passed before we arrived at the Souq, which was located a little outside of Dubai. When our professors released our blindfolds, the sudden brightness blinded our eyes.

We heard Islamic prayers repeated over loud speakers strategically placed on prayer towers, throughout the course of our field trip. Only our two accompanying professors and our bus driver, Abdul, spoke fluent Arabic. They directed us to the best places in the marketplace. When it was close to lunch hour Professor Grjotheim suggested a restaurant at which we could fill our hungry, rumbling stomachs.

Mata'am

When our local waiter brought us the menus, we looked cluelessly to our professors for guidance. "The Nejdi Kabsa is popular among the people of Dammam," Professor Grjotheim said. "This dish is made with chicken, instead of lamb meat. The Yemani Mandi is also popular."

He ordered Shorabah Hareira (Hareira soup,) Madhbi (chicken grilled on stone,) Madfun (literally meaning buried,) Ma'asoob, Magliya (a Hijazi version of Falafel, and Hummus.

All the students looked at our professor with blank stares, not knowing what he was saying. He might as well have been speaking Swahili for all we knew! Our professor continued our education. "Hejazi cuisine is also delicious. Grilled meat such as Shawaman, Kofta and Kebab, Sambousak and Ful are the most popular meals during Ramadan, eaten only after dusk and before dawn. These foods are usually found in Lebanese, Syrian, and Turkish restaurants," continued our teacher.

As soon as the waiter had taken our orders, our Grooming, Nutritional & Diet Professor, Sherlock, continued, "Getting in shape is important and it is especially necessary for all of you who are being groomed for a special task. Two vital aspects of being in good shape are proper nutrition and eating habits."

He continued, "There are a number of different things that can be done to ensure one gets the vitamins and nutrients necessary for a healthy lifestyle. Nutritious meals, combined with an exercise regimen, ensure that one maintains a healthy weight throughout one's life."

Mr. Sherlock advised, "The first tip is to eat a variety of different foods every day. There are over forty different nutrients necessary for proper health. Fruits, whole grains and vegetables should be eaten on a daily basis. Many people do not get the daily, recommended servings of these foods."

He added, "Many times portions are exaggerated and it is all too easy to overeat, especially when dining out. Consider ordering half of a serving or splitting an order with a friend."

Dr. Grjotheim continued to speak, "Between meals, snacking is a helpful way to get needed calories and energy. But snack smartly. Sweet snacks are acceptable as long they are eaten in moderation and in reasonable portions. Moderation is the key."

Finally, our teacher said, "For you to eat properly and have good habits, know your strengths and weaknesses. Know your problem areas. Then, you can monitor yourself, and improve your habits. Keeping a record of what you eat is a good idea."

But he wasn't finished. "Oh! One last bit of information!" But our food had arrived and we were hungry. We dug in, enjoying a delicious, well balanced, and nutritious meal.

Chapter Thirty-one

The Souq

After a hearty lunch at the Mata'am, the freshmen and their accompanying 'big brothers' were permitted to wander around the Souq. Nikee and I decided to walk with Professor Sherlock, because I had a couple of questions I wanted to ask him about vitamins he had recommended in our health and fitness class.

While Nikee was browsing at one of the stalls I asked Professor Grjotheim, "Sir, in class you had talked about the benefits of different vitamins. By the end of your class, I was confused about which I should take since there were so many you spoke about. Can you recommend the ones I should take daily?"

My professor replied, "Young, at your growing age, the easiest and best approach is to consume an already packaged multivitamin each day. Then, you have all the necessary supplements you'll require and you won't have to worry about which ones to select."

I replied, "Well that's easy. What exactly do the multivitamins do for me?" I inquired further.

Dr. Grjotheim smiled and said, "They will assist your digestive function, boost your brain function, give you added energy and help you with weight management (not that you require that at your age, Young). It will also increase your immune resistance and shift hormonal balances in ways which actually slow down the process of aging." He kept on, "Again, this doesn't really apply to you right now, since you are still growing. But when one reaches my age, one must begin paying attention to the balance of hormones."

"Thank you, Sir, for the advice," I said appreciatively.

Nikee's News

Professor Sherlock wandered off to purchase some items, leaving Nikee and me to explore the Souq on our own. My BB seemed to be struggling with his words.

"Young, you know I have applied to several Universities to further my studies. I just found out that I have been accepted to Saint Andrews, in Scotland. The semester commences in a month's time."

"Are you leaving the Bahriji then, for good?" I asked, incredulously.

"I'm afraid so, my young chap. My duties of looking after you are coming to an end. I know you will be placed in good hands after I leave," replied Nikee.

"I'm going to miss you terribly!" I answered, trying to stop tears from rolling down my cheeks.

I knew that Nikee's departure was close at hand because BBs only accompanied their charges to settle them into the Bahriji, for the first three months. After that, a new Valet takes over, when the freshman goes into service at the Households.

My bond with Nikee had always been extremely strong. It was difficult for me to hear my BB say that the time for him to leave was near. I thought my chances of ever seeing him again were slim.

The bus ride back to the Oasis was a welcome relief. At least I could drown in my sorrows behind the blindfold, and no one would notice. For the rest of the journey I said very little. Nikee tried to cheer me up, but I just wanted to be left alone to release the emotional pain within me. I needed to be alone by the Oasis' creek to scream and cry, to let out the heartache and frustration of never seeing Nikee, my beloved big brother and first love, again!

CHAPTER THIRTY-TWO

Art of Sensuality and Foreplay

"The finest clothing made is a person's skin, but, of course, society demands something more than this."
Mark Twain

Art of Sensuality and Foreplay

Professor Andrew Henderson instructed a group of students and our BB's to meet at the grotto, adjacent to the school's swimming pool, a week after our Souq outing. Dr. Julie Colberg, the girls' school's Sex Education Professor, along with several of her students and their 'big sisters', would join us in a practical training session in the Art of Sensuality and Foreplay.

The participants were advised to eat lightly before the event, and to drink plenty of water so as not to become dehydrated.

Every part of our body was thoroughly prepared. We were examined, from head to toe, by our BBs, before venturing to the grotto.

We wore comfortable djellabahs, with speedos under our garments. All jewelry had to be removed for the sensual practicum. The only footwear allowed was a pair of open toed sandals (belugas.)

Professor Andrew had previously advised the male students to restrain from masturbation in the days preceding the training. He did not want us to release semen or dissipate our sexual energies, beforehand. Dr. Henderson assured us that our BBs would have their eyes on us. He stressed the importance of his instructions being followed, to ensure maximum results. He explained that it was important to allow our semen to accumulate within our body, so that we would be acutely aware on every level during foreplay.

When no semen is released for a period of time, the body becomes extremely sensitive to touch, scent, caresses, sight and sound. In such a state, a transformative spiritual event can occur; the experience can transport one into epiphanies of ecstatic sensual and sexual arousal. This, according to our sex education teacher, was the highest good of sensuality and foreplay.

"The use of recreational drugs becomes obsolete, if a person practices the Art of Sensuality," advised Dr. Henderson. He continued, "Some people prefer to label this Tantric Sensuality, leading to Neo-Tantra or Tantric Sex. Remember, boys, we are focusing on the Art of Sensuality and Foreplay, not the Art of Sex, which is another lesson for another time."

We would be kept in a constant, heightened state of sexual arousal, throughout the training. Professor Andrew warned, "There will be times during your sensual foreplay when you might involuntarily ejaculate. It is all right if that happens. But try to exercise restraint when you feel the urge to come. Stop for a few seconds, until the orgasmic urge subsides. This will prolong the sensual enjoyment for both you and your partner, or partners." He reminded us of the required parameters:

- No oral sex or sexual intercourse is allowed during your sensuality practices.
- You can kiss, lick and use your fingers or toes on the periphery only of the genitals and anus. No penetration with fingers of any orifice other than the mouth is allowed.

The Practitioners

There were four heterosexuals, three bisexuals and three homosexual boys in Dr. Andrews' class. For this training, we were split into two groups with five freshmen in each group. The groups trained separately, on different days. Otherwise, the class would be too crowded for our tutors to be able to properly assist us, as well as critique our individual performance.

When I arrived at the appointed practice location with Nikee, all the male students were already present, and so were the girls and their Big Sisters. The swimming pool and grotto were off-limits to others while our class was in session.

The Grotto

The grotto was linked to the pool via a series of streams and waterways. Several entrances, man-made catacombs resembling the interiors of caves, also led into the grotto. A beautiful cascading waterfall, approximately thirty feet in height, was at one end of the grotto. Above the cascading water there were hanging plants with benches, where one could sit and enjoy the surrounding oasis and desert scenery.

The Bahriji grounds were kept pristine by a team of full-time landscapers and workmen. One of their jobs was to ensure that the grotto had no uninvited visitors such as scorpions, spiders, or poisonous snakes.

On the afternoon of our training session, the interior of the grotto was lit with fragrant candles, strategically placed, providing a romantic atmosphere. There was a hidden passageway behind the waterfall, between two large rocks, which allowed access to the caves, catacombs and caverns hidden deep within. Water dripped slowly from stalactite formations, providing soothing sound. In the catacombs, a light sprinkling of water raining down from the rocks created the effect of a misty shower. It was cool steam, in natural surroundings.

Subtle lighting, along with built-in audio equipment placed behind smooth jutting rocks, added to the allure. Sounds of roaring thunder segued into chirping birds during the sensual training. Different lighting effects, a rainbow, even a moonbow, engulfed us. The grotto and hidden caves were built like a movie set, except the props were natural formations from actual caves and caverns, which had been transported to the grotto. Unlike the sets at Universal Studios or Disney theme parks, nothing appeared ersatz about this setting.

Hidden video cameras captured students' performances. The footage was replayed when we had one-on-one tutorials with our sex education professor. During the review, he would advise us on how to improve our sensual techniques. The chance to view ourselves in action was a wonderful tool, helping us learn from our mistakes, and make improvements.

These videos belonged to the school, and were the private property of the Bahriji. Eventually, these tapes would be archived and stored for safe keeping at the Oasis library vault. They could be accessed only by authorized personnel, such as the Headmaster, our sex education professors, or other professors interested in them for research purposes. They were much like secret documents stored in the Vatican's extensive library and high security vaults.

Sensuality in Motion

Three girls from our sister school practiced with Jim and Henry, both heterosexuals, and Abraham, a bisexual. Our accompanying BBs and the Big Sisters were tutors, including Nikee. Henderson and Colberg suggested we pair as couples, as threesomes or as a team of four or five. Jim and Henry went with Deb and Angie. Abraham teamed with Dex, a second year Junior, and Julie. And, Brian and I went with two second year juniors, Josh and Corey.

Our BBs and the BSs were an important part of the teaching team. They demonstrated techniques and guided us on our sensual journeys. They gently admonished us to slow down, to breathe, when we became overzealous, or lost sight of the aim of the practice. If we came close to intercourse, they were there to refocus us, and to guide us back on course.

All the students in the grotto emanated a beautiful glow from their youthful skin as we progressed along candlelit passageways, into the caverns.

Jal, Brian's BB, began a conversation with me. Soon, we fell a few steps behind our group. Discovering a lovely shallow pool of pristine blue water, Jal and I found ourselves stopping by the water's edge. We sat, together, and he nonchalantly put his hand on my leg. He began lightly stroking my upper thigh while I was still fully clothed. I was easily aroused, since I had not come for three days; I was dying to release.

His handsome face was inches away. He leaned over to kiss me. Instead of a French kiss, I felt the sensual tip of his tongue licking the edges of my lips. I responded similarly with my tongue on his lips. His hands slipped beneath my djellaba, caressing my inner thighs. My entire body was tingling. My cock was fully erect, straining for release from the confines of my swim suit. Jal continued sensually stroking me, and I responded by reaching to unbutton his thwab.

I slid my hand into his garment, caressing his muscular chest and erect nipples, which I lightly pinched, sending him into groans of passionate ecstasy.

The other boys and their partners were in various stages of foreplay. I glanced over Jal's shoulder and saw Nikee coaxing Josh onto the path of sensual pleasure. Corey was absorbed in licking Brian's nipples and neck. Both boys mirrored each other's actions, which plunged them into erotic squirms of delight.

Watching the sensuality unfolding, voyeuristically, combined with the romantic setting of the catacombs and Jal's caresses, I was propelled into a marvelous, magical erotic realm.

Jal felt my buttocks, and gripped them, firmly. Arching my tingling body to his every touch, I was awash in my own erotic pleasures as well as the erotica which surrounded me. Every cell of my being pulsed with ecstatic bewilderment. Whatever Jal did, I responded in kind, surrendering to his lead.

He took his time with me. His excellent foreplay made me spontaneously contract; spasms surged through my torso. We continued our erotic play for two hours, slowing only to stave off our orgasmic urges, before resuming again.

This was one of the most enlightening experiences of my adolescent life; the sensual and spiritual epiphanies, along with reviews of what precisely led me and others to that place, are some of my greatest treasures in life.

CHAPTER THIRTY-THREE

Love Knows No Boundaries

"Sexual love is undoubtedly one of the chief things in life, and the union of mental and bodily satisfaction in the enjoyment of love is one of its culminating peaks. Apart from a few weird fanatics, the entire world knows this and conducts its life accordingly; science alone is too delicate to admit it."
Sigmund Freud

It had been a year and three months, to the day, since I met Nikee, my big brother. I had grown from a naïve, innocent pubescent boy into a rapidly maturing adolescent man, in preparation to enter service at the Households in The United Arab Emirates. Nikee spearheaded my maturation process, and I was grateful to him. I could not have asked for a better 'big brother' than Nikee. He was always there to lend a helping hand when I needed moral or emotional support.

Besides being a delightful BB, he was also my first real lover (my relationship with KiWi had been a superficial phase of puppy love). Nikee took me much deeper, revealing many facets of love and sex to me.

Now that Nikee was going to Saint Andrews, we were on the last leg of our loving relationship. I was sad, very sad, to see him leave. But go he must, I knew, to pursue his dreams, as I would. I will always love Nikee.

Last Night Together

Nikee was scheduled to fly away three days after our experiences at the grotto. I wanted our last night together to be extra memorable, so we would cherish the experience for years to come. After a light meal at the school restaurant we decided to take a stroll in the "Hanging Gardens of Babylon," above the grotto.

Nikee began, "Young, you've grown since I first met you. I'm so glad you decided to join E.R.O.S. You made a wise choice to come to the Bahriji. It is an environment in which you already are thriving."

I said, "One of the main reasons I decided to be an E.R.O.S. member was because of you. I looked up to you, always, as my BB and you have a special place in my heart, even though you keep reminding me not to fall in love with you," I gently teased.

He looked at me and said, "You know I will never be able to return the love you have for me. As much as I love you, Young, you are my protégé. Also, I'm not one hundred percent gay. You know I like girls as well as guys. I want to experience different people and play the field. I'm not one to have a long-term relationship with anyone. You should realize that by now," he replied, sounding somewhat as if he were trying to convince himself.

"That doesn't mean I cannot love you," I answered, solemnly.

"I know someone who will be happy to have a loving relationship with you. You are a great guy; you deserve someone who can return your love," Nikee assured me.

"Who is this someone? I'd like to know him. Are you going to introduce us?" I asked.

"You'll find out soon enough, young chap!" my BB said, amusedly.

Making Love

When we returned to the dorm room, Josef, our 'straight' roommate was ready to turn in for the night. Nikee and I really wanted some time together. We asked Josef if he would mind if I slept with Nikee that night. Since all Bahriji students were open-minded and didn't give a damn who slept with whom, Josef was fine with our request.

After showering, Nikee and I jumped into bed naked and we held each other intimately. Our embrace turned to lingering French kisses, and love making. We had always kept a nightlight by the bedside table so none of us would trip in the middle of the night. I could make out, in the dim light, that Josef was watching us. Although he was in his own bed his eyes were transfixed on our every move. For a heterosexual guy, he certainly seemed interested in our male love. I didn't mind having sex in front of Bahriji boys. I had just finished the Sensuality and Foreplay session, with other boys watching. I certainly had no problem with Josef looking on, as Nikee and I made love.

As my BB and I progressed further into our sensual and sexual foreplay, Josef uncovered himself from his duvet, showing us his erect cock. I didn't realize he was a voyeur, until I saw how much he enjoyed watching Nikee and me perform!

Earlier that night, at dinner, Nikee had mentioned he wanted some photographs of us, to better remember our time together. Now the perfect opportunity presented itself. My BB got out of bed, grabbed his camera and handed it to Josef asking him to snap away, while we were in the throes of passion.

As we resumed our play, Josef took photographs with one hand, and with his other he began masturbating. He captured some beautiful moments. I gave myself completely to Nikee that night, like the very first time we made love by Swan Lake at Daltonbury Hall. I look at the photographs to this day and reminisce about Nikee, my beloved big brother in his prime!

Josef

Josef was a second year junior when he entered the Bahriji. He was studying at an exclusive private boarding school in Germany when recruited into E.R.O.S. He was Korean and Taiwanese. His parents immigrated to Berlin due to his dad's bio chemical research work with a medical institution there. Josef's grandparents were wealthy landowners from old money, in Korea.

A young man of five foot, six inches tall, with a boyish frame. When we were first introduced, I thought he was gay; his mannerisms were gentle and polite. He had the "twink" look, which I'm sure many misinterpreted. He said he was 'straight', but the evening he took the photos of Nikee and me, he acted like he wanted to join the party and have a three-way liaison. Do 'straight' boys really do that?

Having been at the Bahriji for two and a half months, I had discovered that many self-professed 'straight' boys seemed to swing either way, under the right circumstances. I believe God created all humans to be equal and there should be no categorization or labeling of different types of sexual preferences. One sexual preference is not more correct than another; the very suggestion that one alignment is superior to another has, historically, resulted in the repression and control of certain groups and individuals.

CHAPTER THIRTY-FOUR

On the Red Sea

"Twenty years from now you will be more disappointed by the things that you didn't do than by the ones you did do. So throw off the bowlines. Sail away from the safe harbor. Catch the trade winds in your sails. Explore. Dream. Discover."
Mark Twain

Lost

The week after Nikee left, I was lost. Previously, my 'big brother' had accompanied me everywhere. Now he was gone, and I had not yet been advised who my Valet would be when I went into service at my first Arab Household. Josef's Valet, Thomas, was acting as my temporary 'big brother' while still keeping an eye on my roommate. He moved into our room after Nikee left. Josef, being a second year junior, already knew the ropes at the Bahriji; Thomas did not have to be at his side constantly.

Our individual Valet would be very much required when a student was at a Household. They would be present twenty-four seven, making sure a student was never in harm's way. If we had any problems, our Valet would step in and take charge on our behalf.

On the one hand I missed Nikee tremendously. On the other, I couldn't help but wonder, curiously, about the identity of my Valet. Most nights, I didn't sleep well. When I had private tutorials with Dr. Andrew Henderson, he noticed my lack of sleep by my reddish, puffy eyes. He knew I was missing my beloved 'big brother'.

One day my kind professor approached me in class. "Young, I'm organizing an outing this weekend with a couple friends. I have invited some of our school's Valets and Freshmen. Would you like to join us?" the Dr. enquired.

"Sure, I'd love to go. Where will we be heading?" I asked.

"My friend, Hadrah Hakim has invited us to spend the weekend on his yacht, The Kahyya'm; we'll be cruising the Red Sea Riviera," replied my professor.

"It will be a fun weekend. Pack light; bring your djellabas and a swim suit," my teacher suggested.

The Kahyya'm

The Friday afternoon we departed was a beautiful clear day. Professor Andrew Henderson, Valet Franco, and I were dispatched in the school's helicopter. We flew over an ocean of desert towards the Red Sea. After an hour and a half of flying, I finally saw patches of blue in the distance. Before long, we were flying over the Red Sea, heading towards a large luxury yacht which cruised steadily along the aquamarine water below. As we drew closer, a couple of the deck hands waved to us, directing our pilot to touch down. The boat's sails were lowered, and as our helicopter started its descent toward the center of the vessel, a solid cover emerged over the huge Jacuzzi, transforming it into a helipad.

As soon as our helicopter was on the pad, we were welcomed with open arms by the yacht's Captain, who informed Dr. Henderson that Hadrah Hakim was waiting for us in the main lounge. The rest of our party had arrived earlier in the morning. A couple of uniformed Abds (servants) unloaded our luggage, and carried the pieces to our respective suites. Professor Henderson was exchanging pleasantries with the Captain and the deck hands.

I was awestruck by the beauty of this floating vessel. A large sun deck on one side of the yacht was the perfect place for sun lovers to soak up rays. If the sun was too strong, an awning, monitored by remote control, would extend outward for shade. This deck also doubled as an extended outdoor dining patio in the evenings. It was a great spot for watching beautiful sunsets as well.

A full service bar, managed by uniformed staff, provided guests with beverages. Since I was underage, I ordered a glass of water. (Although liquor is generally forbidden in most Arab Nations, in certain private quarters, away from the watchful eyes of Islamic law enforcers, liquor flows freely).

We proceeded into the main lounge through spotless glass panels, which revealed an aesthetically pleasing interior. This expansive vessel was paneled in rich, dark wood along the walls. The owner had spared no expense in fitting and decorating the Kahyya'm. She was the highest quality and the most lavish yacht that money could buy.

This was the first in a series of many yachts I would have the opportunity to enjoy during my four years of Household services in the various Arabian Gulf States. All of my Household Masters and many of their family members owned private jets, luxury yachts and fleets of expensive cars ranging from the latest Lamborghinis to Ferraris, from vintage Bugattis to Rolls Royces.

The Party

As soon as we entered the main lounge, Hadrah Hakim, a tall, jolly and robust Arab gentleman, forty-seven years of age, greeted us. He extended his hand for Dr. Andrew to kiss before proceeding to welcome us to his 'humble lodgings on the water,' which was one of the ways he described the Kahyya'm.

He smiled and glanced at me, saying, "Young man, come, sit beside me."

I nodded and went to sit beside the Hadrah. He reached over before I had a chance to settle myself properly, and gave me a big bear hug, which came as a surprise since his greeting with my professor was so formal. As I settled into my seat and looked around at the party, a younger Arab gentleman in his late twenties whom Hadrah Hakim addressed as Habiibi Aziz, his son-in-law, nodded a greeting. Tom, Andy's Freshman charge, was seated next to Habiibi Aziz, while both Professor Henderson and Valet Franco were seated comfortably on separate chaise lounges.

"If Tom was there, then Andy must be present, too," I thought. But I didn't see him around. My mind wondered about Andy's whereabouts, but I was snapped back to reality by a question from the Hadrah.

He spoke in perfect English, "Young, I hope you'll enjoy your weekend here. I heard from Dr. Andrew that your 'big brother', Nikee, left for further education in Scotland. How are you coping?"

I looked to my professor for a response; since I wasn't sure I wanted to reveal the truth about missing my 'big brother' to a stranger. Dr. Andrew came to my rescue. Speaking in fluent Arabic, he turned towards Hadrah Hakim addressing the question. Since I didn't know what my teacher was saying, I kept silent until they finished their dialogue. All the while, Hadrah Hakim, was looking at me and nodding, a wide grin spreading across his bearded face. He seemed a pleasant man, I thought.

Washroom Encounter

I was dying to pee, so I inquired about the location of the washrooms. Hadrah Hakim gave a signal to one of the Abd standing near, gesturing for him to show me to the bathroom. The Abd came over immediately, gave a slight bow and motioned with his hand for me to follow.

As we went downstairs to the lower deck, I passed four spacious, elegantly decorated cabins. One of the cabins contained my luggage. The bathroom which the Abd pointed out was located in my bedroom. There was a Queen and a Single bed in the room. I reasoned I would be sleeping in the single bed; if my 'big brother' had been with me, he would have occupied the Queen.

When I came out of the washroom I was confronted by Dr. Andrew. Standing next to him was Andy! For reasons I didn't quite understand, Andy always made me extremely nervous. I guess it was the potent mental, emotional and physical attraction I had for him.

His six foot three inch stature and his seductive, piercing green eyes intimidated me. He always demonstrated new and different ways of undressing me with his eyes, exposing my inner vulnerability. I was so unsuspecting! He teased me, endlessly, it seemed. I was afraid I would fall madly with him, like I did with Nikee, and that he would not return the love I would openly give. I made a pact with myself not to be shattered, again, by this thing called love! Besides, Nikee had only been gone for a week and I was still mourning his departure. Also, I was unsure of whether it would be appropriate for us to act on the feelings we obviously harbored, intensely, for each other.

I was caught off guard when my professor spoke. "Young, do allow me to formally introduce you to your Valet, Andy. He's going to be your chaperone in the Arab Households when you start, in a week. Andy is a very good guy and I'm sure you'll be in great hands with this wonderful chap," he said, giving Andy a slap on his back as he finished his sentence.

An Abd appeared, informing the Professor that he was required upstairs by the Hadrah. Without another word, my professor departed, leaving Andy and me alone in the bedroom suite.

CHAPTER THIRTY-FIVE

On The Kahyya'm

"Life is all memory except for the one present moment that goes by so quick you can hardly catch it going."
Tennessee William

Andy and I

As much as I had dreamed about Andy I never expected him to be my Valet! I certainly never anticipated him accompanying me to my Household assignments!

Before Hakim summoned the Doctor upstairs, my teacher was in the process of formally introducing Andy to me, apparently unaware that we had already met more than a year ago. Andy, catching me off guard from my nervousness, extended his hand to shake mine, as if it were our first meeting. With an automatic response, I, too, extended my hand to shake his. What I didn't expect was for Andy to hold onto my hand; he was reluctant to release his grip. He held on and subtly used his middle finger to tickle my palm, while flashing me an amused wink with his wicked eyes. Now, I was more nervous than ever, trying to find a way out. Although I secretly desired my new Valet, I never knew how to respond to his myriad sexual nuances. This man scared me tremendously, yet I longed for his intimacy.

My professor seemed oblivious to the secret innuendos happening between my newly appointed Valet and me. All I could master was a lame reply to Dr. Henderson's introduction, "Oh? Isn't Andy Tom's 'big brother'?"

The professor replied, "Franco is now Tom's Valet. Andy applied to be assigned as your chaperone and the board approved his application."

Andy seemed delighted that he had the upper hand in this round of our numerous encounters. He said, "I promise I'll be a helpful Valet to you. I'm at your service." There was a laconic incisiveness in his voice.

I was speechless. I tried to look the other way. I dared not look him in the eye. He was too much of an alpha male for me to handle, right then. I was desperately trying to avoid falling for this man. I needed time to gather myself and to pick up my heart's broken pieces before daring to move forward to a new love adventure.

My former BB had always reminded me to play the field, and not to fall in-love. He said that if I played my cards correctly I would be both emotionally and financially rewarded! Whatever that meant - I never quite understood him when he would say that to me, repeatedly.

I felt the urge to again turn, run and hide from my newly appointed BB. Andy sensed my fear, yet he loved to tease me. The more nervous and intimidated I became, the more he felt a sense of power and control over me, a neophyte. And the more flirtatious he became. As much as I enjoyed the fact that he wanted to win me over, I somehow desired to resist his relentless pursuit even more. Sigmund Freud would most likely have analyzed this as a psychological game lovers loved to play, reducing it to the inverse relationship between attainability and desirability.

Andy, sounding official, announced "My duty as your Valet starts today. I will be sharing this cabin with you." I felt his delivery, viscerally.

I had goose bumps all over me, but I plucked up the courage to reply, "Good! I will occupy the single bed."

My Valet laughed and answered, "Oh no, my sweet boy! You are taking the queen. As your Valet I will be sleeping on the single bed; one of the Bahriji School's rules."

"But you are so tall. Your feet will stick out of the bed," I remarked, trying to sound nonchalant.

Andy continued to laugh and answered, "If you invite me to sleep with you on the queen bed, I am allowed to join you. But, I require your invitation in order to occupy your bed. The Bahriji imposes strict regulations about this rule. The freshman or junior must agree; then it is mutual consent. Otherwise, it might be misconstrued that I imposed upon you. I do not seek out trouble with E.R.O.S. or the Bahriji Board of Directors, be assured. So, young man, the ball is in your court."

It was good to be informed of my privilege. I replied, "I will consider what you have said, and I will let you know my decision, later."

With that remark, I proceeded to walk towards my luggage; I wished to use unpacking as an excuse to escape from my Valet.

As I was starting to unpack, Andy spoke, "Young, from now on you don't have to do any unpacking. Leave this task to the two Abds. You are to enjoy your weekend on the Kahyya'm. All you have to do is be pleasant to your hosts, Hadrah Hakim and Habiibi Aziz; please the two of them and you'll be well rewarded."

With that advice Andy reached over and locked the cabin door. It was a sudden move; I didn't have time to consider his actions. With the bedroom door securely locked he pinned me to the wall, kissing me fully on the mouth. As surprised as I was, I did not resist. Giving in to his tight embrace, I allowed him to take charge. Andy knew I longed for his kisses as much as he longed for mine.

Be Sociable

As much as I did not want Andy to stop our sensual foreplay, I was aware that I had a social responsibility to the party upstairs. Before we got carried away with our passionate kisses, I whispered in my Valet's ear, reminding him that we should return to the party before too long.

When we got upstairs, Professor Andrew gave me a nudge to indicate that I should sit next to Hadrah Hakim, and I dutifully obeyed. The Hadrah was amusing and funny throughout the course of our conversation once we got to know each other a bit.

He asked, "Young, do you ride?"

"You mean horses?" I replied.

"What else do you ride besides horses?" the Hadrah joked. Before I could utter a reply, he continued. "At my ranch (one of several properties he owned), we breed Arabians. You and Andy should view my stallions and ride with me."

"Thank You, Sir! That would be wonderful. I would love to take you up on your offer. Maybe I will learn to ride other things, if you teach me," I answered, wittily.

Finding my remark amusing, he laughed. "We have a race coming up in a couple weeks in the Sahara. I'd love for you and Andy to attend. I'll make sure you receive formal invitations before the weekend is over. Maybe you can ride with me, if you care to join in the fun. It's always very festive. I think you'll like the event," he informed me.

"You'll be part of my entourage," he continued. "Now, my cute boy, go get ready for dinner and I'll see you soon." With those words, he pinched my cheeks, and retired to his Master Suite.

Dinner

The dinner, prepared by the Hadrah's private chef, was delightfully tasty. I was seated next to Habiibi Aziz, who was great company. By the time our formal dinner was over, we had become friends.

"I have taken up photography and I plan to take lots of pictures on this trip," said Aziz. "Tomorrow when we dock by

Shadwan, I'll take some pictures of you boys. There are some nice secluded beaches on the island," he continued.

"Wonderful!" I replied. "Are there any interesting snorkeling or dive sites off Shadwan?" I enquired.

"Oh Yes! I can take you snorkeling; the reefs are some of the most beautiful in the world. I plan to do some underwater photography when we go tomorrow morning," the handsome Arab said.

"We'll take the speed boat to shore. Wear your bathing suit and that should be enough. It's a very private island. Besides, we'll anchor on the side where road access is next to impossible. The beaches are pristine and very beautiful," said Aziz.

"What time are we departing, so I can be ready?"

"Let's make it 7:00 a.m. I like to catch the morning sun before it gets too hot," said Habiibi.

"Ok! I'll be ready. I'd like to see more of the Riviera. Will we be venturing to the towns?" I questioned.

"Sure! We want you guys to explore and enjoy your time with us," answered my host.

Teddy Bears

After dinner, our party sat on the comfortable open deck under the stars, and had a few drinks before retiring for a good night's rest. We wanted to be ready and refreshed, for the next morning's outing.

I returned to my cabin, alone. Andy was still above deck chatting. I found a pair of golden colored 'naughty' teddy bears in the center of the queen size bed. The larger bear's penis was immodestly stuck in the bottom of the smaller bear. In the arms of the copulating couple sat an envelope with an elegant gold brimmed card enclosed, which read:

I'll show you how to ride! Come to my chamber at 10:00 p.m. tomorrow evening,
H H

CHAPTER THIRTY-SIX

Cruising The Red Sea Riviera

"The magic of first love is our ignorance that it can ever end."
Benjamin Disraeli

Shadwan Island

Those in our party who wanted to travel to Shadwan met at 7:00 a.m. sharp, and boarded the speedboat to get to the beach. The Kahyya'm was docked off the coastline waiting for us to return at noon, before cruising to Marsa Alam, Al-Qusair and Shalateen. Franco, Tom, Andy, Aziz and I were adventurers, exploring the beaches and caves lining the deserted coastline. We left Professor Henderson and Hadrah Hakim on board the luxury yacht.

Shortly after we landed on the beach, Habiibi Aziz commenced photographing each of us, individually. The photo shoot started with us wearing our swimming trucks but soon they were discarded, since Aziz preferred to photograph us in the nude. As we were not shy, we stripped and posed naked for our young Arab host.

Tom was first on the list to be photographed, followed by Franco. While the boys were having their pictures taken, Andy and I decided to take a stroll along the beach rather than hang around and watch the photo session.

As we walked along the pristine white sand beach, Andy asked, "Why did you have me sleep on the single bed last night instead of inviting me to join you?"

I replied casually, "I'm not ready for you just yet."

"Why not?" he asked.

Being honest with my Valet, I answered, "I need a little time to gather myself before plunging into another relationship. It is difficult to jump into another person's arms when I haven't gotten over my last relationship."

"Am I sleeping on the single bed again tonight?" asked Andy.

"I don't know. Maybe, maybe not," I teased.

"Oh! I didn't get a chance to tell you I received an invitation from 'you know who' which I found when I arrived in our cabin last night. He asked me to meet him in his suite tonight. What shall I do?"

My Valet grinned, "That naughty guy! I should have known. I didn't expect you to be summonsed so quickly. I thought he would wait until you were in his Household before making his move."

"You mean I'm already assigned to his House without my knowledge?" I asked, surprised by Andy's news.

"My sweet boy, the moment you stepped onto the Kahyya'm you entered the Hadrah's service. That is why Professor Andrew introduced me as your Valet; my assignment was effective immediately," Andy said.

"Oh!" I said. "How should I handle this evening with him?" I looked to my Valet for advice.

"Use what you've learned at the Bahriji and you'll be able to handle the situation just fine. I want you to make your own decisions rather than me telling you what to do," replied Andy.

I asked, "How would you handle the situation?"

He laughed and said, "That is a trick question, you crafty little devil!"

We both broke up laughing and my Valet pinched me on my cheek. Just then, we heard Aziz calling Andy for the photo shoot. I was left sitting on a rock, staring into the Red Sea, looking for an answer to the question I had posed to my Valet.

In The Shower

After the photo shoot, Andy and I showered, as the Kahyya'm journeyed towards Marsa Alam. I turned my back towards him so he could help get the sand off of my back and buttocks. As the soapy water ran down my spine, so did his hands, until they reached and gently cupped my buttocks. Andy began to sensually rub and caress my butt cheeks. I couldn't resist such titillating sensations, so I leaned myself against him, surrendering to his loving touch. His soapy rub was too tantalizing. I couldn't pull away.

His manhood grew hard against my backside, as his beautiful masculine hands encircled my chest. He pinched my nipples, arousing them. He made me anticipate the delight that was to come.

Andy turned my head to the side and slid his tongue into my mouth; he proffered a lingering French kiss that I didn't want to ever end. Our wet bodies slid against each other as my Valet continued his sensual touch over my smoothness. Neither of us wanted the foreplay to end, yet our cocks begged for release.

Andy nibbled at my ear and whispered, unexpectedly, "My beautiful boy, you are not to release. I won't allow it. You have to save it for 'you know who.' That is part of the Household rules. When boys are summoned by their Master, they are not permitted to ejaculate before the visit so they'll be horny and wanting when the time is ripe. This way, your performance will not falter."

By now, my Valet had gotten me very excited with his caresses. I didn't want our union to stop. But we had to, and, reluctantly, we did.

I was glad we held back, because when Andy and I did finally consummate our love it was breathtaking. That unforgettable experience taught me that wonderful things are well worth the wait.

Marsa Alam

Marsa Alam was a good sized town with shops selling trinkets and locally made products. On this trip, Professor Andrew joined our group. Habiibi Aziz, Franco and Tom decided to go shopping and take more photographs while Andy, the professor and I sat in the shade at a cafeteria enjoying local delicacies, and Turkish coffee. My professor directed his question to me, "Are you enjoying the trip, Young?"

"Oh very much so! Everything is new and fresh. It's helping to take my mind off Nikee," I replied.

"Wonderful! I'm glad to hear that," said my teacher.

"How do you like your Valet?" Dr. Andrew looked at Andy with a grin on his face.

"He's OK! He can be a pain in the butt but I think I can put up with him. If he doesn't live up to being a responsible Valet, at least he's good to look at," I replied jokingly.

Andy chimed in teasingly, ruffling my hair, "This boy here received an offer from the boss, to visit his chamber tonight."

"Well, well, well! You are a fast worker, aren't you, boy?" My professor directed his reply to me.

I wasn't expecting Andy to tell the Professor the secret I had confided, and I felt somewhat embarrassed, going red in the face.

Dr. Andrew continued, "The Hadrad is quite charmed by you, Young. He finds you witty, and, judging from my conversations with him, he is quite smitten by you. Play your cards right and you'll go far, young man."

I plucked up my courage to ask my professor for his advice, "How do you suggest I play my cards, sir?"

Laughing, he said, "Do what your heart and inner voice tell you, and you'll not go wrong. Remember and apply what I taught you in class. It's time to put everything into practice." It seemed that no one could provide me with the 'actual' answers I was seeking.

The waiter brought out our dark, Turkish coffee. Taking a sip, I nearly choked on it. It was strong, thick and brown. I had to add lots of crème before I could continue drinking.

My night's adventure might well be like the cup of Turkish coffee; strong, thick and brown, with lots of cream!

PART FOUR

The KOSK Household, Tunisia, Florence, Venice, Tuscany

CHAPTER THIRTY-SEVEN

Seeing Clearly Now

"Whatever is in any way beautiful has its source of beauty in itself and is complete in itself."
Marcus Aurelius

Table Manners

Andy made sure I was clean, dressed in my best djellaba, and fresh as a lark before we proceeded to dine with our hosts and his guest. I felt great after a wonderfully relaxing day in the sun and plenty of sightseeing, as the Kahyya'm cruised to different towns and cities by the Red Sea. My gloom had lifted since boarding the yacht and I was looking forward to the adventure which would unfold that evening.

At dinner, I was seated next to the Hadrah at the head of the table, with Andy next to me. Professor Henderson was directly opposite us. Our delightful photographer, Habiibi Aziz, was at the end of the long table facing his father-in-law, with Tom and Franco on either side. The Abds brought out various delicious appetizing courses as dinner progressed.

I decided to take the opportunity to thank both my hosts for their kind invitation to cruise on the luxurious Kahyya'm. After we were formally seated and drinks were poured, I stood to propose a toast with my water glass to our delightful hosts and the guests.

"I'd like to take this opportunity to say thank you to Hadrah Hakim for being a wonderful host, inviting us on his beautiful Kahyya'm," I said, lifting my glass. Everyone clinked their glasses in unison and cheered the Hadrah, toasting our smiling host.

"I'd also like to propose another toast to Habiibi Aziz for taking beautiful photographs of us today, which I'm dying to see," I continued.

The merriment of the evening began delightfully, with the guests cheering and toasting. Dr. Andrew glanced over at me and smiled. I could see the sparkling glimmer in his approving eyes, appreciating the effort I had taken to ensure that the party got off to a good start.

Over dinner, Hadrah Hakim leaned over and whispered, "Do you like the present I sent to your room?"

I nodded and whispered back, "Yes, very much so. Thank you, Sir!" My Master seemed pleased, smiled, and turned to the professor, initiating a conversation, in Arabic with him.

By the time we adjourned to the upper deck for deserts and beverages it was nearly 9:00 p.m. I needed some alone time, so I excused myself from the group. Standing on the viewing deck of the Kahyya'm, looking out at twinkling lights illuminating ancient cities, I could not help but contemplate the beauty of everything around me. My life had taken such a drastic turn; so much had happened within a short span of time. Within an hour, I would be venturing into the Hadrah's private chambers. What was I to say, and what was expected of me, I wondered?

Deep in thought, I felt a strong masculine hand touching my shoulder. I knew instantly that it was Andy. I could smell his manly scent a mile away. I didn't have to turn around to acknowledge Andy. I knew he was present, making sure I was all right. Beyond that, he understood the fear of the unknown which was running through my head. His presence was most assuring; he reminded me that he would be close if I needed him.

We didn't utter a word the entire time we were together on the viewing deck. The courage I needed for my adventure was standing right behind me, protecting and guiding me. Leaning against me, he gave me a gentle kiss on my forehead before we descended the stairs to Hadrah Hakim's suite.

In The Chambers

I knocked, and a voice behind the sliding doors responded, "The doors are unlocked; come in." Pushing the doors apart, I entered. A delightful scent of sandalwood filled my nostrils as I saw my Master standing, viewing renderings of the renovations for his yacht, which were spread across a desk.

"Close the doors and come over, Young. I want to show you some designs. I plan to remodel the Kahyya'm. My design team has come up with these," he said, pointing to the architectural drawings.

Closing the door behind me, I went over to Hadrah Hakim. He continued, "The Professor mentioned that you are good in art and design. Give me your opinion of these designs," he told me.

I studied the blue prints and answered, "Sir, these are very well drawn, but where is the swimming pool? I don't see a pool in these sketches?"

"You're right! I didn't notice the missing pool. Thanks for pointing that out. Where would you put it if you were designing the boat?" Hakim asked.

"I'm no yacht designer, but if I were to design a new version of the Kahyya'm, I would extend a pool out, just above the ocean. Perhaps I would create one which could be cantilevered off of the yacht's lower body when the boat is stationary. When the boat is in motion, the concealed pool could be electronically controlled to slide into the body of the yacht. If the pool were designed as an optional extension of the vessel, it would maximize your utilization of space. Instead of chlorinated water, pool users would swim and bath in natural sea water, which is much better for the skin, and they would enjoy a natural ocean setting with safe perimeters." I recommended my idea to my Master.

"What clever thinking! Would you be interested in doing some rough idea sketches so you can explain it to my designers?" he asked.

"Sure! I'd love that. When I return to the Bahriji tomorrow afternoon, I will get right on it! Can I show my work to you later in the week?" I replied.

"That'll be splendid! You can show me when you and Andy come to The Kosk (a term Hadrad Hakim used to refer to his mansion)," replied my delighted host.

We discussed at length the design of his new boat as the night wore on. As we got to know each other better, I found that I really enjoyed the company of this educated and charming man. He wasn't as serious as he had seemed when we first met. At times, I would break down laughing at his funny one-liner jokes.

Hakim was a serious art collector, so we discussed the various styles and schools of Art and Architecture. I told him I loved the Ottoman architectural style and design. He said he would introduce me to one of his sons, who was currently enrolled in an Irish architectural college. He would be returning to the Kosk in a couple of weeks, the Hadrah said, during his college break.

We chatted late into the night. The Hadrah casually mentioned, "Why did you come to my room this evening?" Surprised by the question, I answered, "You asked for me, did you not? I received an elegant note on the teddy bears you sent to my room, bearing the initials H. H."

Hakim broke out in roaring laughter, "That naughty son-in-law of mine! The note and the bears you received must be from him. Did you look next to the initials? If you had, you would have seen a small, embossed crest in purple and gold, with his name, Aziz Haashim. That is the Habiibi's full name. He always uses H. H. when he signs his name, which stands for Habiibi Haashim. That is not me!" He continued laughing, as if the mix up was the funniest thing in the world!

His laughter was contagious, and I, too, broke down laughing due to my oversight. Apparently, I did not read the note carefully. Now that the Hadrad had mentioned the crest, I did remember seeing it beside the initials H. H. I hadn't shown the card to anyone else; I just automatically assumed H. H. stood for Hadrad Hakim.

My host laughed so hard, tears were rolling down his cheeks. When his laughter finally subsided, Hakim said, "I like you very much Young. You are so funny! But I also like you because you are so sweet and innocent. You have this beautiful sense of looking at the world with such child-like openness."

"The people I usually deal with are very serious. But when I am in the presence of boys from the Bahriji, I can relax and be myself. But most boys are not as witty as you are. I mentioned to Andrew that I like you and I'd like to see more of you. Both in and out of your clothes," he added.

"Now, pretty boy, stand in front of me and let me see all of you," commanded my Master.

I obeyed and stood in front of him. His six foot tall frame towered over me, as we embraced. He squeezed me tightly. The scent of sandalwood cologne emanating from his bearded chin intoxicated me. Since I had not had an orgasm for a couple of days, my cock became hard immediately when we touch. I felt his hardness under his thawb.

Hakim held me for a long time before releasing his grip. "Take off your djellaba and move for me; show me your beautiful body."

I did as I was told. Hakim continued, "Pose for me; I want to see every angle of your handsome self."

I posed just like I did when I was auditioning for the Ernest Haas photo shoot, showing the Hadrad every inch of my youthfulness. Mesmerized by the sight before him, my Master pulled up his thawb and began jerking his manhood while watching me perform a slow dance.

By the time I left my Master's chamber, it was past one in the morning. I found my handsome Valet sleeping on a comfortable couch next to the Hadrah's bedroom entrance. Dearest Andy had been waiting for me for the past three hours, ensuring that no harm came to me, and that I was safe. I reached over and kissed his forehead lovingly. Hand in hand, we retired to our cabin for the night.

By my bedside table was an elegant tonneau-shaped platinum case, which had been delivered to my room by an Abd earlier that evening. On the case, engraved in dark silver was the label Patek Philippe. The card next to it read,

"With Love & Adoration!"
Hadrah Hakim.

CHAPTER THIRTY-EIGHT

Is It An Empty Experience?

*"Sex without love is an empty experience,
but as empty experiences go, it's one of the best."*
Bernard Tristan Foong

At Breakfast

The following morning, I didn't wake until 10:00 a.m. Andy had already disappeared upstairs for breakfast without waking me. Being a responsible valet, upon returning to our chamber the night before, he had tucked me into the queen and he slept in the single. As much as I had enjoyed my time with the Hadrah, I was chaste throughout my performance. It seemed important to pleasure my host rather than myself. Besides, he did not request that I do so. I was obedient. In truth, I wanted to save myself for Andy, especially after our sensual tantric shower.

This morning, I would have to apologize to my other host, Habiibi Aziz Haashim, for not showing up at the time I was requested to appear. After I washed and dressed, I proceeded upstairs to locate Andy and the rest of our party.

Who should I find sitting alone in the dining room but Aziz, reading the Arabic morning papers, and drinking a cup of strong black coffee. One of the Abds asked if I wanted breakfast. I was ravaged by hunger, and I eagerly accepted the Abd's offer. Off he trotted, to request that the chef prepare a light morning meal to quiet my rumbling stomach.

I took the opportunity to greet the Habiibi, who was overtly polite, and greeted me, in return, with a rather chilly 'Good Morning.'

"I'm so sorry about last evening. I made a mistake, thinking your request was from the Hadrah. I will make it up to you in any way possible, although, I'll be returning to the Bahriji late this afternoon," I stammered, nervously.

Aziz looked up from his newspaper. His pleasantness vanished and he said, sulking, "Meet me at my cabin at 1:00 p.m. with Andy. I'd like both of you to do something for me."

"I haven't seen Andy this morning. As soon as I locate him, I'll inform him. I promise I will appear, with Andy, in your cabin. Once again I'm sorry about the mix-up last evening," I replied, embarrassed and chagrined.

The Abd brought my breakfast. The conversation with Aziz terminated with his announcement that he was going for a morning swim in the sea. The Kahyya'm was anchored off the shores of Nuweibi.

Above Deck

After breakfast, I found Andy and the rest of the Bahriji gang sun bathing on the open deck. I went and sat beside Andy. Before my Valet uttered a word, I told him about last night's mix-up and mentioned that I had apologized to Aziz.

Andy laughed and said, "What happened in the Hadrah's chambers last night? Tell me everything. Did he treat you well?"

I smiled and nodded, "Yes! He was fine and very appreciative. A gift from him was on my bedside table when we returned to the cabin last night. We were both sleepy so I didn't show it to you."

"What did he give you?" Andy questioned.

"I'm not telling you," I jokingly replied.

My Valet started tickling me, trying to make me tell him what the present was. He continued to tickle me until I was squirming and giggling from our childish play. I was getting very aroused while Andy tickled away relentlessly, trying to get the information from me. His hand reached, playfully, into my djellaba and he began jerking my already erect penis while I desperately wiggled and squirmed beneath him, doing my best to avoid his probing hand. We were laughing so hard and loud that our professor came over to quiet us down.

"Hey boys! Boys! Stop mucking around. There are other people on board. You boys behave!" he said amusingly.

Andy paused reluctantly, while I did my best to compose myself, smoothing down my djellaba, which had been pushed up to my upper thighs during our love play.

"Hakim gave me a Patek Philippe watch."

Andy stopped his laughing and replied in a serious tone of voice, "He gave you a Patek Philippe?"

"Yes! He did. It's just a watch," I responded nonchalantly.

Andy was silent for a moment and then responded. "Do you know a Patek Philippe is a rare collectors' watch and is very expensive?" He looked at me, inquiringly.

At that age, I sure as hell didn't know the difference between various brands of watches. I was not a watch connoisseur; how would I know what a valuable watch a Patek Philippe Chronometro Gondolo was? I didn't know the difference between a Patek Phillipe and a Mickey Mouse watch! To me, a watch was a watch and its function was to tell the time, not be a status symbol.

"I see! In that case, can you deposit this precious gift into my safety deposit box, my dear Valet?" I asked, breezily. I acted like it was an everyday occurrence to be given such an expensive gift, by the Hadrah.

In truth, I was delighted by Andy's information. It must be true that the Hadrah found me to be special. My guardian said, "Show it to me when we get back to the cabin. Let me look at it."

"Ok! Ok! By the way, I'm to let you know, we have been summoned by the Habiibi to go his room at 1:00 p.m. He said he wants us to do something for him," I mentioned.

Andy gave me a sly smile and said, "I know. I spoke to him this morning before you were up. We are going to punish you for being negligent last night. You had better obey and do as we command!"

I laughed and replied jokingly, "Yes Sir! 'Big Brother'! Your wish is my command!" I gave my Valet a salute.

After a little sun bathing and a light lunch of fruits and watermelon juice above deck, Andy and I descended to our cabin to prepare to meet Habiibi Aziz Hashim.

Below Deck

At precisely 1:00 p.m., I knocked on the Habiibi's cabin door. No reply. I knocked again. No answer. Andy, standing next to me, gently slid the bedroom door open. We could hear the shower running, in the bathroom.

Andy said, "Let's go in and wait."

I followed my Valet and we slipped inside. A voice from behind the glass shower doors called, "Come in, close the cabin doors and lock them behind you."

Andy did as he was told and the voice continued, "Have Young come in. I'd like him to help me scrub my back."

I looked to Andy, to know how to best respond to the request. My protector gave me a wink, nodding his head towards the direction of the voice, directing me to do as I was told.

Is It An Empty Experience?

My Valet whispered softly into my ear, "Take off your clothes and go. Leave your jockstrap on."

I did as my guardian commanded. Sliding open the bathroom door, I ventured in. The large room was as steamy as a Turkish bath. I could not see in front of me. Before I could get my bearings, a hand reached out from behind me, cupping my mouth, so that I couldn't scream. The voice whispered in my ear, "Don't struggle, I will not harm you. Just do as I say!"

I did as I was told. A wet piece of muslin was strapped across my eyes. I could feel the naked body of my captor rubbing me from behind, as he tightened the blindfold. His erect cock was sliding against my derriere. Feeling terribly excited and aroused by these unchartered paths, my cock jumped to attention, straining against my under garment for release.

As soon as the blindfold was secured, my captor turned me around and kissed me on my mouth. I could feel him rubbing against the fabric of my jock. His neatly trimmed beard brushed against the softness of my skin while hungry kisses filled our lustful souls with forceful desires. The steamy sensuality was too tantalizing for my organ to remain in constraints; it was desperately forcing its way out of my jockstrap. It wanted to be released; it needed attention, and my abductor was delighted to provide.

I heard the glass door open and instantly, I realized my guardian angel had stepped in. Was he sweeping me away from the passionate sensuality that I did not want to end? Was this my punishment? More unreleased sexual tension? My handsome angel Andy and my sexy, strong captor were both hungering to taste forbidden fruits in this opulent pleasure dome, the Kahyya'm.

I longed to continue to be held captive, to be a slave to their every desire. I begged for this dangerous game to last forever! And last it did, for three enticing hours. The exquisite tension built until we united our cores, creating a oneness of Being. Since I had not released for three days I was extremely horny. I responded to every sensual caress and stroke.

By the time Andy and I left the Habiibi's chamber, my abductor had snapped numerous explicit photographs of Andy and me in the throes of our sexual ecstasy. That was the 'something' my captor mentioned earlier, during breakfast, which he wanted Andy and me to do for him.

My angelic protector was happy to oblige our kinky Arabian host. My submission was rewarded with plenty of fireworks and deliciously enticing explosions from all parties involved!

It was definitely a splendid ending to my fun-filled weekend on board the Kahyya'm. It was a weekend I would never forget for the rest of my life.

"Sex Without Love is An Empty Experience?" Whatever would have made me think that!

CHAPTER THIRTY-NINE

This Thing Called Love

Immature love says: "I love you because I need you.
"Mature love says: "I need you because I love you."
Erich Fromm

By the time our helicopter landed at the school it was close to dinnertime. As I unpacked my overnight bag, I discovered two envelopes addressed to me, in the side pocket. The turquoise envelope contained a quirky card with two illustrations of rabbits, on the cover.

A blindfolded bunny was standing on his hind legs with his front paws tied behind a tree. The other rabbit, on all fours, was munching on an erect carrot which jutted out from the groin of the bound animal. On the inside of the card, a third bunny was sniffing the rear end of the munching rabbit. The card read: "Thank You for a Fantastic Time! Let's do it again! And Again & Again!" H.H.

Two folded pieces of paper fell on the floor, as I opened the card. Picking up the papers, I discovered two cheques for the amount of $2,000.00, each. One cheque was made out to me and the other was Andy's. Aziz Haashim's signature was on both cheques. I was taken completely by surprise and felt rather flabbergasted. No one had ever given me so much money before, not even my own parents. $2,000.00 was a lot of money in those days.

A Love Proposal

I showed our cheques to Andy and he responded, "I'll deposit these into our respective Swiss accounts, along with your watch."

I was extremely grateful to my Valet for being such a considerate person. I could not help but give my BB a hug. We held each other tightly. Putting my head on his muscular chest, I leaned against his tall frame and looked up at him. His beautiful green eyes stared back at me. There was a contented smile on his face. Leaning down, he kissed me sweetly. We just stood for a long while, embracing, with an understanding that required no words.

I didn't want to let go, and neither did he. Finally, he spoke softly into my ear, "I love you more than you'll ever know."

I did not respond to his comment. I didn't know how.

"I'll be by your side, making sure you are safe, my dearest boy," Andy spoke softly.

"Thank you for being such a wonderful Valet. You are the best!" I finally said.

My BB answered, "I want to be your lover, and not just your Valet -- to truly love you with all my heart."

I was surprised by that remark. I didn't expect Andy to profess his love for me, beyond just loving me like a responsible Valet. Nikee told me often enough not to fall in love. Now, my protector is telling me he loves me and that he is my lover? The one thing I desired most in my life was for someone special to love me in return and it was actually manifesting in reality! I couldn't believe what I was hearing! And I dared not believe what I was being told.

Love, as I knew it, was too painful. I dared not venture back into that realm. I was too afraid of the consequences of having my heart shattered again. Looking him in the eyes, I inquired, "Did I hear you correctly? Did you just tell me that you want to be my lover?"

Andy laughed heartily and kissed me deeply, not releasing his hold, as if he was afraid I would turn, run and not return.

Staring at me without blinking he continued, "Yes, Young! I want to be your lover and have a loving relationship with you. Beyond being your Valet, I want you as a partner whom you can rely on and call upon. I am here for you through thick and thin. Will you do the same for me?" Caught speechless and confused I kept silent. A few minutes passed. I could not think of any reply.

Finally I was able to answer him. "Yes! I want to do the same for you and with you, too. I've always longed for you to tell me you love me. But, I'm a novice at this Love Game. I am afraid! I don't understand this 'thing' call Love. The last time I was in love with Nikee, I had my heart broken. I'm scared to re-enter this dangerous territory. I don't want to get hurt again."

Andy laughed! Turning to me, he said, reassuringly, "Of course my dearest darling boy, I know how you feel. I want to share everything I know about love with you." Jokingly, he gave me a light slap on my buttocks and said, "Lesson one in love: Go get your bubble butt ready for dinner. I'm starving. Let's go eat!"

With that remark, he released our embrace and we went to dinner at the canteen. I promptly forgot to open the other envelope that was left in the side pocket of my overnight bag.

I was the happiest boy on campus from that moment on. I had a delightfully handsome and kind lover whom I could call my very own. At last, this 'thing' called Love had found me, when I least expected it. It is true: "you can't hurry love." Love certainly doesn't come easy and it is a game of give and take.

This Thing Called LOVE!

After dinner, while the evening sun was lowering its sleepy head over the arrestingly beautiful desert landscape, Andy and I took a stroll to the top of the grotto, in 'The Hanging Gardens of Babylon.' We sat on a bench overlooking the wide undisturbed expanse of sand, contemplating the sound of silence. I was blissfully happy to be with my handsome Valet and protector.

I broke the peaceful tranquility and asked, "What is Love?"

Andy turned, looked into my dreamy eyes, and said, "Love, my dear fellow, is primarily giving and not receiving. Giving is the highest good, Young."

A puzzled look came over my face and I continued to inquire, "Isn't love a two way street?"

"Giving is more joyous than receiving," Andy answered. "Through giving, we feel the most alive."

"Don't giving and receiving happen simultaneously?"

He responded, "True love is all about giving without expecting anything in return. You see, Young, whoever is capable of giving himself, is rich, because he confers the most precious gift he has; he gives his life. He gives his joy, his interests, his understanding, his knowledge, his humor, his sadness; he gives all of the expressions and manifestations of that which is truly alive in him."

"That is a huge responsibility," I said.

A beautiful smile crossed Andy's face as he touched his finger to the tip of my nose. "I care a lot about you, my dearest boy! Care and concern are other aspects of love. But responsibility to another, since you ask, is an entirely voluntary act."

"But you are already responsible for me, since you are my Valet. Does that mean you took this position because you love me?" I was curious to know Andy's answer.

My lover responded, "Love could easily deteriorate into domination and possessiveness, were it not for a third element of love, respect. Respect is not fear or awe; it is the ability to see a person as he is; it is to be aware of his unique individuality, and to honor that, rather than trying to change that person. Young, I respect you."

"Respect entails the desire for the other person to grow and unfold. Respect implies the absence of exploitation. I want you to grow and unfold for your own sake, and not for purposes which serve me.

"I love you and I feel as one with you; I do not need you to be an object for my use. Respect exists only on the basis of freedom, for love is the child of freedom, never of domination."

"Wow! That's a lot to take in. I am curious to learn more," I said, perplexed by his profundity.

Andy said, with love in his voice, "To respect a person is not possible without knowledge of one. There are many layers of knowledge. Knowledge, an aspect of love, does not stay at the periphery, but penetrates to the core. Intimate knowledge must be guided by care and responsibility. Knowledge would be empty if it were not motivated by compassion. It is only possible when one transcends self and sees the other person on his own terms."

"Responsibility, respect and knowledge are interdependent."

I leaned against my protector and asked, "So, was my being in love with Nikee, immature love? It didn't have the components you've just mentioned."

He laughed and answered, "In a way, yes! My darling boy! But you are young and have much to learn.

"Mature love is union which preserves one's integrity, one's individuality. In love the paradox is that two beings become one and yet their individuality remains intact."

"I know that was a lot to take in, in an evening. It's dark; we better get to bed. You have class tomorrow."

We walked back to our dorm room, hand in hand. Josef and Thomas had been relocated to a Household, leaving Andy and me the room to ourselves.

Tonight, I was ready to invite my lover to share my bed.

CHAPTER FORTY

Orgasmic Interlude

"Electric flesh-arrows...traversing the body. A rainbow of color strikes the eyelids. A foam of music falls over the ears. It is the gong of the orgasm."
Anais Nin

Thank-You Notes

The next day, after our return from the Red Sea Riviera, Professor Henderson inquired if I had written thank-you notes to Hadrah Hakim and Habiibi Aziz Haashim. I mentioned that I had not, but would do so as soon as possible, since it was polite to thank our hosts for a delightful time on the Riviera cruise.

As soon as I returned to my room after class, I picked up my pen and drawing materials to create personalized cards for each of my hosts. I sketched an idea for the new design of the Kahyya'm, for the Hadrah's card. I also enclosed sketches, suggesting more remodeling ideas for the yacht. I wrote: "Thank you for the enjoyable weekend, and the generous gift. Our conversation was most enlightening. It was my pleasure to be of service to you. Respectfully, Young."

I asked Andy for a photograph of Haashim which he had snapped during our three way rendezvous. I used it to create the thank you note to Habiibi Aziz. With a black magic marker, I blackened the area across Aziz's eyes. At the back of the photograph I wrote: "The next time, I'll be returning the favor! Thank you for an enchanting afternoon, and your generosity! Young & Andy."

I sealed each card in a separate envelope and handed them to Professor Andrew, to forward to our hosts. Andy and I left for our three month assignment at Hadrah Hakim's Household a week and half later.

Tantric Sex

The final class before we were officially sent to the Households was the "Art of Tantric Sex." Professor Henderson explained the theory behind this practice. Each boy was free to select his own partner to work with on the practical. I chose Andy!

In class, Dr. Henderson explained, "Tantra began as an Eastern practice; as the art became popularized in the West it underwent major transformations. In contemporary Western society, 'Tantra' has become synonymous with 'sacred sexuality,' heralding the vantage point that sex is capable of elevating its participants to a sublime spiritual plane. Though Tantra may adopt many of the concepts and terminology from Vajrayana, or Tantric Buddhism, it often omits one or more of the following: the traditional reliance on guruparampara (the guidance of a guru,) extensive meditative practice, and traditional rules of conduct - both moral and ritualistic."

The professor continued, "Tantric practices were introduced into western culture in the 1800s; Tantra's popularity has escalated, since then. Its essential nature as a spiritual practice is often overlooked. When people mention Tantra they are generally referring to the sexual practices.

"In Tantra, one objective is learning to experience subtle energies. Accessing these energies works to both enhance pleasure and also to challenge the ego, with the penultimate goal of its dissolution.

I couldn't wait for the Doctor to finish, and asked impatiently, "Does that mean I have to meditate before each sexual experience to practice Tantra?"

The professor answered, "Let me finish what I have to say and you will have a clearer picture."

"As I was saying, Tantra cultivates ecstatic consciousness as well as increased spiritual awareness of one's erotic nature. Tantric sexual methods may be practiced solo, in partnership, or in sacred ritual groups. The specifics of these methods have been kept secret, passed down to students deemed worthy, in an oral tradition."

"It must be remembered that in genuine Tantric spiritual practice, sexuality is merely one aspect of a comprehensive spiritual path; the sexual and erotic aspects of Tantra cannot be authentically engaged in without adequate preparation and discipline. Meditation. Yes, to answer your question, Young."

One of the boys, Ka, asked, "Can I practice this during orgies?" The class broke up laughing!

Our professor smiled and said, "I'm sure you can try. Let me know if you succeed."

He continued his lecture, "In summation, Tantric sexuality is just one dimension of a spiritual path that is devoted and dedicated to the challenge of becoming aware, in every moment of our embodied lives, of the Supreme flow of the sacred life force. It can manifest itself through the Sacred Unity of Love."

One of the boys, Jack, asked, "What does that mean, the Sacred Unity of Love?"

Our professor continued, "In Vajrayana Buddhism, Tantric sexual practice, which in Sanskrit is called, Maithuna, is an important aspect of the final stage of the initiate's spiritual path, during which he or she, having already realized the void in all things, attains enlightenment and perpetual bliss."

I raised my hand and asked the professor, "Does that mean that Tantric Sex itself is a form of meditation, if it is part of a spiritual path?"

He answered, "The true use of Tantric Sex is in accessing and activating our energy body, which raises the vibrations of the physical body."

"With an increased vibration, the physical body becomes extremely healthy. As the chakras clear, there is an attendant cleansing of all organs, glands and the central nervous system. The raising of vibration also clears one of negative conditioning from the past."

"Societal rules, more often than not, separate people from their sexuality, leaving much emotional trauma. Due to this, we become cut off from an infinite Source of power, creativity and expression."

I continued asking questions, "Does that mean if I practice Tantric Sex all the time, I will be in perpetual bliss and enlightened?"

The class broke up in roaring laughter, as did the doctor. Professor Andrew replied, "Young, that's a good question! Class, stop laughing and let me explain. Due to sexual and emotional blockages most people do not have the opportunity to cultivate their sexual energy.

"The ordinary male must ejaculate often, or he will become totally preoccupied with sex, frustrated and irritable."

Peter queried, "Does that mean masturbation is good for us, if we don't have sex frequently?"

Dr. Andrew replied, "Yes and no. There are myriad possibilities for expanding consciousness when we prevent the loss of sexual energy."

"The built up energy may, if one practices Tantra, lead to an orgasm lasting for hours. In regular sex, a male experiences a rush of orgasmic sensations through the end of the penis. The amount of sexual energy released, which causes these feelings, is not enough to manifest a full body orgasm. For a full body orgasm to occur, the entire meridian system must be activated, through the cultivation and circulation of sexual energy. This takes time and practice. As you practice, blockages will be cleared and you will be able to build and store much more sexual energy. These far greater stores will be available to release into the meridians during sex, causing some very intense full body orgasms which can continue for a very long time with no ejaculation.

"However, to achieve this, energy blockages from emotional issues from the past must first be cleared. If not, the increase in sexual energies, the kundalini rising, can result in negative states being magnified."

Logan chimed in, "How long do we have to practice Tantric Sex before we have those kinds of orgasms?"

Our teacher continued, "I don't have a definitive answer to your question. Typically, men and women do not cultivate their sexual energy because to do so involves confronting and clearing painful emotional issues from their past. Many who start on the Tantric path give up. This Western's version of Tantra rarely provides enough information on the steps required to clear all energetic and emotional blockages."

"The average person strives for homeostasis; they tend to lose a certain amount of sexual energy and regenerate the same amount of sexual energy they have lost. This stasis maintains the status quo; they become comfortable not being confronted with potent, fresh emotions, negative or positive. Just imagine if all this energy was retained and recirculated instead of being lost through ejaculation. Your energy supply would just keep on expanding."

I continued asking, "How often and for how long do I have to practice before I can achieve better orgasms through this state of consciousness?"

My teacher responded, "Most people think their orgasms are pretty awesome, already. These people haven't been exposed to anything greater. It does take time and practice to achieve greater experiences, but once you have experienced them, you won't want to go back."

"As you progress, you will begin to realize that the possibilities are infinite. The results of proper Tantric practice, which can be done alone or with a partner, are, indeed, far above and beyond just better sex!"

I enquired further, "Is it best to do Tantric practices with somebody I truly love, to achieve heightened states of consciousness?"

Professor Henderson replied, "It will definitely help to practice this with a lover with whom you are truly connected, since you will be circulating and blending sexual energy with this person. Practicing this with one you have already achieved deep intimacy with will definitely help."

"Does this mean I will have multiple orgasms through the Art of Tantric Sex?" I asked, eagerly.

"The feeling of orgasm is the feeling of sexual energy being released; we can actually feel sexual energy, a non-physical substance."

Jack interupted, "How do I clear blockages from my body so I can begin practicing Tantra?"

"Well!" Our tutor continued, "All sexual problems such as impotence, premature ejaculation, lack of libido, frigidity, and problems with self-expression are related to emotional issues associated with our sexuality, according to Freud."

"The repression of sexuality leads to many negative states and imbalances. There are temporary fixes on the market for such problems, from pharmaceuticals to therapies, but most of these are not cures. The only cure for most blockages is a clearing of the emotional and energetic bodies. To do this, Jack, you must begin to cultivate sexual energy; stop its loss and bring awareness to the way it circulates throughout your body and your consciousness. And pay attention to feelings which arise. Be fearless and open, allowing yourself to be informed of your issues through introspection."

Since no students raised their hands to ask further questions, the professor continued, "When we do begin to clear the blockages, cultivate our sexual energy, and raise our vibration, many amazing things may be realized. Tantric Sex has been called Sex Magic; it is the basis for true inner alchemy which can awaken your multidimensional awareness, memory of past lives, even incarnations in other dimensions. Tapping into these higher dimensional forces can free one from all the trappings of the earthly ego and from all illusions, or maya. I encourage you boys to cultivate your sexual energy, to awaken the Kundalini and begin to raise it from the base chakra through the central nervous system, connecting it to your higher Self."

I jokingly said, "Should I perform Tantric Sex day in and day out?"

The entire group laughed at my joke before Dr. Henderson laughingly responded, "It is definitely easier to achieve this state of consciousness when you practice. A lot! Don't expect it to happen overnight."

The good Doctor ended the class by saying, "All emotional issues would begin to be cleared and you could free yourself from all past conditioning. Full body orgasms are only the beginning of the ecstasies and bliss possible through real Tantra. An orgasm in which all boundaries dissolve and partners merge with each other and with their higher selves can occur. At these higher stages of Tantric Sex, experience truly defies description," replied our sex expert educator.

For the remaining four years with Andy, we practiced the Art of Tantric Sexuality, regularly.

CHAPTER FORTY-ONE

The Sahara

"Seize the moments of happiness, love and be loved! That is the only reality in the world, all else is folly."
Leo Tolstoy

Invitation

The Friday before Andy and I were to leave for our three months assignment at Hadrad Hakim's Household, I took out my overnight bag to commence packing. What should I find but the envelope I had left unopened stuffed in the side pocket of my bag! My Abd, who had assisted me in unpacking, had stored my luggage away. I had forgotten about the note. The envelope contained an elegant invitation from the Hadrad requesting that Andy and I join his entourage to The Sahara Festival of Douz. The festivities would begin the next day, Saturday, in Douz, Tunisia, at 9:00 a.m. in the morning. It was already late Friday afternoon when I discovered the invite. I immediately showed the card to Andy who rushed to Dr. Henderson, to see what could be done.

Professor Andrew read the invite and said, "I will consult with Hadrad Hakim immediately."

Andy and I stood waiting while Dr. Andrew spoke in Arabic with Hakim. When my teacher lowered the receiver he looked at us and said, "Young and Andy, go pack your bags immediately. The Hadrah is sending his private helicopter to collect you in an hour. He will fly both of you to Dubai airport to board his private jet to Douz. At Douz, his car will be waiting at the airfield. You will be driven to the Sahara Douz Hotel where you'll be staying for four days, during the festivities. Hakim will make arrangements to meet the two of you and his other guests at the hotel after your arrival."

Andy and I were very excited and started to leave but he stopped us. "Andy, Young, Make sure you pack all you require for your three month stay at Kosk (Hadrah Hakim's residence.) You'll be transported to his lodgings when the Sahara festivities are over. Good luck boys, and have fun! I know you will do a great job."

On that happy note, we left our teacher's office and went straight to our room to prepare for our journey.

Douz, Tunisia

By the time we were in the air, leaving the Oasis, the beautiful orange sun was slipping below the desert horizon in a hazy golden glow reminiscent of a tangerine dream. I sat admiring the beauty of the scenery with Andy, my beloved Valet, at my side. I suddenly remembered what Nikee said before he left the Bahriji.

"Young, there is someone out there who will return the love you are willing to give," he had told me.

And that somebody was Andy, my considerate, kind hearted and good looking Valet. "I am indeed a blessed soul living in this blessed world," I thought. At that moment I was transported into an orgasmic serenity, without having to lose a drop of semen. "Is this Tantric Sexuality?" I wondered. "A joyful heavenly state of blissful consciousness? Had I achieved Nirvana?"

The Simorgh

Hakim's private jet was indeed a luxurious design marvel. It resembled an upscale, sophisticated office, yet it was as comfortable as a bedroom space or living area in an opulent home. With the push of a button, one large room in the interior of this commercial jet liner could be partitioned off, creating a private bedchamber. The soundproof doors provided complete privacy; there was no disturbance, even to the discerning ear.

Douz, Tunisia

By the time we landed at a small private airfield in Douz, it was already nightfall. A chauffeured gold Bentley collected Andy and me, driving us to the Douz Sahara Hotel, the most luxurious accommodation in the Douz vicinity, in 1966. The Hadrah had left a note at the concierge desk informing us to meet him and his group at the lobby the next morning at 7:30 a.m. We would be driven to the festival site with his Lordship in a caravan of open top jeeps.

It was close to midnight when we checked into our five star hotel room. I was exhausted, yet filled with child-like excitement. My experiences had been so fresh, so new and tremendously exciting! I craved to learn more of everything Sahara as the days unfolded. I had a wonderful lover who loved me unceasingly, and a life that promised to deliver all I had wished for!

First Day at the Sahara Festival of Douz

I slept well that night with Andy cuddling me in a safe, peaceful embrace. After a hearty breakfast at the hotel's restaurant I was ready to rock and roll. At exactly 7:30 a.m., Hadrah Hakim appeared, along with an entourage of foreign guests and Household members. This time, my host greeted me warmly with a handshake instead of the bear hug he offered on the Kahyya'm. We proceeded into the Sahara in three separate overland vehicles.

Before long distant noises were heard; drumming musicians and trumpeters blowing their horns filling the once-silent desert air with the vibrancy of a magic carnival. The sounds of neighing horses, rearing and galloping, mingled with the snorts of camels as they appeared on the sandy horizon. Nomadic caravans were arriving from all directions onto the desert scape. It was a splendid sight and a once-in-a-lifetime experience.

Numerous tents were erected around the festival arena. A gigantic stage was arranged, under one canvas covering. It was especially set up for the festival's VIPs. The Hadrah's entourage was ushered to a lavish, red and gold cushioned seating area. Andy and I sat directly behind Hadrah Hakim, our host.

At 9:00 a.m. sharp, a banging gong announced the arrival of a well-known Sheik. He took his place of honor on the stage, then approached the podium to give a welcome speech, in Arabic, before the festivities came to life. After he finished his brief message he announced, with great flair, the official opening of the festival. Musicians began drumming. The emcee took the microphone to inform the audience about a poetry-reading contest including some of the best poets from Tunisia and its sister countries. The topic was "Our youth, and the inculcation of National values."

After the hour and a half long poetry reading session there were photographic exhibits at the cultural house and an Islamic book fair. The Arabic calligraphy competitors were introduced, before the winners took center stage to receive their various awards. The fair grounds were littered with vendors' products from spices, potteries, and rugs to various nomad-made trinkets and knick-knacks.

Our host left his guests shortly after the poetry reading competition, informing us that tomorrow would be the horse racing competitions between various Bedouin tribes. By the time Andy and I finished walking round the festival grounds and checking out the various stalls and exhibitions, we were exhausted, and ready to retire to our hotel for dinner.

Professor Ludwig Abid Safar

One of Hakim's guests was an Arabian German gentleman by the name of Ludwig Abid Safar. He was travelling alone. He had met the Hadrah during one of the Hadrah's business trips to the German city of Dusseldorf. Mr. Safar was an Arabic literature professor at a German university. Andy struck up a conversation with him at the festival. Soon the three of us were hanging out together. By the end of the second day of festivities, we were inseparable. I took a liking to Ludwig, initially, because Andy liked him. He was a humorous and educated man. A delightful smile warmed his handsome, twenty six-year-old face.

Ludwig Abid Safar was descended from a Bedouin tribal leader. He was granted the privilege of pursuing higher education in Germany. Dressed in Bedouin gear from head to toe, he could easily have passed as one of the competing horseman in the parade. As a child, he grew up riding with his tribesmen. He rode with great aplomb, and was, indeed, one of the competitors in the races the following day.

Ludwig joined Andy and me for dinner, where he proceeded to tell us how exciting the following day would be, with horse and camel racing events. Abid asked if Andy and I rode, to which we simultaneously replied, "Yes, we do!"

At the time I did not know the crafty Professor had entered us in the horse and camel racing competitions the following day.

CHAPTER FORTY-TWO

The Parades

*"Do not wait; the time will never be 'just right.'
Start where you stand, and work with whatever tools
you may have at your command, and better
tools will be found as you go along."*
Napoleon Hill

Day Two at the Sahara Festival

The following morning, the Hadrah and his entourage, including Andy and me, once again departed in the jeeps for the festival site. Areas were set up for horses to drink, and hay was strewn, on which the animals grazed. On the far side, away from the horses, were the camels. Arabians and camels were being auctioned to the highest bidder in an adjacent arena. This event was a market place for horse and camel breeders to sell or trade livestock. It was a Bedouin bazaar, in the truest sense of the word.

The morning started with music and folk bands playing traditional Arabian music, while the camels and the horses were saddled for the parades. Andy and I sat in our VIP seats, watching the festivities unfold.

Ludwig, seated a row below us, turned and smiled, acknowledging our presence. He shouted over the noisy crowd, beckoning us to join him, as there were several vacant seats next to his. Andy and I moved down a row, and bid him good morning.

He greeted us saying, "Hi Guys! How are you this morning?"

We told him we had a good night's rest and the hotel bed was comfortable to sleep on. He gave us a wicked smile and winked at me, as if to intimate that he knew about the secret relationship between Andy and me.

Andy asked, "Are you ready for the race today?"

Ludwig replied, "Oh, as ready and prepared as one can be. Besides, the races happen tomorrow. This is the day of the camel and horse parades. The racing competition doesn't begin until the third day of the festival."

Then he added, "You guys better get prepared and be ready to compete!"

Andy and I turned to him, our eyes wide, and said, "What? What do you mean compete?"

The young man broke into loud laughter and explained, "Didn't I tell you I signed you both up to participate in the parades and horse racing competitions?"

Andy and I looked at each other in surprise and said, simultaneously, "You did what?"

Ludwig continued, laughing at the prank he had played on us, and replied, "I said, I signed the both of you up to compete in the horse races, and to join my tribe in the parade of the camels and horses! You'd better get suited up and ready for the parades, which will start in two hours."

Andy and I stared at each other in panic.

"Come with me to my tent and I'll get you guys into your Bedouin outfits. I'm sure our tribesmen have something traditional that will fit you," he continued.

"Come! Let's go!" he ordered, getting up from his seat and waving his hand for us to follow. We had no choice but to trail behind him. As soon as we reached his tent, he waved in a couple of Abds. He spoke to them in Arabic and quickly dismissed them; they ran to do his bidding.

His tent was strewn with Persian rugs and large, ornate cushions were laid casually on the floor. Before long, the two Abds returned with two bundles of clothes. As soon as the Abds left the tent, Ludwig closed the entrance curtain and said, "Now, be good boys and change into these clothes."

He proceeded to sit on the rugs and stare at us while we stripped out of our djellabas. I was getting a little embarrassed from his unblinking eyes, so I turned my back to him, while I changed. Andy, on the other hand, did not mind him looking and stripped in front of Ludwig, brazenly. I wasn't accustomed to being watched by such devouring eyes, like those of a hungry vulture waiting to pounce on his prey.

By the time we finished dressing and were ready to walk out of the tent, Ludwig had filled us in about what was required of us, in the show.

He said, "Do the same as me and you'll be fine. After the parade of the camels, we'll have to change into another set of costumes for the horse show. Then, I'll fill you in regarding tomorrow's races, over our lunch break."

We must have looked shaken because he said, "Relax! You'll have lots of fun. It's not as serious as you think. We're all here to celebrate and be happy! Don't look so grim and worried!" advised the tribesman.

"You already know how to ride. You'll do just fine. It's all for good cheer and light hearted laughter," continued the young man.

In Bedouin Costume

I looked in the mirror and did not recognize the person staring back at me. My Abd thought it was hilarious to see a Chinaman dressed like an Arab boy. I tried draping the Kufiya across my face and, to my surprise, I did look like an Arab boy! I thought, well, even if I fall off the camel, nobody will know it's me. The crowd would probably think I'm a local boy. This thought consoled me a little and I didn't feel so frightened about what was to unfold.

Andy, on the other hand, was enjoying his newly acquired look and was admiring himself in the mirror. Ludwig went over and assisted Andy, draping his Kufiya over his face. We broke out in laughter. I, too, found Andy looking quite unlike himself, dressed in traditional Bedouin garb. It was like playing dress-up for a costume party.

With our faces hidden behind the Kufiya, we walked out of the tent to our camels.

The Camel Parade

At 11:00 a.m. sharp, the drummers began drumming, loudly, and the parade was ready to proceed. Hadrah Hakim and his entourage were already seated in the VIP area. Andy, Ludwig and I were now on camels, looking up at them from the parade grounds. The Hadrad had not noticed his three missing guests, since he was busy entertaining his foreign friends and Household members the entire time of the festivities.

Each Bedouin tribe had a unique flag, emblem and a troupe of musicians following behind the camels. Needless to say, I was associated with the Jebeliya tribe, as Ludwig Abid Safar was a descendant of Emb, one of the four sub families of the Jebeliya. There were twenty members, including Ludwig, Andy and me, representing his family tree in the march of the camels.

Andy and I shared a camel. I rode in the front Andy rode behind me. Dressed in traditional Jebeliya, Emb's family costumes, with our Kufiya shadowing our faces, Ludwig jokingly said I could pass as a cute Arab boy without anyone noticing I wasn't one of their members. With Andy's tanned skin, he could easily pass as a relative.

As soon as the trumpet sounded, the procession started to move. The squatting camel tilted itself forward to rise to the occasion. The beast had a mind of its own and started to follow the other moving camels in front of it, even though Andy was controlling the reins from behind.

As the parade progressed I was enjoying every moment of riding a tall camel named Yuf (short for Yusef). Yuf seemed to have taken a liking to Andy and me, and he would occasionally turn his head to look back at us, while snorting and drooling saliva from his constantly munching mouth.

He was an adorable animal and I loved being on Yuf. The parade seemed to take forever to finish, and when the camels finally took their rest, Yuf lowered his hind and front legs so we could climb off of his back. As I patted him on his head, he glanced at me to acknowledge my presence. I gave him a loving hug and went my merry way with Andy and Ludwig for a light lunch before changing costumes for the horse parade.

The Horse Parade

With a quick costume change Andy, Ludwig and I were now dressed in dark gray and white thobes, kibr and matching accessories and ready to mount our Arabians. Our Abds led out three strong stallions for us to ride. Being dressed in this traditional garb transformed me. For a fleeting moment I felt like Lawrence of Arabia, riding into the Arabian Desert with great strength and vigor, convincing myself I was a young heroic warrior charging into battle. With Andy and Ludwig encouraging me on either side, I also felt like a wandering nomad in the Sahara, a conqueror of wind and sand. These brief moments of fantasy were etched in my memory forever.

As I sat on my charge, pomp and circumstance driving me forward, I could not help but wonder how I had entered this strange new world. I was not born into it but was now somehow a part of it. In my own way, I was grateful to Ludwig for putting me in this unusual situation.

I became the mirror instead of its reflection. I was the watched instead of the watcher. I began to wonder: if all people are connected, a thought our egos are often eager to dismiss, are we all one and the same, regardless of race or color? As my mind drifted the procession began to move and I was jolted back to reality... or was this reality? Had I become the dream and the dreamer, simultaneously?

Suddenly a voice at my side said, "Are you ready to warm up with a trot?" It was my beloved Andy, making sure I was all right.

"Sure! Let's go!" I replied.

The Parade of the Arabians had begun.

CHAPTER FORTY-THREE

The Races

"Love is the irresistible desire to be desired irresistibly."
Louis Ginsburg

Day 3 at The Sahara Festival

The horse races between the various competing Bedouin tribes were to begin at 11:00 a.m. on day three of the Sahara Festival of Douz. Andy and I, under the supervision of Ludwig Abid Safar, changed into traditional white thobe and kibr, with matching accessories in Ludwig's tent. We would mount the Arabians as soon as we finished dressing. The Abd assisting me was a funny eleven-year-old Arab boy who kept giggling as he helped me into my outfit.

Once again, I could not recognize myself once I changed into the Emb's traditional costume. The Abds who were our attendants laughed and joked about our strange appearances. My

Abd had fun mucking around with me while trying to fasten the Kufiya across my face. Andy and I were their amusement for the day. As Ludwig had mentioned, it was all for good cheer and laughter, so I played along.

I was only two years older than my servant, so we chased each other like unruly boys playing a silly 'catch me if you can' game, while I waited for my Valet and Ludwig to finish dressing.

The Competition

The first round of the race consisted of eight horsemen. Each competitor represented one Bedouin family. There would be three winners who would proceed to Round Two. An overall winner would be awarded a large golden trophy, and would bring honor and glory to both his tribe and to the family he represented.

Since I did not understand or speak Arabic I had no idea how this competition was judged or what I was to do. I could only follow my leader's orders. I obeyed whatever Ludwig told me to do without questioning. It's strange: when told to obey orders instead of having to make my own decisions; life became infinitely easier for me. Luckily, I was sandwiched between Ludwig and Andy while our stallions had their final preparations at the lineup, before the race.

Since the Jebeliya Tribe was the oldest and most established, all of the eight competitors from the Emb family, including Andy and me, were the last to compete. We were to race around a half-mile track which was mapped out on the sand with colored paints. The winners from the Emb family would proceed to compete with the three remaining families. These were the descendants of Selim, of Hement and of Nyzinti all from the Jebeliya ancestral family.

Representing the Emb Family

I never dreamed competitive horse racing would be so much fun! As soon as the flag came down, signaling us to begin, I gave my horse, Nasim, (Fresh Air,) a light kick and a whip on his backside. Off the Arabian flew! I was alert and in complete control of my stallion, and myself.

Fresh Air was magnificent to look at and majestic to ride. His shining mane blew back as we shot through the rest of the riders. I merged into spiritual oneness with this amazing animal. The thud of hooves was a roaring, thunderous storm as we ran towards the finish line. I lowered my body over the back and neck of my strong masculine steed as we sped, together, like a bullet aimed at a prized target.

Andy trailed two horses behind. Ludwig was a fraction of a hair ahead of me, to my right. Nasim quickened his pace, giving his all; in a flash we were neck and neck with Ludwig. The two of us led the race.

I was determined to beat my German Arab friend at his game. When I gave Fresh Air encouragement with my spurs, the animal shot across the finish line. I knew I had come in first or second place, next to Ludwig Abid Safar. Unfortunately, Andy came in fifth. Ludwig and I were now slated to compete in the next round. Ludwig's stallion broke away from the other horses and won the race by two lengths.

Awards Presentation

After the initial races, the winners from the various families stood in a row to receive their awards, which were presented by our host, Hadrad Hakim. I wasn't sure if I had stepped out of line as Hakim's guest by competing in the races. If my Master was angry at my misconduct, I had no doubt that I would be reprimanded back at the Kosk, Hakim's Mansion.

As the Hadrah moved down the awards line, handing out the medals, I could not help but feel a sense of remorse for what I had done. I would have to stand up to the consequences, whatever they might be. It was Ludwig who enlisted Andy and me to compete; it wasn't entirely my fault I was in the race, I thought. I kept telling myself this event was meant to be of good cheer and laughter and Hakim would surely understand the situation.

As I was debating within myself, my Master appeared in front of me. He bent forward, slightly, as he pinned a medal to my kibr, and whispered, "Young, I want to see you tomorrow evening on our flight home. Make sure you come to my plane's bed chamber fifteen minutes after boarding."

With that remark, he moved to the next awardee. I was left wondering how serious the trouble was, which it seemed I had gotten myself into!

Sunset in the Sahara

By the time the races were over, it was sundown. To celebrate the end of the races, a huge lantern display lit up the entire festival site. Tea light candles were placed in small containers, like farolitas, arranged strategically on the sand dunes. When the last shadow of orange faded over the Sahara horizon, it was a most enchanting sight.

We cleaned up, and were happily sitting outside Ludwig's tent admiring the beautiful scenery when Ludwig enquired, "Did you enjoy racing today?" I quickly assured him, repeating "I loved it! Loved it! Loved it! I loved every moment of the day. I want to compete more! It was so exciting to be on Nasim. Can I ride him again someday?"

"Of course you can, my boy. I can teach you some tricks about riding an Arabian," he said with a wicked grin while winking at me. His sexy undertone made it clear that he was flirting.

Andy flashed him a knowing smile and replied, "I would like to learn some tricks about riding an Arabian as well. When can these lessons commence?" Andy responded in a take-charge fashion.

"Right now, if you are ready. There is no time like the present; the equipment is ready to go," Abid answered lasciviously.

My Valet didn't break eye contact with Ludwig as he inquired, "Where do we practice?"

"Come in the tent; I'll show you."

The two of them got to their feet and headed into the dimly lit canvas lodging. The scent of Frankincense wafted from the opening. I told them I'd be joining them soon; I wanted to enjoy the tranquil scenery a little longer.

The evening sun was falling behind majestic Mount Sinai. Dusk was fast approaching; the candlelit landscape offered a seductive serenity. I sat, mesmerized, in awe of the natural beauty which Allah had created. Suddenly, a hand tapped my shoulder. Andy, draped in a large cashmere shawl, whispered,

"Come in before it gets too cold, my lover."

He helped me up and we walked into the lavish tent. He closed the curtain drapes behind us, and he wrapped his muscular arms around my waist. Bending down, he kissed me lovingly. I felt my lover's groin stir from our passionate embrace. I knew he wanted me, and I was more than ready for my beloved. His hands reached into my loose garment, lightly caressing the sensitive nipples that were jumping to attention from his gentle, loving touch.

Another set of hands reached for me from behind, lifting my robe, exposing the smooth brown skin of my legs and back side. I held onto Andy tightly when I felt a tongue slide between the crack of my buttocks. I surrendered to the foreplay which lay claim to my body. Foreplay designed for another's satisfaction. My pleasure was much more than vicarious.

My Valet lifted me into his arms and carried me to a satin covered mattress. I was stripped naked by my lover while he French kissed me. My hands were pulled above my head. Our host was tying my wrists with silk cords to the tent posts on either side of the mattress. This sensuality was too irresistible. I desired more! I wanted to memorize every single moment of my passive submission to the demands and delight of my two handsome captors during our night in the Sahara.

I needed to be loved, cherished and desired. I prayed to Allah! "Oh God, please don't let this stop. Plunge me ever deeper into this pool of sensual liquid romance. Yes!"

Yes indeed! My desires were fulfilled beyond measure. My lover and I emerged from the Bedouin tent a little before sunrise. Finding a quiet spot, we sat in silence, witnessing the morning sun rise above the mountain of Moses, while our host slept peacefully, after an exhausting night of love.

My darling Andy shielded me from the chilly morning air with a large Persian blanket and covered our nakedness. We held each other in the most intimate of lover's embraces. Kissing my sweet lips, he whispered softly, "I love you so much, my beautiful boy! I want you to always be happy."

CHAPTER FORTY-FOUR

The Caravan

"As love is the most noble and divine passion of the soul, so is it that to which we may justly attribute all the real satisfactions of life, and without it, man is unfinished, and unhappy."
Aphra Behn

Closing Ceremony

The next day was the closing ceremony of The Sahara Festival of Douz. When Andy and I arrived at the fairgrounds, the ceremony was already in progress. Jugglers and fancy horseback performances entertained the crowd. We left Ludwig's tent while he was asleep, and returned to our hotel to shower. We had to prepare for the camel caravan tour that Hadrah Hakim had organized for his guests.

As we walked towards the festival site to catch the hotel shuttle bus, I noticed separate tents for the women. Throughout the entire event, women were segregated from the men. They observed the parades and the races from a cordoned off section, not mixing with the men. Ludwig had mentioned the day before that the Festival had been set up this way as long as he could remember.

Women Status

"Why are the women's tents separated from the men's tents?" I asked Andy.

He replied, "Just like at the Bahriji and once you are ensconced in a Household, you will note that females are segregated from men for most activities. It is part of the Islamic culture."

"Why?"

"Young, when we arrive at the Households, in the majority of cases, there will be two different wings. One section will be occupied primarily by the Household males and the other by the females. Each wing has private quarters," explained my Valet, as we walked towards the shuttle bus.

Out of curiosity, I continued to ask, "What if they are married? Do husbands and wives not stay together?"

Andy laughed and replied, "Yes, they do live under the same roof, Young, the very wealthy elite have separate living quarters. The men's and the women's harems are located in different parts of their large mansions."

"The men and women have their own entertainment and amusements. Young, you'll soon come to understand that females in this society have very few rights. Most are subjugated by their male counterparts; it is very much a male-dominated society."

"You will find that most Arab men will 'swing' both ways. Since their laws forbid them to have any sexual relationships prior to marriage, most males find alternative outlets to release their pent up energies and tensions. They have boys, like us, on the side. Even if they are heterosexual men, they still have sex with males."

"I thought Islamic laws were extremely anti-homosexual?" My inquisitive mind prompted me to investigate this dichotomy further.

"Yes and no," answered my lover. "The Koran approves of mature men being mentors to boys. Mentorship at times can develop into erotic relationships. If the young man consents to the union between them, then the relationship is deemed appropriate. Now, if the boy doesn't want the mentorship to be sexual and the older man forces himself on his protégé, then Islamic law comes down hard on the older man."

"In the ancient days, the violated boy and his family could sue the mentor for damages. The mature man might be sentenced to care for the boy and his entire family for life under such violation, or there could be other financial compensation."

I said, "No wonder most Arab men I had been acquainted with liked me." Now I was beginning to understand. "I know I still have a lot to learn and I'm glad you are here to teach me and protect me from harm, Andy."

"I'm very attracted to you, my dear lover. You have a boyish innocence which appeals to me, greatly. I was only performing a duty to my previous 'little brother', making sure he was well protected and safe. With you, it's different. You are much more to me than just my 'little brother'. You are my love. I have never loved another the way I love you. I don't know why, but I do," confessed Andy.

I kept quiet until we got on the shuttle. "I love you, too, and feel very safe when you are with me. You should know that by now. Thank you for loving me!"

The Caravan

At precisely 10:00 a.m., the tour guide collected our group, as we were scheduled by Hakim to go on the camel train. Although

Chapter Forty-four

the Hadrah had arranged this tour, he did not join us. He was busy conducting other business while at Douz.

Since we did not see Ludwig in the hotel lobby, we assumed he was still fast asleep in his tent and would not be joining the caravan tour. Mustafar, our well-informed tour guide, introduced us to places of interest as we drove through the city to the desert's edge, to get our camels.

Generally, each person rode on his own camel. Andy requested that we ride together on a single animal, like we did at the camel parade. In the desert, the camel puller walked ahead of the animals, while Mustafar explained the sights along the trail.

Approximately 15 minutes into the tour, we heard sounds of galloping horses heading in our direction. As the horseman drew close, I made out that the rider was Ludwig, racing on Jibril along with two other stallions, to catch up to us. Our caravan stopped and waited.

He apologized for not meeting the group on time. He rode beside us on his Arabian. I was wondering why he brought two extra horses.

He addressed Andy and me, "Good day boys! I didn't realize you'd left so early this morning. When I awakened, you guys were gone."

"I brought along Nasim and Ra'id (Arabic word for leader) for the two of you, in case you prefer Arabians to camels." He gave us his sly sexy smile, emphasizing the word Arabians.

He continued, "Young, I know you asked to ride Nasim again. Here you are! All yours to mount!" he flirted, salaciously.

I looked longingly at Nasim, turning towards my Valet for his approval, to mount the steed. Andy said, "Are you sure you would rather ride Nasim than a camel?"

I nodded pleadingly with my BB, "Please can I ride Nasim once more before we leave Douz?"

"Ok! But be careful. I had better ride with you too."

We handed the camels back to the camel puller. And up I jumped onto my fabulous Nasim! As soon as I mounted the Arabian, he was ready to run. Before long we were galloping ahead of the caravan. I tried to rein him in but he wanted to fly. And fly he did!

Running With Gazelles

I yelled to Andy and Ludwig, "Let's race!" With that, Nasim and I shot ahead as fast as the stallion would carry me. Enjoying the hot Sahara wind blowing, we sped towards the desert dunes. Looking behind me, Andy and Abid were racing at top speed to catch up. The three of us streaked across the desert in the heat of the noonday sun. Our Arabians flew like lightning into the vast open expansiveness of the great Sahara, leaving clouds of fine sand trailing behind us.

Ahead, a herd of thirty Dorcas gazelles watched us fly towards them like arrows. Not knowing what was happening, they stampeded and ran, thinking we were hunting them down. My swift and quick-footed Nasim ran side by side with these amazing animals. We galloped while they raced as fast as they could to outrun us.

I followed the lead gazelle, while my two companions pursued. Once again, my competitive nervous system pumped adrenaline into my body. I thundered across the wide sandy expanse. I loved every second of bonding with "Fresh Air." His determination carried us without my command; he became my Master and I, his slave. We galloped until we were completely exhausted and could no longer compete with the springing gazelles.

Ludwig, Andy and I laughed unceasingly from our joyful exuberance. Our racing game was too much fun for it to end so soon, I thought. By the time our horses slowed to a trot, I was thirsty and needed water badly, as did our steeds.

The Jeweled Dagger

Luckily, Ludwig came prepared. From the side of his saddle he pulled out a camel skin water bag.

"Drink! We'll take a rest under that lone tree over there," commanded Ludwig, pointing to a nearly leafless tree nearby.

Fetching a folded Persian rug out of his bag, he spread it on the ground, while Andy tied the horses to the few remaining branches before feeding the animals handfuls of grain and water. I sat on the canvas looking at the clear blue sky and feeling elated and happy. Shielding my eyes from the blinding desert sun, I relaxed, taking in the excitement of the morning.

Under the brilliant sunshine I noticed a bejeweled dagger case protruding from the leather belt Ludwig wore around his waist.

I remarked, "What a beautiful dagger. May I take a look?"

The German Arab unfastened his dagger from his belt and said, "Isn't this a remarkable piece of art? The case is encrusted with rubies, topaz, sapphires and emeralds; so is the handle," he said, handing me the dagger for my inspection.

"How gorgeous! Where did you find such a lovely piece, and why do you carry such a precious item with you? Aren't you afraid it'll get stolen?" I enquired.

"This is a family heirloom. One of my father's companies mines precious stones and a team of his skilled craftsmen make traditional Arabian pieces such as this," he said.

"There are many dangerous things lurking about in the desert and one must be alert at all times. That's why I carry a small weapon with me."

"You mean to protect yourself from dangerous and naughty men like yourself?" I teased.

Flashing his lustful smile, Ludwig responded, "Yes! There are many lecherous beings crawling about. You never know when they are going to attack. And when they do, I must be ready to defend."

Laughing at his answer, I examined the shining piece of artwork in my hands.

"How long does it take a craftsman to create such an exquisite piece?" I inquired.

"About three to four days. My dad owns a precious gem factory in El Jem. Maybe in the future you and Andy can visit the workshop. We have hired about thirty craftsmen," Ludwig continued, extending his invitation.

"Well, I don't know when I'll have the chance to return to your wonderful country. If I do, I'd love to have you be my guide," I replied.

Handing the dagger back to my friend, I looked at him with a seductive glance before lying down beneath the few shady leaves left on the rotting tree. I closed my eyes to better enjoy my last day in the Sahara.

Danger

Before I could open my eyes, I heard Ludwig's stern command, "Don't move, don't utter a sound! Stay perfectly still." Slowly, I opened my eyes; the dagger was aiming straight at my face! My heart was thumping hard, from fright. My immediate thought was I'm going to be mutilated by the sharp blade of the weapon Ludwig is aiming at me.

The blow was swift and fast. I let out a scream, shut my eyes tightly and did not dare to move. I thought I'd been stabbed! When I finally found the courage to open my eyes, his dagger was inches away from the side of my face, stuck in sand.

Andy pulled me to himself urgently, holding me tight, grateful that I was unharmed. Ludwig pulled his dagger slowly out of the ground, and examined a ghastly looking Sahara scorpion which was wriggling its dying tail on the end of his sharp blade. The Bedouin had saved me from being stung by this deadly creature.

I was so scared, I held onto Andy, not daring to move. Tears of fear began streaming down my cheeks. My lover held me until my fear subsided.

Andy whispered to me, "Thank God you are not hurt!"

Ludwig made sure the poisonous scorpion was dead before flinging the lifeless creature into the desert dunes. Wiping his dagger clean, he turned and enquired, "Are you OK?"

I said, shakily, "Yes! I'm fine. Thank you for saving me."

He smiled and jokingly answered, "You're welcome! You owe me one, pretty boy!"

I went over to him and wrapped my arms around his manly body.

"Thank You, Master! I'm forever indebted to you," I said, with gratitude in my voice.

Smilingly, he questioned, "Is that a promise?"

Before I could response, Andy chimed in, "Are you guys ready to ride back and join the caravan?"

"I'm ready to go!" I cried.

We found our camel train resting by a campsite. Mustafar, pouring Turkish coffee out of a worn flask, invited us to join him. We sat next to the tour guide, on his rug.

He asked smilingly, "Where did you guys fly to? You disappeared rather quickly; we couldn't keep up with you!"

"We just came out of a danger zone. This young guy here (pointing at me) nearly got bitten by a" ,عقرب Ludwig replied.

"My, oh my! I'm glad he came out alive! I'm glad he's all right. Otherwise, I'd be in trouble with Hadrah Hakim. He especially asked me to keep an eye out for this young man. He is very fond of him, you know," commented the guide.

Andy said, "Well you don't have to worry. We are safe and sound." "Good, good, very good!" Mustafar said as he lifted his thumb of approval. "Finish your coffee and we'll move on."

By the time our tour bus dropped us at our hotel, we had less than an hour to pack before the Hadrah's golden Bentley arrived to take us to the airport.

Ludwig had bid us farewell shortly after our coffee break with Mustafar. Since he grew up in the area, he didn't finish the tour with the group. Off he trotted with the Arabians, leading them back to their stable.

A parcel was waiting for me at the Hotel reception desk. Opening it, I discovered the beautiful bejeweled dagger wrapped in silk brocade. The attached note read:

"Carry this with you always. You never know where danger lurks. This weapon is to protect you from Dangerous, Salacious, Lustful & Naughty characters like ME! Already missing you! Ludwig."

CHAPTER FORTY-FIVE

On Board the Simorgh

"Initiative is doing the right thing without being told."
Victor Hugo

At precisely 5:00 a.m. sharp, Andy and I were waiting in the hotel lobby for the golden limousine to transport us to the Hadrah's private jet. Ghali (Arabic for valuable, beloved, expensive), the chauffeur, arrived in a timely fashion. The hotel bellboys loaded our bags into the Bentley as Ghali opened the passenger doors for us to step in.

Andy asked the chauffeur, "Isn't Hadrah Hakim joining us for the ride to the airport?"

In broken English, Ghali replied, "No Sir! He go to airplane already."

With that remark, he closed our car doors and drove to the private airfield. It was sunrise as we arrived; the golden orange sun was casting a beautiful light on the Simorgh, the Hadrah's jet. The two pristinely dressed stewards in white and blue uniforms welcomed us aboard, asking if we would like a drink. I ordered a glass of water. I was dreading the moment I would have to face the Hadrah, in his sound proof bedroom.

Hakim was already seated on a large comfortable sofa, reading a pile of documents in the jet's lavish living room. Without looking up, he motioned us to sit while he continued his business. One of the stewards was closing the plane door when the two pilots were doing routine checks before taxiing down the runway. Since the windows were all double-glazed and totally sound resistant, we could hardly hear the engine noise. Before long we were airborne.

Consequences

My Master had excused himself and retired to his chamber, saying he had a long day and needed some quiet time. I kept looking at my huge, mod Canaby Street watch, dreading the thought that in ten minutes I would have to face the Hadrah's music, alone. Though I wasn't sure why he wanted to see me, my mind thought the worst. Everything negative kept racing and replaying within my head. "Is he going to scold me, punish me or . . . what?" I worried.

I wished Andy could be in the chamber with me, but I knew better. When a 'student' was being summoned by his Master, our Valet always waited outside the chambers, unless invited in by our host. There would be no exception to the rule this time, I was sure. I had to face the terrible consequences on my own.

The Bedchamber

I knocked on the bedroom door and a voice from the other side answered, "Come in."

Andy was sitting on a white sofa next to the doorway entrance giving me a look of love, secretly informing me that all would be well and not to be afraid. Sliding the door opened, I ventured in.

"Lock the door and come over here," said my host who was sitting on large leather recliner.

I did as I was told, and returned to my Master.

Looking at me sternly, he said, "Young, it would have been polite of you to consult me before disappearing to join the festival parades and the horse races."

I started apologizing but he cut me off mid-sentence and said firmly, "When you are in my Household and under my care, I am responsible for your well-being, even if your Valet is with you. If anything happens to you, I have to answer to your school Board of Directors. It would be wise of you to come to me for permission before you go your merry way without your Master's knowledge."

"Sorry Sir! I promise I will consult you before taking the initiative to do anything in the future," I answered, speaking with my head lowered staring, mortified at my stupidity, at the Persian rug on the floor. I felt terribly guilty for what I had done. I wanted to put all the blame on Ludwig Abid Safar but thought better of it since he and the Hadrah were friends. Besides, what was done was done. There wasn't any use blaming anyone but myself, since I was a willing participant in all the activities.

My Master's voice softened to a whisper, "You know, I admire your spunk. You are a very courageous boy. These are qualities I like about you." He grinned as he uttered those words.

"In more ways than one, I admire you taking the initiative to do the right thing, to entertain my friend without being told to. You certainly have determination, and a will of your own. Excellent attributes. And, you are lucky you didn't get bitten by the scorpion," he remarked.

"How did you know about the scorpion?" I asked, curiously.

Hakim didn't reply immediately, but smiled and said, "Now, for your punishment! Let me see you out of your djellaba. Come! Let me hold you. I want to see my beautiful boy."

While I was pulling the garment over my head, Hakim had moved behind me and his hands were already caressing my nimble body. Once again, the sensual tingling sensation stimulated my cock to jump to immediate attention. Standing at my back, he ran his masculine hands over my smoothness with a tender loving touch. His aura surrounded my entire being, encasing me in a glow of warmth. He caressed every inch of my body, leaving no crevice unexplored. I was at the mercy of his soothing fingers, longing for them to reach my groin. Heat radiated from the palms of his mature hands.

Leaning against him, I surrendered myself to my Master's sensual touch. Before long I was moaning for release from his stroking movements. I willingly offered myself as the sacrificial lamb on this altar of sexuality and sensuality, spilling my seed at his command.

Lifting his fingers to his lips, he tasted every delicious drop from my fountain of youth. He seemed deeply contented and rejuvenated. My service to my Master Hakim was complete.

Turning me around, he patted my head and whispered, "Go to your lover. He is waiting patiently outside. Don't keep him waiting any longer. Go quickly, before I change my mind and have you stay."

I did not have to inquire further; he had given his final command.

Hakim was correct; Andy was waiting patiently at the entrance. As soon as I stepped out and closed the bedroom door behind me, my Valet said, "It wasn't as bad as you thought, was it?"

I smiled at him without uttering a word as we retired to the Simorgh's comfortable living room, before a steward announced that we should fasten our seat belts. We would soon be landing at Dubai airport.

CHAPTER FORTY-SIX

The Peacock Chamber

"Love--that divine fire which was made to light and warm the temple of home--sometimes burns at unholy altars."
Horace Mann

On our way back, in the Hadrah's silver and black Rolls Royce speeding towards the Kosk, Andy and I were both blindfolded by Gahli. Hakim spoke little on the journey. Maybe he was tired from his busy business day or perhaps he was simply enjoying the sight of my Valet and me. It seemed like we drove for close to an hour before reaching our destination. When the vehicle came to a complete stop and Gahli opened our car doors, he released our blindfolds. I was standing in front of a very large mansion. The entire building must have been over 30,000 square feet, not including the spacious, meticulously manicured grounds.

Driveway Entrance

The Rolls was parked right in front of the grand entrance. On both sides of the driveway leading to the front doors were sculptures which resembled chess pieces. There were large concrete squares, two different shades of earth tones, on the ground; it was a chessboard on a grand scale. A flight of steps leading up the walkway had narrow water tunnels running down the sides and the middle leading to the front door, a traditional Moorish architectural design feature commonly found in Middle Eastern classically styled buildings.

A young Abd and a male servant were already waiting to take our luggage into the house, to our respective rooms. Since we arrived at night, the mansion was beautifully lit. Subtle lighting placed in areas around the chess pieces created spooky shadowy effects. It was like a surreal Hollywood movie set, right in the middle of Arabia.

The Grand Entrance

As soon as we entered the grand hallway, a pair of curved staircases greeted us. A row of Hakim's servants were lined up by the side of the great oak doors to welcome us. The Hadrad told them that we would be staying at the Kosk for three months, and that during our stay, the servants were to assist us in every way possible, to ensure our comfort. As soon as the instructions were given by our host, the Abd and the servant in charge of our bags showed us to our quarters. We bid our host good night, and followed the servants to our room.

To my surprise, our room was more like a large hotel suite than an average bedroom. Two beautiful crystal chandeliers hung from the middle of the sitting area and also in the bedchamber. It was a bedroom suitable for a prince rather than for a Kuala Lumpur thirteen year old boy, like me. A huge canopied king-size bed sat against a wall. Beautifully upholstered pastel and azure blue settees and chaise lounges sat on lush carpeting. An imposing teak wood desk with a matching high-backed chair stood in one corner of the room. A series of large French windows facing the inner courtyard opened onto balconies, overlooking a swimming pool.

The wallpaper was a subtle pale blue design featuring turquoise, green and white peacocks frolicking in the woods. I was totally mesmerized by the grace and beauty of my chamber when I heard Andy's voice calling from the adjoining bathroom.

The Peacock Chamber

"Young, come over here, there is something I want to show you," called my Valet. "Young, where are you? Come over here!" He shouted again.

Before I had a chance to see what my Valet was calling me about, my jaws dropped in amazement. The bathroom before me was by far the most elegant I had ever seen in my adolescent life. It was decorated from floor to ceiling in azure bluish cream tiles. Tiles featuring pairs of painted peacocks were found in between the plain tiles. It was such a romantic space, and it felt fit for royalty. I had stepped into a fantasy world right out of an adventure tale, Arabian Nights. I had to steady myself to adjust to such beautiful sophistication and elegance which seemed to float around me in a surrealistic fashion.

Although I had been to a few chic places, such as the Parisian Tearoom, The River Restaurant, The Savoy, and the BBC Restaurant in The Langham Hotel, The Kosk was far more opulent and lavish.

The Persian

Andy pulled me back to reality, saying "See what we got here!" Sleeping soundly in a brown wicker basket on the bathroom floor was a beautiful, tiny white Persian kitten. The fluffy 'ball of love' made soft purring sounds and looked absolutely adorable all curled up in its bed. I could not resist the temptation to pick up the beautiful creature, petting his pretty head. Around his neck was a diminutive leather strap, studded with large diamonds, and a tag that said:

"Welcome to The Kosk!
I am Husni.
I am here to give you love and cuddles
When Hadrah Hakim is unavailable.
Love Me!

CHAPTER FORTY-SEVEN

The Kosk Household

"A man can be happy with any woman, as long as he does not love her."
Oscar Wilde

Household Members

The following morning when Andy and I came downstairs we were directed to an opulent dining room for breakfast. Kosk Household members were already seated, eating their Arabian breakfast which consisted of khubuz, fetas, bowls of black and green olives, and cucumber and tomato slices drizzled with extra virgin olive oil. Sweet tea or Arabian coffee served as our beverage choices. I noticed they used their khubuz (bread) to scoop up the white cheese and labneh. Andy and I followed their traditional way of eating when the servants placed our food in front of us.

There were approximately fourteen men and the same number of women in the breakfast group. The women were veiled in niqabs from head to toe with only their eyes showing. When eating, they lifted their thin veils just enough to consume their food, before replacing them to cover their mouths.

The Hadrah was seated at the head of the large oval shaped table, calling for everyone's attention, in order to formally introduce Andy and me as 'students' from the Oasis School who would be staying at the Kosk for three months. Hakim spoke in Arabic to his entourage informing them that our mission to the Household was to learn and experience Arabian cultures and traditions as guests of the Kosk. He mentioned that they should behave cordially and hospitably; they could learn from us in return.

The men greeted us with smiling nods and welcoming gestures. The women appeared expressionless until spoken to by the Hadrah. Since all of them were veiled, except two older teenagers who wore hijabs, I did not know if they agreed or disagreed with what they were being told.

The Kosk Women

The Household women wore white, sea blue, deep mandarin orange or black colored burkas. Since we were strangers in their house, and they were traditional Arabian women, they were expected to be decently and discreetly dressed. It was a week after our arrival before the women wore hijabs, revealing their faces to us. The Hadrah had mentioned to the women that I was good in art and design, especially fashion design, and that I had provided him with some excellent ideas for the renovation of the Kahyya'm.

Their eyes lit up at the mention of fashion. I sensed I would soon be drilled by these ladies on the subject of the latest Western fashion trends and styles. I smiled and gave them a polite nod as the Hadrah spoke. I acknowledged that I was available for fashion consultations anytime, which seemed to please them immensely.

The fashion sessions began a week later, just as I was finishing my daily studies with Ramiz (the Kosk's full time governor and mu'allim). He was also tutoring Gaston and Caroline, two other students from other Bariji schools who were in service at the Kosk along with their Valet and Chaperone.

Our host did not introduce the cast of women by name. Even if he did, I would not have been able to remember them. Between the Hakim's immediate family members and his in-laws, cousins and relatives, there were far too many to register.

The Master's two youngest daughters, who wore headscarves with their faces uncovered, were called Nasreen and Shiya. They were students back on vacation from their boarding schools in Italy and Switzerland. They were the only females within the Kosk who spoke other languages.

Nasreen spoke and wrote Arabic, their mother tongue, English and Italian since she was studying in Italy. Shiya could also read and write Arabic and English, and she was mastering French. Both young ladies were eighteen; their birthdays were only a few months apart. They were half-sisters, from different mothers.

It was difficult for me to differentiate the rest of the women as they were all covered from head to toe; they resembled pear-shaped aliens – their burkas were shapeless. They were blobs of flowing cloth which covered living, breathing beings, underneath.

The Kosk Men

The men were easier to remember, since their faces were not covered. All the men who were introduced were sons, son-in-laws or male relatives of Hakim and his four wives.

Rizq was the Hadrah's grandson. He was learning English and French from Ramiz. The three of us soon became buddies. Caroline attended class separately; I did not become acquainted with her until later.

It was difficult for me to understand Gaston's English because he spoke with a heavy French accent. Most of the time,

I could not make out what he was saying. I became better acquainted with Rizq during our sessions studying the 'Queen's English' by our literary tutor, who was educated at Oxford, graduating with an honorary degree in classical Arabic, as well as English linguistics and literature.

Besides Habiibi Aziz Hashim, there were three other sons-in-law: Habiibi Falah, Habiibi Basil and Habiibi Jabit. Hakim's sons, Ubaid and Wahab had just returned for their vacation from universities in Ireland and France. His third son, Mu'tazz, was about to depart for an accounting college in Switzerland.

It was Ubaid whom the Hadrah had mentioned to me when we were on board the Kahyya'm. He felt that we would get on well since he was studying architecture at Trinity College, Dublin which is one of the best architectural universities in Ireland. The other four males at breakfast were relatives of the Hadrah, as well as two infants, Arfan, three, and Hani, two, were grandsons of our host. The boys' nannies were part of the women's entourage, hired to look after the children.

After Breakfast

After Andy and I finished breakfast, before I was to meet Mu'allim Ramiz for my daily tutorials, I had a chance to ask Andy some questions regarding the Arabian women running through my mind.

As soon as we entered our residential suite, I inquired of my Valet, "Why are all the women covered from head to toe, like aliens from outer space?"

My guardian found my question amusingly naive and said with a voice of authority, "Young, my young one, most traditional Arabian women are very modest. They veil their faces, so men will not be distracted by their sexuality. It is a strong cultural history that women are neither seen nor heard in the company of men. This kind of blind submission is changing, as you can see with the Hadrah's two teenage daughters, Nasreen and Shiya.

"The more educated the women, the more open they are to westernized ways of thinking and behaving. Islamic traditions continue to run deep within their society, due mainly to the country's strong Muslim religion. Women don't have a voice in most matters.

"The majority of the older generations of women are not highly educated and their marriages are often arranged due to family ties between the different tribes," Andy explained to me.

I responded, "In Malaya, where I was born, Muslim women don't generally cover their faces like they do here. Usually they wear hijabs, long sleeve kebayas or baju kurungs. I have never seen anything like what these ladies wear."

Andy replied, "Every country interprets their traditional dress codes differently. In many ways, the burka is a silent sign that women are subjects of the men. They are to obey, without question, their male counterparts. The Quran mentions that women have the same rights as men, but during the pre-Islamic periods women had virtually no legal status. Old customs and traditions die hard."

I was puzzled and scratched my head, and my inquisitive mind urged me to continue this line of questioning, "Does that mean they can't mix with men in social situations? Do they keep female company, exclusively?"

"For many activities, they do," Andy went on. "That is why every wealthy Arab Household has different Harems and recreational facilities catering to each sex. Later, when we walk the grounds after your studies, I'll explain more of the Household practices to you."

"For now, go get your pretty ass ready for your tutorials with Mu'allim Ramiz," commanded my lover.

As I persisted, my lover gave my buttocks a light slap, and off I went to meet my tutor and my classmates.

CHAPTER FORTY-EIGHT

Confessions Within The Mansion

"To look is one thing, to see what you look at is another, to understand what you see is a third, to learn from what you understand is still something else, but to act on what you learn is all that really matters! How do I act?"
Bernard Tristan Foong

Class with Mu'allim Ramiz lasted several hours each day except Friday, which is the Islamic Holy Day, much like Sunday is to Christians. Although the Kosk Household men were required to pray 5 times a day, at times I wondered if they did what was required, diligently. But it was none of my business whether they did or did not pray according to the rules.

The Men's Quarters

After class, Ata, a manservant who spoke very little English, gave Andy and me a guided tour of the Kosk property. The mansion was divided into 2 distinct sections. The front part of the house was a separate property, occupied by the males in the family. It consisted of approximately 17,000 square feet, and had numerous communal living, relaxation and recreational rooms together with a Harem Spa resembling Roman bath facilities. Each male resident had an individual bedroom suite. There were also 12 guest suites, like the one Andy and I occupied. Each suite was decorated with a different theme with living and bathroom facilities attached.

The swimming pool in the inner courtyard acted as the dividing space between the male and the female sections. They were connected by 2 corridors, one, an enclosed walkway and the other, an open-air passageway, both leading to the rear portion of the women's quarters. Men were seldom allowed into the women's inner sanctum. Usually the wives came to their husband's chambers in the front of the house, when summoned.

The Women's Quarters

The women's domain also consisted of numerous bedroom suites. Each of Hakim's wives had her own suite, like an individual apartment, where each wife and her children lived. In other words, there were four separate households located under the umbrella of the main female section of the Hadrah's spacious mansion.

The women's communal areas were similar to that of their male counterparts, with communal living, relaxation and recreational spaces as well as a Harem that was similar to a classical Grecian Spa.

The Grounds

The well-groomed gardens had pathways leading to a gazebo with paintings and carved Moorish sculptural motifs on pillars and wall inserts.

Throughout the garden grounds there were dates and palm trees, plus an array of flowering desert shrubs, looked after lovingly by the Master's full-time gardeners. The property consisted of approximately 30 acres of land, surrounded by a high-walled fortress which ran around the estate. Round-the-clock armed security guards were stationed at strategic hut-like outposts. The security men made sure there were no unwelcomed visitors stealing into the property. They observed monitors with views from cleverly hidden cameras around this walled fortress.

Women's Swimming Etiquette

During my lunch break from my tutorial with Ramiz, an Abd brought Andy and me a couple trays of food that we consumed in our suite. There was some commotion going on around the courtyard swimming pool. I went over to see what the noise was about.

"Look! The servants are erecting a large covered tent covering the swimming pool. Do you know why?" I asked in excitement.

Andy, busy munching a mouthful of food, didn't seem excited over the prospect of checking out the commotion. When he finished eating, he licked his lips and said, "That was delicious!"

I asked again, "Why are the men erecting a large tent?"

This time, my Valet answered my query, "Because the women are going swimming."

"Why do they have to erect a tent when the women go swimming?" I enquired in puzzlement.

He laughed at my question and replied, "So the men can't see them. I already told you my darling boy; it is considered sacrilegious for a female to show her bare skin in the company of men."

Extremely confused, I continued, "What about their husbands? Can't they see their wives naked?"

Andy burst out laughing, stopping only after several minutes and replied in all seriousness, "Of course the husbands and wives see each other naked, in private. But women's flesh is not for public viewing, and certainly not for you and me to ogle." He continued laughing.

"So, do they swim naked under the tent if men cannot see them?" I asked earnestly.

Conversation with Andy

My curiosity got the better of me and I asked, "Are they lesbians?"

This time my Valet burst into uncontrollable laughter, laughing so hard he clutched his stomach, as if in pain. By the time he finally gathered his wits, wiping trickling tears from the corners of his eyes, he said, "Well! I suppose some of them may be lesbians. Young, Young, Young! You must understand with such close female proximity and the fact that they often are not satisfied by their husbands, anything can happen!"

"Are Gaston and Jacques here to satisfy their female needs, if their husbands can't pleasure them sufficiently?" I asked curiously.

He burst out in howling laughter again and could not speak. When he finally calmed his laughter, my lover replied, "In a way, yes! Gaston and Jacques are at times summoned to the women's quarters for the same reasons that the men summon you and me, but it's kept secret. You cannot go announcing to everyone what I'm going to tell you now. These secrets are not to be revealed to anyone. Remember, you and I and every E.R.O.S. member has sworn the oath of confidentially and pledged allegiance to our secret society."

Andy went on. "On the surface we are here to learn Arabic culture, customs and traditions as visiting foreign students. But as members of E.R.O.S., we are also here to satisfy the needs of our Household host and his male entourage.

You see, Islamic rules and regulations go by very strict sets of laws and conduct, but, as the saying goes, rules are made to be broken."

I was fascinated by everything Andy was teaching me. Pieces of the puzzle were starting to come together. He continued, "A good example would be Prohibition in America, when liquor was banned. Many people profited from Prohibition, selling liquor. It was always available, just under the radar. Then, it was made legal."

Andy's Confession

My guardian continued, "In my judgment, the same will happen in any restrictive society. Sooner or later, the majority of people will not tolerate such strict rulings; the society will burst at the seams and a revolution will occur. We are seeing this societally now, in British and American societies."

I sat mesmerized, wanting to learn more. I questioned, "What do you mean British and American societies are changing as we speak?"

"For a start, gay people like you and me are gaining a collective voice, both in the United Kingdom and in America. I'll bet you that several years from now we will be able to openly hold hands and love each other as we please, and not have to live our lives in secret. When that happens, I can come out to my family. At the present moment, my family thinks I am 'straight' and they hope that I will someday find the right woman to marry."

"But that will not happen, because, my darling boy," he paused for a few seconds before continuing, "I'm deeply in love with you! That someone special I want to marry is you!"

I was stunned by Andy's words and didn't know how to respond. I thought we were on the subject of the tent being erected around the swimming pool outside. How did it ended up with my Valet professing that he wanted to marry me? I was a mere young man with much ahead of me, I was not ready to settle down and be a 'housewife'!

Besides, homosexuals were still fighting to be accepted into mainstream society; nobody had even heard of 'gay marriage.' Andy was definitely way ahead of his time, and I was at a loss for words.

Finally, I uttered, "I have to get back to class. I still have an hour with Ramiz before the day's tutorial is finished."

Gathering my books, I trotted off to finish my studies with my Mu'allim, leaving Andy in deep thought, pondering my lack of response to the wish he had revealed.

CHAPTER FORTY-NINE

Talkie, Talk, Talk

*"In this life we cannot do great things.
We can only do small things with great love."*
Mother Teresa

The Ladies

A week after my stay at the Kosk, Ramiz asked one morning after class, "Young, several of the Hadrah's ladies would like to speak with you. Will you have some time to meet them?"

"Of course, I'd be delighted," I replied.

As soon as I finished my morning tutorials with my mu'allmi, Nasreen, Shiya and two of the Hadrah's wives were waiting outside the classroom. Ramiz accompanied us into a living room in the men's quarters where we sat and chatted.

The women wore hijabs (head scarves) without their face veils: I was afforded the opportunity to see the faces of Hakim's wives. Ghaniyah, the fourth wife, was approximately thirty years old and a beautiful woman with big, bright, intelligent eyes and a flawless complexion. She had no makeup on her face, yet she looked as fresh as the morning dew.

Ghaniyah's younger sister, Habibah was equally beautiful. A shy woman of twenty-eight, she was married to one of my Master's male cousins, Tariq. Both Ghaniyah and Habibah wore black burkas while Nasreen and Shiya were in abayas, traditional Islamic garments, still loose, but slimmer in cut, style and fashionable, by Middle Eastern standards.

Fashion Talk

Since Habibah and Ghaniyah didn't speak any English, Ramiz, Nasreen and Shiya became our translators. The women were all excited to be acquainted with Andy and me. Speaking in Arabic to Ramiz, they complimented us on how handsome we were. As they spoke they lowered their gazes and giggled like coy schoolgirls. Ramiz smiled at us while delivering the ladies' message. He also felt a little embarrassed translating their comments. I had a strange feeling that on some level, our translator reflected similar sentiments regarding Andy and me. Being an Arab man, he had to show a masculine facade in order for these women not to suspect his secret lustful attraction towards these two foreigners.

Ramiz began, "The ladies said the Hadrah spoke highly of you. He told them that you are good in art and design and they wondered if you could give them some advice on how to dress well?"

Smiling and flattered by their compliments, I replied, "Thank you for the compliments. I will be delighted to assist in any way possible. I'm not an expert but I certainly am very interested in the subjects of art, fashion and design and I study various Eastern and Western fashion styles and trends diligently."

Nasreen in perfect English, asked, "We were wondering if you would give us some fashion tips on the latest European styles and trends?"

"Sure!" I replied excitedly, since fashion was my favorite topic. With an audience of interested women, I could easily sit and talk shop for hours.

"When would you like to start? We can have an informal discussion - you ladies can ask the questions and I'll do my best to answer," I continued.

While Nasreen was translating to Habibah and Ghaniyah, Shiya asked, "Maybe you can also teach us some techniques to improve our fashion sense. We generally have our clothes made by a dressmaker who comes to the women's quarters, but she is not a designer and we have to tell her what we require. Since none of us are designers, we don't know what will look good on us. Can you give us some advice on this matter?"

"Of course I can assist, but I have to see what's in your existing wardrobes before giving an opinion." I wondered what kind of garments they wore beneath their shapeless burkas.

I was surprised when Shiya exclaimed cheerfully, "That will be great! We'd love to show you what's in our closets and you can then show us how to mix and match!"

I didn't know how to respond to her remark since I had been repeatedly told by my Valet that men were not to venture into the female section of the mansion. Viewing their wardrobes meant I had to be invited into the women's quarters. So, I turned to Ramiz and my guardian for an answer.

My mu'allmi focused his gaze on me and said, "It is OK for you to enter the women's quarters as long as you have permission from the Hadrah."

Shiya added quickly, "We'll talk to my father this evening to obtain his permission. I'm sure it will not be a problem for Andy and Young to view our closets. After all, it was father who encouraged us to approach our fashion consultant here." She gave me an approving nod.

I was curious to see the women's quarters. "I'm available any time after my tutorials," I stated. I directed a glance at Ramiz, who nodded his approval, meaning that he agreed it was wise to attend his tutorials before spending time with the women on what he considered trivial pursuits.

Turning towards me, Nasreen exclaimed excitedly, "Will you also be able to show us what is currently fashionable in Europe, especially London, since you are studying in England?"

"I'll be delighted to! I believe I'm up-to-date with the latest London designer trends. I study the monthly issues of British Vogue and Harper's Bazaar and I'm knowledgeable on the current designers' signature looks."

My enthusiasm must have spread to the ladies. Shiya spoke on their behalf, "Let's start this afternoon at 3:00 p.m. I'll gather everyone and we can have the discussion in our communal room. Will that work for you?"

"Don't you have to ask you father before I venture into the female domain?" I asked, out of respect for the Hakim. After what happened on the Simorgh, I wanted to make sure I had my Master's approval before making an important decision, like venturing into the women's harem.

The older of the two sisters took control and said, excitedly, "I don't think that will be problem. Father knows you and Andy are decent and will do us no harm. But out of politeness, we'll ask. But I don't think it will be a problem."

"Let's tentatively agree to meet at 3:00 p.m. If there are any changes, we'll inform Mu'allmi Ramiz and he will let you know. Otherwise, we'll see you and Andy by the pool."

I smiled excitedly. The women left, elated. I was especially excited about visiting the women's quarters, since it was forbidden territory. Since Andy was my guardian, the women had no choice but to extend an invitation to him, as well.

I was pretty certain Hakim would agree for us both to see the women's closets, since he already knew my Valet and I were lovers. He was a worldly man and had a pretty good sense that we would not be sexually interested in the harem women. If it were Gaston and Jacques, that might have been a different story.

Besides, Nasreen and Shiya were his favorite daughters and, being favorites, they were able to sweet-talk their father into giving in to their wishes. The other female children were not as blessed with the power of persuasion as these two pretty teenagers were.

CHAPTER FIFTY

Fashion! What Fun!

"Those who bring sunshine to the lives of others cannot keep it from themselves."
James M Barri

The Ladies

At 3:00 p.m. that afternoon, Andy and I proceeded to the swimming pool to meet Nasreen and Shiya. They were already sitting under a large cabana sipping ice-cold Arabian coffee. They invited us to join them for beverages so they could brief us on etiquette when meeting the rest of the ladies within the women's quarters.

Shiya started, "We gathered a group of four women to see you this afternoon; they are very excited. We will meet at the Tawus (Arabic for peacock) room. It is quiet and we can talk without any disturbance."

"Wonderful!" I said.

"When you finish your drinks, we will proceed inside, to meet the ladies. I've already gained approval from Father," answered Nasreen.

"As-Salāmu `Alaykum," Andy and I greeted the ladies as soon as we met.

All of them wore hijabs I could see their faces; every one of them had beautiful, flawless complexions. They were already seated on comfortable sofas and easy chairs placed around the ornately decorated room. There was a lingering scent of perfumed; jasmine. Nasreen addressed the women in Arabic, extending a polite welcome greeting to my Valet and me.

She began, "Why don't you start by giving us a little introduction about yourself and then proceed to tell us about the current London fashion trends and the new styles that are emerging."

I provided the women with a summary of how I became interested in fashion, and then inquired if they had been to London. Nasreen translated, as I spoke. One of the ladies answered, "Yes! The Hadrah took us a year ago, for three days. We went shopping in Knightsbridge and Oxford Street. We purchased gowns at Selfridge's and Harrods. I love shopping in London."

The women giggled when Jamilah, Hakim's fourteen-year-old granddaughter broke in, "We subscribe to British, French and Italian Vogues and L'Official. If we like a particular garment, we order it to be sent here."

Surprised that these ladies were already versed in the latest European fashion magazines and trends, I asked, "Where do you wear all the dresses and gowns you buy?" I directed my questions mainly to Nasreen and Shiya. The ladies laughed, guessing what was on my mind.

Nasreen spoke on their behalf, "We have occasions here in the Kosk to wear them. When we go out of the house we are expected to wear a burka but we can wear anything we like underneath the robe. At special celebratory functions such as Eid al-Adha and Eid ul-Fitr, we have a big celebration at our house. My father invites many close friends and relatives to celebrate with us. This gives us a chance to dress up. Or when we visit relatives and close friends during festival time, we also dress for these special occasions.

"As long as the gowns are not too revealing, we can wear anything we desire."

"Fabulous!" I exclaimed.

Designers

"Since all of you like to buy luxury products, designers are catching onto the idea that there is a huge consumer base here that appreciates and can afford to purchase their designs." The ladies were paying close attention.

"Let me show you some examples of what I'm talking about. Can I thumb through copies of your latest Vogue and L'Official magazines?" I requested.

Shiya proceeded to the cabinet and pulled out several European fashion magazines. Handing them to me, she commented, "No wonder the styles we see in these pages are becoming more and more suitable for us. I was never able to buy anything in London before, as the clothes were either terribly short or showing too much skin, which we cannot wear in this country. Within these last couple of years, all the dresses had gotten longer and the sleeves and necklines are covered."

"Now, I can go into Galerie Lafayette in Paris and finally buy dresses I can wear without feeling exposed or being scolded by my father."

Nasreen added, "I can go shopping in London and Rome and am able to buy dresses that have long sleeves and high necklines. We are not conservative women, but our religious laws dictate that we do not reveal flesh."

"Yes. Notice that some of these collections are heavily embroidered and beaded. Many designers are influenced by Middle Eastern cultures and traditional designs. They update and modify them into current trends for women... of your caliber."

Shiya asked, "Does that mean we are the trend setters? Designers are taking our Middle Eastern styles and readapting them into modern contemporary trends, right?"

"I guess you can say that! But what designers did was lift the essence from traditional styles before translating and reinterpreting their ideas into new ways of dressing and coordinating. That is what good commercial designers do. That is where true creative talent emerges," I explained excitedly.

"But fashion can also be Fine Art," I suggested. "How does one differentiate the two?" questioned Shiya.

"Let's take a few British designers and analyze their signature styles to see if I can answer your question," I asked.

Bill Gibb

"Let's start with Bill Gibb. He became popular in the last few years because he was one of the few British designers who took Persian and Arabian influences and interpreted them, creating elaborate outfits such as these," I said, pointing to several Vogue ads.

"See how he uses bright colors and embroidery from traditional Persian motifs, incorporating them into prints on luxurious satin, chiffon and georgette fabrics? Aren't they beautiful?" I continued.

Rabi'ha asked in Arabic while Nasreen translated, "His clothes are gorgeous! But we can't wear them with leggings like these. Women here are not allowed to wear pants or anything remotely resembling trousers."

I replied, "What you see in the pages of fashion magazines are considered the ideal way these clothes are to be presented. In the practical world, the customers who purchase these clothes will wear them with their own unique style. In other words, it is perfectly acceptable to wear a toned down version of the designer's exaggerated looks."

Nasreen lifted her hands to her chin in wonderment and asked, "How will we know how to edit the 'designer looks' to make them work well for us?"

"Ah! That is where a stylist takes charge. If you ladies agree, I can act as your stylist and give you some pointers on dressing a designer look up or down," I replied.

"When can we start?" asked an overly excited Shiya.

"Before we decide that, let me finish introducing the British designers and their signature looks. Tomorrow, or the day after, I can look in your closets; then we can progress from there to work on styling. How does that sound?" I asked.

My audience chorused an overwhelming "Yes," in Arabic.

I continued flipping through the pages of the fashion magazines and came across several photographs of models wearing Ossie Clark, with Celia Birtwell prints.

Celia Birtwell & Ossie Clark

Pointing to a Vogue magazine photograph of a collage of different patterns and prints, designs by Celia Birtwell, I said, "See the mosaic of Eastern influence in these prints and patterns? Textile designer Celia Birtwell works very closely with her fashion designer husband Ossie Clark."

Jamilah exclaimed, "I saw Ossie Clark's dresses at Harrods department store last year."

"Their collections are sold in most of the major London stores, in the designer section. Aren't these prints beautiful?" I responded.

"Bill Gibb, Ossie Clark, Celia Birtwell and a number of other famous fashion and textile designers are graduates from the prestigious Royal College of Art in London. I want to attend the Royal College of Art after I graduate from Daltonbury Hall," I continued.

Nasreen asked, "Are you planning a career in fashion design?"

"Yes, most certainly. It's been my dream since I was six years old. I believe this is my life's calling," I answered with great determination and certainty in my voice.

Nasreen was curious and continued her questioning, "Are your parents OK with you pursuing such an effeminate career?

My father wouldn't let me study law because he believes a woman's place is in the home and laws in the United Arab Emirates are Islamic laws, created and enforced by men. There are no woman lawyers in our country. I want to be one of the first but the Hadrah is totally against my idea."

"How do you plan to convince him?" I asked with curiosity.

Before Nasreen had a chance to answer, I continued, "My father doesn't like me studying fashion design, either, but my heart tells me I have to do it. I will find a way to do what I love doing."

"I will have to find a way to convince my father that it's alright for a woman to be a lawyer. I hope he will come around to my way of thinking." Nasreen looked sad when she spoke. "Let's get back to fashion, which we all love, and we'll talk about our ambitions later," she said more cheerfully.

"Can we reach a stopping point, and continue another day?" Andy chipped in, as he was bored with all this fashion talk and was ready to call it a day. He was more interested in building bridges! Since my Valet could not leave without me, I politely made the excuse that I had homework to complete. I said we could continue our interesting conversation another day when I would return to see the ladies' wardrobes.

CHAPTER FIFTY-ONE

In The Mosque

"There is nothing safe about sex. There never will be."
Norman Mailer

Ubaid

The day after I met the ladies at the women's quarters, Ubaid, the Hadrah's twenty-year-old son who was studying architecture at Trinity College, invited Andy and me to visit a mosque. He described the unique Moorish architectural features which we would find interesting. Hakim had mentioned to him that I was into classical architectural designs, so Ubaid suggested we take a drive to the historical building and he would be our tour guide.

I was terribly excited that morning as we jumped into the new Porsche 914 that his father had recently bought him for his twentieth birthday. Although the fancy vehicle was a two-seater, there was sufficient room for me to sit on Andy's lap. Traffic regulations then were not as strict as they are now, especially in the United Arab Emirates. Being stopped, even for speeding, in this top-of-the-line sports car would not be a problem for the Hadrah's son. Most U.A.E. traffic cops could easily be paid a little 'bonus' money to turn a blind eye, even if our guide was speeding at ninety miles an hour down country roads towards Dubai city.

Being the youngest son of a wealthy oil tycoon, this hot-headed twenty-year-old acted the part of a spoiled brat from a rich and famous family. He loved to take risks and lived the fast life, like many of his young peers.

According to E.R.O.S. regulations, Andy and I were required to wear our blindfolds whenever we left a Household and ventured out, by land. Ubaid convinced us to break the rules, throwing caution to the wind, which we didn't feel comfortable doing since we were brought up as obedient boys. We diligently followed E.R.O.S. and Bahriji School rules. Andy insisted we wear our eye masks as we got into the car, but our guide kept insisting we didn't need to, saying that he would never tell on us.

Just beyond the Kosk driveway, rebellious Ubaid pulled at our harnesses as he drove. My beloved Valet didn't want a car accident to happen due to childish mucking around in a speeding automobile, so we agreed to discard our masks if Ubaid promised not tell the Hadrah. Our naughty guide gave us a crafty grin, nodding his head in agreement.

Off our blindfolds came; it was definitely a relief not to be confined by the cumbersome masks. Feeling a sense of liberation, I drank in the scenery flying by us a mile a minute, my sensible lover held me tightly, making sure I was secured by his strong arms. He didn't want me to bounce off his lap and out of the fast moving Porsche!

It was not easy to have a conversation with wind in our faces, so we kept silent until we reached our destination.

The Mosque

When the Porsche pulled into the parking lot of a beautiful mosque situated on top of a hill, I was amazed by the architectural splendor of this gigantic Moorish building. Tall pillars surrounded the domed structure. Several of the pillars had loud speakers, calling believers to their daily prayers. We entered the marbled entrance. Arabian rugs were strewn on marble floors covered with pairs of shoes and balghas (slippers) left by worshippers who had entered the main prayer hall. It is a sign of respect to Allah for visitors to enter the large prayer room with bare feet.

Since it wasn't Holy Friday, the mosque was not too crowded. Approximately thirty worshippers were prostrate chanting verses from the Quran. Other believers mumbled silent prayers, eyes closed.

As we walked around the edge of the grand hall, I noticed beautiful tiny carved stone stars and crescent moon shaped cut outs in sections of the thick walls. This allowed natural light to create enchanting effects on the floor within the prayer hall. The light seemed an imprint of celestial testimonies cast upon the white marble floors, relating tales of love, compassion and joy for all mankind and the world. I was awestruck by the beauty of this holy place.

Expecting to find Andy and Ubaid at my side, I turned to speak to my Valet. To my surprise, neither of them was around. I continued to explore the great hall, looking for them. On the opposite side of the walkway, I caught a glimpse of my Valet and guide disappearing through a doorway. Silently I followed, some distance behind, through a narrow doorway which the two had entered. I saw a large, open-air courtyard with a tranquil, octagonal shaped fountain of crystal blue water bubbling from a sculpture of a falcon's head. I observed the decorative mosaics and marble surrounding this splendid work of art. In the base of the fountain, I saw inscriptions from the Quran. Golden Arabic calligraphy shimmered under the vibrant sunlight making it appear that the bottom was completely covered in pure gold.

Mesmerized by such beauty, I sat on the fountain's ledge lost in wonder. I could have sat for hours admiring its tantalizing beauty, but I remembered I had to find my Valet and guide. Looking around the open space, I saw four doorways, which I thought led up to the four surrounding pillars in the courtyard. I was wondering which entrance to venture into when I noticed one of the doors had been left ajar, while the others were shut. I decided to go through the opened door.

The Labyrinth

Expecting to find spiral staircases leading to the top of the pillars, I was surprised to find a large room. Red and off-white brick arches and pillars supported the ceiling. The chamber I had entered seemed to stretch for miles. It was silent; no one was in sight. Drawn by the unusual architectural beauty of this space, I quietly tiptoed into the inner sanctum of this holy room. I was transported to a peaceful space within this house of God. I wanted to sit on the cool marble to absorb the beauty of this spiritual sanctuary.

Within the quietness of this expansive chamber I heard faint groaning noises emanating from behind one of the thick circular pillars at the furthest end of the room.

Within The Holy Sanctuary

As quietly as possible I tiptoed closer to the source of the noise. I saw Ubaid and my lover French kissing each other in a heated passionate embrace. The ugly head of jealously rose to the forefront, but I was also excited to witness the scene unfolding before my eyes.

I wanted to go over to separate the two, but my Bahriji training taught me to confront negative feelings, transforming them into positive experiences. My feet felt glued to the floor. I waited; I wanted to see more before deciding upon my next move.

Although the two men were deep in the throes of passion, Ubaid noticed I was standing nearby, watching their every move. My arousal showed underneath my thobe. I voluntarily lifted my garment, exposing my erect penis to my Guide, while they continued their kisses. Ubaid motioned me to join them. Being an obedient Oasis student, I did as was told.

When I was a few inches away from Andy and Ubaid, my guide gently pushed me down on my knees, sandwiching me between the two of them. They lifted their thawb, tying the hem of their garments into knots at their waists, while I lowered their underwear to their ankles, devouring their engorged manhood with a hungry passion I didn't previously know I possessed. The fear of being found in this forbidden act was just as exciting as tasting the juicy fruits of the two mens' loins, which exploded all over me. It would have been high sacrilege if our ménage a tois had been discovered by the Islamic authorities. "There is nothing safe about sex!"

My Bahriji education had served me well. Jealously rears its ugly head and we can choose whether or not to give it power over us. I learned to conquer the negative, and to transform fear and jealousy into positive experiences.

CHAPTER FIFTY-TWO

Redesigning Women

"Get in touch with the way the other person feels. Feelings are translated from body language (55%), tone of voice (38%) and words (7%)."
Bernard Tristan Foong

The day after my mosque outing with Ubaid and Andy I was back at the women's quarters. This time I was invited to view the ladies' wardrobes and continue our fashion discussions in a more relaxed manner. Nasreen and Shiya met my Valet and me at the swimming pool and led us into the Tawus room.

I was taken aback to find twelve women instead of the original we met the other day. It seemed that word had got out that a "fashion expert" were in their midst, and the harem women were out in force to learn more about fashion sensibilities. They wished to obtain advice regarding individual makeovers. Since there were newcomers, Shiya suggested I go over general fashion trend information before reviewing their wardrobes and advising them further on the art of fashion co-ordination and accessorizing.

Jean Muir

"Sure, let's do that," I said.

Nasreen and Shiya had already laid out some new copies of British and French Vogue on the coffee table for me. I casually flipped open one of the pages to a photograph of Jean Muir's designs. Turning the magazine towards the ladies, I pointed to the page and continued, "Jean Muir is currently one of the most sought after designers, although she considers herself a dress-maker rather than a designer."

Nasreen asked, "I've seen local women wearing copies of her designs at functions, here."

"She uses a lot of black and dark colors, which are similar to the traditional black abayas."

"Another element she has incorporated from the abayas is her use of jersey fabrics, which drape splendidly on the female form and can easily be worn by women of different sizes," I replied.

"Many of the women here like to wear bright colors under their burkas," added Nasreen.

"I'm not surprised by this information," I continued, "Wearing bright colors underneath burkas counteracts the sober colors. There always has to be balance in the Universe, otherwise the world will be lopsided." I said, half in jest.

"Have you heard of the Chinese philosophy of Yin & Yang?"

Shiya answered immediately. "I learned a little about Asian philosophy at my Swiss University. Doesn't this concept have to do with the balance of the female and male energies?"

"You are quite right, Shiya. Without balance, we Chinese believe the world will not function properly. The male and female energies can mean many different things in different aspects of life. Elementarily put, it simply means embracing both the negative and positive energies without discarding or ignoring one or the other."

"We love to wear bright colors, and it is very much a part of our tradition to wear decorative accessories to match our garments," Shiya said.

"Well then, I'm sure I'll be in for a treat when I view your closets. Where should I begin?" I responded enthusiastically.

I wanted to see more of the women's quarters as well as to have the opportunity to view their wardrobes. Nasreen and Shiya could hardly wait to have me view their wardrobes. Since their suites were next to each other, I suggested I see the one closest to the Tawus room and then progress down the corridor.

Shiya's Suite

Shiya's sitting room, located adjacent to her bedroom, was elegantly decorated. The wall covering had lilac, magenta and cream-colored orchids intertwined with green vines printed on an off-white textured background. The furniture was upholstered in deep purple velvet coordinating with the patterned wallpaper. Ivory colored rugs were placed on white marble floors.

Lilac and purple orchid plants displayed on the mirrored mantel provided a fresh green house garden environment, giving the room a comfortable feeling. Adjoining the sitting room was a large walk in closet, painted lilac, edged with rose wood. The walk-in was beautifully arranged with the short dresses in a row, graduating from soft to strong colors. The long dresses were arranged in the back of the closet.

Printed dresses lined the opposite side of the huge closet. A built-in dresser had multiple drawers filled with jeweled brooches, bracelets and necklaces, as well as costume jewelry. A full-length mirror with three panels provides the females with a 360-degree view.

Gina Fratini & Ossie Clark

As I looked through Shiya's clothes, I noted that many of the dresses were by British fashion designers, Gina Fratini and Ossie Clark. When I saw these clothes, I was able to decipher a little about Shiya's character since Gina and Ossie's designs were soft, romantic and overtly feminine. Without saying a word, I continued browsing through her closet.

Shiya couldn't wait to ask, "What do you think of my choice of clothing?"

Smiling, I said, "You are certainly a romantic heroine at heart, aren't you? You like being romanced by Prince Charming, and being swept away to his castle far, far away."

Shiya looked at me with her large brown eyes opened wide, saying, "How do you know my thoughts?" she gasped.

"It's not difficult to tell. Your clothes speak of who you are." I replied, delightedly. "What you wear tells who you are. By looking at your wardrobe, I already know you are a very feminine woman. I can also tell you what perfume you like to wear without having to view your dressing table."

"You like to wear L'Air Du Printemps by Nina Ricci and Amor Amor by Cacharel, correct?" I continued.

Shiya said in girlish delight, "Those are two of my favorite perfumes. You are good!"

I replied laughing, "It is very easy to tell because you have this bubbly girlish charm and I'm sure you have many admirers and suitors, ready to ask for your hand. It is little wonder you are one of your father's favorite daughters. I'm sure the Hadrah loves you very much."

Smiling coyly, she turned away and did not reply.

Nasreen's Elegance

Nasreen's suite was as elegant as Nasreen herself was. There were hardly any flowers, except for several pots of cymbidium orchids, placed strategically on a low coffee table. As soon as I entered the room I could smell a familiar scent, reminding me of the perfume my mother wore, Chanel No 5. I knew immediately that Nasreen was a sophisticated and elegant woman without looking at her wardrobe. She possessed a style that was very different from the other harem ladies, but similar to my mother. Most likely she would wear Jean Muir, Yves Saint Laurent and Chanel.

The room was sparsely but beautifully furnished with the purest white, cream, beige and deep browns. Lush cream carpeting with a swirly tone-on-tone pattern covered the entire floor.

As I sat in the pristine white settee admiring a gorgeous Persian shawl draped across the sofa, I couldn't help but think about my mother. Once again, I was missing home (or rather, I was missing my mother and my female cousins). When Nasreen spoke she said, "Young, you seemed lost in thoughts. Are you OK?"

"I'm fine. I'm missing my family in Malaya a little."

Nasreen enquired, "Oh! You are from Malaya? I have been to Kuala Lumpur. I have a Malay girlfriend I met at University who is from your part of the world. It is a beautiful country and in many ways their customs are similar to ours."

"Malaya has Ramadan followed by Hari Raya Puasa and Hari Raya Haji, similar festivals as Eid ul-Fitr and Eid al-Adha, right?"

I nodded as she continued, "Ramadan will be starting in a week's time here. Immediately after Ramadan we have a big celebration, Eid ul-Fitr, to celebrate the end of our fasting season. Maybe you can help us with a fashion makeover and style us for this big celebration party? Father invites a lot of his business friends and many of our relatives to celebrate this festive occasion at the Kosk."

"I would love to. It'll be an honor for me to be of assistance to you ladies," I said excitedly.

Shiya said happily, "That will be wonderful! How long will the make-over take?"

I continued, "Since there are quite a number you and Ramadan lasts an entire month, we can use the month wisely and I can consult with all of you on your individual make-over needs during this period. Then we can unveil the results at the Eid ul-Fitr party. How does that sound?"

"Wonderful!" replied the ladies, joyfully.

True Communication

As I moved down the line through the ladies' closets I was amazed to find all of the most celebrated designer dresses and gowns within the Kosk's women's quarters.

Most of the women possessed a combination of styles and designer choices but several had very distinct personalities and their uniqueness was reflected in their clothing choices. For example, Ghaniyah's closet was filled with Thea Porter and Emilo Pucci dresses. This indicated to me that she was very much a free spirited bohemian woman, wanting to break out of her mold. She wanted to become her own woman, but was trapped and bound by the social and political restrictions imposed on her by the culture and religion into which she was born.

Through studying their choices of fashion and accessories I got an idea of the feelings and state of mind of each woman. It was, indeed, strange to me that fashion reflected so much of the wearer's personality and state of being.

Over the course of my life certain truths became clear:

- The way a person feels is often communicated through the language of fashion.
- In many situations verbal communication is the least expressive means employed to explain one's feelings.
- Body language speaks volumes.
- Tone of voice tells more than the words themselves.

Since I didn't speak Arabic, I did most of my makeovers with the Kosk ladies by reading and observing their body language. I detected their responses through their tone of voice when they responded to suggestions about their individual makeovers.

At the end of the day, I was delighted to have been given this fantastic opportunity to assist the harem women in elevating their (often low) self-esteem, and in bringing some joy into their lives through what I love best, speaking the language of fashion!

CHAPTER FIFTY-THREE

"Pussycat, Pussycat I love you"

"Love knoweth no laws."
John Lyly

Kitty, Kitty, Where Are You?

One evening, several days after my visit to the ladies quarters, Huṣni, my white Persian kitten, disappeared into the garden. Usually, the Abds and servants fed, brushed and looked after my beautiful feline each day. In the evenings, Huṣni would be at our sides, following Andy and me around our chamber, keeping us company. For reasons unknown, on this particular night pussy scratched at our bedroom door, demanding to be let out. I thought he wanted to go into the adjacent sitting room, so I opened the bedroom door for him. Instead, he decided to jump out of one of the large windows that Andy had left open for fresh air.

Since Husni was an indoor cat, I was afraid he might run away and not return. The security guards on the compound had ferocious Alsatians stationed around this huge estate, ready to pounce if they detected intruders. If kitty lost his way and ventured too far, I was afraid the guards' animals might tear my defenseless creature to shreds. I told sleepy head Andy I was going outside to retrieve our Persian.

The Butterfly Lovers

I ran downstairs and out into the inner garden. I did not see Husni anywhere. I started calling the Persian's name softly, so I wouldn't wake the entire Household. I looked everywhere for him but he was nowhere to be found. I checked the shrubberies and behind the mansion walls, but no cat. As I neared the gazebo I saw a flicker of light. Thinking Husni might have gone inside the pavilion, I looked through one of the windows.

In the dim candlelit interior, I saw a sea of moving black fabric. As I stood watching, my eyes became adjusted to the semi darkness. To my surprise I saw two women in black burkas intertwined in a passionate embrace. Although their upper bodies were fully covered in black exposing only their faces, I could see flashes of soft brown skin where the burkas had been lifted above their naked thighs. The couple was making soft moaning noises. Their passionate noises told me a love story was currently unfolding in the heat of the Arabian night.

I was mesmerized by the sexuality before me, when suddenly I heard rustling footsteps approaching my way. I turned round and saw my Valet walking in my direction, looking for me. I quickly put a finger to my lips, gesturing to him to be quiet, and not make a sound. Seeing my signal of silence, he discarded his baghas (Persian slippers) and walked barefoot to my side. I pointed in the direction of the window, so he could observe the happening within the gazebo.

At first, he could not see what was unfolding, but as his eyes became adjusted to the dim light he also witnessed the women making love. We both looked at each other in amazement but kept completely quiet, not wanting to create any commotion and disrupt the passion.

The lovers lay on a comfortable sofa; one woman lifted the other's burka over her head. They wore nothing beneath their dark robes. I immediately recognized the naked lady as Khawlah, the Hadrah's third wife, but I could not decipher who the other woman was, since she was still wearing her burka.

Khawlah parted the legs of the robed woman. She gently stimulated her with teasing fingers, before lowering her lips over her lover's vulva, sucking and licking her. I had never seen two women making love before. I was in awe, and so was Andy.

Occasionally, we would turn to look at each other for a response. We were too stunned by the scenario to consider moving away.

Before long, Khawlah lifted the black robe from her lover. I could see clearly the face of the other woman, who was the beautiful Gharam; she was a cousin of Nasreen and Khawlah's lady-in-waiting. I had assisted each of them in the fashion makeover.

They were often spotted in each other's company, although on the surface they seemed more like friends than lovers. I suppose they were much like Andy and me, portraying a picture perfect male friendship, yet we were lovers in private. In both cases, intimate companions and lovers were all rolled into one.

My Valet and I continued our voyeuristic endeavor. We were Peeping Toms. Both women were in their prime and their shapely naked bodies were delightful to behold. My lover and I wanted to see what lesbian sex was about, so we continued watching the two passionate women. For two gay boys, watching women making out was quite an educational experience. Before tonight, I had no idea what lesbians did when they performed the sex act. I did know that women could achieve multiple orgasms within short intervals. Our professors had taught us that in sex education classes. But I had never, in reality, witnessed women making love, until now.

To me, this looked like a very beautiful experience. Khawlah and Gharam reminded me of butterflies fluttering in and out of each other. With their dark cloaks intertwined around their smooth skin, they very much resembled a couple of monarch butterflies, fluttering in flights of fantasy. Andy and I were definitely enthralled watching the dancing lovers' feminine responses. They were twirling and twisting to and fro from oral ecstasies which both performed enthusiastically.

Later in my adult life, when opportunities arose for me to relate this experience to my heterosexual friends, they always asked if Andy and I joined in the fun with the women. And when my reply was a strident "No," adding that the experience for us was purely educational, they were often shocked that we did not get aroused by what we witnessed that warm Arabian night. My explanation has always been the same: Andy and I are gay. They often replied, naively, "Don't gay men get turned on by female eroticism?"

"No! At least not these two gay men! Women's sexual organs do not excite or arouse us sexually," has always been my reply.

Naughty Pussy

Where did I find the Persian? She was above us the entire time, on top of the tree where Andy and I were standing. The naughty Persian had also been watching the love scene unfolding below; he had a cat's eye view from above. Husni did not make a sound; I felt some bark falling on top of my head and looked up. The wayward kitty was scratching the tree trunk with his sharp claws. My sweet, sweet pussy was waiting for his owners to rescue him.

As soon as Andy tried reaching for him, Husni decided to play one of his crafty little games, jumping into the darkness and heading for the men's quarters. Softly, and as quietly as possible, my lover and I tiptoed away from the pavilion, back to our sleeping quarters. The Persian was leading the way into our peacock chamber.

It was 1:00 a.m. by the time the three of us slipped into deep slumber. My handsome lover was excited by the illicitness of the scene we witnessed and by our voyeurism. He demanded we perform our own private 'sexcapade' while our peeping pussy watched, as he had earlier.

CHAPTER FIFTY-FOUR

Night Clubbing After Sunset

"Dance as though no one is watching you. Love as though you have never been hurt before. Sing as though no one can hear you. Live as though heaven is on earth."
Alfred D. Souza

Since the outing to the mosque, Ubaid had been sneaking into our Peacock Chamber day and night, expecting sex. As much as we enjoyed his company, Andy and I were beginning to wonder if he had any friends to keep him company besides us. One day when he was in our room, he suggested we go clubbing.

Andy being an overly responsible protective Valet said, "Young is shouldn't be going to clubs. He has lessons in the morning with Ramiz."

Ubaid laughed wickedly and said, "No worries mate! One night of discoing is not going to jeapodise his studies, no problemo! Let's go this Friday evening after sunset, before the Club closes for Ramadan, otherwise we will have to fly to Paris to party."

I was curious and excited to go to a dance club since I had never been and was dying to experience Dubai's nightlife. I said excitedly, "Yah! Let's go! I've never been to a nightclub. I want to go!"

Andy, the sensible one of us, was reluctant to put me in the dangerous situation of being an illegal under-aged clubber. With my insistence and Ubaid's persistence, my guardian agreed to go, on the condition that we had to be back at the Kosk no later than midnight, along with several other terms and conditions to which the daring Arab agreed.

Shopping

Although Ubaid promised we wouldn't be out later than midnight, we did not leave the Kosk until 10:00 p.m. that Friday evening. Since Andy and I didn't have any party clothes, Ubaid had taken us shopping at a classy Dubai mall the day before to buy us clubbing clothes so we wouldn't look out of place at the discotheque.

Ghali, our chauffeur, under the supervision of Ubaid, drove us in one of the family's three Rolls Royces to the city's shopping center. Since Ghali was with us, we behaved like good Bahriji students, donning our eye harnesses until we reached our shopping destination.

Ubaid was a big spender; in every boutique, the Arab wanted to make purchases, either for us or for himself. Like his father, he was a generous man and insisted on buying us outfits we liked which looked good on us.

The first shop we went into was a unisex boutique, a rare phenomenon in the Middle East in sixties. It was an elegant shop catering to a new generation of wealthy clients such as our radical young host. Dubai did not have many trendy boutiques since most of the wealthy elites traveled to Europe to shop, where fashion collections were up-to-date. Besides, the prices in the Dubai boutiques were three times more expensive than the normal retail price in Paris or London. Andy and I were desperate to locate something trendy to wear. We had few choices but we settled on a couple of Pierre Cardin and Paco Rabanne outfits.

Entering the CLUB

Once again, we set off in Ubaid's Porsche 914. I sat on Andy's lap while our host drove. We took our eye masks along in case someone spotted us. Then, our plan was to quickly harness ourselves.

Hopefully, no one would notice our truancy. In his usual bubbly fashion, our defiant escort drove towards the city at lightning speed. This time, he drove 100 miles per hour, thundering through the desert.

Instead of going towards the city, Ubaid drove us to a deserted warehouse district out of town, where fences were set up around a large compound. It was an industrial, high security no trespassing zone. When the Porsche drove up to the security gate, two heavily armed guards stopped the vehicle and asked to see the driver's pass. Ubaid flashed his security identification at the guards and handed them a wad of Dirham bills before they opened the gates to let us through. There were already a number of expensive sports cars parked at the back of the building, out of sight.

We entered through a doorway and were confronted by another two security guards standing by a large steel door. They were dressed in black and carrying rifles. This scene reminded me of the James Bond movies Goldfinger, and Thunderball, where Bond and the villains had to bypass security to access secret underground vaults. It was an exciting adventure for me. Andy, being the responsible Valet, had his arm around my shoulders, making sure no harm would befall his lover since we didn't know where our daring host was leading us.

Chapter Fifty-four

The CLUB

One of the men in black took one glance at me and stopped us, even though Ubaid had shown him his entry pass. Speaking in Arabic, our young host pulled out another wad of folded Dirham and handed them to the two men guarding the steel door. They immediately became friendlier, uttering a warm "As-salāmu aleikum" (welcome) to us. Andy responded with, "Aleikum as-salām." As soon as we passed through the steel door, the setting shifted from a stark environment to a warm and cozy atmosphere. I felt as if I had entered Aladdin's cave. In front of us were several sets of moon gates with a curtained entrance over the final gate.

The latest disco hits were blaring loudly throughout this huge space. Disco lights flashed around the dance floor where a large crowd had gathered to dance the night away. My happy feet were already moving to the rhythm. My hips were swaying and I couldn't wait to get on the dance floor to boogie. When my eyes adjusted to the flashy interior, I was surprised to find women in mini-skirts and trendy clothing that I wouldn't have seen outside of this club. This disco was hopping; the club was like a trendy dance club one would find in London, Paris, or Rome. How was this happening in Dubai?

Inside the club was a different world. It seemed like swinging London suddenly landed in the middle of a deserted warehouse in the Arabian Desert. The girls wore belly-dancing costumes and were singing and dancing to popular sixties tunes, but in Arabic. This was certainly a strange, new and exciting world; I was eager to dance and celebrate the night.

Although I had never been to a disco in the United Kingdom, I had seen enough pictures and movies to know what a discothèque looked like, and this club was no different than what I had seen.

We were shown to our seats by a scantily dressed, belly-dancing waitress. Andy and I ordered orange juice, but Ubaid was already drowning himself in a green elixir with a layer of foaming mist on the top, served in martini glasses. He pulled out several large bills to tip the waitress who left us with a smiling face.

Dancing In the CLUB

Since the music was so enticing, I asked Andy if he would dance with me. Women were dancing in groups or with each other, as were the men. There were also men and women dancing together and some danced by themselves. I was flabbergasted by the freedom and openness of this place; males and females were not segregated.

When Andy and I were on the dance floor, a group of Ubaid's friends came over to chat. All his friends were rich Arab heirs and heiresses, educated abroad and exposed to western cultures.

After several extensive dances, I was exhausted. We returned to our seats to watch the dancing and the light show flickering before us. Ubaid's friends didn't seem to mind the intimacy between Andy and me. My guardian wrapped his arms around my shoulders, as we sat in our seats. It was difficult to talk to any of Ubaid's friends with the music blaring loudly. It wasn't until later when we moved into private chambers that we had a chance to become acquainted.

The Belly Dancers

Before we entered the discothèque, our young host handed Andy and me $5,000.00 each, to spend as we wish. He had hinted that we might require some money to tip the wait staff and the entertainers if and when they came over to perform. When the belly dancers started dancing, a couple of the dancers came towards us jiggling their bosoms, bellies and hips. We showered them with Dirham as they swayed their bodies back and forth, rhythmically.

I found it fun and interesting to watch the female dancers shaking and shimmying their voluptuous bodies. I decided to join in the fun. Getting out of my seat I began shimmying with them. The five dancers thought it great entertainment to have a guy shimmy, so they danced round me while I shook my lean hips and trim belly and the audience applauded.

By the time the dancers left, I was in a state of heated exhaustion, and I desperately needed an orange drink to quench my thirst. I moved toward the open-air courtyard to catch some fresh air. I was having so much fun that I completely lost track of my midnight Cinderella curfew, which Andy had made Ubaid promise to keep.

Chance Encounter

As I sat on one of the cushioned benches in the open courtyard, wiping away my perspiration, I noticed a figure standing next to me. When I looked up, I was shocked to see, Habiibi Aziz, Hakim's son-in-law!

He greeted me saying, "Masā' al-xeir", meaning "Good evening."

I replied as calmly as possible, "Masā' an-nūr."

The Arab continued, "Who brought you to here, Young? Where is your Valet?"

"Oh! I came with Andy and Ubaid; they are inside with Ubaid's friends," I finally uttered.

Aziz continued, "I want you to come see me at my chamber tomorrow evening. I have something to show you that I think you'll be interested in."

"Sure! What time should I come?" I asked.

Habiibi replied, "Come at 10:00 p.m. Do you know where my chambers are located?"

I said, "I'm sure Andy will show me."

"I want to see you alone. Andy can wait for you in my sitting room while I take my time with you in my bedroom," he advised.

"I will inform Andy of your request and will see you at 10:00 p.m. tomorrow evening," I answered.

Just then Andy came out to the courtyard and saw Aziz talking to me. Andy greeted the Hadrah's son-in-law politely and said, "I'm so glad to see someone we know here. I think Ubaid has had a little too much to drink. I'm afraid he cannot drive home in his current state. Although he keeps insisting he is able to handle driving, I don't think it's a good idea. Would you talk with him and possibly drive him home in your car? I can drive his Porsche and follow you so we are able to make it back to the Kosk."

Habiibi replied, "Let's go in and see how the rascal is doing."

Just as we were arriving at our table, Ubaid ran past us looking pale and sickly, as if he was ready to throw up. He rushed into the washroom. We followed him in as he was throwing up in a toilet stall. Andy assisted Ubaid in cleaning himself up after this disastrous incident, and Aziz decided it was best for us to leave the club immediately.

Ubaid was so wasted that Aziz and Andy had to carry him out. Getting him into Habiibi's fancy Lamborghini was not an easy task; Ubaid resisted, drunkenly. Eventually, Aziz managed to talk some sense into the young man's rebellious head and he finally relented, leaning back to allow Andy to buckle him in securely.

Since my guardian and I had no idea how to return to the Kosk, we followed the fancy Lamborghini, closely. On the way home, we had to stop several times to assist Ubaid, who threw up when he opened his passenger door at stoplights. I don't think his brother-in-law would have forgiven him if he had vomited in his expensive sports car. Luckily, he didn't.

Conversation in the Porsche

As Andy was driving the Porsche, my curiosity got the better of me and I asked my lover, "Was it alright for us to be openly dancing together and be so intimate with each other in the club?"

My Valet replied, "You may or may not have noticed that it has always been acceptable for two Arab males to hold hands or put their arms around each other when walking down the streets in this part of the world. The majority of people in the Kingdom think nothing of this custom. It is perfectly acceptable for boys and men to be close, unlike in the western world where our intimacy is considered taboo."

"Does that mean it is alright for us to hold hands in public?" I asked.

Andy replied, "It depends on the situation; it is difficult to give you a definite answer as it depends on the circumstances."

As I was contemplating Andy's response, I suddenly remembered Habiibi's summons for me to be in his room the following evening. As I was so absorbed in my guardian's answer, I did not tell Andy about my assignment with Aziz.

When we arrived at the Kosk, it was past 2:00 a.m. Without making much noise, Aziz and Andy carried the drunkard upstairs to his room, stripped him down and laid him on his bed. I couldn't resist taking a photo of this sexy Arab boy in his drunken stupor. It had been an exciting and fun evening; Andy and I were happy to call it a night.

My Valet and I did not know we had gotten ourselves in trouble, until we were summoned to Hadrah Hakim's chambers the following afternoon.

CHAPTER FIFTY-FIVE

Educating a Naughty Boy

"Perhaps a child who is fussed over gets a feeling of destiny; he thinks he is in the world for something important, and it gives him drive and confidence."
Benjamin Spock

During my regular class with Mu'allmi Ramiz the morning after our clubbing episode, one of our Abds informed Andy and me that the Hadrah wanted to see us at 3:00 p.m. that afternoon. My heart sank as I guessed that Hakim must have gotten wind of our illegal clubbing activities. I was in for yet another reprimand.

Conversation with Mu'allmi Ramiz

A few times during class, I couldn't keep my eyes open and my tutor gave me a look that seemed to suggest he knew what I had been up to the night before.

My professor asked, "What's the matter, Young? Are you not well?"

Desperately trying to stay alert, I replied, "I am fine. A little tired that's all."

"I'm not surprised; you guys didn't get in until after 2:00 a.m.," he replied.

I looked at Ramiz, wondering how he knew we had been out so late. He continued, "I saw you at The Club last night; I love the way you danced, very invigorating!"

Shocked at this unexpected information, I blurted out, "I didn't see you last night. Did you see what happened to Ubaid?"

"Yes! I saw everything. I was asked by the Hadrah to keep an eye on all of you.

"That's why I stood some distance away to observe everything that went on. Hakim knows what goes on with Ubaid. That boy is always getting into trouble. He needs friends with a focus, to give him direction. Before you guys arrived at the Household, he had no real friends, other than hangers on, who constantly took advantage of him," my teacher explained.

By now, I was completely surprised at the information told to me by my mu'allmi. I asked, "What about Ubaid's friends at the club? Don't they care about his well-being?"

Ramiz said in a solemn tone, "As you witnessed last night, none of his friends assisted him when he was drunk or advised him to slow down, or even helped him when he was throwing up in the washroom."

"Most of the people he knows are only there for a good time; once they smell trouble, they run and abandon the poor chap."

"If you and Andy and Aziz hadn't been there, he would be wasted, lying in his own puke at The Club."

I said in amazement, "Is that why he's been hanging out with us these past few days? Andy and I were beginning to wonder if he had any friends of his own. His friends seemed like such pals with him at the disco."

I paused and then asked, "Wouldn't you have gone over to help him, if we weren't present?"

Ramiz replied, "Of course I would have assisted him, but my mission there was to observe you guys and report to the Hadrah."

Ramiz continued, "Ubaid is a good-natured boy but he falls in with the wrong crowd of people. What he needs are good-hearted people to guide and assist him, to help him get back on track. He seems to have gravitated to Andy and you. That's why the Hadrah wants to talk with both of you this afternoon."

I continued questioning my tutor, "What can we do? We are only a couple of outsiders who are stationed here for three months. How can we help Ubaid get back on track?"

"Oh! Young, you will be surprised what a few months can do to a person. It can do wonders if he mixes with the right crowd of people."

"I have tried to assist him but he won't listen to me; we have known each other since we were kids. Growing up together can sometimes be more of a hindrance than help. He doesn't think I have the right to tell him how to behave."

"That's why outsiders like you and Andy could be the right people to guide him back on track. I'm sure Hakim will discuss this in detail. I'm only giving you a heads-up, before you head into the meeting this afternoon," Ramiz concluded.

Conversation with Master Hakim

At precisely 3:00 p.m., we entered our Master's chambers. Ubaid was seated in a chair, looking much better than the night before, although he was still suffering from a hangover. Our host welcomed us and gestured for us to sit on the large settee, next to his son.

The Hadrah, sitting behind his imposing desk, started, "My son," gesturing towards Ubaid, "due to his immaturity and insolence, came close to getting both of you in trouble for breaking the Bahriji and Islamic laws. We had a father and son discussion before you entered. As much as I'd like to reprimand you as well as my naughty boy (pointing to Ubaid) for your misconduct, I feel it is not your fault that you landed in this situation."

Looking directly at us, Hadrah continued, "In fact, I want to thank you for tending to this rebel when he was misbehaving last night. I know Andy and you, Yoong, are responsible people. Before I proceed any further, Ubaid has something he wants to say to you."

Ubaid's Apologies

Ubaid, looking embarrassed, said, "I'm sorry for what happened last night. I drove too fast and smuggled you foreign students into a disco club. I want to say I am sorry for being drunk and stupid and for putting the two of you in harm's way. I want to apologize and I also wish to make up for my stupid mistakes. Will you guys forgive my actions?"

Andy and I were shocked by this sudden turn of events and we looked at each other for a moment, before Andy replied on our behalf, "It is not entirely your fault, Ubaid. I could have insisted we not go to The Club. We know you meant well; you wanted to show Young Dubai's nightlife. It was our responsibility to see that you got home safely. We are glad Habiibi Aziz was there to assist."

Hakim answered as soon as Andy finished speaking, "Now that we have cleared the air regarding last night's incident, we will begin afresh. But, mark my words; I don't want this to happen again!"

He continued without pause, "My son likes your company; he likes hanging out with you two. Maybe you'll be able to talk some sense into his rebellious head. I'll be happy to supply you with all the resources you need to help this wayward boy get back on track. Do we have a deal?"

My Valet looked at me before replying, "Sir, whatever we can do to assist, we will, but I'm not sure what is required of us?"

Our Master answered, "Your friendship with my son is a good beginning. Since the three of you have common interests, such as architecture, art, and music, why not take a week away from the Kosk and go to Florence and Venice. A change of scenery for Ubaid, away from his clubbing acquaintances, will be good for him, not to mention it will be an educational experience for all three of you."

We looked at each other with surprise, and he continued. "Ramadan starts tomorrow and nothing much happens during the month; it will be the perfect time for you boys to travel. Make sure the two of you keep a close watch on this party boy here so he keeps out of trouble. I have great faith in the two of you. I'm usually not wrong in my judgment of people. You are beautiful beings and I'd like my son to learn from you."

Hakim outlined his plan: "The Simorgh will fly you to Italy and back. You don't have to worry about expenses; I will be taking care of all logistics. I have requested that Ramiz travel with you as it will be an educational trip. The mu'allmi will also be available to assist you."

Preparation for Italy

The news of our upcoming travels was announced so suddenly that Andy and I didn't know how to respond. First of all, I had committed to assisting the Harem ladies in a month long makeovers for their big presentation during Eid ul-Fitr. Since I was going to be gone for a week, I decided to give the ladies a fashion homework assignment while I was away.

I met with Nasreen and Shiya immediately after my meeting with the Hadrah. My assignment was for the women to pick three outfits in which they felt most comfortable and to coordinate these outfits with shoes and accessories. When I returned, I would work with them, individually, to provide advice and suggestions on the best ways to mix and match in order to obtain the most fabulous results.

Andy and I packed lightly; the following morning, we were ready to board the Simorgh for Italy.

Ubaid was exuberant that we had accepted him into our fold. He had truly enjoyed our company, beyond our great sexual rapport. Andy and I were beginning to seriously wonder if this young man were gay instead of bi, as he kept telling us.

CHAPTER FIFTY-SIX

An Encounter with the Libertine

*"Do not be too timid and squeamish about your actions.
All life is an experiment."*
Ralph Waldo Emerson

I was so excited about the trip to Italy that I nearly forgot my appointment with Habiibi Aziz. I looked out of my bedroom window at 9:45 p.m. and saw Aziz's Lamborghini parked outside the driveway and it dawned on me that he had scheduled a 10 pm meeting with me, in his chambers.

Andy was nowhere to be found. He must have gone to one of several recreational rooms, all of which contained good sized libraries. Since he loved engineering, I presumed he was digesting engineering books to further his knowledge on the subject. I only had fifteen minutes to prepare to meet Aziz, so I decided to go alone. After all, I thought, I would eventually have to do things on my own instead of relying on my Valet for everything.

There were many suites, chambers, corridors and passageways in the men's quarters and it took me a while to locate Habiibi Aziz's suite. I asked a manservant for help and he kindly guided me to the correct door. By the time I knocked on Hashim's door, I was already ten minutes late. A voice from within the room commanded me to enter.

Aziz, sitting at a desk with his back facing me, said, "You're ten minutes late. I asked you to be here at 10:00 p.m. It's now 10:10 p.m. You will, naturally, be punished for not being prompt."

A thought raced through my head, "Oh no! I'm not going to be blindfolded again, am I?" As I uttered an apology to my host, he turned his chair around and noted that Andy was not with me.

"Where is your Valet?" He asked.

I replied, "I don't know. He must be in one of the recreational rooms, reading."

"Good! I wanted to see you alone anyway. Come over here, I have something I'd like to show you," Habiibi continued.

On his desk were stacks of photographs he had taken during our photo shoot on The Red Sea Riviera. As I was looking through the photos, my host asked, "What do think of these, Young? Do you like them?"

"These pictures are beautiful. I like the unusual angles and the spontaneity of the nude photographs of us on the deserted beach at Shadwan Island. You are an excellent photographer!" I said, complimenting him.

Aziz was delighted with my praise and continued, "Select the ones you like and I'll have a set printed up for you."

He continued, "Besides asking you here to look at these photographs, I have some ideas I would like to run by you, to get your opinion. Sit down and let's talk."

Controversial Photography

Aziz continued, "As you know I am a photographer and (as you probably figured out by now) I like to photograph males and females, nude. I love to capture beautiful people in the throes of passion." Aziz paused and looked at me.

"I plan to do a series of photo shoots utilizing sacred places and religious structures around the world, as backdrops. I want to photograph models making love on the Earth's altars. I would also like to publish a series of luxury, limited edition coffee table books. What do you think of my idea?"

I was surprised that my host would ask my opinion on such an important decision dealing with what would certainly be a controversial topic. I looked puzzled as he continued, "You must be wondering why I'm asking your opinion instead of asking Andy or someone else with greater photographic and marketing experience. You see, Young, I don't want to discuss my ideas with other photographers because I'm afraid they might steal this concept before I produce it."

Aziz, looking directly at me, continued. "I know you have great art and design ideas which you demonstrated with your sketches for the renovation of the Kahyy'am. I like your fresh point of view. That brings me to my next question. Would you and Andy be open to modeling for this photography project? My lens would love to capture the essence of your love, that which is sacred.

"I would also like for you to be my apprentice on this project."

Wow! That was a lot to take in and I did not know how to respond to all his requests. I sat on the sofa, trying to sort out all that he had said in order to come up with a sensible reply.

Finally I looked directly at Aziz and said, "I'll do my best to tell you what's running through my head."

"First, I am curious to know in greater detail what you envision. I love the concept of sacred sex in sacred places. It artistically expresses the interweaving of sexuality and spirituality. I am impressed by the concept of presenting 'no separation' between the sex act and the setting. This pushes the limits of current 'acceptable' thinking," I stated.

Aziz interjected, "My photographs are not pornographic, Young, but artistic." "Yes," I continued, "I acknowledge that, but by placing your subjects in shrines and holy centers, well, that definitely adds a new dimension."

The Arab interrupted me. He seemed especially animated and enthusiastic that I "got" his project and that I was willing to participate.

He spoke to me, saying "There are four reasons I would like you to assist me, Young."

"One, I love your spunk and courage to act spontaneously, with apparent ease.

"Two, From the Kahyy'am's renovation to the Harem women's makeovers, you pour your heart into artistic endeavors. Passion is an attribute I want my apprentice to possess."

"Three, I believe we will have a lot of fun working together on this project."

"And finally, I want you to learn to place your trust in me. You can trust me on all levels, Young. I have the resources and skill to manifest my visions, always."

Before my host could continue I asked, "Out of curiosity, doesn't the Hadrah or your wife mind you being associated with what will surely be controversial work?"

With a big grin on his face, he replied, "They won't know if we don't tell them."

Amazed at his craftiness, I questioned Aziz further, "What will they say if they do find out? Will it not jeopardize you and your family's reputation?"

The photographer laughed and replied, "I plan to start the shoots far away from Arab scrutiny, away from this part of the Islamic world."

"I will begin with Europe's famous religious sites, such as well-known Jewish synagogues and Catholic Basilicas and Cathedrals. I will publish and sell the first book in Europe and America. If it is successful, I will do the second series of shoots in Eastern religious temple; Hindu and Buddhist shrines. I'll leave the mosques in various Islamic countries around the world for last."

"If I work on this project outside of the Kosk, I believe I can get away with the Hadrah not knowing what I'm up to. My wife is the easy part of the equation. When we start working together, I can explain to you in greater detail about my marriage and my relationship with my wife."

"Let's just say, for now, that I have everything under control. There is nothing for you or Andy to worry about. All you guys have to do is agree to my proposal."

I took a deep breath and ordered my thoughts. "Personally, I don't see anything 'wrong' with photographing people in the throes of passion in any settings, outdoors, indoors or in holy places, as long as the models are willing participants. We are living in an entirely new generation, one which is rocking the confines of what has been acceptable, societally, for centuries. I am a rebel at heart and I find your proposals extremely tempting."

"As you are aware, my education at Daltonbury and the Bahriji School has taught me freedom of expression which most students my age would have difficulty understanding. I am open to new ways of thinking and expressing, and I think this idea of yours is fabulous!"

"I truly appreciate you asking me to be a part of this exciting project. I agree to be your apprentice and to model for this fascinating project; I just have to run this by my Valet and gain his approval."

Brainstorming

"What concerns me is this," I said. "Won't the religious establishments be up in arms? Will they even let your film crew enter their shrines and temples, to photograph? I don't know the logistics of gaining permission to proceed with such a grand project," my voice trailed off, as I mused.

Hashim smiled and said, "I have many contacts and sources who I believe will be able to pull the right strings for me to accomplish my project."

I thought about my imminent travels and told Aziz, "Ubaid, Ramiz, Andy and I are leaving for Italy tomorrow morning for a week. I will talk with Andy and get back to you when we return from our trip, is that alright with you?"

He replied, "Sure! Let me know when you get back. We'll do more brainstorming upon your return."

Changing his tone of voice and the subject, my punisher commanded, "Now, your punishment for being late; get out of your clothes and get your sweet ass into the bedroom. We have work to do."

By the time I returned to the Peacock chamber, Andy was in a panic over my disappearance. Calming him, I said, "I'm here now and I am safe and sound. There is nothing to worry about. Sooner or later, I will have to take care of myself. Tonight seemed an excellent evening to start!"

CHAPTER FIFTY-SEVEN

At the Palazzo Della Gherardesca

*"Beauty is the wisdom of women.
Wisdom is the beauty of men."*
Chinese proverb

At precisely 11:00 a.m. the next morning, the four of us departed the Kosk, with Andy and I harnessed in our eye masks. We departed for Dubai airport to board the Simorgh to fly us to Firenze, Italy. Once on board the plane, Ramiz handed Andy and me an envelope with a message from the Hadrah, along with $7,000.00 in cash, as pocket money. The message read. "Thank You boys! My son needs friends like you. Have fun in Italy. Be Safe! Hadrah Hakim."

We thanked Ramiz for Hakim's generosity to which the mu'allmi replied, "The Hadrah is a very generous man and always has been. He cares about Ubaid very much and wants him to excel in his career and life. He will do all a father can to get his son back on track; he definitely trusts both of you."

Andy said on our behalf, "We will do whatever we can, to assist Ubaid. I'm sure Italy will be good for him. A change of scenery away from his clubbing pals could do wonders."

Firenze

It was a beautiful autumn afternoon when our flight touched down at the Firenze Peretola Airport. A yellow Rolls Royce was on the tarmac waiting to drive us to the Palazzo Della Gherardesca. The property is known today as the Four Seasons Hotel in Firenze. In the mid-sixties, the property belonged to family members of the Viceroy of Egypt, Ismail Pasha, who passed in 1922. Hadrah's family was close with them; we were guests at the Palazzo when it was still a private home.

As the Rolls drove down the winding streets of Firenze, I was amazed by the splendor of the city's architecture. The medieval fountains covered with beautifully carved marble sculptures of the naked human form were mesmerizing. I was in awe of the history and beauty of this magnificent, magical city.

Andy was in seventh heaven when we drove past the elaborate bridges. He wanted to study the Florentine bridge building techniques in great detail, and he asked our chauffeur to stop several times so he could feel and breathe in the Medici magnificence. Firenze, the city of art and culture, was taking our breath away.

The Palazzo Grand Entrance

As soon as the vehicle arrived at the front door of the Palazzo, a couple footmen and servants greeted us and helped to unload our luggage. The ceiling in the entrance was covered with murals, scenes from the Old Testament, replete with angels. The frescoes were so realistic; I kept looking heavenwards to decipher details, until Andy called me to hurry and follow the group.

A wide ornate staircase covered with plush, deep red carpet greeted us. As the manservants were bringing in our luggage, the butler showed us into the grand salon, which is now The Four Seasons "Gallery Lounge." The spacious room decorated in Italian Renaissance style, included floor-to-ceiling murals and a beautifully carved mahogany grandfather clock, which chimed every fifteen minutes. The salon was filled with such splendid objets d'art and grandiosity that I didn't even notice the two figures seated on the red velvet settee. The men in their dark suits seemed to be part of the décor, until they stood and welcomed our party.

Miraj and Wasim

The older gentleman, Miraj, was the current proprietor of this eleven-acre state; he was the direct descendant of Viceroy Ismail Pasha. The younger man, Wasim, who looked more like an Italian playboy than an Egyptian heir, was one of three grandsons of Ismail Pasha. He was three to four years older than Ubaid. He was suave, full of self-confidence, and stood six feet in height. After our formal introductions, Miraj informed us that Wasim would act as our guide during our stay, since he was born and bred in Firenze and spoke fluent Italian.

After we were seated Miraj said, "Hakim told me that you are here to experience Firenze's art and culture. There is certainly plenty here to see. Have you boys been to our city before?"

Ramiz replied on our behalf, "No Sir! I believe these three young people have never been to Firenze. I was here two years ago. I came as part of a study trip when I was studying in Oxford, to visit the art museums and to learn more about Florentine literature, since literature was one of my majors at Oxford."

Our host answered, "Superb! Then you know where to take these boys. Although I have lived here for many years, I am not so much into the art scene. I travel, frequently, to the Netherlands and Denmark because I own and operate banks in those two countries. It leaves very little time for me to spend in my beloved City."

Miraj, his Excellency, continued, "My other two sons are also involved in the family business. They are stationed in Amsterdam and Copenhagen. Wasim is the only one left in Firenze, along with his mother and our other harem relatives. He will show you the city since he is here for a few days before returning to University, in Rome."

Ramiz continued speaking on our behalf, "That will be splendid, thank you for your hospitality. Would you join us for dinner tonight? Maybe your Excellency or Wasim would be so kind as to recommend a restaurant."

Before his Excellency could speak, Wasim chirped in, "The Relais Santa Croce is a great place to dine. Shall we go there? I know the maître d'hôtel and he'll be able to reserve us a table with a nice view overlooking the Arno."

Miraj answered, "Yes! That's an excellent choice. Unfortunately, I will not be able to join you. I have an important business call to make. You boys go ahead and enjoy yourselves. We can dine together another evening when I'm not bogged down with bank issues."

Wasim continued, "Great! I will make a reservation immediately. Let's meet here at 8:00 p.m. I'll inform Amid (the chauffeur) to bring the Lincoln Continental to the front, and I'll drive us myself."

A manservant showed Andy and me to our suite, called "The Nobel Suite." These were the most luxurious accommodations I had ever experienced. Maids and manservants were on hand to assist Andy and me around the clock. All we had to do was pull a brocade chain by the bedside and the service bell would ring downstairs, where the servants were stationed. Later in my adult years, when watching the British television series, "Upstairs Downstairs" where the Lords and Ladies up stairs rang bells, and the butler, housekeeper, and servants would ascend, from below, to attend to their masters' and mistresses' needs, I was reminded of the Noble Suite within the Palazzo Della Gherardesca.

On the way to Relais Santa Croce

Dressed in evening dinner attire, we met Amid in the grand salon. The open-topped, golden Lincoln Continental was parked in the Palazzo's driveway, awaiting us. Ubaid sat in the front seat next to our designated driver, Wasim. I sat between Andy and Ramiz, in the back. It was a wonderful experience to drive through the back streets of Firenze in a convertible. Although there was considerable traffic, it was a breeze compared to driving through the congested city earlier in the day. As we slowly cruised down cobblestone streets heading towards our dinner destination, Ramiz nonchalantly placed one hand on my lap to see if I would move away. There wasn't any room to move to, as the three of us took up the entire back seat. I surrendered to the situation. I was sure Andy noticed Ramiz's hand; he pretended nothing unusual was happening.

It seemed to me that when Arab men were away from the confines of their restrictive kingdom, they were much more liberal. Ramiz kept his hand on my lap the entire time, as everyone oohed and ahhed at the many breathtaking sites en route to the restaurant.

Dining at Relais Santa Croce

When our car arrived at the restaurant, a uniformed parking valet was standing at attention, ready to open our doors. Lorenzo, the maître d'hôtel, came to welcome us into the dining room. As soon as we entered the sophisticated dining room, memories of the elegance of London's River Restaurant flooded my mind. I was charmed by everything I had experienced, thus far, in Firenze.

As soon as we ordered our food, Ubaid asked, "What kind of exciting things happen here?"

Our host replied, "There are many exciting things to do here in our beautiful City; it depends on what you like to do. There are places to cater to every taste. Speaking of taste, shall we order some wine to drink with our meal?" our host inquired.

Andy quickly chirped, "Order enough for yourself and maybe a glass for Ubaid and me." Looking at Ramiz, my Valet appeared to wonder if he had spoken too soon. He had overlooked our teacher's preference.

Ramiz said, "Just order me a cup of hot tea. I'm not one to drink anything stronger than Arabian coffee. Tea will be fine."

"I'll have tea too!" I added.

Andy was obviously monitoring Ubaid's drinking so the Arab boy wouldn't get himself drink himself into oblivion, again. For some unknown reason, our friend seemed to listen to my guardian's advice. He only consumed a glass of red wine before switching to Perrier water for the rest of the evening.

I noticed Ubaid kept glancing at a couple of young ladies at the bar. After our meal, Wasim suggested we proceed to the lounge, for coffee and dessert. Excusing himself, Ubaid headed in the direction of the bar, where the washrooms were. We made ourselves comfortable on lounge chairs, as we awaited dessert.

Ubaid's New Friends

Looking at Andy and me, Wasim asked, "How did the two of you end up at the Kosk?"

Andy replied, "We are students on a three month study trip at an Arab Household; the Hadrah kindly accepted us as his guests. He is the one who has provided us the opportunity to visit Firenze, to learn more of your city's art and culture."

Wasim continued, "Tomorrow we can visit the Uffizi; you'll see lots of Renaissance art, and sculptures. It is a very beautiful museum containing many famous medieval paintings."

Ramiz added, "The last visit I didn't have enough time to see everything. Now is a good chance to continue my own education at the Uffizi."

I said, enthusiastically, "I'm already in love with Firenze and can't wait to explore the galleries and take in as much as I possibly can."

Wasim laughed at my remark, "You are a very excited fellow, aren't you! You look like you have the energy to explore the entire city! We'll start early in the morning. I'll take you to breakfast before our museum tour. How does that sound?"

"Fabulous! Marvelous! Supercalifragilisticexpialidocious! This is all so exciting!" I cried enthusiastically. They were all laughing at my youthful exuberance when Ubaid returned with two girls by his side.

He said, "Let me introduce Gianna and Allegra; we just became acquainted at the bar." Andy and I looked at each other, smiled and greeted the ladies pleasantly.

Wasim immediately asked, "Are you ladies visiting the city like these four gentlemen?" He directed his gaze at Ramiz, Andy, Ubaid and me.

Gianna replied, "My parents have a vineyard in Tuscany. I'm visiting them for a few weeks before returning to New York where I attend college. My friend, Allegra, is visiting from New York."

Ubaid added quickly, "Since you are visiting the city as well, we can experience this delightful place together!" He gave Andy and me a wicked wink, informing us he wanted to get to know the ladies much better during our time here.

Andy replied politely, "Sure! That will be fun. I'm sure the both of you will enjoy this young man's company," directing his gaze at Ubaid.

We sat and talked until a little after 11:00 p.m., when Wasim drove us back to the Palazzo. I still hadn't found a suitable moment to discuss Habiibi Aziz Hashim's proposal with Andy. I promised myself I would, as soon as the correct moment presents itself. Tonight, I just wanted to enjoy Firenze with my lover, making love in the 'Noble Suite.'

CHAPTER FIFTY-EIGHT

At Gallerie Dell Accademia & Ponte Vecchio

"Believe that it's better to be looked over than it is to be overlooked."
Mae West

Florence at Dawn

Firenze in early dawn has an air like no other city in the world. I awakened at 5:30 a.m. after a wonderful night spent in the arms of my lover. While Andy was still deep in slumber, I decided to venture into the beautifully kept Florentine gardens within the Palazzo Della Gherardesca. I could not help but reflect on how blessed I was that I had decided to join E.R.O.S. I hadn't looked back since I set foot on English soil. My intuition had continually guided me through every situation. The Universe had blessed me in many ways, not the least of which was providing me with a delightful lover who cherished me and looked after all of my needs.

I could not help but wish the same for Ubaid, and for Nikee. I had little contact with Nikee since he left the Bahriji. I had been absorbed in my new life, with Andy, in the Household. Although, Nikee had only been gone from my life for six weeks, memories of our time together seemed distant. As I walked, marveling at the beauty of the autumn landscape, I come across my mu'allmi. He was also up early, not wanting to miss the beginning of a beautiful day. Sitting alone on a deserted bench admiring the golden orange leaves, he seemed to be in a state of deep meditation.

Conversation with Mu'allmi Ramiz

Since I began my studies with my teacher, I had not had an opportunity to know the man behind the books. Our lessons together were solely academic, and our relationship was one of teacher and student. More often than not, I would be in class with Rizq (Hakim's grandson) and Gaston. Normally, after lessons, we uttered our polite thank yous and went on our merry way.

Today was the first time I saw my teacher alone. I wished to take the opportunity to get to know my professor. His eyes were now closed and I did not want to disturb his prayers. I sat patiently on the bench opposite him and watched a couple of squirrels playing on a branch above my teacher's head. Before long, Ramiz opened his eyes.

Surprised to see me watching him, he asked, "Young, what are you doing up so early? Shouldn't you still be in bed? We have a long day ahead of us and you need to be well rested for our day's outing."

I smiled and said, "Sabah el khee (good morning) mu'allmi."

He acknowledged and returned my greeting, "Marhaban (Hi)!"

I continued, "It would be a shame to waste such a beautiful morning hiding indoors. I want to enjoy a breath of the Florentine air before we go into museums and galleries. Do you always get up so early?"

Ramiz replied, "I am used to getting up early to pray. Today is the first day of Ramadan; I want to make sure I had enough to eat and drink before sunrise. I have been up since 4:30 a.m."

"Come over and sit with me," he continued. "Since we are here, I have the opportunity to get to know you better. Is Andy up already?"

"Oh no, he is still sleeping," I answered, while walking over to sit by my teacher.

I asked my tutor, "Although there are many Muslims in Malaya, I don't know much about their customs and religious practices. Do you mind enlightening me about your faith?"

"Not at all; I will do my best to answer your queries. What do you want to know?" replied my tutor.

"What's the purpose of Ramadan?"

My professor laughed as if this was an elementary question to which everyone should know the answer. He began, "It is a month when Muslims around the world fast. The reasons we fast are manifold. First, it is a practice of cleansing our bodies from harmful materials, flushing out toxins like liquor from our bodies."

Before he could continue, I chirped, "I thought hard liquor is banned in the United Arab Emirates?"

He smiled and said, "Although it is banned, it continues to be sold on the black market at a high price and people still obtain it, illegally."

"You mean similar to Prohibition in the United States, in the late 1920s and 30s? Doesn't it make people crave alcohol, if they are not allowed to purchase it legally?" I was curious to hear his answer, since Andy had mentioned to me that the 'American Prohibition' hadn't worked.

Mu'allmi replied, "It is difficult to give you a definitive answer on this topic. With most things in life, people and societies impose double standards about how and how not to behave.

My belief is that it should be up to the individual to restrain from drinking rather than being forced by a government or a religion to abstain, which can often generate a lot of friction.

"Returning to my explanation regarding Ramadan, it is also a time to turn away from worldly matters and devote time to Allah. My personal interpretation of the Quran is it's a time to be at peace with myself, to abstain from materialistic pursuits, and also a time to refrain from sexual practices."

Scratching my head, trying to understand, I questioned, "Does that mean Muslims cannot have sex during the month of Ramadan? What happens to married couples; they don't have sex for the entire month?"

My teacher burst out in laugher and responded, "No, it doesn't mean they don't have sex; it means they don't have sex during daylight hours."

Before he could continue, I chirped, "So they can have sex at night, before dawn and after sunset?"

Ramiz found my question very funny, "Come to my room this evening and I will teach you more regarding the dos and don'ts of Ramadan. For now, we better return to our suites to get ready for our busy day. We have a lot to do today."

By the time I returned to my room Andy was already up, getting ready for our 9:00 a.m. excursion.

"Young, get your cute ass ready, we have to meet the rest of the party in half an hour," commanded my guardian.

Outside Gallerie Dell' Accademia

Since the Gallerie Dell' Accademia was a mere 5 minutes' walk from the Palazzo Della Gherardesca, Wasim suggested we eat a light breakfast at a cafeteria near the Gallerie before venturing into the museum. Although Ramiz, Wasim and Ubaid were all fasting, they took a couple of sips of coffee during breakfast, leaving Andy and me to feast on delicious Italian patisseries.

We had invited the two ladies, Gianna and Allegra, to join us. They arrived late, just as we were purchasing the admission tickets into the Accademia. Looking fresh and beautiful, they sashayed up and greeted us.

As we proceeded into the Gallerie, already admiring the intriguing artwork, our party spilt into several different camps. Wasim and Allgra drifted in one direction, while Ubaid and Gianna went in another, leaving Ramiz, Andy and me to explore the halls together. We agreed to meet at the gallery's foyer at noon, and then visit the shops at Ponte Vecchio and grab a light lunch at an eatery nearby.

Michelangelo's David

There were so many things to absorb and so little time to take it all in. Finally, we arrived at the foot of the famous statue of David by Michelangelo, which seemed to exude a heavy homoerotic undertone. I was curious to know what my teacher Ramiz thought of this gigantic marble sculpture, so I asked, "How do you like Michelangelo's masterpiece?"

Ramiz responded immediately, "It is beautiful how the master carved such an amazing depiction of the male form. I like it very much; every detail and proportion is so well balanced. What do you think of it?"

I replied, "It is amazing. It startles me, how the artist can carve such a perfect statue from a slab of marble. And the sheer size of it baffles me."

Continuing, I said, "I love everything about this statue except his male endowment, which seems tiny compared to the rest of his body, although his buttocks are well proportioned."

My teacher laughed and teased, "Are you larger and better endowed than David?"

I was embarrassed and turned a shade of red. Andy smiled and said, "Trust me mu'allmi, this boy's endowment isn't bad and he has a nice bottom as well."

They both laughed making me even more embarrassed than before. Ramiz jokingly said, "You better show me this evening when you come to my suite, so we can compare notes."

By now I was completely red in the face. I walked away from the two men to avoid their teasing. From a short distance I saw them talking and occasionally turning their glances in my direction. They were obviously discussing my assets.

There were too many rooms and too much interesting art to take in over the course of one morning. I did not have enough time to see everything. I decided to return another day to study more fabulous paintings and sculptures.

At Ponte Vecchio

By the time we found a restaurant at Ponte Vecchio for lunch, more than half the day had passed and we had only seen one museum. There were many more to visit. Even though it was Ramadan, the only person who was observing a strict fast was my mu'allmi. Wasim and Ubaid consumed some food and water. The two ladies, together with Andy and me, ate most of the delicious food that was placed before us.

After lunch, Wasim suggested we look at the Ponte Vecchio shops before calling it a day. Ubaid and Gianna had become inseparable. It was the same with Wasim and Allegra. We agreed on a later meeting place and time before we went exploring again, divided into three different parties.

Andy was more interested in bridge construction research than shopping. He spent a great deal of time analyzing the engineering marvels, leaving Ramiz and me to browse the various shops, without any intention of making purchases. Using this opportunity, I decided to continue studying my teacher.

I asked, "Mu'allmi, are you married?"

My tutor seemed taken aback that I would ask his marital status. Giving a little thought he replied, "I'm betrothed to a lady, Noor, by my parents."

Curious that he should add 'betrothed by his parents,' I continued asking, "You sound like you have no choice in the matter but to marry her. Is this an arranged marriage?" I wanted to find out more information on the subject of arranged marriages.

"If I had my way, I'd remain single. Then I would have the freedom to travel and do what I want to do, instead of being tied down with family responsibilities," Ramiz said sadly.

"Are you the only son in your family?" My inquisitiveness got the best of me.

He replied, "I have two older brothers, a younger brother and three sisters. All my sisters and older brothers are married. I'm considered of age to marry and my father wants me to marry Noor. She is a distant cousin and comes from a well-to-do family. If our union is sealed, our families stand to gain financially from this marriage."

"Do you love Noor?" I asked.

"I haven't set eyes on her since I was six years old and she was four. I don't know what she is like in person, although I have seen pictures of her. She and her family live in Riyadh. She looks pretty in the photos but if I had a choice, I'd rather not marry. I'm just not the marrying type," answered my professor.

"Why would you go through with this betrothal when you don't love this girl?" I asked out of innocence.

"Oh my dear Young, you don't understand my culture. Most of our marriages are arranged to further advance our family's status, and also for the purpose of procreation. Most of the time love doesn't come into the equation. Maybe, if a couple is lucky, they might fall in love after they tie the knot," sighed Ramiz.

"In case you haven't noticed, most men do their own thing and the women do theirs, even if they are husband and wife. Most men don't respect or appreciate their women folk and they often talk down to the females. Maybe that's one of the reasons I don't want to get married."

"But there are other reasons as well which I don't feel comfortable telling you now. Possibly down the road when we become better acquainted, you'll understand," he said with sadness in his voice.

By now, Andy had returned from his bridge building observations and Ramiz changed our conversation to one more light hearted and jolly. By the time we returned to the Palazzo Della Gherardesca, I was exhausted, but still eager to explore more of the palace before our late dinner outing to yet another luxurious restaurant, the Santa Elisabetta.

CHAPTER FIFTY-NINE

At the Ristorante Santa Elisabetta

*"Love is of all passions the strongest,
for it attacks simultaneously the head,
the heart and the senses."*
Lao Tzu

The Palazzo Della Gherardesca was a truly beautiful and historic mansion. As I ventured into the various halls and rooms, some of which were forbidden to male visitors as they were the domain of his Excellency's women's harem, I was in awe. All the wall murals and frescoes had been painted by well-known artists during the Renaissance's Golden Age. They were filled with scenes depicting Old Testament stories, such as Adam and Eve in the Garden of Eden, tempted by the serpent to taste the forbidden fruit of knowledge. Every detail of the stories was painstakingly included in these frescos. I was literally walking through an art museum as I wandered through our accommodations.

Journey to Ristorante Santa Elisabetta

When in Italy, do as the Italians do; one of the things they do is to dine late. At 8:00 p.m., our party gathered at the grand salon of Palazzo Della Gherardesca before heading to the Ristorante Santa Elisabetta for dinner. Wasim wanted to drive his Alfa Romeo Giulia Spider, to impress the two ladies. Although it was a two-seater, a couple of passengers could sit in the rear, on the top of the convertible. In the sixties, traffic police did not arrest passengers for sitting on the tops of sport cars.

Since Wasim and Ubaid went in the Alfa to pick up the girls at their hotel, Amid, the family chauffeur drove Ramiz, Andy and me in the yellow Rolls Royce to the restaurant where we would then join the two couples. We passed by several mesmerizing fountains, and requested that our driver stop the car so we could get a closer look at these gorgeous works of art. Firenze at night was spectacular in every way. The city's romantic illumination and the sensuality of its fountains must have been the catalyst for many romantic flights into sexual ecstasies. How could one not be charmed by such visual delights? We were seduced by Firenze, the city of elegance and sophistication. For a young man like me, it was, indeed, Heaven on earth.

Dinner at Ristoranto Santa Elisabetta

We arrived the same time that Wasim's Alfa Romeo pulled up to the parking valet. The restaurant, located inside L' Hotel Brunelleschi, was once part of the Torre Bizantina della Pagliazza, a Renaissance style building located in the heart of Florence. Since it was past sunset, our three Arab friends were able to break their fast and eat. I was surprised they didn't binge, since they had had nothing to eat or drink for most of the day.

Since Ubaid landed in Florence he seemed much better behaved than in Dubai. I wondered if his rebelliousness at home was due, in part, to the fact that he was forbidden to cross religious boundaries; therefore, he insisted on proving that he could. Or was he trying to impress Gianna, his new girlfriend? Whatever the reason, this bad boy was behaving himself for a change.

He imbibed one glass of red wine throughout the entire meal, again drinking Perrier water for the rest of the evening.

Ubaid also cut his smoking down to one cigarette after dinner instead of consuming half a pack every evening. Whatever had swept over this young man, Ramiz, Andy and I were happy to see it. Personally, I think Gianna had much to do with Ubaid's sudden change in behavior. Her presence in his life seemed to have a most positive influence on my friend.

Invitation to Villa Le Papavero

During dinner Andy asked the two women, "Did you ladies enjoy the museum today?"

Gianna and Allegra replied almost simultaneously, "We had a marvelous time. Did you?"

Andy replied, "Yes, very much so. We'd like to visit the Uffizi tomorrow. Will you ladies be joining us?"

"We'd love to," Allegra said, looking at Gianna, hoping that she would agree.

Gianna replied, "Of course we'd love to, since tomorrow is our final day in Florence before I have to return home to visit my parents in Tuscany."

I chirped, "How exciting, I wish I could visit Tuscany. I've seen pictures of the Italian countryside and it's beautiful. Don't they grow grapes there? I wish I could go with you!" I spoke rapidly, with great excitement.

Gianna suddenly said, "In that case, why don't you guys come for a visit? I'm sure my parents would be delighted to meet you."

Chapter Fifty-nine

My eyes opened wide with excitement at the thought that I might be in for another grand adventure, when Ramiz responded, "It would not be polite to impose on your parents, having us barge in, uninvited."

Gianna said immediately, "Don't be silly! It's not a problem. My parents are always having guests at Villa Le Papavero. And I'm sure they would love to meet all of you, especially this exuberant young man (looking at my direction). I'll call them tomorrow to inform them that you guys are coming for a visit. I'm quite positive that it will not be a problem."

Andy added, "Young wants to go everywhere and he is not shy to tell you. We certainly don't want to put you on the spot and make you feel you need to invite us."

Gianna laughed and said, "Don't be ridiculous! It is really not a problem. My parents live approximately an hour outside of Florence. You can make it a day trip. If we leave early the following morning you can return to the city in time for dinner."

I saw Ubaid's eyes sparkle at the thought of being able to spend another day with his girlfriend and getting to meet her parents in the process. He quickly agreed that it would be a nice outing for us to troupe to Italian wine country.

Wasim was also delighted to be able to spend a little more time with Allegra before he had to return to his university, in Rome. He was all for the idea and agreed that it would be a nice way to see the vineyards with someone who was familiar with the region. By the time dinner was over, we had already planned our day's outing to Villa Le Papavero.

As we sat in the restaurant lounge enjoying our coffee and desserts, serenaded by an excellent pianist and violinist, playing Italian arias, Wasim suggested, "Let's go dancing. I know a great disco club where we can have a good time. Besides, the night is still young!"

Ubaid, bubbling with enthusiasm replied, "What an excellent idea. Let's go!"

Andy quickly added, "I'm afraid, Young and I will have to pass; we have another full day tomorrow and we need to catch some rest. You should all go and have fun."

I was disappointed to be left out of such a fun experience but my Valet called the shots and he was right about having a full day ahead tomorrow.

The ladies were quick to agree to clubbing, since they didn't want the evening to end so soon, either. The only person who didn't seem keen on joining the couples was Ramiz. As much as he didn't fancy the idea of staying up late, he reluctantly agreed to go. I believe the main reason he went was to keep Ubaid in line. After all, he had promised to keep a watchful eye on Hakim's son, making sure he didn't go overboard drinking and partying. If Ubaid did overindulge, Ramiz could minimize the damage and save his childhood friend from embarrassing himself and his family, in public.

Ramiz seemed sad that our evening's appointment in his chambers would not occur. But, I was sure there would be other occasions for us to get to know each other, intimately.

Since there were five in the party, it was decided that Amid would chauffer them in the Rolls, while Andy drove us back in the Alfa. I was glad to have some alone time with Andy; it was the perfect opportunity to discuss Habiibi Aziz's photography proposal, as we experienced Firenze by night in the convertible.

Conversation with Andy

It was such a rush of adrenaline, traveling in the Alfa Romeo with Andy at the wheel. Always a cautious driver, unlike Ubaid, Andy proceeded slowly. This gave us a chance to talk on our way to the palace.

I started the conversation as he made his way around a traffic circle featuring a beautifully lit fountain at its center. "You remember the evening when you went into a panic when you couldn't find me?"

"Yes! I remember. Where were you?" enquired Andy.

Replying with confidence in my voice, "I had been summoned by Habiibi Aziz to his chambers, and, since I couldn't find you, I decided to venture to his room alone."

"You know you are not supposed to go to any of the Household chambers without your Valet present! I need to be close by to make sure you are alright. You disobeyed E.R.O.S rules!"

"I'm sorry but I was in a hurry and I forgot to inform you beforehand that I had been summoned," I apologized.

"Aziz has a rather unusual proposal for us. He is planning to do a series of photo shoots involving models making love in sacred places, such as famous basilicas, temples and mosques around the world. Isn't that fascinating?" I was bubbling with excitement over Habiibi's ideas as I announced them to Andy. He was curious to know more and asked, "How does he plan to get away with that?"

I replied, "He said he has connections and the resources to pull this off. He wants to start his initial shoots in Europe, away from his family, so the Hadrah will not know about it. Then he asked if we would be part of his modeling team. And, he asked if I wanted be his apprentice on this project."

Andy took his eyes off the stirring wheel and glanced at me briefly before speaking, "This is fascinating; it is a huge project to undertake. If it were anyone else, they would have insurmountable problems pulling it off, but Aziz has the financial resources to make this project a reality. How do you feel about it?"

"I didn't promise him anything. I wanted to ask your opinion first. I would love it! To participate would be exciting and interesting, but how are we going to work on it if we are only stationed at his Household for another month and a half?" I asked.

My Valet advised, "This is a very controversial project, we have to consider carefully what the consequences might entail. I love you and will support you in anything you want to do. I would love to do it too. I love to make love to you everywhere, all the time! We are adventurous people, Young, and modeling during lovemaking would not be a problem. I'm just a little skeptical and concerned about possible fallout."

Andy, being responsible and cautious, would consider every possible scenario before taking action. I was sure of that.

I added, "We don't have to give him a reply until we arrive back at the Kosk. We still have time to consider all of the possibilities."

"Good! Let's sleep on this and when we return, we can talk more with Aziz. I'm glad you asked me before you gave him a definite 'yes.' You are such a good boy. I love you very, very much." With that he leaned over giving me a kiss on my cheek while driving.

I smiled happily and said, "I love you very much, too, and you look very handsome all dressed up in your fitted suit this evening." I slipped my hand onto his lap and gave him a kiss back.

Before long, we arrived at the Palazzo Della Gherardesca like a couple of star-struck lovers. Lao Tsu's words certainly rang true for us: "Love is of all passions the strongest, for it attacks, simultaneously, the head, the heart and the senses."

CHAPTER SIXTY

In Anticipation Of Things to Come

"Of all the ways of defining man, the worst is the one which makes him out to be a rational animal."
Anatole France

I woke early again the next morning, on our second day in Firenze. The early Florentine hours held a rare beauty I hated to miss. I ventured into the gardens of Palazzo Della Gherardesca, to enjoy the songbirds' delightful melodies as Andy, my beloved, slept. Again, I saw my teacher, walking the grounds. I caught up with him as he was entering the gazebo to perform his daily prayers. I considered leaving him alone but I was quite curious to discover how the previous night had unfolded, so I followed my tutor into the pavilion.

Chapter Sixty

Conversation with my Teacher

"Good Morning, mu'allmi," I said.

Ramiz turned around, surprised to see me. "Oh! Good morning to you, too. You are up so early again!"

"As usual, I don't want to miss these beautiful Florentine mornings. I'm surprised you are not sleeping, as you were out late last night, I suppose. How was the dance club?" I asked, cheerily.

He replied, "It was fine. The couples enjoyed themselves. I would have preferred to be at the palace, but duty called. I had to keep an eye on our naughty friend."

"Did he behave?" I asked, eager to find out what had transpired.

"Yes! He did, and I'm surprised. Usually, he becomes quite unruly when he goes to those places, but last night he behaved. I think he is keen on Gianna, and wants to make a good impression," Mu'allmi replied.

"Come to my suite tonight after dinner; I want to see both you and Andy. I missed you last night, and had difficulty sleeping."

"Yes! We will come. I'll inform Andy as soon as he gets up," I replied.

Out of curiosity I asked my tutor, "Are you always so diligent, praying five times a day? Don't you get bored and not want to do it sometimes?"

He laughed, seeming to think my line of questioning was rather childish. "Young, my dear, young man, there are many things in life for which I need Allah, to give me strength and guidance. The more I pray, the more insights I receive from the Almighty. To be truthful, Allah is the only solace in my tumultuous life."

I couldn't understand how my teacher could possibly have any difficulties in his life. He was from a wealthy family, he didn't have to worry about finances, he had a teaching position he enjoyed - what more could anybody want in life? My simplistic mind and curiosity egged me on. "Mu'allmi, you already have everything in life, what can possibly be tumultuous?"

Looking serious, he said, "My dear boy, I envy you. You are the one who has everything in life, not me. You are getting a great education and experiencing all the wonders life has to offer. And you have a special person who loves and cares for you, dearly. I, on the other hand, crave things I cannot openly discuss with anyone."

I gazed at my professor in bewilderment and said, "What can that possibly be, Sir?"

Ramiz sighed, "Oh Young, Young, Young! Yes, I love my job and all the material things my family can supply, but the things I crave have nothing to do with that."

"For a start, as I told you, my parents want me to marry Noor, for whom I have no special feelings. Maybe I am an ungrateful son, but I have seen what true love is and I want that. I'm not interested in being stuck in a loveless marriage for the sake of status, position or procreation. Yet, it is my duty to be a loyal and obedient son."

"I pray diligently to Allah to free me from worldly bondage and concerns."

My simplistic young mind immediately responded, saying, "That's easy. Just stand up to your parents and say no to the marriage and do what you want, instead."

Ramiz broke out in laughter, patted me on the head and replied, "You, my dearest boy, are the sweetest and cutest of all my students. If it were only that simple, no one would have any problems, would they? Unfortunately, life is complicated and years of religious tradition and Islamic culture are not discarded, overnight. Besides, my father holds a powerful position in the government. If my siblings or I step out of line, it would bring shame and social disgrace to my family. That is why I am unsettled, and have to ask Allah for constant guidance. Hopefully he will show me the correct path to take."

I looked down on the ground in deep thought before questioning him again, "Why don't you run away to create your own destiny? Then you would not have to answer to anyone except yourself."

He found my suggestion funnier than my previous solution to his problems, and laughed even more loudly. When he calmed, he said, "You are so darling; that's probably why I enjoy your company so much. There is much more than meets the eye. Like I said, when we become better acquainted, we'll exchange more of our life stories. How about that? Maybe this evening when Andy and you come to my chambers you'll have the opportunity to understand me a little better."

"That will be splendid. I'm always eager to learn about everything except bridge building, which Andy is so fond of. I don't understand his love for engineering," I said.

My teacher smiled and advised, "My young one, you don't have to understand bridge building to love Andy. All you have to do is to accept him as he is. I'm sure that's all he asks of you. I believe he doesn't understand your love for fashion design, either, but he accepts it because he loves you. Do you understand? Now, run along and let me do my prayers before we leave for the Uffizi. I'll see you at the Grand Salon at 9:00 a.m."

As I walked back to my room, I could not help but wonder what could be bothering my mu'allmi, making his life so confusing? Suddenly a thought flashed through my mind. Maybe Andy and I were sent by Allah to bring solace?

Galleria Degli Uffizi

Our party gathered at 9:00 a.m. sharp, including the two ladies. I wondered if they had stayed at the palazzo last night after clubbing. They were wearing freshly pressed street clothes instead of their evening gowns from the night before.

Since the Galleria Degli Uffizi was a twenty minute walk from the Palazzo, we declined a ride. By the time we arrived, there was already a crowd queuing to get in. Wasim suggested we grab something to eat inside the galleria. Once inside, I was amazed at the foyer's extraordinarily high ceiling. It made me feel minute in comparison.

We found a table and ordered morning coffee and pastries. Italian pastries are some of the best in the world; lovely to look at and marvelous to taste. Being a greedy boy who was not observing Ramadan, I consumed a large piece of cannoli and a brioche, together with a cup of cappuccino.

As we walked the halls of the Uffizi I couldn't help but think what a rich city Florence had been during the Renaissance. We came across the famous painting, by Sandro Botticelli, The Birth of Venus. I asked, "Can you explain a little about Botticelli's painting, mu'allmi?"

Ramiz thought for a while before answering, "The Goddess of Love, Venus, depicted here, is also known as Aphrodite in Greek mythology. Some art experts believe the painting is a celebration of the love of Giuliano di Piero de' Medici for Simonetta Cattaneo Vespucci, who lived in Portovenere, a town by the sea, reputed to be the birthplace of Venus."

"This is interesting," I said, "It reminds of the James Bond movie, Dr. No."

"How so?" asked my curious professor.

"In that movie, the sexy actress Ursula Andress rose up from the sea, much like Venus in this painting." Andy and my teacher laughed. When Ramiz's laughter subsided, he said, "You are quite right. I saw that movie in London; Venus and Ursula do share similarities. Maybe Ms. Andress was influenced by this painting!"

"She definitely was! I'm sure of it!" I was confident of my viewpoint.

Andy and my Mu'allmi laughed again, before my Valet quipped, "Young also came out of the sea, like Venus, when we were photographed by Aziz during our trip to the Red Sea on the Kahyya'm."

"Really?" my surprised teacher turned to me, continuing, "You'll have to show me those photos. I'm sure you are a sight to behold." They both teased me like they did when we looked at Michelangelo's statue of David.

"Ask Andy to show them to you. I don't think I have any copies."

This remark brought on more laughter so I decided to walk away and leave them to their jokes. Before long, Andy came up to me and said, "We can't help but laugh at your remarks. You are so funny."

I replied in as serious a tone as possible, "There is nothing funny about me at all!"

Andy laughed even more while I tried to keep a straight face. It took him a few moments before he proceeded, in a serious voice, "I spoke to Ramiz. After dinner he wants us to go to his chambers. Before we go, I'll fill you in a little about your teacher. We'll talk when we are alone." I was more curious than ever to hear what my guardian had to tell me, but I asked nothing more.

Corridor of Statues

As we continued our tour, we came across a hall lined with male busts and statues of nudes. I thought to myself, "Oh, oh, here we go again with the teasing." Surprisingly, the two behaved quite well until we came to a statue of naked wrestlers, one subduing the other. My professor said, "Hmm! I like this." His eyes lit up as he spoke.

Andy gave him a sly grin. "And you shall have your wish this evening."

Wondering what their little secret was, I eavesdropped on their conversation while pretending to study the various statues.

Mu'allmi continued, "The brute force is fascinating. See how he dominates the other?"

"That can be arranged. We'll locate a hardware store to purchase the necessary equipment for our rendezvous tonight."

Ramiz eyes glistened at that remark. "Buy a pair of handcuffs while you are out."

Andy said, "That will definitely spice things up!" They exchanged knowing nods before their conversation returned to art appreciation and history.

Basilica di Santa Maria del Fiore

After a light lunch at a restaurant near the Basilica di Santa Maria del Fiore, we proceeded into the large domed Cathedral. Rather than disappearing in separate parties, we stayed together. I finally had a chance to speak with Gianna.

Andy fell in step with Ubaid. "I haven't had a chance to talk with you since we arrived. How are you enjoying the trip so far?"

"It's splendid! I couldn't expect more from this trip," replied Ubaid, giving Andy a wink, implying he was having a great time in Gianna's company.

Since Gianna and I were walking together, I engaged her in conversation. "Are you looking forward to going home to visit your parents?" I enquired.

Gianna, looking happy, replied, "Yes! I haven't been home for a year and I miss the beautiful Tuscan countryside. My parents' house is lovely; it is quiet compared to the street sounds of New York. Don't get me wrong, I love the Big Apple and I have met many new friends, but it's nothing compared to the tranquility of my home, the Italian wine country."

I asked, "Is that why your parents moved to Villa Le Papavero - for peace and quiet?"

Gianna replied, "The property belonged to my grandparents and when they died, my father inherited the land and became a wine maker. He had learned the art of distillation from my grandparents."

"Are you one hundred percent Italian? You reminded me of a distant cousin who is part Chinese and part Spanish." I asked curiously.

Gianna smiled and replied, "I'm part Chinese from my mother's side. She escaped Shanghai just before the Communists took the city. She fled to Florence. That is where my parents eventually met."

"I'm Chinese from Malaya," I added.

"I know. Ubaid told me a little about you and Andy. He said that you are on a three month study program in an Arabian

Household. I would like to visit the Middle East someday," she replied.

I didn't want to give her a negative impression of women's status in the Middle East, so I said, "I'm sure Ubaid will be able to show you around when you travel to The United Arab Emirates. He knows all the trendy places to go."

Ubaid and Andy caught up with us as we took photographs of each other posing by the ancient relics and sepulchers before we called it a day. When we arrived back at the palazzo Andy informed me that he and Ramiz had to run a couple of errands and I should prepare for our evening dinner sojourn.

CHAPTER SIXTY-ONE

Notte Sadomasochistico

> *"Courage is resistance to fear, mastery of fear, not absence of fear."*
> Mark Twain

When Andy returned from his errands he sat me down in our luxurious sitting room and began speaking. "Young, there is something we are going to do this evening that is different and could be shocking to someone like you."

I was curious, "I'm all ears; tell me more."

Mu'allmi Ramiz's Story

Andy said, "Before I begin I have to fill you in a little about Ramiz. You probably already know he is a very religious man and has a number of issues surrounding his sexuality, which he has trouble confiding to anyone.

Chapter Sixty-one

"When he was young, his father found him playing with himself, and also with another boy in his Islamic religious school. His father was very angry and used a leather whip to beat him, thinking that by doing so he would stop what Islam considered sinful."

"Ramiz could not control himself and kept falling back into his 'sinful' sexual habits. Being whipped actually encouraged his sexual thoughts involving another man. After masturbating or a sexual liaison with a male, he would secretly whip himself. He began to crave pain associated with the sex act, self-inflicted or other-inflicted."

I was shocked to hear what my Valet was telling me, but I was also intrigued, and listened attentively.

Andy continued, "When Ramiz was at Oxford University, he stumbled across a homosexual leather bar in London and was amazed to learn that there were others, like him, who liked to roleplay as dominants and submissives."

I asked, seeking clarity, "You mean like what Professor Henderson taught us about sadomasochistic behavior?"

Andy replied, "Yes, something along those lines but in Ramiz' case, it is associated with repentances from his sins. Now he has become addicted to being whipped and abused. After punishment he feels cleansed from his bad behavior until his sexual urges return and the cycle begins all over, again."

I questioned, "Is that why he couldn't sleep last night and got up early to pray? Does he ask Allah for forgiveness because of his sinful, homosexual thoughts?"

"I suppose," replied my Valet. "He became a regular at the London S & M underground dungeons, playing the role of 'slave.' Back home it was next to impossible for him to meet people who behaved in a similar fashion. Then, he met us. We, being educated in varied forms of sexual expressions, are open to experimental ways of thinking and doing things. He asked me to play the role of Master, to handcuff him to the bed and to lash him with a leather whip."

Fascinated by this incredible tale, I enquired, "What am I supposed to do? Where do I come in?"

Smiling, my guardian replied, "You, my darling boy, are to play the part of the savior, to console his pain and anguish during the whipping. You'll soothe him and tell him that he can bear the pain and that the ordeal will soon be over. Gently tell him to be a good man and let his Master have his way with him until his sins are completely cleansed."

I couldn't help but burst out laughing! In my mind it seemed so absurd. My Valet reprimanded me for laughing at such a serious matter and said, "Young, you cannot laugh when we are role playing. You have to be dead serious; otherwise your professor will never forgive you for embarrassing him. Our standing at the Hadrah's Household could be jeopardized."

I continued asking, "Does Hakim know about Ramiz?"

"I don't know. Maybe you can ask your mu'allmi after we are done. For now, we must get ready for our evening at Ristorante La Fonticine," Andy commanded.

At Ristorante La Fonticine

As we sat, waiting for our food in the lavish open air ristorante, I could not help but think of Ramiz's story. I was looking at my teacher, wondering how in the world this gentle man got himself into a sadomasochistic addiction. Was it years of repression that caused this? Or was he born with such an unusual inclination, the way I was born an effeminate boy? All these thoughts ran through my mind like wildfire, as I wondered what our after dinner-rendezvous would bring.

On one hand, I was curious to find out what happens during sadomasochist play-acting, and I secretly anticipated the meeting. On the other hand, I was worried someone might get hurt, since I had not a clue as to what might happen in such a dangerous game. Although Professor Henderson had given us lectures on such behaviors, class studies are vastly different from reality. All I could do was wait to witness, firsthand, what would transpire in the Conventino Presidential Suite, mu'allmi Ramiz's chambers. For now, I concluded, I might as well enjoy a fabulous meal, push my fears aside, and let the evening unfold itself.

Within The Conventino Presidential Suite

Andy and I wore thobes without any undergarments when we proceeded to my teacher's suite at eleven. When we knocked on the chamber door there was no reply. Andy knocked again but there was no response. As we stood, we could hear some groaning noises faintly, through the doors. My Valet decided that we should creep into the room, unheard.

The sitting room was nearly pitch black. The only light was a dim blue nightlight shining from within the bedroom. We tiptoed towards the bedroom door without making any commotion. The door was partially ajar. The television was playing and I could hear moaning and groaning noises, as if someone was in pain.

Ramiz, lying in bed naked, was busy masturbating while watching a pornographic S & M movie. Completely absorbed, he seemed not to notice us standing in the room, watching him play with himself.

When he discovered we were there, he panicked and tried to cover himself, but my Valet was already pinning him down onto the bed. As the two men struggled, I saw Ramiz purposely allowing my guardian to force him into submission rather than trying to wiggle away from his muscular captor. I also noticed that mu'allmi's cock was extremely aroused during the wrestling.

Andy snatched a pair of handcuffs from the bedside table and cuffed my teacher's wrists to the bedposts, face down. Although Ramiz continued to thrash about, his Master controlled him, binding each of his ankles to an end post of the bed. The victim was now under the control of his handsome, dominating Master. Andy blindfolded his conquest with a piece of black material so he could not see who inflicted the blows.

The Master took a black leather horsewhip from a bedside drawer and began whipping his victim's hairy buttocks. With every wallop, the slave let out a whimpering moan, and his captor commanded him to shut up. He would inflict a tougher punishment if he continued squirming, disobeying his commands.

Andy said in an angry voice, "How many times do I have to tell you not to masturbate or watch those nasty movies?"

Ramiz whimpered, sputtering in a barely audible soft voice, "I'm sorry, Sir! I promise I will not do it again."

With each plea of apology the Master gave his slave lashes on his buttocks until the poor man was sobbing with remorse. Andy motioned for me to go over to my teacher and lay his tearful face on my lap, so I could console the victim with soothing words of love and understanding, telling him that his ordeal would soon be over if he did as his punisher commanded.

Mu'allmi cried for the whipping to stop. "Please, please Master! I'll do whatever you command. Spare me this pain and release me."

"No, you ungrateful man! Allah will never forgive you for your sins." Andy scolded angrily while raining another blow down on the man's naked buttocks, yielding another whimpering yelp.

I continued stroking the slave's handsome face, consoling him with compassionate words, leaning down to kiss him on his lips and mouth as he endured another wallop on his backside. Ramiz looked so pathetic that my heart genuinely reached out to him.

The more I consoled my teacher, the further I took on the role of the protector, begging my guardian to stop beating him. Yet, Andy was relentless. Severe blows pelted the man's bottom until it was red and raw from the whipping and spanking. At times, Andy would reach his hand out, to stroke his slave's engorged penis, jerking him nearly to the point of orgasm, then stopping to strike his buttocks again, unrelentingly.

I could tell Ramiz was enjoying all the attention showered upon him from Andy and me. My guardian savored the role of the punisher, and I was the perfect consoler, allowing Ramiz a mouthful of semen from my fountain of youth. I sensually kissed and caressed every inch of Ramiz' body during his punishment.

The Final Ecstatic Torment

By the time we left the Presidential Suite it was almost 3:00 a.m. We were scheduled for an early start to Tuscany that morning. Ramiz seemed deeply satisfied after his punishment. Andy and I were emotionally and physically drained after doing our best to assist Ramiz, who was tangled in remorse, desire and guilt. At least we brought some solace to his tormented soul. We were, indeed, glad we were not in the mu'allmi's shoes. Despite the wealth, education and career success a man may have, he is unsatisfied without the blessing of true love.

"When love and skill work together expect a masterpiece."
John Ruskin

CHAPTER SIXTY-TWO

The Rape of Shanghai

*"The greater our knowledge increases,
the greater our ignorance unfolds."*
John F. Kennedy

Early the next morning we departed Palazzo Della Gherardesca and headed south. Wasim drove Allegra, Ubaid and Gianna in his Alfa Romeo while Andy drove Ramiz and me in a Mini Cooper S. The Mini was all the rage in the 60's. I believe Wasim bought this vehicle as a toy sports car instead of an automobile to use on a daily basis. As we sped out of Florence, the cityscape transformed into beautiful countryside. We drove through stretches of vineyards. The fresh country air and autumn sunshine moved me. Looking adoringly at my lover, seeing his handsome face and elegant figure, I longed for his gentle loving touch. I turned to study Mu'allmi Ramiz, who had a contented grin on his face after last evening's rendezvous. I decided to take this opportunity to find out more from him.

Gentlemen's Word of Honor

I asked my mu'allmi, "Did you enjoy yourself last evening?"

My teacher bristled, slightly, when I brought up the subject of the previous evening. He turned to look out at the scenery as if he hadn't heard what I said. It was a while before he cordially responded.

"Thank you. I had a delightful time and I would like to share similar experiences down the road."

I said, "Forgive me for being forward, but I'd like to ask a rather personal question."

"What is it that's on your mind, my student?"

"Does Hakim know of your sadomasochistic inclinations?"

He replied rather embarrassed, "I believe not, since I'm not in the habit in confiding my sexual preferences to anybody other than those I trust to keep my personal matters confidential."

I quickly answered, "You can definitely trust Andy and me. We will not tell anyone, especially not the Hadrah."

"Good, my boy. I know you will keep my secret. I am glad I can openly talk with you. I like the two of you very much. You are good people," replied my teacher.

Andy responded, "Thank you mu'allmi. Your sexual inclinations are safe with us. You have our word of honor."

At The Villa Le Papavero

Before long, we were driving up to an immensely large Villa with an array of out buildings all painted a shade of dusty pink, glowing splendidly under the hazy Tuscan sun. There was an outdoor swimming pool and a ranch with horses grazing in the meadows around acres of vineyards. It was the harvest season. The grounds were filled with purple and green clumps of juicy grapes. I had never seen countryside so beautiful and could not help but stick my head out the car window, feeling the freshness of the day as the gorgeous scenery floated by my windswept face.

As we pulled up the driveway a middle-aged couple was already standing by the entrance to the main house, ready to greet our party.

"Salve," Signor Giuseppe Di Luca, Gianna's father, greeted us with a huge grin on his face. He spoke broken English with a heavy Italian accent. Signora Lillian Zhang Di Luca, on the other hand, spoke perfect English with a Chinese accent that I had no problem understanding. They welcomed us into their home and guided us onto an open terrace where their servants had prepared a table of delicious treats. I inhaled mouthfuls of Italian pastries and Chinese cookies. I had missed those cookies terribly since I left Malaya.

Signora Lillian laughed when Andy apologized for my rude table manners and said, "I'm glad someone enjoys my baking. Eat, young man, you are a growing boy. It would be a shame to see my cookies go to waste. Dig in, don't be shy."

I continued eating happily. Mrs. Di Luca said, "Gianna tells me you are visiting from Dubai. How are you enjoying Italy?"

Andy replied, "We have loved every moment of our time here. Thank you for inviting us with such short notice."

Lillian answered, "Oh! We are happy to meet all of you. There aren't many Chinese people in this part of the world and I miss speaking Chinese."

She spoke in Mandarin, directing her gaze at me. "Ni shi na guo ren"?

Clearing my throat of a piece of cake, I replied "Malaya Wǒ shì cóng Malaya lái de (I'm from Malaya)."

When I had filled my stomach I was ready to chat further with Signora Lillian. I asked if I could have a tour of her beautiful property. Madam took me on a personal tour of the various buildings. This gave us a chance to get to know each other better.

Signora Lillian Zhang Di Luca

As she showed me each of her beautifully decorated rooms, I asked how she came to settle in Tuscany. "Gianna mentioned you escaped from Shanghai during the Communist takeover, and came to Italy. How did that happen"?

The signora was quiet for a while before she replied with sadness in her voice, "It's a long story. Are you sure you want to listen to an old woman talk about her past?"

"Of course I do. My mother told me some wonderful things about Shanghai when China was under the Kuomintang rule. She said Shanghai was the Paris of the East."

Lillian answered with sadness in her eyes, "Your mother was absolutely correct. Shanghai was a very cosmopolitan city and my family belonged to the literary elite of that era. Unfortunately, when the Communists took power, they destroyed a tremendous amount of our cultural heritage. I was a teenager when I fled to Hong Kong and then to Italy."

With tears forming, she sat down in her spacious living room, dabbing her eyes with a silk handkerchief before she continued, "It was a very sad time for my family. I was the only one who managed to escape when the Communists came to arrest my parents. They had committed no crime except to speak out against the Communist Party and for being wealthy, educated intellectuals."

I was curious to know how she escaped arrest.

Mrs. Di Luca reminisced, studying the landscape as she answered. "I was lucky. The evening the soldiers came to our house, I was going out for dinner with my fiancé, Li. He had just arrived to collect me and we were driving out from the back garage entrance onto the main road when stones were thrown through our living room windows.

"Before I knew it, I saw my parents being dragged onto the street and our house set on fire by the scoundrels. I begged Li to stop and help my parents, but it was too late. The soldiers came at us with bayonets. Li stepped on the gas as they fired at us, hitting him. We drove at top speed to the British embassy. Since we both held Hong Kong British passports we prayed that the embassy would help us once we got onto their grounds."

I was intrigued. "Did you make it to the embassy?"

She continued, "When we arrived, the embassy's gates were closing. Li sped like crazy and we just made it through. We were the last people to make it into the British embassy. By this time Li had lost a lot of blood and fell unconscious. There was so much commotion around us that I could not find doctors or nurses to help him."

Lillian was now sobbing uncontrollably, so I put my arm on her shoulder to comfort and console her as I had done for my teacher the night before. This time, the tears were from reliving a tragedy instead of from pain inflicted as punishment.

Wiping away her tears, she began again, "Li died in my arms that night. I was devastated, but had no choice but to board the helicopter and fly immediately to Hong Kong. I caught the last flight out. Luckily, my family had relatives there with whom I could stay until an aunt who was living in Italy sponsored me, and I came here, to study in Florence."

"Is that where you met and married Signor Di Luca?" I asked.

"That is right. Giuseppe is a good man, a wonderful husband and I am lucky to have him in my life. I don't know you and I'm telling you about my life's misfortunes." said the Chinese lady.

She continued, "You are such a good listener. I never knew I could tell my sad story to one so young."

I replied, "Maybe it's because I'm Chinese and I understand a little about Chinese history and culture. I'm fascinated by what you told me and I want to learn more about my Chinese cultural heritage. Even though I am from Malaya, our forebears were from 'Hor San' in Mainland China. I think at times it takes a person of similar background to know another of the same."

By now Signora had dried her tears and we decided to return to join the happy party talking and laughing out loud, enjoying the late morning sunshine.

Chapter Sixty-two

Italian Hospitality

Lillian prepared a wonderful light lunch with various cheeses, hors d'oeuvres and plenty of wine from their vineyard. I stuck to lemonade and water. Even Ubaid was a good boy and drank moderately.

Gianna's parents were most hospitable, and asked us to spend the night at the villa. Of course Ubaid welcomed the idea so he could spend more time with his girlfriend. We swam in the large heated pool, went horseback riding around their huge estate and enjoyed an early evening country walk with our hosts. During our stroll, I returned to the subject of Lillian's parents after their Shanghai house was set on fire. I fell in step with the signora and asked, "Mrs. Di Luca, I'm curious to know what happened to your parents after they were arrested."

The lady turned towards me and sighed, "My parents suffered a terrible fate. They were thrown into prison and remain there."

I said, "I'm so sorry to hear that. I hope they are out of prison now?"

Lillian's eyes turned red, tears rolling down her cheeks as she replied, "The latest news from my relatives from Hong Kong is they are being dragged out onto the streets of Shanghai and openly denounced by the Red Guards, who are no better than animals honing in for the kill."

My heart reached out to my host, who had suffered such great loss. When I learned that her family suffered such misfortune, I tried to comfort her with my youthful words. "Isn't there any way to get them out of China?" I asked, not realizing that the Republic was locked and closed to the rest of the western world.

"Trust me; I have been trying to help them but my motherland is now operating under a strict regime and a closed door policy. But I am determined to get them released. This I promised myself. Giuseppe is using his connections within the Italian government, and hopefully we will secure their release. I'm praying this reign of terror will be over soon," replied Mrs. Zhang Di Luca, dabbing her eyes again with her handkerchief.

During the rest of the stroll I did not press her for more information. The poor woman had suffered enough relating her story and I did not want to upset her further, so we went on enjoying the countryside with more lighthearted conversations.

That evening we were treated to a wonderful Tuscan dinner at Terrazza Limone. Signor Giuseppe drove us in his yellow Bentley; it was a charming terrace restaurant surrounded by a grove of lemon and orange trees in full bloom.

CHAPTER SIXTY-THREE

Romeos and Juliets

"Love is eternal as long as it lasts."
Vinicius De Morais

After a scrumptious meal at Terrazza Limone, we had time to kill before retiring to bed. Gianna took out her guitar and played a sweet Italian Ballard for us to enjoy. She had a wonderful singing voice and she played flawlessly. When it was time to say good night to our hosts and party, Ubaid asked if he could borrow her guitar on the pretext that he also wanted to try his hand on the strings. She agreed and we trotted off to our respective chambers.

We were staying at the guesthouse a couple blocks away from the main house where the Master and Mistress slept. Villa Le Papavero was a huge estate; the girls' chambers were located next to the guest building.

In the middle of the night I was awakened by strumming sounds from an instrument being poorly played. Andy was dead asleep after a hectic day. Though I was sleepy, the noise was keeping me awake, so I looked out the bedroom window to see who was making such a disturbance. I saw a figure standing below a balcony of the adjacent building. From the verandah all I could make out was a dim light coming from one of the upstairs bedrooms. Rubbing my eyes to decipher the figure, I thought I saw Ubaid's silhouette. Curious to find out what he was up to in the dead of the night, I sneaked out of my room into the garden.

Mr. Romeo

I made myself invisible by lurking in the shadows. Ubaid's guitar playing was atrocious; I had to cover my ears to dull the noise. I should have guessed who would appear on the landing: Gianna. Obviously, the Arab was doing his best to serenade his girlfriend. I could hear Gianna laughing at the scratchy "music" the guitarist was making. Putting down the instrument, he began reciting a poem, but I had no idea what it meant since he was speaking Arabic.

Clearly Gianna didn't understand her romantic suitor's ballad either because she kept laughing. Her laughter only served to encourage him to be more bold and brazen with his actions. When he finished his poetry he blew air kisses to his love-stricken lady who, by now, was completely charmed by Ubaid's romantic gestures.

The Fallen Lover

Before I knew it, Romeo was climbing a tree to try to reach Gianna's balcony. I feared for my friend's safety, as every step he took moved him closer to a branch that I was sure would not support his weight. The break was going to happen sooner or later. The next thing I knew the branch snapped with a thunderous cracking noise, sending Ubaid tumbling down toward the ground. This will surely wake the entire household, I thought.

Ubaid managed to cling to a branch during his fall and was now dangling from the tree without any foothold. I wondered how long he could last, hanging there. Gianna was panicking, unsure of what to do. As she rushed inside to solicit help, I decided to play a prank. I carefully climbed up a few branches behind Ubaid. He was doing his best to hold himself steady, looking for a way down. I reached over and pulled down his pajama pants, exposing his nakedness. He gave a surprised cry, trying to hold onto his trousers and to see who had done this treacherous act. He saw me laughing at the prank I had just played and he started cursing me in all the languages he knew. Yet my friend could do nothing since he was holding on for dear life. Dangling in mid-air, exposing himself and cursing me with every breath, the would-be-Romeo finally begged me to help him get down.

The Dangling Wee Wee

While Ubaid was cursing and begging, I descended several branches down the tree. Seeing his pants were half way down his legs, I did the most embarrassing thing I could do to my friend: with a forceful yank I caused his trousers to fall completely to the ground. Now he was totally naked from his waist down. He screamed more obscenities at me but I was already on the ground, laughing so hard I could not contain myself.

Just then help arrived in the form of Allegra, whom Gianna had beckoned. They found the situation hilarious and were laughing at the dangling male when they saw me running to hide in the bushes. As the girls extended their hands towards the compromised minstrel, he inched himself towards the balcony. By now, both ladies had an eyeful of Romeo's well-endowed equipment and were laughing so hard tears were rolling down their cheeks. The embarrassed Ubaid tried to cover himself with both hands before Gianna threw him a shawl. I, too, was laughing hard at my playing such a great prank on my friend.

I was surprised an angry Romeo did not come chasing after me. I suppose he was just glad he was rescued by the ladies and had managed to enter his girlfriend's chamber. Before long the commotion was over. I was also surprised that we did not wake the entire household. I returned to my chamber and into bed next to Andy, who had slept through the entire commotion. But I could not get back to sleep after all the excitement that had transpired.

Peeping Tom

After an hour of tossing and turning I decided to sneak out to the garden again. With a full moon shining brightly, I headed to the tree from which Ubaid had hung an hour ago. As I passed the stable barn, I saw a light flickering within so I quietly entered the stable to see if there was anything exciting and interesting to explore.

On top of a haystack lay two figures passionately making love, their elongated shadows casting haunting images upon the wooden walls against a dimly lit oil lamp. I stood mesmerized, trying to see clearly who these two lovers were.

I was expecting to see Ubaid and Gianna until I got a closer look. Who should I witness but the handsome muscular Wasim on his back with the sexy Allegra straddling him.

I was indeed surprised to find so many Romeos and Juliets in the span of a single evening.

As I had not witnessed heterosexual lovemaking before, I decided to stay and watch, hoping to learn something new from this liaison that I might have missed during my sex education studies. I soon came to the conclusion that there wasn't much difference except the penis penetrated an orifice located in the front with a female and in the back with a male. After hanging around a while, I was bored and decided to see if anything was happening around the tree the other Romeo had climbed earlier.

Ooh la la!

As I headed in the direction of the first Juliet's balcony a dim light was visible from within. Then, below, I saw something that made me curious. Romeo had climbed a tree to obtain entry into his girlfriend's room. I wondered if he realized that there was an easier way to ascend to the balcony. Did Romeo want to show off his bravery by climbing a tree or had he failed to notice the cast iron ladder screwed into the side of the balcony wall?

My brilliant observation allowed me to take the easy way up, so I mounted the ladder. Once on the terrace, all was revealed to me. The entrance into Gianna's bedroom was a floor to ceiling French door. With a clear view, I witnessed the star studded lovers in various Kama Sutra positions. They starting with the 'missionary,' changed to 'doggy,' transformed into 'spoons,' reversed into 'cowboy,' then progressed to the 'suspended congress,' and finally ending with 'The Perfumed Garden.' Passionate explosions were heard from within the chamber.

Who would have thought such wild 'Fireworks' would go off at the Villa Le Papavero within a short span of a night? I certainly didn't! Unfortunately Andy slept through it all.

CHAPTER SIXTY-FOUR

At Albergo Danieli Venezia

"The best way to get something done is to begin."
Bernard Tristan Foong

We did not leave until 9:00 a.m. the next morning. As we thanked our host and hostesses, Ubaid held back his displeasure with me, in front of Gianna's parents, pretending that nothing unusual had happened. But when we drove off, Ubaid was ready to kill me for embarrassing him the night before. Ramiz and I were seated in the back and he and Andy were in the front. Ubaid turned and reached for me but Ramiz intervened and stopped him before he got to me. Since Andy was driving and couldn't hold him back, he begged the Arab not to punish me for the prank I played.

As soon as we had awoken that morning I had told Andy about the various episodes from last evening. He, too, had a good laugh from Ubaid's losing his pants and dangling in mid-air. Now, in the car, Ubaid was again cursing me, threatening to never forgive me for the trick I played. I found the entire incident extremely amusing but in order to keep peace, I apologized to lover boy as he continued to fume and bombard me with curses. Although I was laughing secretly, I put on a serious face and pretended I was truly apologetic for making him lose face in front of the ladies. After much negotiation with Ramiz and Andy, 'Mr. Romeo' finally calmed down, but for the rest of our journey he did not speak to me.

Albergo Danieli Venezia

When we reached Venezia Marco Polo Airport a helicopter was waiting to fly us directly to Albergo Danieli Venezia. Hadrah Hakim knew the owners of Venice Hotel Danieli and had arranged VIP treatment for us. A valet and two bellboys were standing at attention on the hotel's helipad to collect our luggage. We did not have to check in at the front desk; those logistics were assigned to the valet who showed us personally to our respective suites. Ubaid, Ramiz, Andy and I occupied three separate suites. Andy and I shared the Lagoon Suite.

Hotel Danieli, in an earlier incarnation, was the Palazzo Dondolo, owned in the 1400s by Doge Enrico Dondolo. It was beautifully restored by 1966, when we stayed at the magnificent palace. After we freshened up, we agreed to meet in the hotel lobby for a shopping spree in this gorgeous city of canals. While Andy and I were waiting for our friends, I decided to explore the hotel before departing to Piazza San Marco. The lobby was magnificent. An abundance of Murano glass chandeliers hung beneath ornately painted ceilings, and decorative pink marble columns studded the spacious lobby. Large wooden doors lead to the stone streets. Gas lamps lit romantic walkways across bridges and along alleys.

The Handsome Italian

After snapping pictures of the grand palazzo's foyer, I returned to Andy. I found him chatting with a handsome Italian man who introduced himself as Count Mario Conti at the exact moment that Ubaid and Ramiz showed up. Before Count Mario bid us Arriverderci, he handed Andy a business card and asked him to call.

Evidently, the Count had noticed Andy from the bar, and decided to approach him to ask if he would be interested in modeling for L' Uomo Vogue. The Count was a photographer for various Italian magazines, he informed Andy. They struck up a conversation. The Count also mentioned that he was a location scout for an upcoming big-budget movie, Franco Zeffirelli's Romeo & Juliet. It would start shooting late '66; he was looking for suitable locations to recommend. I was fascinated by this news.

Shopping at Piazza San Marco

As we walked to Piazza San Marco, the passing gondolas and their gondoliers fascinated me. The boats were exquisitely crafted; each was a work of art. The black and white striped T-shirted gondoliers with red kerchiefs round their necks serenaded the passengers. Venetians redefined romance. It took my breath away. I was in love again, with Venezia.

There was such an array of charming and unique shops at the Piazza. I wanted to venture into every one of them but time did not permit. Browsing in Chimento, an exclusive jewelry store, I came across a series of delicately crafted, limited edition Faberge eggs which were originally designed for Tsar Alexander III, of Russia. They were rare collector's items considering the craftsmanship and history behind each egg. I was looking at the beautiful Russian heirloom collection when Ramiz came up next to me. "Young, which one do you like best?"

"They are so incredibly exquisite; each has its own uniqueness. It's difficult to decide which one I like best," I replied. Ramiz continued, "Select one. I want to know your taste."

The Hen

Going through the entire collection, I finally saw an egg that was simple in design and style, possessing clean lines that were modern and contemporary. I pointed out the "Hen" to mu'allmi, not expecting that he would ask the saleslady to release it from under the locked display case. As soon as the "Hen" was out of its display case I could see that it was even more beautiful and elegant than it first appeared.

Ramiz held it in his hands, looking closely at this costly luxury item. "How much is it?"

The signora looked at the price tag. "It is US $3,800.00." That was a lot of money in 1966.

My professor held up the egg, examining its simple contents before replying, "Please wrap this for me. It is a gift for someone very dear to me."

As the saleswoman took the expensive egg to be boxed and wrapped, I asked my teacher, "Are you buying this for Noor, your soon to be betrothed?" He smiled without saying a word as he continued to look around the shop for other items to purchase.

At Caffe Florian

Taking a break from shopping, Andy and I went into one of Venice's oldest and most popular cafes to sample their lovely patisseries and drink their famous dark hot beverage. It is made from a special bean called 'kahve', introduced to Europe by Constantinople. Since Ramiz and Ubaid couldn't eat or drink until after sunset, they continued their shopping.

I was curious to find out more about the handsome Italian Count, so I pressed Andy for information. I began, "Are you going to do some modeling for him?"

My Valet smiled and answered, "Don't you want me to?"

"Yes, of course! It will be interesting to see how a professional fashion photographer works. After all, if we are going to model for Aziz and if I'm to be his apprentice, we have to know what we are getting ourselves into, don't we?" I asked, testing the waters, to see how he would take my remark.

The waiter came to take our order. I continued, "Call him as soon as we return to the hotel and arrange a meeting; I'd like to get to know him better."

Andy gave me a sly grin and said, "I believe you are more interested in being with him than you are in finding out more about modeling and photography, correct?" He poked at the tip of my nose.

I smiled craftily and answered, "How did you know?"

"I saw your longing eyes checking every part of him when we were talking. You are dying to see what he is made of, in bed, aren't you?" he said teasingly.

"That would be nice. He is so sexy and handsome. I'll bet he has a big one, don't you think?" I said mischievously.

My lover laughed, "Yes! I'd like to see it too. I'll call him to arrange something, during our time in Venice." By now, our coffee and pastries had arrived. We ate, and our party headed back to the hotel to prepare for our 8:00 p.m. dinner reservation at Terrazza Danieli.

CHAPTER SIXTY-FIVE

At Terrazza Danieli & Ponte Di Rialto

"Every accomplishment starts with the decision to try."
Bernard Tristan Foong

As we looked at the Terrazza Danieli's menu, deciding what to order, the Ristorante's Maître d'Hôtel came over to bid us welcome. His name was Lorenzo. "Benvenuti al ristorante. How are you this evening?"

Ramiz tried answering in Italian, "Siamo bene, la ringrazia."

Lorenzo replied, "Molto Bene! You came to Venice at the perfect time. We have a festive fireworks display tonight."

Andy asked, "What's the special occasion?"

The happy Maître d' said, "Tomorrow our city celebrates Regata Storica. There will be festivities, gondola races and water floats on parade. You are just in time for our autumn festival."

My eyes lit up to learn that there would be lots of new and exciting things to see and do while we were in Venice. I jumped in and asked Lorenzo, "What happens during Regata Storica?"

He smiled. "First, there is the historical boat procession then the racing competition. It is comprised of historic boats from the 16th century manned with oarsmen in period costumes. The Grand Canal will be packed; the best place to see the parade is from here."

By now, I was totally engrossed and could not wait to find out more about Regata Storica. I continued questioning, "Can I go on one of those parade boats?"

He laughed. "Maybe the hotel concierge can arrange something for you, Sir."

"Can they?" I could not contain myself and was looking at Andy for approval.

Andy replied, *"Thank You, Lorenzo. We'll check with our hotel valet."*

By the time our dinner arrived I was doing my best to convince our party that it would be a great experience for us to be in a parade boat. To me, it was such an exciting prospect, a once in a lifetime experience. Andy promised he would check into the matter.

Fireworks Display

After a delicious gourmet dinner, we sat on the open-air terrace enjoying the breathtaking view of Venice. As we were relaxing and having our coffee, Ubaid said, "I'm going clubbing. Anyone care to join me?"

Ramiz chimed in, "I'll go. I'd like to experience some of Venice's nightlife."

Once again Andy and I decided not top join the group but took a stroll on the streets below the hotel. Suddenly the sky lit up brilliantly with huge balls of thunderous fireworks. Handel's Water Music accompanied each burst of glittering color. It was one of the most enchanted evenings I've ever experienced.

After the brilliant firework display, Andy and I ventured back to our Lagoon Suite to make arrangements with our valet regarding the parade.

In The Lagoon Suite

Before Andy could contact our valet, he noticed there were two messages waiting for us at the front desk. The first message informed us that packages awaited us at the reception desk. The other was from Count Mario Conti requesting that we return his call immediately.

While Andy was on the phone with the Count the doorbell rang. I answered. Standing there was our hotel valet with two beautifully wrapped gifts in hand. Passing me the small packages wrapped in silver and gold paper, he inquired, "Is there anything else I can do for you?" Andy finished his conversation with Mario, tipped our messenger and sent him away.

I was surprised he did not ask the valet about the boat parade. He responded, in a hurried fashion, "Let's go out." I left the gifts on the large mirrored mantelpiece without opening them, as Andy hurriedly ushered us out of the suite.

At Ponte di Rialto

As we walked towards Ponte di Rialto Andy said, "The Count is meeting us at Rialto Bridge so he can fill us in on some activities tomorrow."

"What kind of activities? Tomorrow is Regata Storica and it is a public holiday."

Before we knew it, we were already at the bridge. Mario was standing at the foot of the bridge waiting for us. He bid us good evening and suggested we locate a cafe where we could sit and chat. As soon as we ordered our beverages, the photographer commenced, "I'm doing a fashion shoot for Italian Vogue. The Festival is the backdrop. Would you be interested in joining me?"

Excited at the opportunity to witness a professional fashion shoot, especially one for a major fashion magazine, I replied enthusiastically, "Yes! We'd love to come. Do we get to go on one of the parade boats?"

Mario laughed. "Correct! Vogue Italia has commissioned a float especially for this fashion photography session. We have three female models on location and I thought, if Andy is agreeable, he could be an accompanying male model. I had not thought of using a male model until I met this handsome man."

Andy, lost for words for a moment, spoke. "I have never modeled before. I wouldn't know what to do."

"Oh, don't worry. It's not difficult. It's like play-acting. Just be yourself and let the camera do the rest! You'll be reimbursed for your work, and I'd also like to treat both of you to dinner tomorrow evening, as a token of appreciation, for helping out."

Before agreeing, Andy said, "Young and I would very much love to dine with you but we must consult the rest of our party; we can't abandon them." The Italian added quickly, "Not to worry, ask them to join us, too, since the female models will be dining with us as well."

I spoke before Andy could reply. "Yes! We'd be delighted. Where will we meet tomorrow morning for the shoot?"

The Count responded, "I'll pick you at 6:00 a.m. We will begin at the Vogue Italia parade boat. I want to try to finish up in half a day, because the gondolas start racing in the afternoon, once the parade is over."

Andy agreed, "OK! It will be fun. Besides, my charge here is into fashion. Seeing him so excited excites me as well. We'll meet you at our hotel lobby in the morning."

Turning towards me, Andy continued, "We'd better get going to catch an early night's sleep. I want to look well rested and fresh."

"You both already look sexy and delicious enough to eat," the photographer flirted.

Andy, in his quick witted fashion, replied, "We'll leave the delicious eating until tomorrow evening. For now it's time to say good night." With that, we bid our suitor good evening and returned to Albergo Danieli Venezia for our beauty sleep.

CHAPTER SIXTY-SIX

At Regata Storica

*"Happiness is an effect of doing what you love;
not an end goal to be achieved."*
Bernard Tristan Foong

Preparation for the Fashion Shoot

I was so excited about the upcoming photo shoot that I forgot about the gifts sitting on top of the mirrored mantelpiece. At 6:00 a.m. sharp, Mario sent his assistant to collect us from the hotel lobby. He ushered us to the dock where a team of models, hair and make-up artists, stylist, helpers and our photographer were already stationed.

A tent was set up as a make shift changing room for the models to do their preparation. Hair and make-up were done within this 12' × 12' fabric enclosure which sprouted electrical cords for hair dryers and electric rollers, necessities for "bouffant" hairdos.

I was mesmerized while watching different colored eye shadows, face powders and lipsticks painted onto the females. Seeing glamorous pictures in a glossy magazine was one thing but witnessing first-hand how it was applied was quite another. The hours of preparation that went into preparation for each model included in a photograph stunned me.

Fashion Education

By the time these super model, super tall girls were ready to change into their outfits it was close to 8:30 a.m. The parade was due to begin at nine. A smaller changing room was erected on the "Countess Cornaro", our ornate parade boat, which was ready to join the other parading vessels in the Grand Canal. Within the tiny changing space (four poles draped with fancy velvet) hung a dozen fabulous couture gowns from internationally well-known designers such as Christian Dior, Givenchy, Chanel, Yves Saint Laurent, Valentino and Emanuel Ungaro. I was in seventh heaven having this rare and unexpected opportunity to study and scrutinize these exquisite designer dresses. I turned every garment inside out to see how they were sewn, beaded and constructed. That day, floating in a parade boat along other vessels in the middle of the Grand Canal in historic Venezia, my fashion schooling had begun. It was the first day of my professional fashion education.

Man with the Magic Camera

Count Mario Conti had his camera in hand when the 'Countess,' rowed by six oarsmen, joined the flotilla. His assistant had his camera umbrellas ready and was holding up a large silver foil shade. All the models were preening and posing while Mario clicked away, twisting this way and that, upward, downward and every which way in order to capture the perfect shot.

Not surprisingly, Andy was a natural in this modeling game. Like a well-trained Bahriji grad, he worked his seductive charms while posing with the three females, exuding an unmistakable flair and panache at every turn. Viewing the photographs later, I was definitely fooled by Andy playing the role of a 'straight' man. It was strange for me to see how photographs trick the eye. I saw, until I analyzed it, exactly what the creator wanted me to see, and believe.

The rolls of film told a glamorous story, a make-believe fantasy. The reality was quite a different tale than that which was portrayed on the glossy images of Vogue. I must admit I was a sucker for the superficial, for illusions, back then. Now that I'm older and hopefully wiser, glamor has taken on a different meaning in my life. In the sixties, it was love at first sight between me and the fashion world.

On the "Countess Cornaro"

The large crowds lining the Grand Canal cheered as each decorative vessel rowed by to the courtly sounds of blowing trumpets and sounding bugles. As the "Countess Cornaro" floated past, I could not help but feel like a royal prince who was being welcomed into Venezia by my loyal subjects. I had seen film clips of Queen Elizabeth II waving her hand when her royal carriage passed, to the loud cheers of well-wishers during her numerous royal visits. I started waving my hand like the Queen, as if I were of royal descent. It was such an exhilarating moment in my adolescent life, playing the role of an aristocrat. I would have happily accepted, if ever I had found myself suddenly assigned a title. I waved, picturing myself as the Royal Heir to a monarchy, cherished by its happy and contented citizens.

It was past 2:00 p.m. by the time the parade ended. We had an hour's break before the gondola races were to begin. Andy and I were already exhausted so we decided to rest and relax in the comfort of our suite for a few hours. We watched the races from our balcony before our next round of excitement.

Since the Count wanted to shoot more pictures of the girls on land, and Andy's presence wasn't required, we arranged to meet the photographer at 8:00 p.m. in the lobby, to travel by gondola to Ristorante Da Raffaelle for dinner.

Our Clubbing Friends

As soon as we entered the Lagoon Suite there were a couple of messages on the house phone. One was from Ramiz and the other was from Ubaid. The two clubbing boys did not return to the hotel until nearly dawn, and slept through the entire boat parade, which took place below their bedroom windows.

Ramiz woke at noon and could not locate us, so he went sightseeing alone. Ubaid was still in bed with the one-night-stand he had picked up at the disco, the night before. Andy left them messages to join us for dinner.

The Faberge Eggs

As I sat looking at the gondola races below our chambers, Andy called to me. "Young, what are these two packages on top of the mantelpiece?"

I replied, nonchalantly, "Oh! I forgot to mention that our valet brought them to us last evening when you were on the phone with Mario, and then you were hurrying me out the door before I had a chance to open them."

Andy looked at the presents and said, "One is addressed to you." He began to unwrap his gift.

"Who are they from?"

"I don't know, open yours and see," replied my lover.

Andy undid the silver wrapping on his parcel and I carefully opened the gold package. A beautifully crafted box lay beneath the tissue papers. Elegantly scripted in platinum, on top of each box was the FABERGE label. To our amazement we discovered two limited editions of Faberge eggs. One was platinum and the other was pure gold; within each egg was "The Hen". My jaw dropped, knowing full well that these presents came from Ramiz. I looked at Andy in astonishment, lost for words, before he read out loud the two gift cards tucked inside the boxes:

"You are amazing! Thank You. Ramiz. P.S. Let's get together for twice weekly sessions at the Kosk."

CHAPTER SIXTY-SEVEN

Ristorante Da Raffaelle & Beyond

"Sex is like money; only too much is enough."
John Updike

Ramiz, Ubaid, Andy and I met the Count in Albergo Danieli Venezia's lobby before traveling by gondola to Ristorante da Raffaelle. For me, it was a joy ride, as I had never traveled by gondola before. As soon as we arrived at the ristorante, the maître d'hôtel greeted Mario with a warm hug. He welcomed us to their establishment, showing us to our table which looked across the Grand Canal onto Piazza San Marco. The gorgeous models were already at the table. After formal introductions we took our seats at the beautiful table filled with fragrant white and pastel peach-colored flowers and candles.

Venezia Gay Clubs

Ubaid, seated between two of the women, was as happy as a lark. I could tell he was giving it all he had, in hopes of another night of unbridled sex with one, two or all of them. I knew he was the type who agreed that 'the more the merrier.'

Ramiz, on the contrary, acted prim and proper until he got to know the Count a little better. Then he began to loosen up, and soon was enjoying our dinner conversations. I asked the Count how long he had been a photographer.

"Close to six years, now. I started taking photos of Venice's nightlife, people in trendy clubs and bars, when a friend recommended I approach Vogue Italia and show them my portfolio. They loved what they saw and hired me on the spot. My assignments were to photograph that which was considered cutting edge, places frequented by Gays, Lesbians, Bisexuals and Transgendered people."

"How exciting," I said. "Are there many gay clubs and bars here?" I asked.

Mario smiled. "There are a few upscale trendy clubs that are 'unbiased.' There are also several regular gay dance clubs and a few S & M leather bars."

The very mention of S & M leather bars made Ramiz' eyes light up and he asked, "Where are the S/M bars located? I'd like to check them out."

"There is one called Porto de Mar. On our way back, we will pass by the place. You will need a membership pass to enter. However, I know the manager and owners of that club. I can speak to them and get you in. They are very friendly people; since you are visiting for a few days, I'm sure they will be happy to entertain you. They speak a little English, all you'll need to understand," explained our host.

I could tell Ramiz was excited that he would soon be visiting an establishment where 'birds of his feather flocked together.' For the rest of the evening he had a happy grin on his face, knowing he would soon be a slave again.

Venezia Art & Culture

Andy asked the Count, "On our way to the restaurant, we passed an Opera House and it looked beautiful. Are there any interesting performances happening there?"

Mario replied, "Teatro La Fenice is Venice's most famous Opera House and I believe they are currently playing Verdi's La Traviata. Are you interested in operas?"

Andy answered, "Yes! I'd like to see a play or an opera while in Venice. It would provide this one (pointing at me) with some cultural education. Since Young likes fashion and costume designs, I'm sure he'd love to see an opera." I nodded in agreement with what Andy said.

"Well then, let's go to the Opera tomorrow night. I can get tickets through the magazine's editors. We will be assured of good seats. Would your friends, Ramiz and Ubaid, like to join us?" asked the Count.

Ubaid was in his own world, busy flirting with the models and Ramiz was absorbed with the idea of visiting the leather bars. I could tell he was more interested in having a fun time at Porto de Mar than joining us at Teatro La Fenice. So it was settled that the Count, Andy and I would venture to the theatre the following evening, leaving our friends to arrange their own fun.

After dinner, on our way to the hotel, we dropped Ramiz at the leather bar. Mario introduced him to the owners, Carlos and Rico, and asked them to take good care of him. Ubaid and the young women went for a night of partying to the trendy Bacaro Jazz Bar.

As we dropped each group off at their respective club and bar, I couldn't help but peep into each establishment to see what the interiors and the patrons looked like.

Bacaro Jazz

Ubaid and the models were the first party we dropped off. As the night was still young, there were only a handful of patrons in this establishment which the Count said was usually jam-packed. A young man stood on a ladder in the middle of the dance floor hanging a selection of women's bras and panties, and men's underwear on clotheslines, near the ceiling. Apparently, it was Braless and No Undies Night at Bacaro Jazz. It was funny to see bras and panties dangling above a dance floor.

Ubaid's party seemed to find this fun as the models started unhooking their bras. Many stared at their voluptuous bosoms and ogled as they took off their underwear, while leaving on their mini dresses. Ubaid, the extrovert, dropped his jeans and then dropped his briefs, in full view of every one. All the patrons were *ooh*ing and *aah*ing, cheering them on.

More people who entered did the same. I stood by the entrance watching the strip show unfolding. Soon the bouncer came up to usher us off premises since I was not supposed to be inside in the first place. We were just waiting for Mario to introduce Ubaid to the manager.

Porto de Mar

By the time we reached Porto de Mar, there was a long queue waiting to enter. Since it was a holiday, the leather guys were out in full force, dressed in leather from head to toe. They were showing off their hairy bear chests, thick mustaches, beards, leather caps, straps, chaps and boots. Ramiz was salivating, dying to enter the 'MAN' club. This night, he couldn't be bothered with Ubaid's wellbeing. He reasoned the girls would be able to look after his friend while he enjoyed a night of sexual debauchery.

Mario seemed to know everyone who was anyone in the city. Jumping the queue, he ushered Ramiz into the smoky premises and introduced him to the manager, Alberto.

Alberto was a friendly character and offered to show us the interior of the club, even though I was not legally allowed into the venue.

The ground floor had a bar, which was already filled with half-clad leather Bears, Masters and Slaves drinking and smoking. A floor down was the dingy smelling dungeon. Hanging on the walls, I saw a variety of whips and torture equipment which I had never seen before. There were already a number of Masters and Slaves waiting for some hardcore sex.

We sailed away from Porto de Mar leaving Ramiz to his sexual explorations, anxious for ours to begin.

CHAPTER SIXTY-EIGHT

Lido Excelsior Di Venezia & Plazzo Contessa Rosa

"Love is the wine of existence. When you have taken that, you have taken the most precious drop that there is in the cluster."
Henry Ward Beecher

As our gondola rowed out of Porto de Mar, we were free from our evening's companions, except for our alluring host. The Count began, "My dear boys, it's been an exhausting day. I had hoped to spend an evening of love making with you two handsome men but, alas, tonight is not the night. I'm tired and am retiring early, on my own. What plans do you have tomorrow?"

Andy answered, "We have nothing planned tomorrow except for some sightseeing."

"You should come visit me at my palazzo in Lido, and spend the day on our charming island," the Count suggested.

I was very excited by this invitation, as I had heard of the famous Lido Excelsior di Venezia, from Mother. She spoke highly of this luxurious hotel where she had a lovely afternoon tea at the Tropicana Restaurant, overlooking the sea. I was eager to experience this spectacular hotel for myself. I said enthusiastically, "We'd love to spend the day in Lido and visit your palazzo. I'm sure it is beautiful."

Andy, turning to Mario, added, "Are you sure it's not too much of a hassle for us to visit? We don't want to impose on your hospitality."

Count Conti smiled. "Not at all boys; I'd love you to visit so we can spend some quality time together. I will collect you in my speedboat tomorrow morning. We will have breakfast at the Lido Excelsior di Venezia. I don't think your friends will be up early to join us after painting the town red. I can have you boys all to myself. I'm a greedy lover." He smiled seductively.

I couldn't wait to answer. "Yes! Where will we meet you?"

"Meet me by your hotel pier at 7:30 sharp."

Lido Excelsior di Venezia

Like Florence, Venice at dawn has an air of grace and elegance, especially in the autumn months. As Andy and I sat on the pier we couldn't help but notice a speedboat flying in our direction at exactly 7:30 a.m. The suave thirty-three-year-old Mario was at the wheel. Docking his blue and white water vehicle by our side, he extended his hand to help us board. He then turned the boat around towards the Lido Excelsior di Venezia. It was a perfect Venetian morning with strong gusts of wind blowing on my face. Andy wrapped his arms around me, keeping me warm the entire way to our destination.

When we arrived at Lido Excelsior's pier, a uniformed boat valet was on hand to assist us and park the boat. Another staff member guided us to our table at the Tropicana Restaurant. We sat, overlooking the beachfront. I could see the beautiful domed steeple of Saint Mark's Cathedral in the distance hazily camouflaged by the morning sun.

As soon as we ordered, the Count began, "I'm so glad you came to visit me today. Last evening, I was too tired. I didn't want to spoil the evening; you are both too delicious for a casual fling. I want to spend quality time making love without having to rush. Now, we have the entire day."

Andy and I looked at each other and smiled at Mario's charming compliments before changing the subject.

I responded, "This is indeed a beautiful place."

Andy added, "I read Death in Venice by Thomas Mann and I believe the story is set in Lido di Venezia. Have you read the book?"

The Count replied, "I know the novel well. In fact, I just got wind that Hollywood is planning to make a movie here based on Mann's novel."

"You mentioned you are a location scout for Franco Zafferelli's Romeo and Juliet. Have you found suitable locations yet?" I asked.

Mario smiled, reached over close to my ear and whispered, "I believe I have found Romeo and Juliet's lovemaking bedroom."

"Really? Where?" I questioned excitedly, "Will you show us?"

Laughing, Count Conti answered, "Of course I'll show you but you'll have to keep it a secret. I cannot have the entire world learning about it before the movie comes out. Can you keep a secret?"

"Of course I can. I'm very good at keeping secrets," I whispered back into the Count's ear.

"OK, then! I will show you the place as soon as we finish eating."

Palazzo Comtessa Rosa

We boarded the speedboat toward Palazzo Comtessa Rosa, Count Mario Conti's home, inherited from his parent's after their passing a couple of years previously. The palazzo's main garden faces the sea and as we docked, the Butler came to receive us. "Here we are: my home sweet home. Let me show you around," the Count said.

As we entered his spacious mansion, I was awed by the numerous antiquities hanging on the high walls, stored carefully within glass cases or displayed on marbled mantelpieces. Each item was a treasure, passed down for generations.

After the tour, he invited us to the Terrazza Gardino for refreshments. I was curious to know more of the Count's ancestry. "Is your family from Venice?"

Our host replied, "My great grandfather was a successful merchant in Venice; he made his money trading gold. My grandfather and my father inherited the family business. My father married my Spanish mother, Comtessa Rosa, in Barcelona. He bought this palazzo for her as a wedding gift and named it Palazzo Comtessa Rosa."

I continued asking, "Do you run the family business in addition to being an accomplished photographer?"

Mario laughed and said, "Oh no! I have no interest in my family's business. My brothers have taken over the operations. Alfonso, the eldest, lives in Rome and manages the foreign dealings of the enterprise. Pietro, my other brother, lives in Florence to oversee the day-to-day operations. That leaves me, the prodigal son, to do as I wish. I leave my business shares in their charge. As long as I get my monthly stipend, I'm happy to let them run the family business. Besides, I love Venice and most of my friends are here."

I was eager to see the movie location, which the Count had promised to divulge, so I enquired, "When are we going to see Romeo and Juliet's bedroom?"

Mario laughingly replied, "Be patient boy. It will soon be revealed. For now, take your tea."

Casanova Count Mario Conti

We proceeded into his private chamber which was as luxurious as the Count, himself. His king-sized bed was covered with a fur bedspread, lined with brocaded silk satin. His photograph collection covered an entire wall. I was amazed to discover that all the photographs were of our host in various sexual positions with different men. He lined his bedroom wall with images of his sexual conquests.

Now, that's a true blue-blooded Casanova if ever I met one! As I was examining the beautifully framed erotic art, I felt a pair of hairy arms reach round my waist, holding me tight. Before I could turn around to see whose muscular hands they were, Andy was in front of me, kissing me on my lips. My excitement rose in anticipation of the sensuality and sexuality that was unfolding.

In truth, I've always preferred good-looking, well-groomed mature men and the Count definitely fit the description of the perfect man in my sexual fantasies. He was strong, yet his arms had the gentle touch of a man of distinction. Reaching forward he undid my trousers, easing them to the floor, before removing Andy's pants.

My erection was grinding against my Valet's. I unfastened Mario's belt and unzipped his pants, feeling his throbbing hardness against my palms. Since he wore no undergarments, I could feel him bouncing in rhythm to my every stroke.

Before long, we were merging into passionate three way embraces, changing positions every so often. We were accompanied by classical music which played softly throughout this sensual Venetian chamber. We made love slowly, gently, softly, allowing ourselves time to explore our most erotic parts, in synchronicity. Mario, well versed in the art of lovemaking, was the best lover I'd ever had the privilege of experiencing, apart from my beloved Andy. I had the crème de la crème with these two expert lovers trained in the sexual art of Kama Sutra.

Each interlude led to fuller and better orgasms than the last, yet we desired more. Count Mario Conti definitely lived up to the reputation of a great Italian lover of men, like the infamous Giacomo Girolamo Casanova de Seingalt was to women.

Needless to say, our lovemaking flowed unceasingly until the final hour we were scheduled to depart to Teatro La Fenice, to attend the evening's performance of La Traviata. We unwillingly left the comfort of the king bed to dress. I did not want our lovemaking to ever end.

CHAPTER SIXTY-NINE

Teatro La Fence & The Gondola Experience

*"Love is not what the mind thinks,
but what the heart feels."*
Greg Evans

The Count's speedboat whisked us back to the Hotel Danieli. Our host invited us to stay at his Palazzo whenever we returned to Venice. He suggested that Andy and I celebrate February Carnival with him – the nights of festive jubilation, preceding Lent. "Young will love the theatrical costumes and masks. There will be grand balls and masquerade parties," said Mario. "The whole city will be out in full regalia."

I replied, "How wonderful! I want to come back soon. It is such a grand city. I'm sad tomorrow will be our last day here."

The smiling Count continued, "I'm glad you love Venice. It is, truly, one of the most elegant and sophisticated places on earth. That's why I choose to live here."

Andy added, "I, too, have fallen in love with the great beauty of this city."

We returned to our suite to change, before departing on a special gondola Mario had arranged for us. We were picked up and delivered to Teatro La Fenice in style.

The Gondola & Gondolier

Mario's gondola was waiting for us at the dock. This gondola was a restoration of a nineteenth century Venetian boat. It featured an enclosed canopy, and deep red organza curtains which could be closed, for privacy. It was ornately decorated with gold cherubs set on highly polished ebony.

Unlike the tourist gondoliers who dress casually, our gondolier was elegantly attired. He wore long black pants and a long-sleeved red and black fitted shirt which highlighted his physique. Callisto was a tall, elegant man, with a full head of jet black, wavy hair and beautiful bone structure. He sported a thick, waxed mustachio which gleamed with his bright eyes. He reminded me of Inspector Hercule Poirot, the armchair detective in Agatha Christie's murder mysteries. He wore a red kerchief around his neck which bore Count Mario Conti's initials. The family crest was a gold image of King Neptune holding a Triton.

Callisto extended his hand to assist us into the exquisite gondola. The heavy, red velvet curtains at the entrance were also emblazoned with the Count's initials and Crest. Floor to ceiling zebra wallpaper rose from above furs strewn casually over the white carpeted floor. A huge bear rug, along with black and white velvet cushions trimmed with gold braids and tassels lined the gondola. Red candles made with essential oils of rose petals created a delicate, romantic glow. The ceiling was midnight blue, studded with diamonds resembling twinkling stars in the night sky. Vases of red roses in full bloom added the finishing touches to this enchanting vessel.

I felt bewitched in the opulence. Andy and I automatically removed our dress shoes, before entering this love chamber. Callisto presented us with soft burgundy red velvet slippers, also embroidered with the Count's initials and crest. Mario removed his shiny patent leather shoes and donned his own embroidered slippers.

"Gentlemen, welcome to my gondola, Il Tritone, The Merman."

I gasped, "This is your private gondola?"

The Count laughed and replied jokingly, "Yes, my friend this is my, how do you say in Americano, my 'Love Boat'?"

I replied, still absorbing everything with all of my senses, "This is definitely a Love Boat! I've never seen anything so romantic. I feel like Prince Charming in this gondola!"

"Well, you are, my darling boy. Both of you are my royal Princes Charming, this evening. Let's celebrate with Proseco!" said our charismatic host while popping the champagne cork, letting the intoxicating liquid flow freely over the mouth and down the glass neck of the bottle, before pouring it into our glasses.

Although I don't drink, tonight I wanted to try some champagne. I wanted to experience the night through a haze of romantic dizziness. I was convinced the flowing, bubbly Proseco would further enhance my experiences.

Andy was surprised to hear me request champagne. He tried to persuade me not to, but Count Casanova convinced Andy that a few sips wouldn't harm me. "Besides, we should toast our friendship," said the Count. Andy consented to breaking the E.R.O.S. rule for a night. He knew me well enough to know I had my mind made up.

Teatro La Fenice

I saw everything through a rose lens after finishing off my flute of champagne. Everything looked even more perfect than before. My head was spinning like an antique carousel where horses, camels, elephants and storybook animals came to life.

I had never been to a large-scale opera performance in an historical theatre. Teatro La Fenice dated back to 1792. It was ornately decorated; even the cloakroom was trimmed in gold. Those bygone days, theatre staff wore perfectly pressed outfits, similar to footmen in the gilded age. The dizzying splendor spoke to my soul. Everything was elegant and in pristine condition; it was beautiful and larger than life. I was hooked on opera before La Traviata even began.

The audience, dressed in their fineries, appeared sophisticated beyond anything I had seen in the top fashion magazines. Mario, 'The Count,' greeted his acquaintances and friends with charisma and charm. I was already secretly in love with this Casanova. However, I guarded this secret cautiously. I assumed my lover saw telltale signs of my desires and romantic attachments in their infancy. Surely he had seen how I looked at the Count during our passionate lovemaking moments at the Palazzo. Andy, my beautiful Andy who loved me unceasingly, was the most unselfish lover I would ever know. He allowed me the joy of running away with my fantasies. Bahriji boys were well trained in the art of self-control; my lover and Valet stayed completely open, with no thought of self, expressing no jealousy.

La Traviata, the Opera

The curtain opened revealing Violetta Valéry, the courtesan, in a glamorous party scene. I fell in love with her, as well! She sang with an enchanting voice, like a nightingale. I sat, spellbound, weeping in the private box.

By her untimely death, I was crying my eyes out. Was it the champagne, the sets, the costumes, the singing, the story or the overwhelming sensory input of the entire day which brought my tears? I wasn't sure, but my body convulsed. I was trembling with sorrow, joy and love. Andy held me close, for he, too, was moved by the romantic tragedy of this beautiful heroine.

When the curtain finally came down and the audience cheered their bravas and bravos, calling for encores, tears were streaming down my cheeks. Andy reached over and kissed me lovingly, reassuring me that my life would not end the way Violetta's did. I was touched by my calming angel.

The Gondola Experience

When the performance ended, we returned to the comfort of the Count's gondola, and celebrated the beauty of the evening with more champagne. By now, I was head over heels in love, bewildered by beauty. What had been an enchanted day turned into an unfathomable evening. The organza curtains were drawn, shielding us from the departing theatre crowds. Romantic candles burned as we began, again, the love dance left incomplete, on Lido.

Mario's expert hands blissfully caressed every inch of my smooth body as Andy lowered his expert mouth on my growing organ. I wanted both the Count and Andy, together, at the same moment. As the gondola sailed out into the wide expanse of the Grand Canal, both lovers were inside me, moving in tandem with the rhythmic sounds of waves lapping against the Love-Boat.

I surrendered myself wholly to indescribable sexual ecstasy, rocking to the motion of their sliding cocks filling me to the brim. I wanted them and I desired every drop of their precious seed to feed my deepest center.

I was awakened by the chirping sounds of two love birds perched on the gondola's window. My lovers lay in deep slumber, their arms draped around my naked body. I gently lifted their arms, and sat up. I saw the majestic steeples of Saint Mark's Cathedral. The singing larks turned long enough to look at me with knowing smiles. I had been to heaven; I did not want my night's pleasures to end.

CHAPTER SEVENTY

At Mercatino dell'Antiquariato & La Cupola

"Forget love; I'd rather fall in chocolate."
Bernard Tristan Foong

We did not return to our suite from our fantastic gondola experience until after dawn. When I awoke, in bed, Andy was already up, dressed and gone. He left a note for me to join him at the hotel's breakfast room. I was suffering a slight hangover from the champagne, and throughout the day I had a foreboding feeling that everything in my life wasn't as rosy as I had thought the night before.

I was suffering from the bondage of being in love. Without being fully aware of how it happened, I had fallen head-over-heels in love with the charismatic Count. I was sad all day, but I couldn't put a finger on my sudden melancholy. I kept telling myself that it was the after-effect of the Proseco, but the truth was I wanted to be with the Count! I didn't want to leave Italy so soon. Ten days had flown by too quickly.

At Breakfast

Our friends were already at the breakfast table with Andy, awaiting my arrival. Ramiz and Ubaid did not eat. They watched me finish my breakfast before we set out to explore the Mercatino dell'Antiquariato, Venice's largest antiques fair. As much as I tried to be enthusiastic about our outing, everything that happened made me miss the Count.

Andy noticed my melancholy. "Young, you're not yourself today. What's wrong?"

I took my time to answer, "Nothing. I'm fine. Just a little hang-over from last night's champagne."

Ramiz looked at me. "This chap had champagne last night? What was the celebration? He normally doesn't drink."

Andy jumped to my defense immediately. "He took a couple of sips since it was his first time to attend the theater. There was cause for celebration," he said, hoping his answer would suffice.

I changed the topic quickly. "What did you do last night?" I asked, directing my glances at Ramiz and Ubaid.

They both smiled as Ubaid answered. "Well! I spent the last couple of days with the models and had a fabulous time, mostly in bed."

"Great! What did you guys do?" I was trying to find out more, though I already knew what had happened in his bed.

Ubaid laughed. "Wouldn't you like to know, you rascal? After you embarrassed me at Villa Le Papavero, I haven't fully forgiven you. If not for the three girls keeping me busy, I would have been boxing your ears these last couple of days!"

I grinned slyly and asked, "So, you fucked them all?"

Ramiz responded with a pretended stern look on his face, "Hey! Boys! No vulgarity at breakfast!" We all laughed.

Andy continued, "What did you do, professor?"

My teacher smiled but said nothing. Obviously, he did not want Ubaid to know what he had been up to, in case his friend blabbed about his S & M activities to everyone in The United Arab Emirates. Instead, Ramiz changed the subject and said, "Let's visit Mercatino dell'Antiquariato. I heard there are quite interesting things to see and buy."

Mercatino dell'Antiquariato

By the time we arrived, it was close to noon. The fair was filled with tourists and locals, all looking for bargains. Although there were flea markets in England, I had never been to one. The numerous stalls with antiquities and curios fascinated me. Although there were many interesting distractions, my nagging melancholy continued.

I came across a stall that sold antique dolls, and the mere sight of these dolls threw me into a deeper depression. Tears formed in my eyes.

"What's the matter, Young? Why are you crying?"

I leaned against Andy and wept. Holding me close, he comforted me. "It's alright boy. It's alright; nothing is going to harm you." He soothed me with his gentle words. Staring into my tear-filled eyes he continued, "Tell me what's wrong."

I finally said, "I'm going to miss this city. It's been so wonderful and I don't want to leave Venice."

He turned to face me and ruffled my hair, "You silly boy. We will come back soon. I will miss this place also, but we'll be back for Carnival. Now cheer up and stop crying. Big boys don't cry."

I did not have the heart to tell my lover I had fallen for the Count. I was afraid that if I let on, he might change his mind about returning for Carnival. So I did my best to cheer myself, but looking at the antique dolls brought another flood of tears to my eyes.

The Miseries of Falling In Love

Between my sobs I confessed, "I'm sorry! Looking at these dolls bring back memories of my childhood. I miss my mother."

Andy comforted me and replied, "Soon it will be Christmas and we'll be back homes with our families. Now, stop being so sentimental and let's enjoy our final day in Venice. What would you like to do?"

Just then, we were passing a chocolatier and I was drawn to the arrays of goodies on display. I suddenly had a voracious appetite for chocolate, which I later would realize was transference from my sexual desire for the Count. I suggested we go into the chocolate shop. Since Ramiz and Ubaid couldn't eat during daylight hours, they continued browsing the antiques market while we ventured into the store. There were so many temptingly delicious chocolates; I couldn't squelch the urge to try as many varieties as possible.

I was using chocolates to drown my sorrows for being stupid enough to fall in love with an Italian Casanova. Why was I missing this 'man-izer,' when I already had a fabulous lover standing by my side?

I sat at a corner table drinking latte and eating choc olates, gobbling the delicious sweets, my comfort food.

"Young, I'm worried about you. You're behaving very strange today. I've never seen you eat like a mad person. Tell me what's wrong. I want to help."

Tears began flowing again as I continued to stuff chocolate after chocolate in my mouth. How could I tell my beloved what was happening inside my head when I myself didn't know what was wrong with me? The more I cried, the more I ate. I consumed dozens of chocolates.

"I don't know what's wrong with me. I'm a silly stupid boy!" I started banging my head against the wall where I was leaning.

Andy looked very concerned and commanded, "Young! Stop it! You are hurting yourself. Stop this nonsense at once!"

I blurted out, in the midst of sobs, "Is parting always such a difficult thing to do?"

Andy, not realizing I was grieving over Mario, caught hold of my hands and whispered into my ears, "My sweet darling boy! I'm here, aren't I? And I'm not leaving you anytime soon."

Wiping my tears I said between sobs, "I know, I know! You are the kindest person in the world and I love you very much."

"Well then, stop this silly crying."

Albergo Carlton, La Cupola

I calmed down during the rest of our time at the market. Andy decided to take me for Afternoon Tea at La Cupola at the luxurious Hotel Carlton. Our friends decided they wanted more shopping and sightseeing.

As soon as we sat down at La Cupola a waiter pushed a trolley full of delicious cakes, tarts and pies our way. I began to order desserts. Andy looked at me, his eyes wide, wondering how in the world I could consume all the chocolates and still order more sweets.

After eating, I said to Andy, with urgency in my voice, "I have to use the restroom."

"Do you need me to come with you?" Before I could answer I was running towards the washroom, trying to keep from throwing up.

Andy followed after me. My guardian did his best to clean me up, swearing under his breath that he should never have allowed me to eat all the junk food. I was too breathless and exhausted to argue with him, so I kept quiet during our sojourn back to our hotel, where I lay down to rest for the evening.

Ramiz and Ubaid came in to check on me before they departed for dinner, leaving my lover to care for his lovesick boyfriend. I felt like Violetta Valéry, the love-stricken courtesan in La Traviata.

CHAPTER SEVENTY-ONE

That's What Friends Are For

*"Man only likes to count his troubles
but he does not count his joys."*
Fyodor Dostoyevsky

Andy and I were scheduled to check out of the Hotel Danieli at 9:00 a.m. We arranged to meet our group in the lobby before departing, via helicopter, to the Airport. From there we would catch the Simorgh to Dubai. At 9:30 a.m., we were still waiting for Ubaid, but there was no sign of him. Ramiz called his room on the house phone, but got no response. We were getting worried. We waited another fifteen minutes and still, no Ubaid.

Ramiz and the hotel valet went upstairs to search. Andy and I waited in the lobby, in case Ubaid came in. When the men returned there was still no sign of Ubaid. We were panicking, wondering if he had met with an accident.

Ramiz imagined the worst-case scenario - that he might have been kidnapped for a ransom! While we were discussing whether we should inform the police, Ubaid came breezing in, arm-in-arm with one of the models. As soon as we saw him, Ramiz rushed over, asking him where he had been and why he wasn't ready to depart.

Ramiz and Ubaid

Ubaid looked surprised. "Oh! Are we leaving today? I thought it is tomorrow."

Ramiz gave him an ugly, scolding look and said, "We were worried you had an accident, or were kidnapped."

Our friend seemed amused by that remark and laughingly replied, "I spent the night with Christina and just got back. I'm sorry I alarmed you. I'm going to take a shower."

My Mu'allmi said in an annoyed tone of voice, "We'll wait for you here. Be quick about it. The helicopter has been waiting for over an hour."

Ubaid obviously did not like the idea of leaving today any more than I did. He went to his suite with Christina, while we all sat and waited for him. Again.

Shaking his head, Ramiz said, "That guy is so irresponsible when he is having a good time. He obviously isn't ready to leave Venice."

I asked, "Is he always such a poor timekeeper?"

Evidently, it was Ramiz' turn to be emotional. He surprised us, saying "If I were not so much in love with him, I wouldn't care what he did or didn't do!"

I asked, "Are you lovers?"

Ramiz could no longer withhold the truth. "I will confide in you. Remember when I mentioned my father punished me for playing with another boy in school? That boy was Ubaid. We have been friends since childhood. One day while playing we decided to go skinny-dipping in the pond. We thought no one was around to see us.

"One thing led to another and we started fooling around, touching each other's penises. As I was about to suckle his member, I saw another boy scamper away. In a flash, our teacher appeared, threatening to tell our fathers what happened. I was terrified of my father's anger. That's when he began to whip me to get me to stop sexual games with other boys."

Ramiz told us that because of Hadrah Hakim's prominence in political, business and social arenas, the teacher didn't tell on Ubaid, and the Hakim never knew what transpired.

"So you and Ubaid are fuck buddies?" I asked, trying to determine the truth of the matter. Andy elbowed me furtively, intimating that I should not be so blatant in my inquiries.

Ramiz looked embarrassed but replied, "Well, I suppose you can call it that but the more we continued, the more I found that I was in love with him. As you already know, Ubaid is hot-blooded, and is into both men and women. I suppose I'm smitten. He frustrates me. He has no reservations about doing whatever he wishes, no matter the consequences. He is rebellious. Maybe that's why I'm attracted to him. He'll never return my love but that does not deter me. I'll always been drawn to him."

I was fascinated and wanted to ask more but Andy stepped in. "Is that why you are employed at the Hadrah's home – to continue your liaison with him?"

"He needs someone to keep him in check so he won't get too out of hand. But, to answer your question, yes. I love him unconditionally. I suppose that is the main reason I took the governor's position; I can be close, and also keep an eye on him."

Andy and I were indeed surprised by this piece of news which my teacher made us promise to keep confidential. We solemnly gave him our pledge.

Reasons for staying in Venice

We boarded the Simorgh with saddened hearts; each of us had our personal reasons for wanting to stay in Venice longer - except for Andy, who just wanted to be wherever I was.

Ubaid reluctantly bid a sad arrivederci to Christina. They made promises to keep in touch, but deep in their hearts they knew it was their final farewell. Ubaid did not want to return to the Kosk before returning to University. The Hadrah imposed restrictions upon his life, which he saw as limiting. Ubaid's life, as he liked to live it, hinged on sexual conquests.

As for Ramiz, I could tell he would miss the S & M establishments. Returning to a conservative and socially restrictive society such as the United Arab Emirates was like returning to a life of imprisonment for him. Ramiz' freedom shrank under the watchful eyes of his family. Soon he would probably go through with the arranged marriage to his cousin.

My reason for staying longer in Venice was simply that I was utterly smitten with the Count and wished to spend more time with him. I should have been counting my blessings, content with my beloved who loved me unconditionally. But I was too immature to appreciate my good fortune.

I suppose we humans are seldom satisfied with our blessings. Most of us choose to search for and believe in greener pastures, which, more often than not, only exist in our imagination. I was easily taken in by fantasy at the tender age of fourteen.

On The Plane

During our long flight to Dubai, Andy and I had a chance to discuss our upcoming photography project involving Habiibi Aziz. I had absorbed many great notions, having been influenced by art in Italy, and I was eager to share them. Finding a private, quiet corner I began, "I have been giving Habiibi Aziz' project a great deal of thought. I want your opinion."

Andy said, "Fire away."

"While looking at the fantastic set designs at the opera, an idea occurred to me. Rather than photographing copulation and sacred sex acts within existing religious structures, why not have sets built to resemble the locations? That way, Aziz wouldn't need to get permission."

Andy responded excitedly, "What an excellent idea. That would eliminate the time factor of having to obtain written permission. Gaining approval would no longer be an obstacle! Excellent thinking, Young!" He encouraged me to continue dispensing my ideas for his consideration.

"Aziz could possibly have sets built, like movie sets in Hollywood. They certainly would have excellent props craftsmen who could build sets to resemble the real locations, don't you think?" I continued, with zest.

Andy answered, "Aziz can definitely afford to build these sets instead of going to the trouble to film in holy spots around the world." He seemed reflective. After a pause, Andy continued, "I wouldn't mind travelling the globe to visit the actual locations and experience the real venues."

"You just want to see the bridges over every river in the world!" I jested, playfully.

"Couldn't we suggest for him to do both?" Andy asked. Couldn't he photograph the explicit scenes in the studio and shoot the less controversial pictures on location?"

"Sure." I answered. "Let's suggest these ideas to him and see what he thinks."

"I have another idea having to do with photography. Perhaps we should introduce Aziz to Mario? Both of them enjoy taking nude pictures of beautiful people in the throes of passion; they might enjoy each other's company and could, possibly, collaborate on this project."

"My clever boy. Another superb idea! Let's set up a meeting with Habiibi as soon as we get back to the Kosk and get this in motion. Your ideas could land us in Venice sooner rather than later!"

My eyes brightened at the thought of returning to Venice to see Mario again, but I did not tell Andy my thoughts. Instead I smiled charmingly at my beloved letting him know I loved him very, very much.

CHAPTER SEVENTY-TWO

The Two Brothers

"The search for the perfect venture can turn into procrastination. Your idea may or may not have merit. The key is to get started."
Bernard Tristan Foong

To overcome my sorrows from missing the Italian Casanova, Count Mario Conti, I used the armor of protection I was the most familiar with: WORK, WORK and WORK! As soon as I returned I resumed my regular studies with Mu'allmi and scheduled a meeting with Habiibi Aziz and Andy. I also resumed my regular visits to the harem women's quarters to continue working with them on their makeovers for their big presentation at the Eid ul-Fitr.

I had another item on my agenda: I started to write a personal journal. I poured out my pent up emotional turmoil over unrequited love, thinking that this private document would be for my eyes only. I kept my writing under lock and key inside my desk in the Peacock Chamber.

Our meeting with Aziz was scheduled for the following evening, a day after our return from Venice. Our host was delighted to see Andy and me, greeting us with a warm nose-to-nose welcome, a traditional Arabic greeting.

Andy and I were not expecting anyone else and were surprised to meet Aziz's older brother, Thabit, for the first time. Thabit was married to one of Hadrah Hakim's distant cousins. He and his family lived in Abu Dhabi. Thabit was in Dubai on business and decided to spend a few days at the Kosk.

The Meeting

After introductions, Aziz inquired about our trip to Italy. We told him we had a fabulous time and hoped to return to Venice soon. We shared stories about our new friend, explaining that he was an accomplished Italian photographer whom we would like to introduce to him. Since we did not know if it was appropriate to discuss Aziz' photography project in the presence of his brother, we waited until Habiibi gave us the green light before we brought up the subject.

"Who is this person you'd like me to meet?" enquired Aziz.

Andy replied, "He is a photographer who works for several Italian fashion magazines. He is also doing photographic work similar to your planned project."

Aziz said excitedly, "Really? I'd like to know more about him." Seeing our hesitant faces, he continued, "You can talk frankly in front of my brother. We are very close and tell each other everything. He is well aware of my photography project. Actually, he is partnering with me."

I turned to Thabit and asked, "Oh! Is that what brings you to Dubai, your Excellency? Are you here to discuss this project?"

Thabit smiled. "Well, I have other business to attend to while I'm here, but I am very interested in Aziz's project and want to catch up with him on the details. He mentioned that he wants to shoot in Europe first. I'm all ears; what is your input?"

Andy and I proceeded with our proposals. Both men were very excited with the idea of building sets of famous religious places instead of having to go through the red tape of getting approval from different religious authorities. We also proposed that the less controversial pictures be shot on location.

Andy brought up the matter of logistics and time constraints. "We will be allocated to different Households in five weeks so it might be difficult for us to commit to seeing the project to fruition. However, we will do our best to assist you while we are here, and into the future," Andy offered.

Wazir Thabit

After listening attentively, Thabit said, "You can be assigned to my Household in Abu Dhabi and continue on this project after you leave here. I can have a word with the Bahriji School and have you allocated to Sekhem (Thabit's palatial residence). It won't be a problem."

Aziz added, "That would be great, Thabit! Then we'll be able to proceed without any hindrance or interruption. I can always come to Abu Dhabi to work on our project. How do you feel about this arrangement?"

I was excited with the prospect! Andy and I agreed wholeheartedly. Wazir Thabit would request our presence at Sekhem when our service at Hadrah Hakim's was complete, and, with the Hadrah's blessing, we would then move to Wazir Thabit's Household.

The Harem Spa

After our meeting had adjourned, Aziz suggested we proceed to the Kosk Male Spa for some relaxation and pampering, with massages and men's beauty treatments. Andy and I had never taken advantage of the services offered at the men's spa, although during our tour of the Kosk we had seen the facility. We did exercise in the gym regularly.

The brothers enter the Jacuzzi; Andy and I swam in the lap pool before joining them. Since the spa was solely a male domain, it was fine to strip naked to enjoy the various facilities. As I entered the hot tub, streaming jets of bubbling water pulsated all over me. My forlorn, lovesick tension over the Count slipped behind me. Closing my eyes, enjoying the soothing, piped-in music, I found that I was relaxing into a better state of mind.

I felt a couple toes nibbling at my groin. I did not move nor did I open my eyes. It felt good to be caressed under the warm currents. Soon the wriggling toes crept towards the base of my scrotum. This playfully titillating sensation made me fully erect. Before long, two hands were touching my body under the jets of circling aqua. I kept my eyes closed, not wishing these sensual sensations to end nor needing to know whose hands they were. Soon, a sweet mouth leaned over, kissing me tenderly, sending tickling shivers down my spine.

Whom should I discover leaning over me but the good-looking Thabit, with his hair and beard wet he looked like a tanned Poseidon rising from an ocean of bubbling love. His longing gaze sent shivering chills through my wet, dripping body. Melting into his manly arms I gave myself to him as fully as I had to the Casanova Count.

I did not see Andy or Aziz in the tub. Thabit whispered into my ear in a gentle voice, "Your friends are in the massage rooms getting their body rubs. We are here alone."

"Happy Endings"

By the time Thabit and I finished making love in the Jacuzzi, I was ready for my massage. I headed into one of the private chambers and laid face down, ready for my full body rub to commence. The expert hands of Julian, my Filipino masseur, felt good on my relaxed skin. Before long, I fell into a light slumber while he worked his magic on my back.

I was gently awakened by a delightful tingling sensation on my cock and scrotum, sending me into another full erection under Julian's oil filled palms. He leaned over and asked in a soft, barely audible voice, "Sir, do you prefer a 'Happy Ending'?"

Not knowing what a 'Happy Ending' was, I said nothing. Julian continued his excellent stroking motions on my already engorged manhood. I felt delightfully relaxed on the massage table. Before long, I had my night's second orgasm. I spilled my seed onto my heaving belly at the request of his nimble fingers.

The Filipino wiped me clean with a wet towel. "Thank you Sir. Whenever you require my service please provide me with an hour's notice and I will be available for you." On that note, he left the private room, providing me a chance to rest peacefully until Andy came to escort me to our Peacock Chamber. I slept like a restful child throughout the silent night.

CHAPTER SEVENTY-THREE

The Rite of Passage

*"Sexuality poorly repressed unsettles some families;
well repressed, it unsettles the whole world."*
Karl Kraus

Not long after our return to the Kosk, Andy and I were summoned to the Hadrah's chambers. As soon as we exchanged our formal greetings Hakim began, "Boys, how did you enjoy Italy? How did my son behave?"

Andy replied, on our behalf, "We had a wonderful educational experience. Thank you for sponsoring our trip. Ubaid did very well; he curbed his drinking and smoking. The change of scenery was definitely good for him."

"Wonderful! Maybe I am too hard on my boy, but members of my household must be responsible. I know Ubaid gets out of hand at times. I must make sure he doesn't bring any offense to our family name. I do love him and care for him, and I appreciate the friendship you have offered him as well as your guidance."

Hakim smiled, and continued, "I have another matter with which I'd like your assistance."

Male Mentorship

Before the Hadrah had a chance to tell us what he expected Andy answered, "We will do our best to assist in any way possible. How we can be of service?"

Our host was grateful and continued, "My grandson, Rizq, is of age, which is celebrated in Muslim tradition by his circumcision. The day of his surgery I will be throwing him a Rite of Passage celebration party. I wish for you to provide him with some male sensual and sexual education.

"Would you be willing to take on this task of being his mentors? I have asked Gaston and Jacques to educate him in heterosexual lovemaking."

Andy looked at me for a response. I nodded so he replied, "We will assist this young man to the best of our ability. Thank you for trusting in us to take on this mentorship role. We are most grateful and honored."

"Well, that is wonderful. I'd like Rizq to have a few sexual experiences before his circumcision, and then again after he has healed from his surgery. That way he will better understand the different sensations, before and after circumcision," he replied.

Discussions with Andy

I asked Andy, "When the Hadrah said he'd like Rizq to experience both males and females 'like most of the males in his Household,' are you sure he doesn't know the relationship between Ubaid and Ramiz? Are most of the Kosk men bisexuals?"

Andy laughed. "Young, as you probably know by now, most Arab men are versatile due to the segregation between males and females. Most men have had sexual experiences with both sexes even though it's done in secrecy.

"Hakim is a wise and worldly man and I am sure he is well aware of what goes on in his domain, even though many think he doesn't know their secrets. He is shrewd; he doesn't let minor issues disrupt his household unnecessarily. I believe he knows of Ramiz' and Ubaid's relationship but he chooses not to meddle in their affairs." I continued, "How do you propose we mentor Rizq?"

After a brief pause Andy added, "Maybe now is a good time for you to begin learning the art of being a 'big brother', in preparation for when you take on the role."

"I'll do my best. I have the best teacher standing right next to me."

"Good! We can kill two birds with one stone." My Valet said.

Latif's Visit

The next day Latif and Ramiz paid us a visit after class. After our formal greetings Ramiz said, "Latif would like to have a word with you regarding his son's upcoming ceremony. Since his English is not so proficient, I'll interpret."

Latif said, "I want to thank you for taking my boy under your wings. I just visited Gaston and Jacques to give them my blessings in their assistance in mentoring Rizq in heterosexual love making."

Andy politely replied, "Sir, it is our pleasure. We will do our best to help your son. He is an intelligent young man and I'm sure he will learn quickly."

The boy's father looked delighted and responded, "I want my son to have a rounded education, not only in heterosexuality but also within the male realm. This will provide him with a better understanding of the world. I don't want to risk him being misguided or misinformed as he grows into adulthood.

"When I was growing up, I only experienced a heterosexual way. Since marrying Iman, my beloved wife, and living in the

Kosk, I have become more enlightened in my world view and I want that for my son.

"The Hadrah is a very intelligent and understanding man. I am grateful to him for helping me see the world in a different light."

My Valet replied, "Be assured that Rizq will be in good hands. We will set a good example for him and assist him in all he wants to know about the male ways of the world." Thanking us, Latif bid us farewell and said his son would pay us a visit tomorrow, after his visiting the Islamic school, which was preparing him for his upcoming circumcision ritual.

Mu'allmi Ramiz

As soon as Latif was out of sight I asked my teacher, "Why did Latif wait to talk to us until after Hakim met with us?"

Ramiz laughed, "Young, you must understand; the Hadrah is the patriarch of this Household and the patriarch has to be consulted first. He gives his approval or disapproval in all family matters. It is he who is the final voice for his family. That's why Hakim approached you before Latif came to give his personal blessing for your mentorship."

"Latif mentioned that the Hadrah understands worldly matters regarding male and female sensuality and sexuality. Are you sure he doesn't already know about your relationship with Ubaid?" I tested the waters to see Ramiz's response.

My teacher gave me a serious look. "Even if Hakim knows, he will not say a thing. As long as his prominent public standing is not threatened by any scandals, we men can do almost anything we want.

"You see, Young, there are double standards in the Arab world. As long as things appear proper on the surface, men can do whatever we like. I will soon be married to a respectable girl. I will have credibility in my social standing even if I continue to live my secret life.

"When Ubaid is of marrying age, he too, will have to take a wife, whether he loves her or not. After marriage, he can resume his other life, outside of our country. But he cannot do it openly, discrediting his family's good name. He will most likely have many men and women whenever he travels abroad. This is one of the unspoken facts of life in my country. Why do you suppose he was so unhappy about leaving Italy?"

"Well then, you don't have to worry about marrying Noor. You can still do whatever you wish after marriage," I said, grasping for understanding.

My teacher shook his head and sighed, "I feel terrible for Noor because I will not be able to provide her with the kind of love she deserves, and I risk ruining her happiness. Besides, I will be living a lie, and I find that difficult to accept. I don't want to think about it." We bid farewell, but not before he reminded us that our bi-weekly appointments in his chamber would commence tomorrow evening.

CHAPTER SEVENTY-FOUR

Sex Before Circumcision

*"I hear and I forget, I see and I remember.
I do and I understand."*
Chinese Proverb

Rizq

Rizq and I were in tutorials together; I had known him for eight weeks. I noticed he was taller than before I left for Italy. Before, he behaved like a child instead of a young man about to pass through his Rite of Passage. When he called on Andy and me a couple of days after our discussion with the Hadrah, he seemed grown up and more mature. We invited him into our suite to talk.

Andy said, "Rizq, don't be shy; tell us how we can be of assistance to you. We are here to help."

He replied, timidly, "I know. My grandfather and father told me I could ask you anything."

I asked, "Have you been to see Gaston and Jacques yet?"

The young man answered, "Yes! They are very kind and helpful. They introduced me to Caroline, who taught me many things."

"Did you like it?" I enquired.

Rizq smiled. "I liked the sensations but I still want to try making love with a man. That's why I'm here."

Andy chipped in, "Yes. We've been asked to help. What do you want to try first?"

"Well, what can you teach me? I'm ready to learn anything."

Andy asked, "When is your circumcision day"?

"The day after tomorrow. I'm here before my foreskin gets cut; my Islamic teacher tells me I will have to practice Fitrah (cleanliness) and be shaved before my circumcision can begin."

"Well, in that case, we will have a lesson now. Is that good?" suggested Andy.

"Come sit with us. Start by telling us your fantasies when you have sexual urges," he said with a calming voice. "Do you think of a female or a male when you masturbate?" asked my guardian.

Rizq awkwardly lowered his head and closed his eyes, giving Andy's question some thought, but not knowing how to respond. He kept his eyes closed while his body froze and tensed. He gripped his hands tightly in his lap.

Instinctively, I moved over to him and slowly licked his lips. He did not move away, neither did he open his eyes, so I continued to gently kiss his tender lips. He let out a low moan and laid his head back on the settee, inviting me to continue.

Andy moved Rizq's hands away from his lap and unbuttoned his thobe, revealing a smooth, hairless chest. Before long, his briefs and trousers were lying on the floor. I fondled his tiny nipples. He obviously liked the sensation. His eyes remained closed as we continued our sensual foreplay. Rizq's body slowly began to relax as he enjoyed our gentle, loving caresses. Soon we were completely naked, with me on top of him, licking and caressing every part of his youthful body.

Rizq was fair-skinned for an Arab boy, although he had tufts of dark colored pubic and armpit hair that were just beginning to grow. We knew it would not be difficult to show him the technique of shaving.

Andy gave me the task of educating my friend. I was surprised at myself by getting so easily aroused by a boy my own age. Usually, I preferred older, mature men but with Rizq I seemed to have taken on an erotic mentorship role; it came to me naturally.

Holding my friend's hand, I led him into the bedroom and continued where we left off on the sofa. Soon we were making love passionately, switching positions without discussion as to what roles we were to play. Sometimes I was on top and at other times I was below. By now, Rizq had relaxed and he was having a wonderful sexual experience under my tutelage. Andy remained on the sidelines, like a sex educator. He viewed us through his camera lens, clicking away and recording Rizq's first male-on-male sexual encounter.

As Andy clicked away I was further aroused, observing my lover watching me have intercourse with this youth. The tutorial took less than half an hour; our friend released soon after we lay on the bed.

I knew in my heart, that without the professional training from the Bahriji School I couldn't have done this. Most men were not educated in the Art of Sensuality and Sexuality. I was glad I attended such an excellent male finishing school, and had the privilege of having the finest and most proficient teachers. I was, indeed, one of the lucky selected ones.

After the First Lesson

Andy and I wanted to know how our friend liked his beginner's lesson in male lovemaking. "Did you enjoy it, Rizq?" Andy asked.

Chapter Seventy-four

The adolescent retreated into his shell again, not daring to look into Andy's eyes. "It was nice and I liked it. It was definitely different than having sex with a girl."

Never having been with a female I asked, "How is it different?"

"When I was with Caroline, I did most of the work, although she responded to my approaches. With you, Young, it was more mutual giving and receiving."

Andy enquired, "Which do you prefer?"

For the first time since entering our chambers, Rizq looked less serious. "The experiences were vastly different. Maybe I should try experiencing both at the same time and see how it feels. That might be fun!" he responded.

A thought raced through my mind. "Maybe you should try Caroline, Gaston, and Jacques, together. Then you can be both dominant and passive, at the same time."

"I'm more interested in my next lesson with you," replied a delighted Rizq.

Andy continued, "Since your surgery is imminent, we should meet again tomorrow. I'll teach you how to shave; then you will be Fitrah ready for your ceremonial ritual. We will be by your side, providing moral support."

"Thank you. It will be nice to have friends by my side to see me through my initiation."

"Are you ready for the circumcision? You know it will hurt, right," I enquired.

"I'm ready as I can be, I suppose. I am looking forward to taking my place within my Islamic community. I know I will be cleaner after the surgical procedure."

"Excellent. We will see you tomorrow." We both kissed him on the cheek, as he departed.

CHAPTER SEVENTY-FIVE

Fitrah and Khitan

*"It is not because things are difficult that we do not dare;
it is because we do not dare that they are difficult."*
Lucius Annaeus Seneca

The following afternoon, Rizq returned to our chambers. I was curious to find out how his experiment went (his foursome with Caroline, Gaston and Jacques). "Hi Rizq. It is good to see you; how did it go with your four-way?"

Rizq looked at the floor, searching for words to describe his experience. "I found it hard to concentrate, as there were all these hands caressing me and everything happening all at once. I lost my concentration. Although I enjoyed the various interactions, I prefer to stick to one-on-one.

"I did enjoy being inside Caroline with Gaston in me, from behind. This was very stimulating."

I replied, "At least you tried and you can now best decide your preference."

Andy asked, "Now, Rizq are you ready to be shaven?"
"Yes, I am."

Fitrah

Andy had laid out a towel, a can of shaving foam and a few razors on the bed. Rizq stripped and lay on his back facing Andy, who sprayed the shaving cream around our friend's groin. With utmost precision, my Valet slowly shaved the region around Rizq's penis as it began to grow; he obviously liked Andy's attention. When his pubic hair was completely gone, Andy told Rizq to spread his legs and lifted them in the air so he could get to the base of his scrotum and around the edges of his anus. As Andy continued shaving, the boy became more and more aroused, as was evidenced by his pre-ejaculatory fluids.

Rizq's excitement aroused me, so I, too, disrobed and began sensually caressing my friend. I fed him my cock.

Andy started clicking away while Rizq and I made out passionately. This time Rizq was totally passive, allowing me to dominate him without any resistance. Without pubic hair, Rizq seemed to feel more vulnerable.

Seeing Rizq's clean look, I decided that I, too, wanted to experience what it felt like to be shaved. My lover complied with my wishes. When Andy made love to my clean-shaven body, after the Rizq's departure, I suddenly was aware of my fragility. I felt vulnerable. It is indeed a strange phenomenon that hair could have such an impact on one's psyche.

Khitan

Early the next morning, I heard drumming coming from the men's section of the household. By the time Andy and I arrived, a large group of relatives and friends were gathered for the Khitan (Circumcision.) The servants and Abds served beverages and food while waiting for the ceremony to begin. Andy explained that the drummer's role, besides playing celebratory music, was to drown out Rizq's cries when the Circumciser performed the procedure.

The Imam, the spiritual head of the Hadrah's mosque, greeted the invited guests. The bearded, mature man conducted the Khitan ritual. He began with a recitation from the Hadith. Guests recited chants, after him. Rizq appeared, looking like a wide-eyed fawn. He began the descent, down stairs, followed by his father, Latif, and his grandfather, Hakim. My young friend knelt in front of the Imam, who began reading from the Qur'an. Rizq recited each verse after it was read.

After the recitation the Imam leaned Rizq backwards, and kissed him, fully, on the mouth, in front of the congregation. The happy relatives cheered with excitement. Rizq was then led to an adjacent room which was set up for the procedure. Andy was asked to enter the chamber. I stayed outside with most of the guests. I could not handle the sight of my friend's foreskin being removed. The sight of blood upsets me.

As the drumming grew louder and more intense I knew the scalpel was ready to draw blood. When the drumming decibels lowered, I knew the procedure was complete. Guests filed into the operating chamber to wish the newly initiated a speedy recovery. I waited until the last well-wishers had left before I entered the chamber to see my friend. Wiping his tears, I held his delicate hands in mine and whispered a *Jinn* into his ear. I pressed a tiny crystal into his palm as a protective amulet. Rizq gave me a weak smile before closing his eyes to rest.

At that instant, Rizq looked more vulnerable than ever. I kissed his soft cheek and felt like singing a little lullaby to ease him into peaceful slumber. Andy put his hands on my shoulders, assuring me that Rizq was going to be fine.

The Man Who Lays Golden Eggs

While Rizq was healing, Andy and I met Ramiz for our bi-weekly sessions. At some juncture of each rendezvous, Ramiz would lay two golden eggs he had inserted into his anus! After they had been cleaned, these eggs were presented to us as tokens of appreciation for our service. They were crafted by Chimento, the luxury purveyor from whom Ramiz had bought the Faberge eggs. The shop made two dozen of the hollow, twenty-four carat gold eggs. He stuffed several hundred dollars in each of them.

Andy nicknamed him 'The Man who lays the Golden Eggs.' Like the golden goose in 'Jack and the Beanstalk', my teacher never failed to lay golden eggs during each session.

After Circumcision

When Rizq finally came to visit us, a week after his surgery, the young man looked delighted. I asked him why he had a Cheshire cat's grin on his face. He replied, "I like the feeling of being circumcised. The head of my penis looks larger and the length seems longer during erection. Do you want to see it?" Without waiting for our response he dropped his trousers to display his prized possession, which, indeed, looked more impressive than before.

Andy asked, "So, my friend, are you back for more lessons?" Rizq beamed as he displayed his bulbous crown.

"I'm ready for action. Let's give it a go to see how it rides." He seemed to have turned into quite a cheeky devil, reminding me of his Uncle Ubaid. I began to wonder if this rite of passage had removed the last vestiges of a boy and turned him into a man.

We proceeded into the bedchamber. It became immediately clear that he was the aggressor. Rizq was a handsome and virile young buck, with stubble.

CHAPTER SEVENTY-SIX

Eid al Fitr & The Nubian

"When it is dark enough, you can see the stars."
Ralph Waldo Emerson

Before I knew it, Eid ul-Fitr was upon us. Andy and I were up early to join the Household members for a hearty breaking of fast meal. Men, women and children ate together; it was a joyous celebration with well wishes of Eid Mubarak. The festivities lasted for three days. The first day of celebration was the most important. The Kosk's big party would be held that evening in the grand ballroom. Servants, Abds and caterers were busily transforming the huge hall into a festive arena.

    Vendors delivered the finest cuts of meats, fresh herbs and vegetables, to the kitchen entrance. Florists arrived at 9:00 a.m. to decorate the house and gardens. Tents were erected and workmen built an open-air dance floor and podium for musicians and belly dancers who would provide the evening's entertainment. Electricians set up fairy lights in the garden and gazebo. It seemed the Gods had taken a sparkling wand and waved it, turning the Kosk into a Magic Kingdom where Snow White, Cinderella, Princess Jasmine and all their Princes would feel right at home.

Makeover

This was the day of the Kosk women's makeover debut. Professional beauticians provided facials and beauty treatments for the ladies while I checked accessories, shoes and clothes. As soon as each finished with hair and make-up, I helped them dress, detailing their ensembles. It was a considerable amount of work to style sixteen women in four hours. My enthusiasm more than made up for my lack of training as a professional stylist.

I absorbed everything with enthusiasm. The women and I were pleased with the results. Their husbands congratulated them on their beauty and style. I felt satisfied and happy that I had managed to bring more joy into their lives.

Hadrah Hakim

Hadrah Hakim's eyes sparkled when he saw his harem of beautiful women looking so gorgeous, as they paraded around the party. To him, they were prized trophies and this was an opportunity to show them off. The Hadrah was proud as a peacock with his colorful fanned tail wide open. I was sure he was one of the happiest men in the Arab Kingdom during those three days of festivities at the Kosk.

Hakim showered expensive gifts upon his entire family. The servants and Abds wore joyful faces probably in part due to generous monetary rewards from the Hadrah. He rewarded Andy and me handsomely for mentoring his favorite grandson. Our Eid Mubarak greeting card read: "Please accept this gift and a week's vacation to anywhere you'd like as a token of my appreciation for the friendship and guidance you so kindly provided

to my grandson. The Simorgh and the Kahyy'am are at your disposal. (Signed) Hadrah Hakim."
Enclosed were two cheques for $3,000 each.

The Silver Cabriolet

As the evening festivities progressed, more guests arrived at the grand entrance, in fancy, chauffeur-driven vehicles. Large sections of the driveway and grounds were allocated for parking. From my room, I had a perfect view of these rare and expensive automobiles. Nestled among the fancy cars, a silver 1930s sports car caught my eye. I'd never seen such a gorgeous vehicle before. I went downstairs to have a closer look.

Ghali, the Hadrah's chauffeur, was assisting one of the arriving guests. He saw me admiring the vehicle.

"Good Evening and Eid Mubarak, Sir. The vehicle which has caught your eye is a rare 1938 Sport Cabriolet." An elegantly dressed gentleman walked over, and chimed in. "Yes! Isn't it stunning? I don't think they make these anymore. It's a Horch Erdmann and Ross," he said.

I didn't know the names and models of cars at this time. I was simply fascinated by the look and condition of this car.

"Who does it belong to?" I wondered.

Before Ghali could reply, the Nubian gentleman jumped into the driver's seat and was searching for something in the glove box. "He is a business associate of Hakim. He owns several oil rigging enterprises in the Emirates and in the United States."

"I see! He sure has great taste, at least when it comes to cars." I commented.

Just then Ghali was called away to meet other arriving guests; I was left with the black man who now carried an elaborately wrapped gift under his left arm. "I believe we have not met. You are?" he asked, extending his hand to shake mine.

"Hello Sir! I am Young, a student from England. The Hadrah has very kindly taken me and my guardian, Andy, into his

Household. It's part of an exchange program, through our school."

The gentleman said, "So nice to meet you. I hope to make the acquaintance of your guardian."

"I'm sure you will. He is probably looking for me as we speak. Andy doesn't like me out of his sight for too long."

"Understandable. Shall we head in, and join the other guests?" He guided my arm as we proceeded toward the mansion.

As soon as we entered the foyer, which was overflowing with guests, the gentleman was cornered and pressed upon by many people who greeted him warmly. I looked around and saw Andy. He was speaking entertainingly to guests who seemed to adore him. When Andy saw me, he excused himself and asked, "Who is the handsome black man you were standing with?"

"He says he is a business associate of the Hadrah."

"What's his name?" My Valet enquired. I just looked at Andy blankly. I hadn't a clue. "The Nubian?" I framed my response as a question.

As the evening progressed the band began to play. Couples were filing onto the dance floor, arm in arm. Males and females mixed openly, as this was a private function at a private mansion; strict Islamic regulations were thrown to the wind. Liquor flowed freely.

Shall We Dance

I danced with several of the Harem women whom I had befriended. Shiya, Nasreen and Ghaniyah danced with Andy and me, as a group. I had such a wonderful evening. I completely forgot about the Nubian, until the evening was drawing to a close.

I noticed the black gentleman bidding the Hadrah and his wives farewell. He leaned over to whisper something in Hakim's ear before Ghali pulled up in his silver Cabriolet. He saw me, smiled and waved goodnight before disappearing down the driveway.

I slept well that night, knowing I had accomplished another milestone in my fashion future. I looked out my balcony and couldn't help admiring the beautiful stars twinkling against the expansive night sky.

Hidden beneath the dark gloomy burkas, abayas and hijabs were plenty of brightly colored twinkling stars. These stars, these heavenly beauties, were the harem women. I was so gratefully glad to have helped bring out their brightness on this starry, starry night.

CHAPTER SEVENTY-SEVEN

Merci Beau Coups and The Visitors

"Do not anticipate trouble or worry about what may never happen. Keep in the sunlight."
Benjamin Franklin

With the Eid ul-Fitr festivities in full force, the Hadrah's family was busy entertaining visiting dignitaries, as well as relatives and friends who came to pay homage to Hakim. The harem women seemed to exude a newfound enthusiasm and confidence which the Kosk men, especially the Hadrah, found especially charming.

On the final day of the festivities, the group asked to meet me. When we were gathered, Nasreen spoke first. "We'd like to say 'Shokran' to you for assisting us with our make-overs."

Above the applause Shiya added, "Young, we are happy to present you with a small token of our gratitude." I assumed prayer position, head lowered and hands clasped, signifying my humbleness for their generosity. Nasreen placed an envelope in between my hands.

"It's been my pleasure to be of service to you and to be given this opportunity. I am eternally grateful," I assured them.

Invitation to Paris Couture Fashion Week

After the pleasantries and the individual shokrans from the various ladies, Nasreen announced, "Young, we are going to Paris to the Couture Fashion shows in a couple of weeks. Are you and Andy interested in coming with us? We'd like your suggestions and opinions on what to purchase at the shows."

I was, indeed, surprised at this unexpected invitation. "I'd be more than happy to accompany you to the Couture shows. When do we leave?"

Nasreen laughed at my no holds barred attitude. "Next week Shiya and I will return to Europe, to university. We'll meet you in Paris the following weekend. Father can send the Simorgh to collect you," Nasreen suggested.

"That's splendid. It will be wonderful to see the fashion shows and to be of assistance to you." I was jumping with joy as I agreed to Nasreen's invitation.

Shiya chipped in, "Wonderful! Our cultural attaché to Paris will make arrangements with the fashion houses, informing them that we'll be attending. They will also provide us with a list of designer ateliers. I'll organize everything immediately."

"Fabulous!" I kept my cool, acting as if designer shows in Paris were an ordinary item on my agenda. I was screaming with happiness on the inside.

The Dilemma

When we returned to the Peacock Chambers, Andy said, "The Hadrah wants to see us as soon as possible. Can you go now?"

I placed the envelope from the ladies on my desk, and Andy and I headed for Hakim's chambers. As soon as we entered, the Hadrah began, "I have a dilemma. Ubaid disappeared on the Simorgh leaving a note saying he had gone to Italy to be with his girlfriend, Gianna. He wants to elope with her. I have asked Ramiz to go immediately to track him down. Will you go talk some sense into his thick head? He is more apt to listen to your advice than mine!"

Distraught and angry, Hakim bellowed, "This son of mine is too radical and impulsive. He doesn't think things through. I want him back at the Kosk immediately before a scandal breaks out!"

Andy immediately responded, "Sir, I will go with Ramiz to find Ubaid. Rest assured we'll talk sense into him. I'm certain we can convince him to return at once."

Our host looked gratefully at Andy. "I've told Ramiz to prepare to depart within the next hour. Ghali will drive you to the airport to board a commercial flight to Florence."

As soon as we left the Hadrah's chamber Andy turned to me. "Young, I think it is best you stay here. It is pointless for you to go, since there is not much you can do. Stay and enjoy the rest of the festivities; leave me and Ramiz to handle Ubaid."

It was true that my presence would not assist in bringing the rebellious prodigal son home, so I agreed to stay at the Kosk until their return, which he promised would only be a few days.

Ludwig Abid Safar

Andy left with Ramiz. I went to join the endless flow of guests coming to wish Hakim's family "Eid Mubarak." One guest in particular was Professor Ludwig Abid Safar, whom I met during the Sahara Douz Festival. He was delighted to see me, and motioned for me to walk beside him. Smiling he said, "Let's go out to the terrace and talk."

We sat on a shaded bench. "I am here to pay homage to the Hadrah, of course. I want to wish him well on this festive occasion. But most of all, Young, I came to see you and Andy."

I replied, "Andy just left for Florence with my teacher, Ramiz. They are on urgent business and won't be back for a few days." I was careful not to disclose that Ubaid was missing in action. I understood secrecy and the value of privacy when it came to dealing with family matters. Privacy was especially important in the Hadrah's household. It would be unforgiveable to reveal unsavory tales of Hakim's son's private life.

Ludwig smiled again. "Well so much the better. I can have you all to myself. I am staying at an apartment in the city. Would you care to have dinner with me this evening?" I decided to accept Ludwig's offer. He continued, "I will pick you at 7:00 p.m., and we'll have dinner in the city."

Nirob

Ludwig and I returned to join the other guests. The handsome Nubian was in a hallway, having just left the Hadrah's office. He noticed me, and stopped to speak. Ludwig was ahead of me, already mingling with guests.

His name was Nirob. I caught that as he shook my hand, mentioning how happy he was to see me. He asked when he might have a chance to meet Andy. Again, I found myself explaining that Andy was away, temporarily, and would not return for a few days.

Nirob also seemed delighted with this news! He said, "Will you have dinner with me this evening? I'm staying at a hotel in the city for a few days before flying to Texas on business."

I politely declined, explaining that I already had a dinner engagement that evening. I suggested meeting the next day. Nirob looked disappointed that he couldn't see me that night but agreed to meet with me the following day, for lunch.

Thank-You Card

Later, as I sat in my room contemplating the day's events, I began to wonder why these men were so eager to meet me when

Andy wasn't around. All sorts of strange and unsavory scenarios raced through my mind. I envisioned the worst. Are they going to corner me and rape me, since I am not accompanied by my guardian? Or are they going to sell me to slave traders, once they had their way with me? All these weird fears ran through my head; I began having second thoughts about going on my dates. I wished Andy were making these decisions with me, and that he was here.

Then, I reasoned: I am old enough to take care of myself. I can be brave and act like a man instead of a sissy boy who constantly has to have my guardian make my decisions. It is time to start taking charge of my life, and deciding things for myself.

While these thoughts were creating havoc in my head I remembered the card from the harem ladies which I had left on my writing desk. When I opened it, a cheque for $16,000 was sandwiched between an Eid Mubarak card and a beautifully scripted message by Nasreen, on behalf of the harem women. It read: "Young, Thank you for your contribution to our make-overs. Please accept our humble gift." All of the women had signed it. I was touched by this lovely gesture of gratitude and I promised myself then and there that I would make fashion my career. I would help women show their shiny beautiful selves to the world in shiny and beautiful couture!

CHAPTER SEVENTY-EIGHT

Ludwig, Oberon and Nirob

"Worrying is the same thing as banging your head against the wall. It only feels good when you stop."
John Powers

It was, indeed, true that worrying was the same as banging my head against the wall; it felt great when I stopped. Fortunately, none of my worries manifested. Both dates yielded the opposite of all my fears.

At precisely 7:00 p.m., Ludwig drove up to the Kosk in a top of the line Mercedes. He had asked the Hadrah's permission to take me out, since Andy wasn't around. Hakim told him our arrangement would be fine as long as he returned me safely home no later than midnight.

When we reached the restaurant, a good looking German man by the name of Oberon was already seated at our table. He was a newly appointed Law professor, celebrating his thirtieth birthday by accompanying Ludwig to Dubai. The two had become lovers a few months previously.

Ludwig and Oberon

Ludwig was hoping that Andy would also be present, for a potential 4-way liaison. He had thought of it as a gift, for Oberon's birthday. But since my Valet wasn't around, it was to become a 3-way liaison instead. Although I did miss Andy, I was well cared for and appreciated by these two gentlemen. No harm came my way. Instead it was love, love and a lot of ecstatic love-making before the clock struck twelve.

During our Lebanese dinner, Ludwig enquired, "How do you find Middle Eastern life, Young?"

I replied, "A lot has happened since we last spoke. I've been to Italy, and in twelve days, I'm leaving for Paris for the Couture Fashion shows. Life couldn't be better; I have new experiences daily. Never a dull moment."

"I'm happy for you! Do you have to watch out for lecherous men like me lurking about?" Ludwig asked, jokingly.

"Ah! I keep your jeweled dagger by my side as my protective weapon, in case men like you should suddenly attack. I am well protected; thank you for your precious gift." They both laughed heartily at my remark.

Oberon added, "You are funny, Young, I like you."

"I'm glad you do! I am forever indebted to Ludwig for saving me from a deadly scorpion in the Sahara. I owe him one."

Ludwig took this opportunity, "Well, now is time to pay up! Let's have a threesome!"

I looked at the handsome Oberon, then glanced back at Ludwig. I answered, "Your requests are my commands!"

Chocolates

Their laughter was infectious! Ludwig continued, "Christmas will be here soon. Would you and Andy like to visit us in

Tubingen where we teach? We can attend the ChocolArt Festival in early December."

Curious, I asked, "What is the ChocolArt Festival?"

Oberon explained, "It's one of the biggest festivals in the world for chocolate lovers. Artists create chocolate art; there are chocolate competitions and lots of delicious chocolate to eat."

Without thinking, I said, "I'd love to come and I'm sure Andy will agree! Chocolates are my all-time favorite! When does the festival begin?"

"It's the first week of December. You and Andy can stay with us as our guests." "Yes, yes and yes! I will definitely come. I was delighted to be invited to spend Christmas in Germany.

After dinner, we proceeded to the professors' room. We began our lovemaking in earnest. This time, instead of falling in love with a person, like I did with Count Casanova Mario, I fell in love with the idea of all the chocolates I could manage to eat. I could hardly wait for December to arrive!

Husni

True to his word, Ludwig delivered me safely to the Kosk at the stroke of midnight. Our sweet cat, Husni, kept me company. We slept through the entire night without any disturbance. He seemed to know I needed his love more than ever, since Andy was away. For the next few days and nights, the Persian snuggled close to my side and purred contentedly.

Nirob

One in the afternoon rolled around quickly. Nirob's Sport Cabriolet appeared in the driveway to collect me for our lunch appointment. He, too, had requested permission from the Kosk patriarch for my leave. I was excited about the opportunity to ride in such a beautiful automobile. As I was lacing my eye mask, Nirob asked, "Why do you have to wear that strange contraption?"

Chapter Seventy-eight

Without a thought I responded, "Oh, it is one of the Bahriji school rules. Whenever we leave a Household, on a land journey, we are to be blindfolded."

Nirob said, "What if I drove you away and never brought you back? You'd never know how to return to the Kosk, would you?" That thought had never entered my mind.

I said, "Oh, I've never thought of that! I trust you will neither sell me into slavery nor bring harm to me in any way. You are a trusted friend of the Hadrah and he is like a father to me. You wouldn't risk his wrath."

Nirob laughed and said, "You are exactly right my dear boy; I will not harm you. I will love and cherish you. Just like this car of mine. I care for it with utmost love. I'm drawn to beautiful things, Young, as is the Hadrah. He and I work well together; we both have similar tastes and objectives."

As I buckled myself in my harness, my date continued, "You will meet my girlfriend when we get to the restaurant. She is there now, waiting for us."

I was surprised to hear the news. Nirob could not see my bewilderment. I kept my cool. "Why didn't your girlfriend come with you to the Eid ul-Fitr party at the Kosk?

My date answered, "She wasn't invited to the party; Hakim doesn't know about Kismat. I did tell her about you and Andy, though, and she is eager to meet you both."

I asked, "I'm curious; what is the reason for this lunch appointment? What's on your mind?"

Nirob smiled and continued, "We'll, let's see what transpires over lunch." He was silent for a bit, and then continued. "I hope you like her; she is a very nice person. Some people might not understand her unique ways, but I believe you and Andy will."

I was really curious, and probed further, "What do you mean that Andy and I will understand her unique ways? What are her unique ways?"

The Nubian continued, smiling. "I'll leave that for you to figure out when you meet her."

Before long, we arrived at Cafe Persimmon located in a five star hotel, where Nirob and Kismat were staying.

Kismat was dressed in the latest fashions and she was one of the most beautiful women I'd ever set eyes on. I could not decipher the unique ways that her boyfriend had gone on about. What's there to understand about her, I wondered? She seemed perfectly charming and nice; I liked her company.

After the delicious lunch and a delightfully friendly conversation, I did not see the Nubian and his girlfriend again until after Andy returned from Italy. It was then that the truth came out about the gorgeous Kismat's unique ways.

CHAPTER SEVENTY-NINE

Kismet and Friends

"We are all a little weird and life's a little weird, and when we find someone whose weirdness is compatible with ours, we join up with them and fall in mutual weirdness and call it love."
Dr. Seuss

Andy returned a few days later with Ubaid in tow, kicking and cursing. Both Ramiz and Andy had to strong arm him to get him to return home. Of course, the Hadrah gave him a good scolding and grounded him for the rest of his time in Dubai. Our friend couldn't bear living under his father's iron fist. Hakim had round-the-clock bodyguards watching his son, making sure he would not repeat his disappearing trick. Our poor lovesick friend was back to his old tricks, smoking and drinking heavily. Ramiz, Andy and I tried our best to console him and cheer his tortured soul, but depression had him in its grip.

The week and a half in the Kosk, before he returned to Trinity College, was hell for him. He was not allowed to communicate with Gianna – his father commanded he cut off all ties with her. The more the Hadrah clamped down, the more Ubaid wanted to escape to see his beloved.

Andy and I felt sorry for our friend and Ramiz was secretly heartbroken to see his beloved so devastated. Several times Ramiz tried using sex as a diversion, to help Ubaid. The amelioration of his mood was quite temporary. It lasted only as long as the sex. The deeper remedy for Ubaid's depression came in a most unexpected fashion.

At Al Falconry

I promised Nirob and Kismat we would get together when Andy returned. Nirob called on the Hadrah a few days after our lunch date. We spoke and arranged to formally introduce Andy to Kismat and Nirob. Since Ubaid was in such an unhappy frame of mind, we asked the Hadrah's permission for his son to join us. We mentioned our friend's lovesickness to Nirob, and he had a splendid idea.

"Kismat could introduce Ubaid to a couple of her female friends who are in town from Paris," he said.

Ubaid joined us at the elegant Al Falconry restaurant that evening. Kismat's friends, Lamei and Wannie, were already seated at the table. Ubaid immediately started flirting with them. All of the ladies were of Asian descent. They spoke French and a little English. We managed to communicate sufficiently through gestures and a few words. Nirob was our translator.

Dinner Conversation

After formal introductions, Nirob said, "Andy, it's so nice to have a chance to meet you. Young speaks so highly of you."

I responded, "I couldn't have a better guardian than this man. He's responsible, and cares for me well."

"That is good to know. I care about Kismat very much too. Although we only met a few months ago, we have grown very close. We have a delightful rapport, don't we, love?" added the black man.

"How did you meet?" Andy asked.

The Nubian looked at Kismat, grinned and continued, "We met at the Folies Bergere in Paris. Kismat is a dancer. She is one of the prettiest and most talented showgirls in the troupe. We are very open-minded. We like to experiment with others when the right situation arises." He was testing our response.

My guardian smiled and said, "Like you, we are also happy to try new experiences when the appropriate occasion arises."

"Andy and I are going to Paris in 10 days. I'd love to see Kismat perform at the Folies. Would that be possible?"

Nirob turned to Kismat and spoke to her in French before answering, "She will be delighted to have you attend her performances. When you are in Paris contact her at this number, and she'll arrange to get you in a show." Kismat smiled graciously showing her approval.

I couldn't help but to clap my hands in excitement. "Fabulous! Andy and I will definitely contact you," I said, acknowledging her nodding smile.

We all laughed when the Nubian said, "Let's order the main course. After dinner we can decide on the kind of dessert we'd like to experience." He stressed the word 'experience' and gave us a flirtatious wink, signaling that he couldn't wait for 'dessert.'

Foursome

At the opposite end of the table, Ubaid and the girls were having a great time. They were busy flirting and laughing; it reminded me of how he had acted with the models in Venice.

We were not surprised when Nirob suggested we return to his suite for dessert. Ubaid agreed, eagerly, but he was already scheming; he planned to rent a room to have a night of sexy fun and games with Lamei and Wannie.

Ubaid and the two Asian ladies checked into a suite of their own, rather than join us. The four of us proceeded to Nirob's luxurious penthouse. As we sat on the comfortable sofa, he offered Andy and Kismat chilled champagne from an ice bucket. I drank water.

A few glasses of champagne later, our friend began kissing his girlfriend on her lips and neck. Soon her dress was half way down her waist showing off her voluptuous breasts. As Nirob continued his sensual foreplay, Andy and I were getting aroused. We started our own love game, right next to the couple. I could feel my lover's excitement as he kissed me, while watching the erotic heterosexual scene unfold before us.

The Nubian eased off his girlfriend's panties. 'She' had an engorged penis pointing upwards, instead of a wet vagina waiting for attention.

This Lady Boy mesmerized Andy and me; we could not take our eyes off of Kismat's sex organs. I had never witnessed a real life transsexual before this moment.

Nirob was enjoying every moment of their foreplay. He certainly had no qualms about making love to a transsexual. Before long, we were in a four-way liaison. As much as I was aroused by the good-looking Nirob and Andy's erotic kisses and caresses, I could not get into the mood for sex. I kept glancing at this half female, half male. I found the experience disorienting.

Andy began losing his erection, and wasn't able to perform. For me, the allure was Kismat's unusualness. My erection was waning. If not for Nirob and Andy's alpha attention, I would not have been able to continue. I'd rather have been a voyeur, watching Kismat and Nirob, than an active participant.

Nirob was completely turned on having a Lady Boy and a Pretty Boy simultaneously. He asked Andy to take photographs, thus providing him the perfect excuse to shy away from sexual participation (as he had totally lost his erection). He embraced the camera, clicking away, capturing our three-way action.

Sex with a transsexual was not my lover's forte, nor was it mine. I enjoyed Nirob's masculinity, and scent. I secretly wished for a three-way with Andy and the Nubian.

Driving Home

After our sexual soiree, Ubaid drove us home in his Porsche. I asked our friend how his evening had been. Smiling, he said, "It's been a very interesting evening."

I was curious to find out if he had had a similar experience as us, so I probed, "How so?"

The Arab continued, "It turns out that the two Parisians were Lady Boys, and I had a lot of fun with them. They knew just how to make me feel good. I wouldn't mind visiting them at Le Crazy Horse de Paris. They are showgirls."

"Why do you like having sex with them so much?" I asked.

Ubaid said humorously, "I like them half female and half male. That way I have the best of both sexes in a single person; to me that's sex-citing! I'm completely sexed out. It was like an all you can eat buffet. They sure know how to please a man." He licked his lips, demonstrating to us how they pleasured him.

"When do you plan to go to Paris to see them?" I inquired.

"Maybe I will spend a weekend in Paris after my return to Ireland. My sisters told me you are joining them at the French Couture Fashion Shows. Should we meet in Paris and have a fun weekend?"

Andy responded, "That would be great. At least I'll have some company while Young is at the shows with the women."

By the time we reached the Kosk it was settled. We would meet in Paris. For the next ten days I excitedly looked forward to a romantic rendezvous in good ole Paree.

PART FIVE

Oasis, Daltonbury Hall, Paris

CHAPTER EIGHTY

Back At The Bahriji

*"Life can only be understood backwards,
but it must be lived forward."*
Soren Kierkegaard

The ten days passed very quickly. Before I could blink, my three months' service at the Kosk was coming to an end. The day before we were scheduled to leave I felt sad and somewhat depressed. I had found a family away from home, but it was time to say good-bye. I had to move forward to garner new experiences and seek new adventures.

Ma'a Salaama Hadrah Hakim

Before Andy and I returned to the Bahriji, we met Hadrah Hakim to bid our farewells and to thank him for the hospitality he and his Household had so generously showered upon us. As soon as we walked into his chambers, the Hadrah came over and gave us bear hugs. He began, "It seems only yesterday you came to the Kosk and now you are already leaving. I want to tell you that your presence in my Household has been most delightful."

Andy responded on our behalf, "Young and I are eternally grateful for your hospitality and kindness and we'll always be at your service. Please do not hesitate to contact us if you ever need us." Bowing with both hands clasped, we lowered our heads and kissed the Patriarch's hand. "I wish you a safe journey in your other Household assignments," he said, with great warmth.

"Don't forget that you have the use of the Simorgh and the Kahyya'm for a week whenever you are ready to take me up on my offer. You are good boys; I wish Ubaid was responsible, like you." He turned his gaze to Andy.

"Although he is impulsive at times, I'm sure, with age, he will be like his wise father," my Valet said, with determination in his voice.

Our host sighed before answering, "I pray to Allah daily that this is so. You have my blessings to go to the Sekhem; may good fortune be with you both, always."

I finally got a chance to thank the Hadrah, who had become like a father to me. I lowered my head and in a standing prayer posture I said, "IL-Hamdu-Allah" (Thanks be to God) for your kindness and generosity during our time here. It is my sincere wish that you have a long life and many years of fulfillment and happiness." He looked lovingly at me, and moved towards his large desk to pick up an envelope.

Handing me the package, Hakim kissed me on my lips and said, "Accept this as a token of our Household appreciation for both your and Andy's contributions here, and Inshallah (God willing), we shall meet again."

Ghali loaded our luggage into the yellow Rolls Royce and we sped towards the airport to board the Hadrah's helicopter to the Bahriji School, on an oasis in the middle of the desert.

At the Bahriji

Andy and I spent five days at the Bahriji before returning to Daltonbury Hall for a week. I was delighted to see my Oasis teachers again. Professor Henderson had grown a beard and looked even more handsome. He was eager to find out how things progressed at the Kosk Household during our time in service. We gave him a summary of our three months at the Kosk and provided detailed descriptions of our relationships with the various Household members.

It was our responsibility to provide a detailed assessment of our treatment during our residence at each Household. These recorded accounts were documented and archived in the school's extensive security vault. The school authorities made sure that each Household complied with the E.R.O.S. rules and regulations. The same applied to each student and his or her guardian. Any complaints filed by any of the three parties would be investigated fully. The E.R.O.S. organization ran smoothly and efficiently, on every level. There were many checks and balances.

Andy and I also had private meetings with Dr. Henderson. In this setting we could confidentially divulge personal issues. The day of my individual meeting with the Professor, he made sure I was satisfied with my Valet's performance. He asked about Andy's handling of different situations throughout our assignment. He wanted to know whether or not Andy performed his Valet duties to the best of his abilities. Of course I provided an excellent account of Andy's conduct and mentioned that he handled every situation with excellent skill, understanding and positivity.

My comments were a report card on his performance which would be presented, officially, to the Bahriji and E.R.O.S. Board of Directors.

If there were complaints from a student or the Household, the Valet would be kept under surveillance or terminated. My professor continued, "Young, you are growing up so quickly! I want to hear all about your experiences with Hakim; he is one of our school's most generous supporters. Past students in his service had a very positive rapport with him and his family. Did he treat you well?"

"Oh yes, Professor! It could not have been better; he is a very generous man. He showered us with gifts for which I am very grateful. His family is delightful. They gave me chances to put my theoretical studies into practice." I grinned cheerfully.

"How so?" my teacher enquired, with curiosity.

"For a start, I had the opportunity to see a little of Tunisia and Italy. Soon, I will be experiencing France and Germany. I have learned so much since making the decision to be an E.R.O.S. member!" I reported, joyfully.

"Also I met a charming transsexual whom I will be meeting again in Paris. I learned a little about the art of S & M role playing. But, the most delightful gift was finding a father figure who accepts and loves me just as I am."

The Dr. looked pleased. He continued to enquire, "Are there any issues bothering you? You can tell me honestly since this is a confidential meeting. You can speak about anything. The school and society will assist you if there are any difficulties you are facing."

Without hesitation, I replied, "No, nothing at all. I am one hundred and one percent satisfied and happy with the way my life is going."

"Very good, then! In that case I will have the allocation documents ready for you and Andy for your next Household, which will be at the Sekhem, Wazir Thabit's residence. After your Christmas break you'll return to Daltonbury for a week, then you will come back to the Bahriji. From here you'll be transported to the Sekhem.

"Have a wonderful and Merry Christmas, if I don't see you before you leave for Daltonbury Hall." My session with Professor Henderson ended with a farewell kiss on both cheeks.

Several days later my Valet and I were flown via helicopter to Dubai airport to board the Daltonbury Hall private jet back to my English boarding school.

Game On

During the 5 days at the Bahriji, I had time to catch up on activities I missed during my stay at the Kosk. I resumed my fencing lessons with Professor Lichman.

My teacher was just wrapping up a class in the fencing studio when I walked in. He was delighted to see me and came over to give me a big hug. I felt tingling sexual energy during our intimate embrace. I caught a whiff of his masculine scent when I leaned against the side of his neck, and whispered, "So happy to see you, professor." We held each other for awhile before my teacher threw me a sword and said, "Let's duel!"

Without suiting up, we started fencing. He threw me a foil and I retaliated. We laughed like friends who had not seen each other for a long time, before stopping to catch our breath.

He put his arms around my shoulders and looked directly into my eyes. "It's so good to see you, Young. Will you help me tidy up the studio this time around, as well?" He queried, giving me a wicked wink. We both remembered what had happened the last time I offered to help him store his equipment, in the right places.

The Incredible Professor Lichman

I laughed and said, "Yes Sir, definitely Sir!" I helped him pack up the fencing equipment while catching up on his news.

"Did your first Household assignment go well?"

"Very well Sir. Better than I expected! I've gained more experience, especially in the art of body language," I teased.

"That's good to know. Perhaps you can teach this old dog some new tricks," he flirted.

"Sure, that can be arranged. When do you want your lessons?" I asked alluringly.

"Now is a good time. Let's finish cleaning up and go to my apartment for a shower."

"Fabulous. It'll be great to continue where we left off." I smiled, sexily, at my fencing professor.

Before long we were kissing lovingly. Warm water sprayed upon our perspiring bodies. Our lingering kisses were titillating. We found fresh ways to explore all of our hidden crevices, leading to new heights of sensual and sexual ecstasy.

I had matured in the art of lovemaking and this time, we enjoyed each other's company more than we did the first. In my five days at the Bahriji, besides attending to my regular studies, I assisted Professor Lichman many times. We were very pleased with the results! Whenever I returned to the Bahriji, we continued our liaison where we had left off.

CHAPTER EIGHTY-ONE

Oscar! What Am I To Do With You?

"The eye is the mirror of the soul."
Proverb

The day after Andy and I returned to Daltonbury Hall we had an appointment for medical check-ups with Dr. William Hunton. The two nurses at the *Rabbit Hole*, Felicia and Mary, greeted us with hugs and warm welcomes. We then entered separate examination rooms for blood work and various physical exams.

    A few days later, when my Valet and I returned to the *Rabbit Hole*, the doctor informed us that we both had clean bills of health. Andy was stationed at Yates Fraternity's dormitory and was temporary allocated as 'big brother' to Steward, a Yates junior of Indian Portuguese decent. He was not an E.R.O.S.

member. My Valet was looking after Steward until his regular 'big brother', Leonard, returned from Christmas break.

It was difficult for Andy and me to be separated since we had been sharing the same bed for three months. My sweet Husni wasn't around to keep me company, either. We had decided to leave Husni, temporarily, at the Kosk since we couldn't have animals in our dorm rooms. Husni would be returned to our care when we were stationed at the Sekhem, a month and half later. I missed my Persian and I missed Andy in bed with me.

I was glad to be back in England. The wet, chilly British air was a pleasant change from the dry, hot U.A.E. climate. Back at the Tolkien Brotherhood dormitory I met my new roommates: a cute but timid junior Latino boy named Pepi, and his handsome six foot tall BB, and athletic build. His name was Oscar. I was immediately attracted to him.

I knew instantly that Pepi wasn't an E.R.O.S. member; he did not possess the qualities sought by the secret society. I could not decipher Oscar, so I asked Andy, when our paths crossed, about him. He had no idea either, so my curiosity remained piqued until an unexpected situation arose.

Rooming with John

John, my old roommate, had just returned to Daltonbury Hall and was in a Tolkien Brotherhood dormitory. We were excited to renew our friendship and hung out that week. John's Valet had taken leave for Australia to be with his family, prior to the school holidays. John was left in his dorm room alone, so I decided to take the opportunity to room with him instead of Pepi and Oscar.

Since my time at Daltonbury Hall was only ten days, I quietly changed rooms, only informing Oscar (my temporary BB) who did not mind. Oscar agreed to my room swap because it fit in perfectly with his plans. Oscar said that he would be checking on us when he had time away from his duties to Pepi.

Oscar

The following evening, after I moved in with John, Oscar dropped by to see how we were doing. I was in bed reading when he entered.

Without glancing up I responded, "I'm fine. It's good to have some time to catch up with John; after all I haven't seen him for over three months."

Oscar said, "I just returned from Abu Dhabi a few days before your return. I don't like this damp English cold one bit."

Closing my book I looked at him and replied, "I'm sorry to hear that, Oscar. I go to Abu Dhabi after my Christmas break. What's it like there"?

The BB continued, "It's a great place to be! The Arab family I stayed with was wonderful. The patriarch is a Wazir and his home is an amazing palace. I'll be going there again after the Christmas break with a new charge. Which family are you assigned to in Abu Dhabi?"

I wondered if the Wazir's household was Thabit's. "I'll soon be assigned to a home called the Sekhem; the owner is Wazir Thabit."

Oscar said with a surprised look on his face, "That's where I was. I was with Roy, my charge, but he didn't adjust well to that household so next term he's going to Bahrain instead. But I liked the Wazir's household and requested to return to the Sekhem with a new charge. I don't know who I'll be taking care of, yet. Who is going with you?"

"Andy, my Valet from Yates Fraternity. He was with me at the Kosk, my previous household," I answered.

The BB sat next to me on the bed as we talked, giving me some insight into Thabit's household, and his experiences there. As I learned more about Oscar I sensed he was a person with whom I could very easily fall in love, so I tried to keep my distance.

I could tell that Oscar was developing a strong liking for me. As our conversation progressed, he inched closer and closer. I was doing my best to avoid looking directly into his eyes as we spoke because I knew my eyes could not keep my secrets. Soon, he had moved so close his scent flooded my nostrils. Desperately trying not to betray Andy's love, I moved away, bit by bit. The further I moved, the closer Oscar advanced. When my resistance was at its weakest, John entered the room; Oscar and I were about to ignite a fire with our first passionate kiss.

Pulling away, we greeted John as if we were just having a casual conversation. John's presence definitely changed the dynamics and soon our conversation turned from flirtation to casual inquiries. Because of the dissipating energies, I said to Oscar "Don't you have to return to your room to see how Pepi is doing?"

The BB smiled and answered, "I guess you are right, I better be going as it's getting late and we all have a full day tomorrow; you guys better get some sleep."

Getting up from my bed, he bid John and me good night and departed. As soon as the door closed behind him, John asked inquisitively, "You have the hots for each other, don't you?"

I was taken by surprise by that remark. "I don't know what you're talking about. He's my temporary guardian; obviously he is concerned about my well-being, nothing more than that."

John laughed and gave me a wicked grin before speaking, "I think there is more to it than what meets the eye."

Trying desperately to deny my strong sexual desire for Oscar, I responded, "Don't be silly; you are reading too much into it. I am devoted to Andy and I will not cheat on him. I tell Andy everything."

That was a lie. I did not tell Andy everything. Instead I told my diary everything. And it was locked in my desk.

That night I had difficulty sleeping. I fantasized about Oscar and felt terribly guilty for thoughts about cheating on Andy. A sense of foreboding swept over me the next day. I did not mention any of my feelings to my beloved. I put on a brave face, keeping my secrets under wraps, hoping that my forbidden desire would disappear if I hid it long enough.

I kept telling myself that Andy and I would be in Paris next weekend and then we would be in Germany and Switzerland for 3 weeks. The chances of an affair with Oscar would be impossible and everything would be all right – or so I thought.

CHAPTER EIGHTY-TWO

My Mystery Lover

"A heart that loves is always young."
Bernard Tristan Foong

Oh Oscar, why did you make me fall in love with you? I desperately tried to resist your charm! The weekend before Andy and I left to join Ubaid and the Kosk Harem ladies in Paris, I was torn between two men: Andy and Oscar. What did I do to deserve this kind of attention? Many would love this experience. I had two men vying for my attention. Was it because of my youthful heart that loved freely and openly, without reservations? I wondered.

After Oscar visited my room I could not get him out of my mind, so I consoled my pent up emotions with my diary. Somehow writing down my thoughts calmed my nerves. Although I saw Andy daily, I did not mention my distress. In my innocent mind I thought my stress would disappear if I ignored it. Life would then resume as it was before Oscar. Unfortunately, emotions seldom work that way. The nagging desire to pursue a deeper relationship with my temporary guardian did not wane, nor did it magically dissolve into nothingness. Instead the plot thickened and boiled over like a pot of overheated stew.

In The Bath

After a hectic day attending classes, I was glad for a chance to relax, after a late supper. I decided to enjoy a soothing hot bath at my dormitory's communal bathroom. Our bathtubs had no curtains or partitions. I decided to settle into a tub located some distance away from the bathroom entrance, in a secluded corner so I would not be disturbed if anyone entered the facilities. It was wonderful to soak in a steaming tub of bubbly hot water when the temperature outside was freezing cold.

Before long I was happily soaking in the water, wearing only an eye mask to block out the bright overhead lights. I was humming a popular melody, enjoying my solitude, when I felt a pair of hands massaging my groin. With the mask shadowing my eyes I could not see this mysterious person. This tantalizing feeling was extremely soothing and stimulating. Relaxing into the tub I allowed the massaging hands to continue. These seductive hands soon found their way to my scrotum and engorged penis. Before I could discard my mask, the tempter's sweet lips were on mine, prying my lips open, forcing them to surrender to his lusting mouth. I just wanted to enjoy these sensual sensations, and flow to the rhythmic motions of this mysterious interloper.

The next thing I knew my tantalizer was in the tub on top of me. The risk of being discovered by fellow students served to heighten my erotic pleasure. Our passionate kisses teased our senses, leading into forbidden sexual ecstasies. The point of no return was a necessity. Our essence mingled, uniting us into a single entity of unified passion. The mystery of not knowing my lover sent shivering chills down my spine; I had no desire to discard my mask. I wanted the mystery and longed for more unseen ecstasies to unfold.

Minds play tricks when eyes do not see. Uncharted sexual fantasies swam in my head like schools of fish devouring plankton. I wanted this man and he me; I didn't care who the stranger was; I was delighted to surrender myself to this mysterious being.

I let out an ecstatic whimpering moan and released my pent up energies from my exhausting day. At that very moment, he spilled his sex onto my soaked belly dissolving us in our liquid warmth.

My fantasies were too wonderful to spoil, so I kept my mask on long after my lover departed, leaving me to savor the afterglow in the relaxation of my intoxicating bath.

My Mystery Lover

The next few nights, after the majority of the dorm students had washed and retired to their respective rooms, my mysterious lover appeared, without fail, during my late night baths. Each time I wore my bathing mask, not wanting to identify my seducer. In my mind I hoped it was Oscar, but I did not want to admit it.

During the daytime when we saw each other we never alluded to our nightly liaisons; instead we chatted about nothing, like casual acquaintances. When I was with Andy, I behaved normally without creating suspicions, although there were times when he and I met secretly in my room when John wasn't around.

John was not blind nor was he unaccustomed to the ways E.R.O.S. students lived, in 1966. He was fully aware of our cavorting in the room when he wasn't there. I was sure he did the same with other boys when I was not present. We made cheeky remarks and teased each other. Our outlook was that boys will be boys and sex is a natural act we enjoy, not an issue to get hung up on. John never inquired again about my relationship with Oscar after the night he initially suspected we had the hots for each other, yet I feel he knew more than he let on.

Picture Perfect

A few evenings into my bath time assignment, I heard clicking sounds from a camera shutter, every few seconds. As curious as I was to know who the photographer was, I was also excited by his voyeurism. It was curiosity versus exhibitionism; I wondered if I should discard my mask or just continue to be mystified and enjoy my lover and the voyeur. As the sounds of clicking magnified within my head, I rose to the occasion, giving a performance to whom-ever was viewing my lover and me through his lens. My overwhelming curiosity was too much. Whispering into my partner's ear I said, "Tell me, who's taking the photographs."

My seducer replied, "A friend who already knows our deepest darkest secrets."

"Who and what might those secrets be?" I whispered into his ear in the heat of our passionate caresses.

"Someone whom we adore -- you will find out when we return to your room because he is joining us tonight."

That message made me more excited and aroused than before my questioning. The clicking soon stopped, and my lover assisted me out of the tub. He dried me off and wrapped us both in large towels. Taking my hand, he guided me to my room. As soon as I heard the door close, my mystery lover released my mask. In bed, snuggled under the duvet, was my sexy roommate John, naked and ready for a night of unbridled sex with Oscar and me.

Needless to say, we had a fun filled evening with little sleep and lots of play. By the time Friday rolled round, I had unwittingly plunged myself into a muddy pool of forbidden love.

During the course of my Christmas vacation, which followed, it created much uneasiness which I had not anticipated.

This is the nature of life. Just when we believe we have it all, life throws us a surprise, so we can learn valuable lessons in another chapter of life, making us stronger and more resilient than before.

CHAPTER EIGHTY-THREE

Ou La La Mon Paree

*"Life is not a problem to be solved,
but a reality to be experienced."*
Soren Kierkegaard

Friday afternoon before we broke for Christmas vacation, Andy and I boarded the school's helicopter. We flew to London to catch the Simorgh to Paris. Ubaid was already on the plane waiting for us. He had helicoptered in from Dublin. Our Arab friend was in good spirits during our 45-minute journey to Charles de Gaulle airport. On the flight I was curious to find out if he had defied his father's wishes and continued to see Gianna. I asked, "You must be happy to be back at university, judging from the look on your face."

"Yes, that is true. I am very happy. Gianna flew to Dublin to spend several days with me before she left for New York, with Allegra."

"Well, it sounds like you had fun with your girlfriend. When will you see her again"? I asked.

Ubaid gave me a sly grin and replied, "Wouldn't you like to know, you inquisitive devil!"

After a brief pause, he continued, "I plan to visit her in New York, during the Spring holidays. We'll spend a couple weeks travelling the U.S."

"What about your father's wishes? Are you going to defy him again?" I asked.

"He won't know if you and Andy don't tell."

With strong conviction in my voice I replied, "That, you don't have to worry because our time at the Kosk is completed and it's very unlikely we'll have a chance to see the Hadrah anytime soon. I promise I will not tell Aziz or Thabit when I am at the Sekhem."

Ubaid laughed and responded, "Very good then, I have nothing to worry about. Tonight, let's party. We can go to L'Arc; it's one of the best discos in town."

I shrieked with excitement, "That'll be fun, let's go, I'm game!"

Andy, being sensible, said, "Have you forgotten what happened at The CLUB"?

Our friend laughed, "This is Paris, not Dubai. Our attaché will arrange for him to get in. A word from our embassy and I can get Young in anywhere."

My guardian shrugged his shoulders and reluctantly agreed; after all, he, too, wanted to experience the nightlife of Paris. Since Andy was chaperoning me and I don't drink or smoke, he relented. And that evening we partied.

Paris Ritz Carlton

When the Simorgh landed on a private airstrip at Charles de Gaulle a shiny black Bentley sat waiting for us. Tariq from the U.A.E. embassy was waiting to greet us. He said, "The Kosk ladies have arrived and have checked into their suites at the Ritz

Carlton." Andy and I shared the Windsor Suite and Ubaid had the Prince of Wales Suite.

A section of the hotel floor was cordoned off especially for our entourage of five men and eight females. The women were Shiya, Nareen, Ghaniyah, Hazar (Hakim's second wife), Hakim's granddaughter, Jamilah, and Kukus, a cousin. The men were Ubaid, Andy, Siddiq, Mu'in (Hazar's cousin) and me.

The Windsor Suite

The Windsor Suite, named after the Duke and Duchess of Windsor, was a beautiful chamber consisting of a living room and a bedroom. From the large French windows we had a tremendous view of romantic Paris. We couldn't have asked for a better room. As soon as the bellboys deposited our luggage there was a message from Nasreen requesting us to join them for dinner at 8:00 p.m. at Restaurant Espando, downstairs.

It was wonderful to be in Paris. Mother had talked about the romantic air of Paris on her world tour and now, seeing Paris with my own eyes, I found it even more spectacular than her lovely descriptions.

At Restaurant Espando

It was wonderful to see the Kosk ladies again, and to catch up on their news. As we sat down at the dinner table, Shiya asked excitedly, "Young, how do you like Paris?"

"Without leaving my suite I'm already in love with Paris. The view from my room is spectacular. Thank you for inviting Andy and me to join you."

Nasreen laughed, "You are like a brother to us. You always have a delightful sense of grace and poise, and you are always happy, unlike Ubaid." Ubaid was not with us. Instead he was at the Hemingway Bar, consuming an aperitif, on the lookout for someone to pick up.

I smiled graciously. "Thank you!" I said to our hostesses.

Shiya said, "Tomorrow we have a full day ahead with three Ateliers to visit. Our first appointment is with Chanel, followed by Christian Dior, with a lunch break before going to Emanuel Ungaro. We can then maybe have tea at Cafe de Flore and in the evening we are free to do our own exploration of the city. Let's meet at the lobby at 9:00 a.m. Our attaché has arranged limos for us."

I replied with excitement in my eyes, "Be assured I'll be ready. I can't wait for our day of fashion to begin."

Andy didn't want to go to the Couture Showings. He went sightseeing the following day instead.

Walking By the Seine

After dinner, we bid the ladies good evening and Andy and I ventured outside to explore. Ubaid chose to hang around the Hemingway Bar for more drinks to kick off our night of partying.

Florence smelled sweet in the wee hours of dawn; Paris smelled of romance in the small hours of the night. I couldn't help but hold on to Andy's hand as we walked along the Seine looking across to the famous Notre Dame de Paris. I should have been blissfully happy, but the nagging memories of Oscar would not leave my head. I had a wonderful boyfriend who adored me yet I was missing another across the Channel. Why can't I have two pieces of cake and eat them both?

If I had been truthful with Andy in the beginning it would have been a different matter. Yet, my fear held me back from telling the truth. Wise men say, "The truth will set you free." I should have taken their advice.

A Night At L'Arc Paris

A long queue had formed at L'Arc. Back then, the disco was more a gay establishment than the metrosexual club it is today. It attracted an international gay and lesbian-friendly crowd, many who were either celebrities or on the way to becoming famous. Ubaid had promised our cultural attaché for us to enter L'Arc. The bouncers were more than happy to usher us through, treating us like royalty.

Once inside we were waited on hand and foot. The staff had obviously been advised that we were very important people. Ubaid gave generous tips to those who provided us impeccable services.

The Arab had picked up a good-looking French man, Alain, at Hemingway's. It was difficult to talk with the loud music blaring, so I people-watched as fantastic scenarios unfolded before my eyes. Before long, Alain led Ubaid into the back rooms where a lot of 'unspeakable' acts were played out in the darkness. I did not enter with or without Andy's supervision.

As the evening progressed the music became louder and the party became wilder. Couples of all colors and races were kissing and tonguing each other with abandonment. It was the first time I had witnessed such unbridled sexual acts of wantonness in public. I was fascinated by everything I saw. Andy stayed by my side, making sure no unsavory characters bothered me, soliciting salacious sex.

I was happier being a voyeur than an active participant, although I did dance with Andy when Ubaid and Alain were in a backroom. I did not see them emerge until the Go-Go Boys dance show was over. The performance consisted of several muscle guys clad in the briefest briefs, adorned with pheasant feathers from head to tail. They performed an African war dance routine, reminding me of the fabulous "Black Pearl," (Josephine Baker) who was popular in Paris during the late 1920s and '30s, the golden Jazz Age. Everything in the club was so Parisian! I ate it up like a spoon full of sugar.

My Protector

There were certainly a number of men who gave me "the eye" but I dared not stare back. Since my handsome guardian never left my side, none of these men dared to venture forward. If they had, Andy would have fended them off. Yet, a nagging longing for Oscar loomed large behind each disco face I saw.

I wanted to bang my head against the wall like I had done in Venice. Oscar was in my thoughts throughout my fun-filled Parisian weekend as well as during my vacation in London, Germany and Switzerland. I was in emotional turmoil.

By the time our limo returned our party to the Ritz, I was exhausted. Alain spent the night with Ubaid for further sexual fun and games. With Andy cuddled next to me, I slept like a baby.

CHAPTER EIGHTY-FOUR

A Haute Couture, Chanel, Dior Emanuel Ungaro

"Fashion can be bought. Style one must possess."
Edna Woolman Chase

Three beautiful Rolls Royces, one pearlescent white, one metallic silver and the last a pale matte gold, pulled up to the front of the Paris Ritz Carlton at precisely 9:15 a.m. the next morning to collect the Kosk ladies, the two chaperoning Arab gentlemen and me. We were driven to Chanel, No. 31 Rue Cambon. Three hours later, they returned us to the Ritz. The ladies changed into Christian Dior couture before heading to No. 30 Avenue Montaigne for our next appointment at the House of Dior. Afterwards we had a light lunch at the Ritz before they donned Emanuel Ungaro couture and proceeded to our final appointment for the day at No 2 Avenue Montaigne.

At Chanel

As soon as we arrived at Chanel, a couple of vendeuses came to greet our group, welcoming us into their establishment. Once inside, the Harem ladies discarded their burkas, revealing elegant Chanel couture outfits which had been made to order by Chanel the previous season. The women knew their fashion etiquette well.

An unspoken couture fashion rule was that it was polite for a client to wear the designer's label while visiting their establishment. That was the primary reason the ladies changed outfits when visiting the designer houses. However, this also gave the women an excuse to wear several different outfits per day. It was very much like a competitive sport between the ladies, to see whose look was the most outstanding. And, like with the fashion houses, rivalries could be fierce.

We were ushered into an elegant room decorated with floor-to-ceiling mirrors. This was one of Coco Chanel's trademarks. She had an abundance of mirrors in her Salon. Once we were seated on the comfortable leather sofas, the vendeuses offered us champagne, petit fours and a few minutes of social chitchat before guiding us into the main salon for the private viewing. Since we had a French - English - Arabic-speaking interpreter, Adele, whom the UAE cultural attaché had organized for our entourage, we were able to communicate with the Chanel staff efficiently.

A couple of rows of gold chairs were arranged around a low platform for our fashion presentation. In the old days, music was not the norm at couture fashion shows. The head venduse introduced each outfit as the models paraded by. Besides walking on the catwalk they also walked past our chairs for us to feel the fabrics or examine the details closely. It was, indeed, a luxury to attend a private couture viewing in those halcyon days of haute couture fashion.

A total of fifteen outfits were presented, from day wear to the most exquisite evening dresses. Each outfit was a work of art in and of itself. I was in heaven. It reminded me of Count

Mario's Vogue Italia photo shoot, when I could turn every couture gown inside out to study details of the workmanship.

I was seated in the comfort of the Chanel showroom, being treated like a young prince purchasing couture outfits with my sister princesses in tow and absorbing everything with awe. When the final model appeared, I was so excited I couldn't help but clap! The Kosk women kept silent.

Apparently, it wasn't customary to show jubilation, as this was a serious buying spree. Fortunately, all forgave me since it was my time attending a couture fashion presentation. The venduses smiled at my exuberance. I knew I had won them over; one of the sales ladies offered to show me the sample rooms if I was interested in seeing, first-hand, the process of couture dressmaking. Of course I jumped at this rare opportunity and said, "Oui Madame, J'aime beaucoup voir il!"

While the Harem ladies were busy discussing the styles they planned to order, Marie Laure guided me upstairs to view the workroom, which was normally out of bounds to customers.

There were approximately ten skilled sample machinists and sewers, two pattern makers constructing paper patterns and a couple of toilers draping fabric on dress forms. This visit galvanized my determination to pursue a fashion design career. I wanted to cut, drape, sew and learn everything there was to know about the couture fashion industry. By the end of our Chanel visit there was no doubt in my mind that this was my life's calling. All I had to do was to answer the call to become a part of this exciting high fashion world.

At Dior

We started with small talk, then petit fours and a private fashion presentation. Each designer's showroom was equally as glamorous as the one before. They were all competing for the Harem women's business. The young, talented Yves Saint Laurent had left Dior to start his own couture house. The creative director at Dior that fall was Marc Bohan, a prolific designer.

After the showing, Monsieur Bohan came to greet the ladies. I was speechless, since this was the first time I had met a real-life international designer, face to face. I was tongue tied and did not utter a word. After a brief conversation with the ladies, Mr. Bohan noticed that I was staring at him so he came over to extend his hand. I was so nervous my palms started perspiring when he said, "Soyez bienvenus à la Maison de Dior, le jeune homme. Quel est votre nom?" (Welcome to the House of Dior, young man. What is your name?)

I replied, timidly, "Mon nom est Jeune."

Monsieur Bohan continued in French, "I am delighted to meet you. Tell me, is there anything I can assist you with?"

Now my palms were complete covered with sweat and I was speechless. "You don't have to be nervous; I'm not that frightening, am I?"

By now, my French was pushed to its limits, but I finally uttered, "This is a beautiful salon. I am so honored to have a chance to meet you in person."

Marc handed me a tissue to wipe my perspiring hands before patting my back, saying, "Would you like to see more of the salon? I can show you after I finish speaking with the ladies."

I was elated when he said he would show me the place. I replied, in a shaky voice, in my shaky French, "Le Merci. Thank You that will be wonderful. Can I visit the workshop?"

He continued in French "Normally, I do not show customers the workshop, but I detect you are interested in fashion. Are you planning to become a fashion designer someday?"

I responded shyly, "Oui, je suis. Yes, I want to grow up to be like you, designing haute couture."

This seemed to tickle his interest. "Well, in that case I will make an exception and show you. I like to feel that, in some small capacity, I am educating the next generation of designers. Give me a moment and I will take you upstairs."

I was completely enamored when it came time for the tour. I had many questions to ask Mr. Bohan, which he answered to the best of his ability. I was so determined to enroll in a prestigious fashion school, as my mentor recommended.

At Emanuel Ungaro

By the time we arrived at Emanuel Ungaro I was two hundred percent sure that fashion was going to be my career. In a short span of three months, since entering the Kosk, I had soared in my understanding of high fashion, and I craved more.

After the showing, Monsieur Ungaro came to greet us. After he departed, the venduse took over the discussion and Ungaro disappeared to his atelier. By then, I was bold enough to request a showing. I put on my most charming persona, applying my art of flirtation to persuade Mme. Fleur, a saleswoman, to show me the workings of the couture house. When she allowed me to have a peek into Monsieur's sampling room, the designer was in the middle of fitting a dress on one of his models.

I stood at the entrance to his studio watching, while Mme. Fleur asked the designer's permission for me to watch him work.

Monsieur nodded in my direction. "No problem Mme. Fleur. He can enter."

She motioned me over and left me standing by the designer, who spoke in broken English, saying, "You are a Prince from Arabic?"

Taken by surprise, I decided to play along. I smiled and lied, "Yes, I'm Prince Young. The women you met are my sisters."

"You are handsome Prince, you look chinoiserie, no?"

I continued the game of deceit and jokingly replied, "I am part Arab, part Chinese."

"Ah! You like fashioonee?"

"Yes I do. As a matter of fact I plan to study fashion design after secondary school," I replied.

As he pinned and draped, the designer never lifted his eyes from his toile. He asked, "Where you want study fashioonee? Paris?"

"Oh no, in England, that's where I go to school now," I responded.

As he continued to pin and drape, he advised me to study in Paris if I wanted to learn the Art of Haute Couture, since Paris was the epicenter of the fashion world. The problem was, my French wasn't good enough to enroll into the Ecole de la Chambre Syndicale de la Haute Couture, the most prestigious fashion institute in Paris. I would have needed to study one to two years of French before I was ready for that. In England, I could enroll in an Art and Design College immediately after my studies at Daltonbury Hall and my services at the Arab Households.

CHAPTER EIGHTY-FIVE

J'Aime Mon Paree

"Happy boys are the handsomest."
Bernard Tristan Foong

After our first day of couture viewing, I returned to the Ritz Carlton full of hope, wonderment and encouragement due to the advice from Monsieurs Bohan and Ungaro. Besides receiving the valuable mentoring from the designers, I had also given solid suggestions to the women, helping them best choose outfits which were flattering to their figures. They ordered from various designers, and returned to Paris several weeks later for their fittings. I was able to attend the fittings also, since I was in Paris working with Aziz on 'Sacred Sex in Sacred Places.'

After dinner with the Kosk entourage at La Fermette Marbeuf, an elegant Art Nouveau restaurant, Ubaid, Andy, Shiya, Nasreen and I decided to visit Maxim's while the rest of our entourage returned to the Ritz.

Maxim's de Paris

As soon as we walked into the legendary Maxim's de Paris, I was struck speechless by the elegance. The establishment, still owned by the original creators Monsieur Maxime Gaillard and Madam Irma de Montigny, drew a crowd from the "Who's Who" in Paris. It reminded me of the infamous Hong Kong Repulse Bay Hotel where the island's rich and famous gathered.

Maxim's, like the Repulse Bay Hotel, was a vibrant society venue. In one corner sat the aging Maurice Chevalier, dining with Lana Turner. Looking around the room, I saw a gaggle of well-known movie directors and cinematographers of that genre. I was in seventh heaven as we walked by each famous personality on the way to our seats. There were models, designers, actors, actresses, opera singers and ballet stars, each competing to appear more beautiful than anyone else in the room.

I was dressed in my most handsome formal attire, yet, I felt almost threadbare in the midst of all the elegant and glamorous people in this opulent venue. Maxim's was also a dance club, and soon, Ubaid gravitated towards the bar. Before long he was chatting with several beautiful men and women, laughing and flirting with these gorgeous people.

Since we had already eaten, we ordered desserts and coffee. Andy and I, being polite gentlemen, invited Shiya and Nasreen to dance. Our friends, wearing their glamorous couture evening gowns, looked spectacular. I was amazed how quickly they discarded their burkas. If I didn't know better, I would have never guessed they were abayas and burkas wearing women. They blended perfectly into this chic establishment.

To me, it seemed strange and suddenly not strange at all, that many people have double lives. No one would guess Andy and I were male courtesans allocated to Arabian harems to service their household. Certainly at Maxim's we were disguised as two well-groomed aristocratic gentlemen having fun dancing with young ladies. I didn't realize that many others in this opulent hall were courtesans and cicisbei, just like Andy and me.

As we were dancing on the crowded floor, a suave gentleman came over to me and whispered a request. He wished for the pleasure of a dance, with Nasreen. I politely answered for her, in French, "Sure that's not a problem. I will be more than delighted to oblige." We were at Maxim's not for a long time, and my friend did not seem to mind this stranger's forwardness; in fact, she seemed more than happy to be pursued by Edouard.

This good-looking Frenchman whisked her away from me into a waltz. I could tell from Nasreen's expression that this admirer, not from her clan, charmed her.

As I returned to my seat, a hand reached out from the crowd, tapping me on my shoulder. When I turned, I recognized Wannie, one of Kismat's friends, standing behind me and smiling. I struck up a conversation with her and her friends, who spoke English fluently. She invited our party to join them at La Belle Epoque; she would be participating in a beauty pageant there later that evening. Without consulting Andy, I agreed to meet their party at Maxim's entrance, to depart for La Belle Époque.

As soon as Andy returned from the dance floor I told him about my plans for us to go to La Belle Époque. Since I had never witnessed a beauty pageant before, Andy relented and agreed that we would go. Shiya decided that she and her sister would join us, too, but Ubaid was nowhere in sight. Andy went looking for him. When he returned, he informed us that Ubaid was otherwise engaged.

The five of us, including Edouard, trooped to La Belle Époque with Wannie and her friends. Edouard drove us in his white vintage Roll Royce. We left the Ritz's limo at Maxim's, for Ubaid.

At La Belle Epoque

La Belle Époque was a cabaret dance hall, much like the famous Moulin Rouge and Folies Bergere. We didn't know that the evening's Beauty Pageant was a competition for The Lady Boy of

Paris. The winner would proceed to compete at a flamboyant gala Lady Boy of the Year Award, held in Berlin on New Year's Eve.

When we arrived, the place was packed. If we had arrived on our own we would not have gained entrance; this was a private function. Wannie got us in through the back stage entrance. The security guards could tell we were wealthy patrons, so they allowed us in. Edouard tipped them generously as we trooped into the theatre.

Wannie led us to the Captain, who offered us an excellent table. She had obviously informed the Captain of our status. The hall filled up quickly. By the time the performance began, it was jammed to capacity, and people were clamoring at the front entrance. The event began with choreographed dance routines by the club's regular performers. Then, the MC announced the pageant commencement.

The Beauty Pageant

The French speaking MC announced, "Welcome ladies, gentlemen and all those in between sexes, to La Belle Époque. Tonight, we have many fabulous contestants from around the globe. A wonderful group from Thailand is here to perform for us later in the evening. Please, give our contestants a big hand as we begin our pageant with the swimsuit competition."

As the music started, each beauty queen paraded in front of the judges and audience. Loud cheers came from all directions. There were wolf whistles, catcalls and an assortment of cheers which encouraged the competitors forward. Each 'queen' seemed to have perfect everything, including well-developed bosoms and male genitals.

How unfortunate that the heterosexual world felt threatened by these unique beings! They possess courage, and face life with gusto and bravado.

I was surprised to find the beautiful Kismat and Lamei in the contest. Unlike most heterosexual female beauty pageants, where contestants are often rivals, these lady boys were friendly and respectful of each other. Years later, I was invited to judge female beauty pageants. I didn't observe the kind of camaraderie and cordiality that these lady boys displayed toward each other amongst the female contestants.

Each evening gown worn was as beautiful as the person who wore it. Most of the dresses were exquisitely crafted and designed. Some came from well-known couturiers and others were sewn by the contestants themselves, or by their friends. Under the flattering stage lights it was certainly a difficult task for the judges to select one winner.

A sexy French lady boy by the name of Jacqueline beat the other contestants and took the crown. The runners-up were Kismat and her Thai friend, Arie. We all cheered the winners and blew them air kisses, which they blew back.

It was certainly an eventful first day in Paris, the city that never sleeps. Andy and I were glad to return to the Ritz. We decided to take a romantic stroll along the Seine at 2:00 a.m. in the morning, feeling exhausted and extremely happy to be together, and so much in love with each other.

Does this saying really hold true? Are "happy boys the most handsome?"

CHAPTER EIGHTY-SIX

Un Spectacle Historique de Beaute a Paris

"Love does not consist in gazing at each other, but in looking together in the same direction."
Antoine de Saint-Exupery

The following morning, Andy and I did not wake until 10:00 a.m. We had been out late the past two nights, and desperately needed to catch up on our beauty sleep. Paris had been exhilarating from the moment we arrived. We didn't go down to Le Brunch, a restaurant within the Ritz, until almost eleven. Our companions had a similar idea; they were just being seated at a large, round table when we joined them.

Ubaid was nowhere to be found. I presumed he was still in bed with whomever he had picked up the night before. His sexual appetite never failed to amaze me. Much like the Road

Runner, our friend could keep going and going, day in and night out, without showing signs of exhaustion. I wondered how he did it. Viagra was not available in those days. Maybe he employed aphrodisiacs, I mused. It remains a mystery to me to this day.

At Le Brunch

Shiya was seated next to me. I politely enquired, "Wasn't it a fun evening at Maxims and La Belle Epoque? Did you and Nasreen enjoy yourselves?"

She smiled. "Yes, we did! And, today after brunch, Edouard is coming to pick us to show us Paris. Will you and Andy join us?"

"Sure!" I answered excitedly.

Andy replied, "We don't want to impose."

Nasreen laughed, "Don't be silly, Andy. It will be great if you guys can join us. You can be our chaperones."

Always the perfect gentleman, he added, "Of course we will be happy to be your chaperones. We are at your service whenever you require us."

"Eduoard suggested we drive round Paris, and if time permits he will drive us through the countryside, outside the city."

I replied, "That's fabulous! I haven't done any sightseeing yet. Andy did some when we were at the Ateliers yesterday. Where did you go yesterday?" I turned to gaze at my Valet. I continued, "To see bridges, I presume?"

Andy smiled. "Clever boy, you know me well. I spent time on the Pont Alexandre III, checking out its construction. Later, at the Musée des égouts de Paris, I found more information and engineering documents related to bridge building and old Paris's underground sewerage system! I spent the morning looking at the museum's archival documents."

Sightseeing in Paris

At 1:00 p.m., Edouard, along with his pal Jules, collected us in his Rolls Royce as well as a blue vintage Lincoln Continental convertible. As soon as I saw Jules's fancy Lincoln, I wanted to ride in it. Andy and I got into the back, leaving Shiya to sit in the front with Jules. Edouard had set up this road trip as a double date for Nasreen, him, Jules and Shiya. Since Andy and I tagged along it became a triple date outing.

It was exhilarating to ride in the eye-catching Lincoln and it certainly turned a lot of heads!

In Basilique du Sacré-Cœur

Our first stop was the famous Basilique du Sacré-Cœur. In those days, cars could drive up to the front of the Cathedral for passengers to alight. Today, vehicles are permitted only during sanctioned events. The view looking down at Montmartre from the top of the hill was breathtaking. Memories of looking onto the Fragrant Harbor from Hong Kong Peak came flooding back, and I missed the presence of my mother. I leaned against Andy for comfort, and he put his loving arms around my shoulders, acknowledging my sentimentality. He was such a kind and compassionate man.

There was an afternoon Mass in the Basilique. Our friends went exploring, leaving Andy and me on our own. I was in a state of reverence as I reflected on the grandeur and history of this Cathedral. Intoxicating incense wafted through my nostrils and the heady religious rituals reminded me of my E.R.O.S. initiation ceremony.

We sat on one of the pews, and when I looked at Andy, tears came to my eyes. My lover was obviously thinking similar thoughts. This time around, I wasn't running away from his loving presence. I looked at him with love and gratitude in my heart that our paths had crossed, and that we were heading in the same direction. Within my heart I knew better times lay waiting for us, but I also knew I had to find the correct moment to confess to Andy my secret regarding Oscar.

Instead of telling Andy right then, I went into the confessional booth and confessed my secrets to a priest, who spoke little English but was a good listener. My sins cleansed after confession, he suggested I make a donation to the church before leaving the sacred premises. Although I didn't belong to any religious faith, I felt more at ease after my confessions, and, with a grateful heart, I left a generous offering in the collection box. Unfortunately, this temporary fix did not chase my guilt away; it came back with a vengeance throughout my time in Europe.

At La Tour Eiffel

There was a long queue waiting for the elevator up the Eiffel Tower, so Jules suggested we walk up the wrought iron staircase. It became windier and windier. Before we reached the first floor, Shiya and I were already suffering from severe acrophobia. We decided to descend, while the others continued. As much as Andy and Jules wanted to go on, they offered to accompany us down the wobbling staircase. Andy held my hand while Jules wrapped his arms around Shiya's shoulders guiding her to the ground. The two courageous souls, Nasreen and Edouard continued their climb.

The enclosed elevator ride was less unsettling than the walk, but I could feel the lift vibrating to the sounds of the howling winds. When we finally arrived on the second floor, I was too scared to venture out of the elevator. I decided that it was better for me to wait at the ground floor ticket office. Since I didn't want to spoil Andy's Eiffel Tower experience, I encouraged him to take his time exploring the tower while I waited inside the warm enclosure of the downstairs gift shop. Andy reluctantly agreed.

Pierre Et Luc

While I was looking at the trinkets and books in the gift shop a well-dressed gentleman approached and started a conversation in French, "Good day, it is cold and windy today."

I smiled but didn't reply. He continued in French. "Young man, why aren't you at the tower looking at the beauty of Paris?"

I politely replied, "It is so windy and I'm afraid of heights. My friends are above and will be joining me soon."

"I don't like heights either; that's why I'm here waiting for my friend, Luc. He wanted to venture up to see the view — like you, I'm here waiting. Where are you from"?

"I'm from England, and you?"

As our conversation progressed, my French was becoming more and more unwieldy, so I said, "Do you speak English?"

It turned out he was from Aubigny-sur-Nere and spoke English, with a French accent. He was in Paris with his friend, Luc, who was three years older than I. They had come for a day of sightseeing. When my party returned, Edouard was surprised to see me talking with his friend, Pierre. Coming over to greet Pierre, he joked in French, "Pierre. You naughty devil, I see you are already soliciting my friend, Young. Where is Luc?" Just then, Luc appeared from behind our group and both Edouard and Pierre formally introduced us.

It turned out that Luc was Pierre's latest boyfriend; they had been together for six months. After a casual conversation, we departed. As Pierre was leaving, he turned around and secretly gave me a flirtatious wink and smile. I smiled and gave Pierre and Luc friendly nods before going on our merry way, thinking that was the last time I would see these guys.

At Giverny

Jules suggested taking a drive out to the country. It was a beautiful autumn day and the lazy afternoon sun cast a hazy glow on the Parisian landscapes. It was a perfect day to see Giverny, Claude Monet's residence, which was now a museum. In those days, it was a private residence.

The owners were Jules' and Edouard's family friends. The drive to the country in Jules' blue convertible was lively. Shiya, behind her sunglasses, Givenchy headscarf blowing in the wind, looked like Audrey Hepburn in the movie 'Roman Holiday.' Jules was definitely smitten by her beauty; I was sure a romantic liaison would soon begin.

It must be that the Parisian air makes people fall in love. Andy kept looking at me, throughout the journey, as if he couldn't get enough of me. I could tell he was undressing me with his eyes, like in the early days before we became lovers; his charming grins gave his desires away. I, on the other hand, felt guilty for cheating on my lover. 'What's the matter with me? Why can't I just come clean and tell Andy the truth?' I thought. It was not the correct moment to do so. I regretted not giving truth a chance to set me free.

Monet's historical house and gardens were more stunning even than his Impressionist paintings were. It was the epitome of French country living, a place where the courtesan, Violetta, in La Traviata would be most happy frolicking with Alfredo.

The beauty of the gardens sent me into fits of sorrow, like the first time I saw the opera at Teatro la Fenice. Andy noticed my weeping and held me to his chest, comforting me like his little brother, telling me to hush and reassuring me that all was well. He'd never allow me to suffer the same fate as Violetta.

As Andy sat comforting me on a bench, a hand tapped my shoulder. When I turned to look, it was none other than Pierre, with Luc at his side. They had the same idea as us. They chose to come to Giverny, before heading back to Aubigny-sur-Nere.

Andy and I were surprised to see them. As Andy spoke with Luc, Pierre asked in English, "Why are you crying in such beautiful surroundings? What's unsettling a beautiful boy like you?"

Putting his hand on mine, he continued, "You should be celebrating instead of crying. Come visit my home and we'll have high tea."

Wiping my tears, I looked towards Andy for a response. My Valet said, "That is very kind of you to offer. If we were not with company we'd love to visit your home but since we came with friends, we'll have to pass on your invitation this time around."

As we were having our conversation, Edouard and Nasreen strolled towards us hand in hand; overhearing Pierre's request,

Edouard said, "That's not a problem; let's all return to Paris for high tea at Cafe de Flore. They serve the best high teas!"

The party agreed and we were soon at Cafe de Flore for a scrumptious High Tea Français. Darling Andy was looking in the same direction as me. It was me who had the problème.

CHAPTER EIGHTY-SEVEN

Café De Flore et Le Folies Bergers

*"There goes a saying, and 'twas shrewdly said,
'Old fish at table, but young flesh in bed'."*
Alexander Pope

High tea at Cafe de Flore was inspiring, to say the least. Café de Flore was a Parisienne establishment where the famous and well-to-do came to see and be seen. It was also a place where 'Cougars' came, before they were called cougars, for their supply of handsome hot studs. It was also the place where 'Sugar Daddies' came to find their long lost Twinkie sons or Lolita daughters. In short, it was a mad house, fun-filled to the brim.

Nowadays this establishment is a tourist destination like many other joie de vivre Parisienne venues which were tres chic, but later turned into mainstream attractions. Luc, Andy and I enjoyed the ambience and the attention of every admirer who swept passed in addition to the wonderful patisseries. The bistro, beautifully decorated, full of French je ne sais quoi, was charming to both the mature and the young. This 'pick-up' joint was filled with beautiful young flesh looking for wealthy daddies and mummies to provide for them.

From the turn of the twentieth century to the late 1950s, it was a watering hole for intellectuals such as Ernest Hemingway, Jean-Paul Sartre, Simone de Beauvoir and artists like Pablo Picasso and Albert Camus. With such a distinguished array of controversial liberal figures, this historic café was bound to bloom into the mod scene which it became in the 1960s and '70s.

At Cafe De Flore

As soon as we ordered, I could see Pierre's roving eyes darting around the room, shopping for his next conquest. Luc, on the other hand, was busy casting for the next big fish to finance his extensive buying sprees. I was simply in awe, bewildered and wide-eyed, taking the scenario in.

Male and female eyes gravitated towards Andy as soon as we walked into the café. He was certainly the crème of the crop and I was the lucky one who got to take home the trophy.

Edouard and Jules had no problem fitting into the scenery as they grew up with French liberals, and most of their friends were sexually liberated people. Nasreen and Shiya had been educated in Europe; they were comfortable absorbing the different lifestyles the world had to offer. They were also seeing the world through the eyes of their father, Hakim. They understood, innately, the way their own culture embraced dual lives. These westernized Middle Eastern women seemed accepting of the ways of the world and I believe they fully understood the meaning of, "When in Rome, do as the Romans do and when in Arabia, do what the Arabs do."

Pierre turned to me and asked, "What brings you to Paris?"

"Andy and I are guests of Shiya and Nasreen. I'm privileged to be their fashion consultant and Andy is my companion."

"How do you know Edouard?" I enquired of the Frenchman.

"I've known Edouard since our school days; we used to hang out together. Now, I'm looking after my estate in Aubigny-sur-Nere since my parents died. You must come and stay at Chateau Rouge. It's a beautiful property and we can go hunting. Do you like to hunt?"

I answered, "You mean foxes?"

Pierre laughed, "No, we are not like the English. We hunt pheasants and this is the perfect time of year for this sport."

"I have never hunted foxes or pheasants. It will be a new experience for me."

"How long are you staying in Paris?" questioned the Frenchman.

"Unfortunately, we leave the day after tomorrow for England. We are also travelling to Germany and Switzerland over the next few weeks. But we should be back in Paris soon, for two projects," I told Pierre.

"Give me a call when you are back in Paris and come spend some time at Chateau Rouge. I'd love to have you boys for company," he said, giving me a flirtatious grin to indicate that he wanted more than just a platonic friendship.

I gave him a knowing wink and replied, "Sure, we will contact you when we are in Paris again. I'm sure Andy would love to visit your Chateau."

By the time we finished High Tea, it was time for us to return to the Ritz to dress for our evening's outing to the fabulous Folies Bergere.

At Le Folies Bergere

As Edouard's Rolls Royce drove up to the main entrance, the theatre was beginning to get crowded. Cars were waiting in line for passengers to alight. Our tickets were waiting at the ticket office as Kismat had previously arranged.

When we entered the performance hall, a sexy waitress guided us to our assigned tables. Round tables were neatly arranged in rows, lit dimly with red glows giving the grand hall a cabaret feel, much like the famous 1965 French movie 'Viva Maria' with Brigitte Bardot and Jeanne Moreau playing the lead roles. Our party consisted of Shiya, Nasreen, Edouard, Jules, Ubaid, Andy and me. Ubaid came sans partner so he would be free to party and pick-up showgirls for a frolicking good time after show.

Kismat got us front row tables. In typical French fashion, every festivity starts with champagne and this was no exception. A live orchestra began playing as soon as the theatre was filled to capacity. With a loud bang a glamorous girl was shot from a huge cannon onto a net on the stage. The show had begun.

Flamboyant costumes, lighting and dancing brought the set to life. The showgirls, decked in faux jewels and sparkles that barely covered their nipples came out in chorus line-up formations. Tall, leggy, slender and gorgeous, they looked just like the beauty queens from the other night. Feathers, furs, more feathers and more furs were the costumes derigure.

I sat mesmerized by this spectacular parade, especially during the Can Can number. I did not move from my seat until the show was over. This was top-gun glam compared to my Griffin Inn shows, which were amateurish, of course. For the first time in my young life I was witnessing professional showmanship. What better place to learn than at The Folies Bergere? "I watch, I absorb, I decipher and I create" has since been my life's motto in all I do.

Après Le Spectacle (After The Show)

After the performance, Ubaid, Andy and I went backstage to the girls' dressing rooms to congratulate Kismat and the beautiful performers. Before long, playboy Ubaid became our crowd pleaser. Like an excellent snake charmer, he wasted no time charming a group of showgirls into fits of giggles and laughter.

I knew that our friend wouldn't be sleeping alone tonight. Which girl wouldn't want to have the opportunity to be a potential candidate to become a wealthy oil heiress married to a sexy Arabian stud? The Folies ladies certainly knew what they wanted and were not shy about their ambition of hooking a rich heir.

At the opposite end of the spectrum, I was amazed by the backstage workings of the show, from lighting to sound control. I wanted to understand the functioning of sets and props and to learn the various duties and responsibilities, from that of the head costumer to the alterations staff.

This was my initiation into the professional world of theatre. In later years I had the opportunity to design stage costumes for major theatrical productions. I obtained a full postgraduate scholarship in theatre costuming studies at the prestigious Fitzgerald Theatre at the University of Hawaii.

Paris is Jazz

Nasreen, Shiya, Edouard and Jules were at the Folies Bergere bar, waiting for us to leave Kismat's dressing room. Ubaid, like the evening before, had the use of the Ritz's limousine to chauffeur him and his entourage into the evening.

Andy and I joined the couples at L'Absinthe, a jazz club where Edouard and Jules had suggested we go for a nightcap.

Paris is Jazz and Jazz is Paris! The smoke filled L'Absinthe had a jazz band in full swing. I expected the famous Edith Piaff to appear at any moment, singing one of her raspy-voiced ballads. Everything in Paris was new and exciting, and I was mad about Paris. Throughout my life I have returned to this enchanting city many times over; each visit has been more exciting than the last.

Since we had a full couture day ahead of us, our party stayed at L'Absinthe for an hour before calling it a night and heading back to the Ritz Carlton. I was glad to be alone with Andy. That night we made passionate love. This romantic city had seduced lovers over centuries. This night I only had Andy on my mind. I was relieved.

CHAPTER EIGHTY-EIGHT

Les Maisons de Givenchy, YSL et Jean Patou

*"A new dress doesn't get you anywhere;
it's the life you're living in the dress."*
Diana Vreeland

Sunday, while Nasreen, Shiya, Edouard, Jules, Andy and I were out sightseeing, Ubaid was busy having sex. The rest of the Kosk entourage went shopping with their translator, Adele. And shop they did, according to Adele, who snapped a picture of the shopping burka ladies buying the entire boulevard.

On Monday, at precisely 9:15 a.m., the Rolls Royce took us to Le Maison Givenchy located on Avenue George V. Dressed from head to toe in Givenchy outfits beneath their shapeless burkas, the Harem ladies marched out from the Ritz into the Rolls, only revealing their splendid Givenchy couture once inside the designer's foyer. Ghaniyah and Nasreen had final fittings this visit and I had the opportunity to witness the process.

At Le Maison Givenchy

The venduse brought out the exquisite ball gown hung on the beautifully padded satin hanger that Ghaniyah had made to order from her previous trip. There were tacking stitches around the hem and on certain areas of the fitted bodice. If alterations were required these areas could be easily unpicked without ruining the expensive fabric. A couple atelier assistants, accompanied by the head venduse and Monsieur Givenchy, were already waiting for Ghaniyah to change into the dress. When their client finally appeared from the spacious dressing room, the venduse assisted her onto a low platform so the Monsieur and seamstresses could work on the adjustments to the dress length with the shoes Ghaniyah brought along.

Her decolletage was too high, so the seamstresses altered the neckline to the requested shape. The correct undergarment support was added, padded and molded to flatter every part of Ghaniyah's body.

This attention to detail gave every client confidence and self-assurance. Besides being truly glamorous, the psychology of wearing couture is very powerful. Haute Couture is the epitome of high style; no garment ever comes close in comparison to a made-to-order gown. I saw the Kosk women's physical, mental and emotional transformation when they wore their couture outfits. The burkas made them feel timid, submissive and meek, while the latter brought on confidence, self-assurance and vitality. This huge contrast was an amazing visual and psychological learning process for me.

YSL - Mondrian Haute Couture

The girls changed into Yves Saint Laurent outfits at the Ritz before the three Rolls took them to the House of YSL. This was the year his famous Mondrian Haute Couture Fall-Winter '65/'66 collection was hailed as Yves best work to date. The geometric color blockings, influenced by the painter Mondrian, were the epitome of mid 60's fashion. I managed to persuade Nasreen and Jamilah to order several pieces from this world-renowned collection. They are now collectors' items.

The Mondrian collection was a major turning point in the world of fashion. Interpreting street fashion and translating that into haute couture outfits had never been done before the Mondrian. In the past, it was always haute couture trickling into high street fashion.

At La Maison Yves Saint Laurent

After the maestro's fashion presentation, the man himself came to greet us. I was again in awe, as I was when I met Monsieurs Bohan and Ungaro. I stood speechless, mesmerized by the slender elegance of young Yves, not knowing what to say or do. Nasreen and Shiya motioned me over to introduce me. Nasreen told the maestro I was an aspiring fashion designer and she asked him to take me under his wing.

Yves responded, "Si agréable de vous rencontrer. So nice to meet you. As you know I have only been a designer for a short time. I don't know if I am capable to provide any valuable advice to you lad."

Terribly nervous, I did my best to reply in French, "I am so honored to meet you. I am an admirer of your work."

"Dites merci! Thank You! You are too kind. I am delighted to answer any questions you may have regarding fashion."

Not knowing what to ask, I requested timidly, "May I take a picture of you and your staff?"

He smiled cheerfully and nodded, "We'll be delighted. Where would you like us to stand?"

"How about standing on the staircase?"

True to his promise, after his conversation with the Kosk ladies he gathered his venduses and a couple of his seamstresses for a photo. Voila! I had a picture of the famous Yves Saint Laurent and his Maison staff as a remembrance of my first visit to this legendary designer's salon.

Afterward, the designer asked one of his venduses to show me the L'Atelier as he had a meeting to attend. This week was definitely one of those rare occasions on which fantasy met reality; never in my life would I have imagined I would have had the opportunity to meet all these great fashion designers who shaped my career in their unique ways.

L'Atelier Jean Patou

Our last Couture House was La Maison Jean Patou. Monsieur Patou had passed thirty years before. The House was now famous for its designer perfume, Joy. Yet faithful clients such as Hazar (Hakim's second wife) and, at times, Ghaniyah, remained loyal to this designer's Maison.

The couture dress that Hazar had this L'Atelier make was a duchess silk satin ball gown, exquisitely beaded. Her understated traditional and classic style suited Hazar's personality perfectly. Unlike Ghaniyah, Nasreen and Shiya, who had model-looking figures, Hazar's dimensions and fashion sensibilities matched Patou's designs well.

Les Deux Magots

After our final couture appointment the white Rolls drove Nasreen, Shiya and me back to the Ritz. The other two Rolls drove the rest of the entourage for more shopping at Saint-Germain-des-Pres. For the past couple of days, Edouard and Jules seemed to have become chaperones - for lack of a better word - for Nasreen and Shiya. Ubaid, for the most part, disappeared. Unless we were headed to fun places such as L'Arc, Le Folies Bergere or Maxim's, he was nowhere to be found.

Andy had taken off that morning to visit more engineering museums. He was waiting for me in the Windsor Suite when I returned to the hotel. I informed him that Edouard and Jules were on their way to collect us for High Tea and we were to meet in the hotel lobby in half an hour.

As we ordered our food and drinks at Café Les Deux Magot, Andy posed a question to the men, "Do you happen to know what is playing at The Palais Garnier? I'm hoping to take Young to an opera either this evening or tomorrow night."

Jules replied, "I believe Salomé is playing at Opéra de Paris. Shall I call to see if we can get tickets? My friend Marcel is the manager of the theatre and I'm sure he can get us tickets for this evening's performance. Would you ladies like to go?" He turned to Nasreen and Shiya.

Shiya replied excitedly, "That will be fun, what do you think Nasreen?"

She happily answered, "Yes! That sounds exciting. I have to return to the hotel to change. Do we have sufficient time to ready ourselves for the performance?"

"I'm sure we can make it. I'll call Marcel to see if he can get us good seats at this late hour," Jules answered cheerfully.

While Jules made his way to the phone booth to call Marcel, our array of pastries and beverages arrived. Since I was a hungry bear, I munched away at the delicious éclair, mousse au chocolat and a tarte aux fruits plus, all of which were terribly decadent.

By the time Jules returned with the good news that he had secured the tickets at the Opéra de Paris we had already finished High Tea and were ready to return to the Ritz to dress for another fun filled evening in 'Gay Paree'.

CHAPTER EIGHTY-NINE

Au Revoir Mon Aimee

"I shall be telling this with a sigh – somewhere ages and ages hence: two roads diverged in a wood, and I - I took the one less traveled by, and that has made all the difference."
Robert Frost

My experience at the Opéra de Paris was as wonderful as the time spent with Count Mario and Andy at Teatro La Fenice. I had the opportunity to grow in understanding of the workings of theatrical designs during each of my stays at households. This experience influenced my art, fashion, and costume work, profoundly. The early encounters with international Haute Couture houses laid the foundation for my professional practice and my fashion philosophies in the artistic world I've influenced for five decades. The attention to detail in shape, form, color, pattern and style that I witnessed in Paris fueled my perfectionism. I had seen the impeccable work of masters. My sights were set high.

Without these extraordinary introductions and behind-the-scene opportunities, it would have been difficult for me to comprehend the work that went into fashion, art, theatre sets and costume design.

While my choice to enter a secret forbidden society at age twelve was unconventional, looking back, I am grateful that I decided to take the road less traveled and venture into an unknown world. Without my harem experiences, my life and career path would have been vastly different. The fashion and costume design success I've enjoyed over the years I attribute to the opportunities afforded to me in my adolescent years. I am grateful to all my guardians on my life's journey who guided me through my young years into adulthood with ease and grace. I am, indeed, one of the lucky few to have had such excellent mentors and teachers, who opened professional doors for me.

The Hadrah Hakim

The last I saw of the Hadrah was in the summer of 1967, when Andy and I decided to take a week's vacation and tour the Greek Islands. Hakim kept his promise of a week's use of the Simorgh and the Kahyya'm, and sent his plane to collect us at Heathrow. My Master was on his way from London to Monte Carlo, where the Kahyya'm was docked.

I was deeply saddened when news reached me that the Hadrah had passed from cancer, in 1976. He had been a wonderful surrogate father to me. I had desperately needed a mature male figure in my life. This understanding man accepted me. He did not try to change me; instead he encouraged me to see the world through my own, fresh eyes.

He provided me the opportunity to shine in the field of fashion and design by introducing me to his harem, sending me for art appreciation lessons in Italy and on Haute Couture fashion trips in Paris. I loved the Hadrah. He taught me to appreciate and live life, seeing each day as a new beginning.

Hadrah Hakim provided me many opportunities to live the width of my young life during my time in his Household; I was, and always will be, most appreciative.

Sayonara Ghaniyah & The Harem Ladies

I was sad to bid farewell to the rest of the harem women, especially to Ghaniyah, the Hadrah's fourth wife. We did not speak much due to our language barrier, but her gestures and body language more than made up for the lack of verbal communication.

She was the most beautiful woman in the harem, and certainly the one with the kindest heart. I learned that throughout the course of her life she did much charity work, assisting the less fortunate with financial contributions as well as visitations. She was certainly beautiful both outside and inside. My admiration for her has not waned over the years; her legacy continues to live on in my heart.

My Friend Ubaid

Ubaid's perennial womanizing and "man-izing" continued. He defied his father's wishes by not returning to Dubai. Ubaid finished architectural school at Trinity College in Dublin, and then married Gianna, after graduation. Their marriage ended in divorce a few years later, because of his infidelity.

The day Ubaid returned to Ireland for his architectural studies he was the happiest I'd ever seen him, at the Kosk. He couldn't wait to be away from his father. His feelings about his father reminded me of my own feelings and how I felt when I left Kuala Lumpur and my father's clutches. Although Ubaid bade his father farewell, he did it as an obligatory gesture.

Even though we had a funfilled weekend in Paris, I was sad that I would not be living in close proximity to him as we had been at the Kosk.

Our Paris trip was the last I saw of my friend, I received occasional news regarding his wellbeing when I worked on "Sacred Sex in Sacred Places" with his brother-in-law, Aziz.

Ubaid travelled extensively in Europe, attending parties and functions across the continent before settling in Florence. Hakim's death required his return to the United Arab Emirates to oversee his father's extensive business enterprises, in which he had no interest at all. Like his father, he eventually took four Arab wives and oversaw his ever-expanding male and female harems.

In some indescribable way I missed Ubaid and our times together. He opened my eyes to a lifestyle that I had never witnessed before I met this playboy. If not for his wanton behavior, the Hadrah would never have sent us to Italy. For this I am grateful to "Mr. Romeo."

Bye Bye Rizq

The last time I saw my young friend Rizq, he was happy as a lark. His circumcision, attendant ceremony and exploration did wonders for his mental and emotional state. He was no longer the shy boy who came to us, but a handsome buckaroo, constantly adding sexual adventures to his repertoire. His Cheshire cat grin still is imprinted on my mind, forty-five years later. I am sure he is now a successful business entrepreneur, walking in his grandfather's footsteps.

To this day I am bewildered by the act of circumcision and the rite of passage. Does it really convert a boy to a man, or is it just the mind playing a magic trick? I'll never know, since I didn't personally experience Khitan.

The Elegant Nasreen

I saw Nasreen and Shiya when Andy and I were in Paris assisting Aziz in his project. The Kosk ladies were viewing the new fashion collections. I was able to revisit the Ateliers and continue to learn the art of Haute Couture.

These two ladies were instrumental in providing me with the opportunity to delve into the world of fashion styling. They offered me the chance to observe High Fashion L'Ateliers operating in French Haute Couture arenas.

I was delighted for Nasreen when Hadrah Hakim finally relented to her wishes, allowing her to pursue her law degree in France. Nasreen and Baron Edouard Fontaines' relationship deepened over the years while she was studying at the Sorbonne Law School. They secretly married with a small gathering of friends, away from the eyes of the Hadrah. He did not know his beloved daughter married a French nobleman until the ceremony was over.

When Hakim first discovered the marriage he threatened to disown her, and banned her from returning to the family fold in Dubai. He went so far as to say that she would be stoned to death under strict Islamic law if she appeared. Fortunately, that did not happen; Nasreen didn't return until many years later. This beautiful woman changed her name to Baroness Marie Fontaines, and gave birth to two heirs.

Over the years, the Hadrah accepted the Baron and forgave Nasreen for defying him. His love for his daughter never waned, even when he threatened her in the early period of her marriage. In his will, Hakim left his daughter a sizable portion of the family business and estate, knowing that she would continue expanding the family's various enterprises. He also knew that Ubaid would leave most of the administration of his inheritance to his entourage of lawyers and advisers, while he gallivanted around the world in pursuit of sexual conquests and the 'good life.'

The Angelic Shiya

Shiya's relationship with Jules soon ended; she discovered her boyfriend's infidelity. After volunteering for the Red Cross and living in Europe for several years after graduation, Shiya returned to her homeland. Unhappy with Middle Eastern women's inequality, she took on the cause as an activist fighting for women's rights. Although the Hadrah did his best to match-make his daughter with a suitable Arab husband, he did not succeed. Shiya's refusal to be subjugated as the property of a traditional Arab husband made marriage nearly impossible. She remained single until her sister secretly arranged a blind date for her with Viscount Sebastian Baptiste. She fell in love.

The Hadrah, for fear of losing another daughter, agreed that Shiya could marry the Viscount. Having both daughters married into European aristocracy in many ways elevated Hakim's family connections in European society. He gave an elaborate wedding reception for the happy couple and accepted the Viscount into the Household with open arms.

Shiya continued her charity work, especially for Middle Eastern women's equality. In subsequent years, she was bestowed an award equivalent to the Légion d'Honneur by the French government for championing women in France and the Middle East. She bore three lovely children. Nasreen and Shiya made France their home, commuting between Paris and Dubai, regularly.

Ramiz's Ma'a Salaama (Good bye)

My Mu'allmi was one of the most difficult people for me to bid ma'a salaama. I felt I'd known him longer than three months. My teacher was sad to see us leave. We had bonded with each other, not just as tutor/student but also as friends assisting each other in a time of need. I never saw my mu'allmi again.

All the golden eggs have been sold, but I am very grateful and thankful to the man who laid them! Those valuable eggs afforded me the opportunity to attend college, where I earned a terminal degree in fashion. I later became a known fashion designer. Thank you, Ramiz, for laying a dozen of these eggs for me.

Habiibi Aziz

Aziz was thrilled that Andy and I were stationed at the Sekhem, Thabit's palatial residence, for our next Household assignment. This gave him the opportunity to work with us away from the scrutiny of the Hadrah's domain. Aziz travelled to Abu Dhabi frequently. He used the excuse of needing to spend time with Thabit on various business ventures. It was really an escape from the restraints placed on him by his father, wife and children.

We had many fun times together working on "Sacred Sex in Sacred Places." We travelled to photography exhibitions around the world, and published a coffee table book. Our work provided Andy and me with fabulous travel opportunities. We visited many parts of the world, and experienced a variety of cultures and different ways of living which opened new horizons for us both. I am, indeed, grateful to Aziz and Thabit. My service at the Sekhem helped me to mature, and it was there that I became an adult.

"Daddy Dearest"

During my summer vacations to Kuala Lumpur, Father continued to force me into different physical exercise programs. He never stopped trying to change me, or to "butch me up." From basketball to weight-lifting to football, the list was endless, as were his disappointments. In the majority of these classes I started falling for a handsome guy instead of concentrating on being manly. This, of course, did not sit well with this controlling, disappointed man. He couldn't accept that I would never "turn" heterosexual, and he never accepted me.

I didn't want to return home during my summer vacations, but I went for my mother. I endured my father, and focused on the fact that I would soon be back in Andy's arms.

I detested the Methodist Boy's Summer School programs I was forced to attend. I had grown in every way due to my secret Bahriji experiences. The local boys, even though they were older than I was, were no more mature than when I first left for school in the UK. I could not talk about where I had been and what I had done and I had no interest in their immature pursuits. We had nothing in common, much like my father and me.

One summer, I arrived home to discover I had a half-brother, Kitson, and a half-sister, Irene, both children of Father's mistress, Annie. No one had told me Annie had a condition which could prove fatal; she had a hole in her heart.

Father tried his best to save her short life by sending her for treatment to one of the best hospitals in England, but she did not make it through surgery. She died in his arms, leaving their children, a nine and a ten-year-old. Father did his best to look after his children, but his businesses were failing and he was also ill. Years of heavy drinking and smoking were taking a toll on his health. Father suffered a major heart attack not long after Kitson and Irene came to live with our family.

After being in a coma for a week, Father died, at age 53. This left only my Mother to care for the children, which she did splendidly. Mother brought up Annie's children until they were grown, educated, married and settled, with families of their own.

My father left deep debt, bills and lawsuits for his son, James, to clear up. Mother and my brothers advised me not to return home for father's funeral, as funds were limited. I was glad to be spared the agony of having to pretend to mourn a man with whom I had no real affiliation. His passing was, in some ways, a relief. I knew that when I next returned home I would not have to go through the agony of being butched-up and put down.

Darling Mummy

At times, Mother came to visit me in London during my Spring or Christmas break. We shared wonderful times, together with Uncle James, visiting new and interesting places in the United Kingdom and Europe. Mother's friendship with Uncle James continued until his passing in 1980; he died in a plane crash.

Mother and I were incredibly sad. Uncle James had never remarried after his wife's death. I think he was hoping that one day he would have Mother's hand, but that did not happen. Mother stayed in her marriage. For a woman of her time, it wasn't appropriate to leave your husband for another.

I asked Mother why she brought her husband's mistress' children into our home. She replied, "My heartache with your father had nothing to do with them. They were innocent but unfortunate, caught up in our drama. I felt a responsibility to do my best for them. I ask you to do your best to accept your half siblings as your own brother and sister. They deserve the best our family can offer."

Mother's wish of having a beautiful daughter came in the form of my half-sister, Irene, whom Mother adored. My abundance of dolls and girly things were left in my lovely sister's care.

As much as I had promised myself that I would never return to Kuala Lumpur, after college I found myself working there for a large corporate fashion company from 1992 to 1994, before Mother's passing. I needed to spend time with the only woman I ever loved, a woman who was loved and cherished by many.

Mum died peacefully in her sleep from Alzheimer's at age seventy-six, in a nursing home, unable to recognize any members of her family. To honor her, I decorated her wooden casket with one hundred and one red roses: one hundred lined the outer edges, representing those she had loved and been loved by. The one I placed near her heart was from me; the effeminate son who thought the world of her.

As cliché as it sounds, to me, my mother was one of the greatest women who ever lived. She continues to be with me in spirit, occasionally visiting me in my dreams. I feel her presence. She is always there when I most need her.

My 'Big Brother' – Nikee

My handsome Nikee graduated from Saint Andrew's in Scotland. He achieved many accolades in the field of sociology and psychology. He spent his life researching human behavior, and in later years authored a series of books on relationships.

The months I spent under the guidance of this charismatic man provided me with the first real taste of protection and love. Nikee was much more of a big brother than my own brothers were. They were busy pursuing their studies abroad, and had no time for me.

Nikee taught me to give, freely, and to never give up hope when times were rough. He loved with an open heart and an open mind. Nikee encouraged me to have faith that there would always be light at the end of darkness.

He taught me to live life "lightly." His words of wisdom when I felt sad or depressed were always, "Young, do you know why angels can fly? Because they take themselves lightly."

His philosophy has stayed dear to my heart, and over the years not only did I fly, but I soared. For this and more, I am thankful to Nikee, the best guardian any young man could ever have!

Oscar, My Temporary 'Guardian'

I continued my affair with Oscar while in service at the Sekhem, where Andy was also stationed. When Andy discovered the affair, which was documented in my diary, he asked me to never keep any secrets from him, again. He lectured me on the ethics of honesty, insisting that the truth would always set me free. He forgave me, over time, even though he was deeply hurt. He was more hurt by my lies than he was by my love of Oscar. Andy's love for me never waned; our relationship improved with each passing year.

Oscar was a Valet to a Bahriji student stationed at the Sekhem. He soon realized that my bond with Andy was too strong to be broken. With heavy hearts, we decided that it was best not to continue our love affair. After three months, Oscar left to further his medical studies. He became a well-known cosmetic surgeon. Although we corresponded for a period of time after his departure, we eventually lost touch.

Oscar was one of the gentlest souls to ever walk this planet. He was very much like the guardian angel I dreamed of the night before I agreed to join the Enlightened Royal Oracle Society. His loving aura continues to surround me, bringing rosy memories of our time together. He constantly whispers in my ear to not be afraid, to call his name and he will be there, beside me, in spirit. He has kept his promise. When I am unsure of myself, I call upon him and his spirit fills me, dissipating my anxieties and reminding me to receive each day with enthusiasm and vitality.

My Valet and Lover Andy

How can I ever forget Andy, with whom I spent four wonderful years of my life? Our separation was one of the most difficult decisions I've ever had to make. It was devastating to Andy, as well. To this day, I still have the occasional regret that I did not accept his sincere, loving proposal to be his life partner. He asked me to live in New Zealand with him.

Andy was destined to be an international engineering expert in bridge building, and I was destined to be a fashion designer. As much as I had come to love him, I knew instinctively, at my core, that New Zealand was no place for me. I had to be in London or Paris.

He obtained a scholarship in 1970 to engineering school at the prestigious University of Canterbury.

My memories of Andy continue to be a reminder about what it means to live generously and to love unconditionally. Until Andy, I didn't know this kind of love and commitment existed. I found it noble, and filled with integrity.

Magnanimous Andy provided stability and a road map for me, who desperately craved love. During our four years together he found my soul, and cherished it. I will always remember my Valet, my lover and mentor, as God in human form.

He performed his Valet duties well. I grew into a confident, responsible and successful man, who follows his own footsteps, never walking in those of others.

Breaking up with Andy was the hardest thing I ever did, but it was the right decision then.

As For Me

I went on to finish my fashion studies at Harrow College of Art & Technology before obtaining my Master Degree in Fashion Design at the prestigious Royal College of Art, in London. I fulfilled my ambition of making a mark in fashion both as a fashion professor and a known designer in London, Hong Kong, Singapore, Malaysia and Hawaii.

When I was studying for my 2nd Master Degree in Theatre Costuming at the Fitzgerald Theatre at The University of Hawaii, I met my life partner, Walter Bissett, a successful realtor and, also 'God!' An Andy archtype! We have been together for sixteen years. We currently reside on the beautiful island of Maui, Hawaii.

I made a choice to follow my life's calling. There have been many trials as well as numerous successes along the way. There were times when I wondered how my life would be if I had followed Andy to New Zealand. My decision to come into my own and to be "me" was definitely a better choice than that of living in the shadow of another man's dream. As the saying goes:

> *"A person who walks in another's tracks leaves no footprints."*
>
> Young

Author's Biography

Bernard Foong is, first and foremost, a sensitivist. He finds nuance in everything. To experience the world he inhabits is an adventure which is mystical, childlike and refreshing. He has a rare ability to create beauty in a unique fashion. His palettes have been material, paint, words and human experiences.

By Christine Maynard (screenwriter and novelist).

Bernard Tristan Foong, alias Young, is an accomplished fashion designer. After graduating from The Royal College of Art, London, England, he worked as an in-house bridal wear designer for Liberty's of London for four years.

The Hong Kong Polytechnic/University offered Mr. Foong a fashion design professorship for the next six years. He was a founding member of The Hong Kong Fashion Designer's Association; consultant to numerous fashion companies in Hong Kong ranging from lingerie, furs, womens-wear designs, to his specialty – romantic and ethereal bridal ensembles.

During his lecturing sojourn in the United States of America, he was recruited by The University of Wisconsin-Madison as an associate fashion professor. He was also a visiting lecturer at The Minneapolis College of Art, Minnesota.

In 1994 to 1996, The Singapore Temasek Polytechnic recruited Mr. Foong to organize the school's fashion design and merchandising department. He was also the acting fashion development manager for Parkson Grand department stores in Kuala Lumpur, Malaysia.

The designer was offered a scholarship to complete his Master in Theatre Costuming at The University of Hawaii in 1996. Since then he has made Hawaii his home. He resides on the beautiful island of Maui with his life partner of sixteen years, Mr. Walter Bissett, and their 'Goddess' daughter, Ms. Kali Durga (a fluffy Himalayan).

He is a full-time writer and has recently completed Unbridled, Book II of A Harem Boy's Saga, sequel to Initiation, to be released soon. He is currently working on Book III.

A Harem Boy's Saga is a series of five books documenting the designer's life.

Acknowledgements

In January 2011, an interminable urge overtook me to document a segment of my adolescent life which had been kept secret for forty-two years. I was compelled by an unseen power to write A Harem Boy's Saga.

Ms. Marji Knowles, a friend and confident, intrigued by my story, encouraged me to proceed. Not only did she offer me assistance in editing my manuscript, she also provided sound advice and suggestions throughout my writing process. I am grateful for the months of hard work she devoted to Initiation. Her cogent arguments spearheaded my determination to complete the first in a series of A Harem Boy's Saga.

Thank You to Ms. Devorah Rubenstein for her professional Market Read on Initiation. She provided me with numerous commercial and personal insights on improving my writing and storytelling skills.

Ms. Christine Maynard, my editor in chief manifested from Louisiana. She is a genius in keeping my youthful voice intact while transforming my story onto the pages of this book. I have grown to cherish and love this amazing woman during the months we spent editing. We laughed, cried, and sometimes cursed but forgave, as we cleaned and scrubbed this manuscript to perfection. We have since become close friends. A quote by William Blake:

"Opposition is true friendship."

I am grateful for the valuable information on publishing, marketing and promotional advice from Mr. Ghalib Shiraz Dhalla.

I would also like to take this opportunity to say "Thank You" to all my friends and supporters who continue to have faith in me and support my revelations during the past eighteen months of grueling work, before this memoir came to life.

Last but not least, I am indebted to my life partner, Mr. Walter Bissett, for his steadfast unwaivering support, encouraging me to tell my story truthfully. In his words:

"The truth will set you free."

Book II – <u>Unbridled</u> – details the author's experience in the second Arab household to which he was assigned.

This print book is available in ebook form from the following:

Apple iBookstores
Barnes & Noble
Amazon
Kobo ebooks
Rainbow ebooks
Sony Reader Store
OmniLit ebooks
Google Play
Bookstrand
Coffeetime Romance

Made in the USA
San Bernardino, CA
17 September 2013